The World of George Sand

GEORGE SAND AT NOHANT © *Françoise Gilot 1986*

The World of George Sand

OCTOBER 16-18, 1986

HOFSTRA UNIVERSITY

HEMPSTEAD, NEW YORK

HOFSTRA CULTURAL CENTER • HOFSTRA UNIVERSITY • HEMPSTEAD, NEW YORK

THE WORLD OF GEORGE SAND

Edited by Natalie Datlof,
Jeanne Fuchs, and David A. Powell

Prepared under the auspices of Hofstra University

HOFSTRA
UNIVERSITY

Contributions in Women's Studies, Number 122

GP

GREENWOOD PRESS
New York • Westport, Connecticut • London

Library of Congress Cataloging-in-Publication Data

The World of George Sand / edited by Natalie Datlof, Jeanne Fuchs, and David A. Powell ; prepared under the auspices of Hofstra University.
p. cm. — (Contributions in women's studies, ISSN 0147–104X; no. 122)
Proceedings of the 7th George Sand Conference, held Oct. 16–18, 1986, at Hofstra University.
Includes bibliographical references and index.
ISBN 0–313–27584–X (alk. paper)
1. Sand, George, 1804–1876—Congresses. 2. Novelists, French—19th century—Biography—Congresses. 3. Women and literature—France—History—19th century—Congresses. I. Datlof, Natalie. II. Fuchs, Jeanne. III. Powell, David A. IV. Hofstra University. V. George Sand Conference (7th : 1986 : Hofstra University) VI. Series.
PQ2412.W6 1991
843'.7—dc20
[B] 90–46700

British Library Cataloguing in Publication Data is available.

Library of Congress Catalog Card Number: 90–46700
ISBN: 0–313–27584–X
ISSN: 0147–104X

First published in 1991

Greenwood Press, 88 Post Road West, Westport, CT 06881
An imprint of Greenwood Publishing Group, Inc.

Printed in the United States of America

The paper used in this book complies with the Permanent Paper Standard issued by the National Information Standards Organization (Z39.48–1984).

10 9 8 7 6 5 4 3 2 1

Copyright Acknowledgments

The editors and publisher gratefully acknowledge the following sources for granting permission to use copyrighted material:

Excerpts from *Lélia* by George Sand and translated by Maria Espinosa, 1987. Courtesy of Indiana University Press.

The frontispiece is courtesy of artist Françoise Gilot.

"The Great Chain" is courtesy of Marilyn French.

Chapter 1 by Anne Berger was previously published in English under the title "Let's Go to the Fountain: On George Sand and Writing," in *Writing Differences: Readings from the Seminar of Hélène Cixous*, edited by Susan Sellers, Open University Press, 1988, and in French under the title "L'Apprentissage selon George Sand," *Littérature*, no. 67, October 1987. By permission of Open University Press and courtesy of *Littérature*.

Contents

Preface ix

Keynote Address: George Sand, Our Contemporary xi
HENRI PEYRE

Special Address: The Great Chain xxi
MARILYN FRENCH

Part I: Rustic Novels

1. Apprenticeship According to George Sand 3
ANNE BERGER

2. *La Petite Fadette*: A Pre-Feminist Dialectic of Tradition 15
BRIGITTE LANE

3. The Language of Loss in George Sand's *Le Meunier d'Angibault* 27
WENDELL McCLENDON

4. François Comes of Age: Language, Culture, and the Subject 35
JANE A. NICHOLSON

Part II: *Lettres d'un voyageur*

5. Imaginary and Symbolic Orders in "Sur Lavater et sur une maison déserte" 45
MARY ANNE GARNETT

6. *Lettres d'un voyageur*: Traveling with George Sand 51
SUSAN H. LÉGER

Part III: Autobiography

7. Positioning the Self in Autobiographical Writing: George Sand as Model for Marguerite Yourcenar 59
   PETER CHRISTENSEN

8. *Histoire de ma vie*: George Sand and Autobiography 67
   GITA MAY

9. Aurore Inscribing Aurore: A Reading of "La Reine Coax" 75
   LYNN KETTLER PENROD

10. George Sand's Poetics of Autobiography 85
    MARILYN YALOM

Part IV: Text and Ideology

11. George Sand and the Romantic Sibyl 95
    MARIE-JACQUES HOOG

12. *Consuelo* and *La Comtesse de Rudolstadt*: From Gothic Novel to Novel of Initiation 107
    ISABELLE NAGINSKI

13. *Consuelo* and *Porporino*, or the Influence of Change 119
    DAVID A. POWELL

14. Intertextuality: *Valentine* and *La Princesse de Clèves* 127
    LUCY M. SCHWARTZ

Part V: Political Affinities

15. *Nanon*: Novel of Revolution or Revolutionary Novel? 137
    NANCY E. ROGERS

16. Reasons of the Heart: George Sand, Flaubert, and the Commune 145
    MURRAY SACHS

17. Freedom Smuggler: George Sand and the German Vormärz 153
    GISELA SCHLIENTZ

Part VI: Sexual Politics

18. *Elle et lui*: Literary Idealization and the Censorship of Female Sexuality 163
    MARIE J. DIAMOND

19. *Mademoiselle Merquem*: De-Mythifying Woman by Rejecting the Law of the Father 173
    CLAUDE HOLLAND

20. Healers in George Sand's Works 181
ANNABELLE M. REA

21. The Divided Self in *Lélia*:
The Effects of Dualism on the Feminine Psyche 193
WENDY ANN RYDEN

22. *La Petite Fadette*: An Epicene Cautionary Tale 199
MAÏR E. VERTHUY

Part VII: Contemporaries

23. George Sand and Alfred de Musset: Absolution Through Art
in *La Confession d'un enfant du siècle* 207
JEANNE FUCHS

24. George Sand's Multiple Appearances in
Balzac's *La Muse du département* 217
JANIS GLASGOW

25. George Sand's Reception in Russia: The Case of Elena Gan 227
KEVIN J. McKENNA

26. George Sand and Flaubert: Inspiration and Divergence 235
MARY RICE

27. The Important, Little-Known Friendship of
George Sand and Alexandre Dumas fils 243
EVE SOURIAN

28. Two Monologues from *Dialectic of the Heart* 255
ALEX SZOGYI

29. Fanny Lewald and George Sand: *Eine Lebensfrage* and *Indiana* 263
MARGARET E. WARD and KAREN STORZ

Selected Bibliography 271
DAVID A. POWELL

Program of Conference 279

Name Index 303

Subject Index 307

About the Editors and Contributors 313

Preface

The Seventh International George Sand Conference, held at the home institution of the Friends of George Sand, Hofstra University, on October 16–18, 1986, brought together scholars from all corners of the United States as well as from European and Asian countries. We are proud to offer in this volume a collection of essays that represents "The World of George Sand." These efforts give testimony to the steadfastness of our organization on this tenth anniversary of its inception.

After ten successful years, the Friends of George Sand look forward to providing a forum for further studies of Sand's works, life, and influence. Ongoing scholarship will continue through biennial conferences and symposia. The ensuing publications of the conference proceedings and the journal *George Sand Studies* will provide an additional vehicle for scholars.

The proceedings of the 1986 George Sand Conference opened with two special addresses, by Henri Peyre and Marilyn French, which link George Sand and her world to the world around her, from her contemporary surroundings to the present. The twenty-eight conference papers and an excerpt from Alex Szogyi's original play *Dialectic of the Heart* compose the body of the proceedings. They fall loosely into seven main categories: The Rustic Novels, *Lettres d'un voyageur*, Autobiography, Texts and Ideology, Political Affinities, Sexual Politics, and George Sand's Contemporaries. The wide range of topics reflects the breadth of scholarship demonstrated at the Seventh International George Sand Conference as well as the wealth of inquiry open to Sand scholars today. The numerous nationalities of the contributors also bear witness to the worldwide interest in George Sand studies that continues to grow in academic centers. It is also gratifying that this volume includes the work of newcomers and young scholars alongside the contributions of well-established *sandistes*. We are confident that this collection of essays advances George Sand studies and will prove useful for future work on the Berrichon author.

All these George Sand projects have come to life and flourished during the tenure of Hofstra University's president, Dr. James M. Shuart, and to him we all owe our deepest gratitude.

Our editorial tasks were made lighter by the special talents of Edwin L. Dunbaugh, professor of History, and Alexej Ugrinsky, codirector of the Hofstra Cultural Center and adjunct assistant professor of German.

It saddens us to announce that since our last George Sand publication (1982), three of the Hofstra University founding members of the Friends of George Sand have died: Joseph G. Astman, professor of Comparative Literature and Languages and director of the Hofstra Cultural Center; Frank S. Lambasa, professor of Comparative Literature and Languages; and William S. Shiver, associate professor of French. Professor Joseph Astman was not only a charter member of the Friends of George Sand but also the founder of the Hofstra Cultural Center. It is his vision of interdisciplinary and intercultural inquiry that continues to inspire the programs created by the Center. Professors Frank Lambasa and William Shiver were also instrumental in the founding of the Friends of George Sand and were key figures in shaping the scholarly and philosophical goals of our organization; they also served as editors of previous conference proceedings. We cannot close without recognizing the work and influence of the late Professor Henri Peyre, whom we wish to honor as well. His contributions to Sand studies are too numerous to list here, but we shall always be grateful that he so generously lent the prestige of his international reputation to our undertaking. It is to these four distinguished scholars that we dedicate this volume.

The publication of these proceedings has been made possible by a generous grant from the French Cultural Services of the French Embassy in the United States. We are deeply grateful for the continuing support the French Cultural Services has shown the Friends of George Sand since its inception in 1976.

The Editors
Natalie Datlof
David A. Powell
Jeanne Fuchs

Keynote Address: George Sand, Our Contemporary

Henri Peyre

During the first half of the twentieth century, George Sand's reputation had sunk to a low ebb. Three or four of her novels, the pastoral ones, were given to children to read but were eventually discarded or half forgotten by them when they reached adulthood. Academic scholars, psychologists, and psychoanalysts had not yet learned how to decipher the secrets in *La Mare au diable* and *François le champi*. Parents insisted on believing in the unsullied purity of childhood; yet it was the fashion to deride as incredibly naive and as a temporary aberration Sand's social fiction and her faith in the hidden talents among the working classes. Surveys of the modern French novel chose to ignore a representative of what Charles Maurras and his followers on the right of the political spectrum scornfully termed "le romantisme féminin," nor were Pierre-Joseph Proudhon and other leftist advocates of revolutionary change any more favorable to women who had the audacity to compose novels instead of living them or, at best, after having repented for living them.

Gustave Flaubert himself, who exchanged warm, friendly letters with the aging maternal author (respectfully alluded to as "la bonne dame de Nohant"), evinced no interest in the fiction of that predecessor who had found words of praise for *Salammbô*, who had shrewdly commented on *L'Éducation sentimentale*, and whose *Indiana* had in several respects anticipated *Madame Bovary*. Sand's novels, one remembers, were among the readings that had led Emma astray into romantic dreams. Later, the revelation of Flaubert's own early unrepressed romanticism and of his own Bovarysm was to betray his affinities with the author of *Lélia* and *Jacques*. It is not surprising that neither Anatole France nor his successor at the French Academy, Paul Valéry, and neither André Gide nor Montherlant or André Malraux expressed much interest in Sandian fiction, or in the female ego in general. One may regret, however, that French women novelists, from Gyp and Colette to

Nathalie Sarraute, Simone de Beauvoir, and Marguerite Yourcenar should have proved so utterly disdainful of their predecessor and, worse, so unconcerned with depicting convincing female characters in their own fiction.

Things changed with the second half of this century. The rehabilitation of George Sand, not necessarily as a practitioner of the art of fiction as Flaubert, Henry James, and Thomas Mann have redefined it, but as an autobiographer and an incomparable letter writer, is due to a few French and other European biographers: André Maurois, Renee Winegarten, Joseph Barry and, above all, to the indefatigable and bold Georges Lubin, to whom all scholars of nineteenth-century French literature are heavily indebted. It is due also to a number of scholars, writers, critics—courageous and enterprising minds—who have been gathering around Hofstra University. Unmindful of trends and fashions that, elsewhere in the New World, preached other cults and favored philosophical, sociological, linguistic, or hermeneutic approaches to literary works, the Cultural Center of Hofstra University has preferred simplicity and a modest spirit of inquiry. Without any fanfare, it has drawn researchers from several continents. It has brought them to a center deeply committed to the whole of the nineteenth century rather than only Sandian studies, a center that has become the focus of an admiration not exempt of a little envy by other and more traditional universities. Its publications are read and appreciated by scholars everywhere. A huge debt of gratitude is owed by all researchers and lovers of literature to the president of Hofstra University, James M. Shuart, who immediately sensed and encouraged the importance of the Hofstra Cultural Center when it was created by the late Professor Joseph G. Astman. Natalie Datlof and Alexej Ugrinsky have devoted immense efforts, much imaginative and ingenious zeal to the gathering of more than fifty international conferences—three of which have been devoted to George Sand and her times. Through them, and the devotion and enthusiasm of scores of scholars from American and European universities, George Sand has regained her rightful place among the early advocates of the rights of women. A group of Sandian scholars is active in Holland at the University of Amsterdam. A renewal of interest in Sandian fiction has surged up in the land of one of her faithful readers, Dostoevski, where the poetic achievement by women in this century surpasses in depth and emotional power all other feminine poetry. Between 1850 and 1950, the French had been liberally given credit in the United States for having discovered, naturalized among them, and imposed on other cultures Edgar Allan Poe, Walt Whitman, and William Faulkner. Americans in return have rehabilitated and reinterpreted both Denis Diderot, long neglected by his compatriots, and then today, thanks to Hofstra, George Sand. She is now truly our contemporary.

The feminist movement has played its rightful role in this process of rejuvenation. George Sand, however, cannot be treated primarily as a feminist propagandist. A courageous article by Annabelle Rea entitled "George Sand Misogynist?" appeared in the 1983 volume of the Hofstra *George Sand Newsletter*. Avowals in Sand's *Histoire de ma vie* bluntly confess that she was unable to put up very long with the company of women, who, she felt, exhibited narcissism and nervous tenseness. Without any allusion to sexual attraction, on which she was usually very discreet, she says she preferred the company and the conversation of men and she claimed to believe in the possibility of friendship between males and females "when the age of passion is over." Still, it is undoubtedly one of the positive achievements within the rich array of biographical and critical scholarship now available (written mostly by women) to have at last rid Sand studies of the anecdotes, slander, cheap sneers, and perfidious suggestions that had long cluttered the story of George Sand and her times. Even the serious and, in its day, original biography by Maurois, *Lélia* was not immune from these blemishes. Superior to it, and to any work on Sand by male writers, is the lively and truthful volume by Renee Winegarten, *The Double Life of George Sand, Woman and Writer* (1978); the bulky, erudite work by Thérèse Marix-Spire, *Les Romantiques et la musique: Le cas George Sand, 1804–1838* (1955); or the comprehensive and pioneering book by the late Ellen Moers, *Literary Women* (1963).

Thanks to such a patient critical achievement and to a greater degree of maturity in the reading public, we have at last, a hundred years or more after her death, buried the once popular clichés about George Sand's male attire, her pipe smoking, her relations with her husband and children, her treatment of her galaxy of lovers, her close female friendships, or even the alleged frigidity which inadequate males often attribute to their partners. Early in her career, in 1835, she voiced her protests against the conspiracy of society that curbs the senses and the passionate élan of women and relegates them to being pious churchgoers and chaste, submissive wives. She expressed rebellion, in a letter to François Rollinat, against the intolerance of heartless and cowardly members of her sex who condemn those who attempt to break their chains. In vigorous language, she took issue no less scornfully with self-righteous males who, no longer wishing for devout and self-effacing female companions, still do not yet accept enlightened and educated women, and who hypocritically sing the praises of a fidelity by which they themselves refuse to abide. Later, during her tempestuous liaison with Michel de Bourges, she showered on that married man, who hypnotized and humiliated her, some of the most burning and pathetic love letters composed by any literary woman. She had submitted to him meekly and obediently, "half-stifled with virtue." She had suffered from being humiliated and from being neglected by him. "I have had most enervating dreams," she wrote him from Switzerland. "Blood rushed to my head incessantly. . . . There is fire in my blood, . . . my flesh is assailed by a thousand twinges of desire." In her voluminous correspondence and in several of her novels, Sand voiced her passionate urge and poured the remembrance of sensual ecstasies embittered by acute pangs of regret. She spurned the expression "physical love," aware as she was of the role played therein by sentiment and the intellect, by the "wisdom of the heart," as Henry Miller was to call it. She well knew that the stirrings of the imagination cannot be divorced from the pleasures of the senses.

Her British admirers have contrasted her frank acceptance of sensuality with the feverish dreams of solitary, exasperated English virgins like the Brontë sisters, Christina Rossetti, and, on another continent, Emily Dickinson. Indeed, Charlotte Brontë herself expressed her admiration for Sand: "She has a grasp of mind which, if I cannot fully comprehend it, I can very deeply respect." She judged the French woman to be "sagacious and profound" and much preferred her to Jane Austen, whom she declared merely "shrewd and observant." Continental readers of Jane Austen (whom some of her English admirers in the academic world have at times ranked next to Shakespeare) experience a similar reluctance to see true and complete women in the vapid heroines of Austen's novels, who are forever and insidiously competing for gallant squires to be lured to legitimate betrothal. By contrast, Sand's heroines do not harbor any illusions about their male partners, much as the author herself did not. She was not long blinded by males, neither by the mediocre individuals like the one whose name she adopted for her nom de plume, nor by the glamorous writers and artists whose egoism and vanity she quietly perceived. Her novel *Lucrezia Floriani* courageously and lucidly offers a fictional portrait of Frédéric Chopin with his childish and imperious caprices, which she accepted as the ransom for his genius. Sand was aware of the inadequacies of Alfred de Musset, even if she never belittled his qualities. She could be patient and devoted. Musset himself, long after their Venetian adventure, remarked to Heinrich Heine that George was endowed with a rare talent, and practiced a very winning technique: "She never gave anything away in conversation." Instead, she pretended to listen meekly while men spoke—inevitably and chiefly of themselves.

Sand stands in contrast with a French woman novelist of the twentieth century, Colette, who in *L'Entrave*, confesses, "I have not known any of those women who are called great." Colette, whose prose in her best moments stands remote from the fluidity and verbosity of Sand's, failed to express much appreciation for her predecessor. Implicitly scorning her literary achievements, perhaps, she insidiously ventured her puzzled curiosity on another point: "What contraceptive did she use?" However, if Colette depicted teenagers and some women reluctant to mature, very seldom, if ever, did she draw a man in whom proud and thin-skinned males would agree to recognize their own ilk. The stuffy world of *Chéri* and the titillating milieu of *Gigi* have no equivalent in George Sand's fiction. Sand did not ignore the egoism of the males who dupe themselves with the eloquence with which they clothe their desires, however. Indeed, she could remark about one of her characters, Raymon (in *Indiana*), "He expressed passion with art and felt it with warmth. But it was not passion which rendered him eloquent: it was eloquence which made him passionate." Many of her male characters are endowed with that infinite capacity for weaving tissues of lies and contriving to believe in themselves. Their female partners are at first enraptured by the male eloquence of desire. Then, they voice their disappointment and see lucidly through them. Usually they forgive, and magnanimity becomes their privilege. Inevitably, a number of the women characters in Sand's overabundant fiction do not escape conventionality, yet an unbiased reader who laments the relative absence of fully true and convincing women in nineteenth-century fiction (Honoré de Balzac and, perhaps, Flaubert's Emma Bovary excepted) may avow that one finds in her novels more complexity and more fully "round" characters, as E. M. Forster might have called them, than in the whole range of Victor Hugo's fiction: Esmeralda, Cosette, and the pallid, sexless heroines of *Les Travailleurs de la mer* and *L'Homme qui rit*. Hugo pursued through his long career of a tireless faun a long series of female partners from all social classes, but he seldom created any real ones in fiction. It may be that unhappiness in love can be a boon for a creator.

The revival of interest in George Sand in our time will not, and does not attempt to, rehabilitate the whole of her enormous fictional output. It has enabled us to read with fresh eyes and a zest of discovery novels that had long been slighted. *Consuelo*, the greatest of the novels on the theme of music outside those of Balzac, Romain Rolland, and Thomas Mann; *Lélia*, *Indiana*, and even *Jacques*, which was once praised by Matthew Arnold and termed by Renee Winegarten "a landmark in the cultural history of the nineteenth century." The pastoral fiction of Sand deserves the esteem of adults for its descriptive pages and the subtlety of its psychology, and it may still be enjoyed by teenagers, even in this age of sophisticated mechanical toys and computer games. Fans of Sand's fiction experience thrills of adventurous novelty with *Mauprat* and *La Comtesse de Rudolstadt*. It is fair and probably accurate to assert that, next to Balzac, Sand did more than any one before Emile Zola to extend the dominion of the novel in the French language. Few of the possibilities offered by the genre were left unexplored by her enterprising spirit. Her social and political fiction has undergone the fate of much writing on and around questions which, once solved or formulated in different terms, cease to interest us. Still, even in her enthusiasm for Pierre Leroux, whom she hailed for a time as a new Plato or a second Christ, the crusader in Sand evinced a keener insight and a more generous understanding than most of her contemporaries (who chose to prefer banal and unadventurous academics like Victor Cousin or Villemain).

Posterity is only now granting Leroux his due, but George Sand never stinted her admiration for him. Stimulated by him, she undertook rash ventures into the realm of the fantastic, at the risk of bewildering her readers in the age of positivism. Her *Laura, ou voyage dans le cristal* in 1864, late in her career, has in our time been reprinted and hailed as one of the boldest attempts to "leap beyond the limits of our sidereal world" and to marry the two souls that may be ours, the one within ourselves and the other existing outside in a world of radiant splendor. It was reprinted and interestingly presented by Gerald Schaeffer in 1977. Long before it, when she was just leaving for Majorca with Chopin, with youthful audacity and well aware that she was courting failure, Sand had published her own *Faust, Part II*, entitled *Les Sept cordes de la lyre* (1838), a lyrical epic that, among a surfeit of poetical visions, voiced a plea for social justice and the total renovation of society.

George Sand's most impressive work along similar religious and mystical lines awaits to this day a modern critical edition. It is *Spiridion*, the first of her novels to have been appreciated across the Channel. It was completed at Valdemosa, in Majorca, in a monk's cell. The strange hero, Father Alexis, upholds the claims of "fervor and asceticism, the two things which are most feared around him." He has fled the secular word because he was too strong to submit to it and feared that his uncurbed passions would have turned his strength into a near madness. The flesh, if spurned, resists and fights against the spirit, asserts this rebellious monk. His words are reminiscent of the disturbing verses of Saint Paul in the *Epistle to the Galatians* (6: 12) on the flesh lusting against the spirit and the spirit lusting against the flesh.

Under the sway of Pierre Leroux's mysticism, which discarded the timidity of conventional faith, Sand went so far as to praise "the intellectual greatness of atheists, those deeply religious souls who become weary or waylaid in their soaring flight toward heaven." Ernest Renan, in 1850 and soon after renouncing his clerical vocation, praised *Spiridion* as "one of the books which are most dear to me." Alexander Herzen and other Russian thinkers were equally impressed by that disturbing novel, which seemed to be pointing the way for humankind to convert to the one true religion, fraternity. There are anticipations of the monks of *The Brothers Karamazov* in it. Jean Pommier, who wrote assiduously on Renan and taught in our time at the Collège de France, and Isabelle Naginski in this country, have in the last two decades redirected our attention to that singularly original novel. English biographers of Matthew Arnold have revealed that, in 1882, toward the end of his life, the Victorian critic pondered over *Spiridion* and transcribed extensive passages from it in his *Notebooks.* Arnold also owed to Sand his earlier discovery of Etienne Pivert de Senancour's *Obermann*, which impressed him lastingly when he was at Dover Beach, listening to "the melancholy withdrawing roar of the sea of faith" in the Victorian age.

In bringing George Sand back to us, as the twentieth century nears its demise, her many interpreters who are grouped around Hofstra University have vindicated her from the relative neglect of our predecessors. We have brushed aside the complacent blame once heaped on her life and her championship of women's rights. We atone for the blindness and the injustice of several of her contemporaries, among whom was Charles Baudelaire himself in his rancorous moments. The poet, an outcast himself, pursued her with heavy-handed sarcasm concerning the many good reasons she had for refusing to believe in Hell. He even begrudged his own admiration for the masterpiece that his great hero, Eugène Delacroix, created when he painted Sand's portrait. The poet of *Les Fleurs du mal*, deeply Catholic himself in his sensibility and ever torn between God and Satan, failed to acknowledge in Sand a spiritual yearning for the irrational and a heart driven by charity. He chose to praise the sentimental *chansonnier*, Pierre Dupont, rather than George Sand, who fought for the recognition of hidden talent among workers and peasants.

Others among the famous men of the middle of the century and later had more insight, or more fairness. Alexis de Tocqueville was one of them. Invited to meet Sand at a luncheon organized by a prominent British visitor to Paris, Richard Moncton Milnes, the stern statesman was, much to his surprise, charmed by the conversation of the dreaded woman novelist. She opened his eyes to the legitimate grievances of the Parisian workers who were threatened by unemployment and starvation wages. More clear-sighted than the politicians then at the helm, she foresaw the explosion of the June 1848 riots which rocked the Second Republic. Later, while a new wave of discontent swept the Parisian population and announced the upsurge of the Commune, Ernest Renan, in a firm and dignified letter to the German historian Theodore Mommsen (who had condemned the defeated France as decadent), rose in defense of the other face of France. The date was March 17, 1871. There was, Renan retorted, vitality and nobleness in a culture that could boast of George Sand along with Jules Michelet, Hippolyte Taine, Claude Bernard, and

Berthelot. In June 1876 Renan was grieved by her death and went with Flaubert to her funeral. He recalled how, at age fifteen and a pupil in a Catholic school in Brittany, he had watched the priests mention her name with horror and display a lithograph picturing the woman writer clad in black, trampling a crucifix under her feet. He proclaimed her passing in 1876 as a loss for humanity. "She had given life to the yearnings of those who felt but could not create," he asserted. "She was the inspired poet who clothed with a body our hopes, our grievances, our errors, our groans." Taine, who was seldom appreciative of the modern French novel (except for the two demigods, Balzac and Stendhal, to whom he had been the first to assign their future rank) made a signal exception for Sand when he stood at her funeral in 1876. He praised her novels as "providing the moral history of our times." Hugo, in a high-sounding tribute, celebrated in Sand the living proof that "women can have all our virile gifts without losing any of their angelic ones."

The correspondence exchanged, during the last years of her life, between George Sand and Flaubert (who was seventeen years her junior) has been lavishly quoted. It includes some of Flaubert's most outspoken statements on his aesthetics and some equally blunt and ill-tempered comments on the political and moral condition of his country. Sand had, not without originality and courage, praised *Salammbô* as soon as it came out, in March 1863, as "strange and magnificent, rich in both darkness and bright éclat." She had voiced legitimate reservations on *L'Éducation sentimentale* which, if properly understood, hinted that its author might have spared France his own destructive rage during the Commune. In his letters, he harped on his favorite themes, in particular the imperative necessity of absenting oneself from one's writings and banishing sentiment. Against those irate curses, Sand (of the two by far the less authentic representative of the bourgeoisie) tirelessly asserted the need to understand, to offer sympathy and to love. "Not to love is to cease to live." The masses are not necessarily and universally bestial and ferocious, ignorant and foolish. If they are, it falls on us to remedy that and to fight strenuously against any inequality of condition and opportunity. Judged both as testimonies of a broad heart and even as statements on literature, Sand's assertions may be deemed to be more generous and even more profound than Flaubert's repetitious declarations. He had ridiculously overvalued friends like Louis Bouilhet and even Georges Feydeau, but he did not overpraise Sand. While he asserted repeatedly that he wrote for ten or twelve people only, she retorted that she would wish to be understood by far more readers than the nobles and the middle class, whom she held in low esteem. "One does not curse and scorn one's species. Humanity is not an idle word." There is probably no letter in the whole published correspondence of Balzac, Hugo, Flaubert, and Baudelaire comparable in nobleness of spirit, breadth of understanding, and sheer intelligence to the long epistle from Nohant and dated September 14, 1871. It had been written as a manifesto, her ultimate one in many respects, and it appeared in *Le Temps* on the following October 3, 1871, and later in Sand's *Impressions et souvenirs*.

The reappraisal of George Sand in our times is remarkable for having been anticipated by outstanding writers in the English-speaking world and for being shared today, one hundred twenty years later, by the foreign participants of the

Hofstra conferences. One of the earliest of these writers in Britain was no other than John Ruskin, who had set himself up as a moralist, reserving the privilege of creation to those whom he called "right-minded artists." While traveling in France in 1856, he became familiar with Sand's novels. He read *François le champi* aloud to his mother. Interestingly, Ruskin's French admirer and would-be translator, Marcel Proust, was later to do likewise and share his sentimental emotions in reading Sand with his own mother. Both of them perhaps recognized in the work of the perceptive woman author revealing insights on the complexities of mother-son relationships. Ruskin eventually conceded that Sand "is often immoral, but always beautiful."

George Eliot, herself emancipated from the legal bonds of wedlock, approved of the Frenchwoman's unorthodox views as to the position of woman both in society and in the realm of religion. She felt flattered to be associated with George Sand in the views of several serious critics, one of them the father of Virginia Woolf, Leslie Stephen. The English George may have well been more skilled in the craft of fiction than her French predecessor and a more spare and calculating stylist. However, one is entitled to conjecture that she probably remembered some of Sand's novels when she composed her *Scenes of Clerical Life* and *Mill on the Floss* (which was to bring tears to young Proust's eyes). Indeed, Sand's ascendancy among British women writers was considerable. Charlotte Brontë did not hesitate to disparage Jane Austen when comparing her to the French author, for whose "grasp of mind" she proclaimed greater respect. She even declared Sand's brain to be "larger than that of Balzac and her heart warmer than his." Queen Victoria herself declared *Consuelo* "dreadfully interesting." Did she share the second part of that novel and its adventures set in a colorful German castle with Prince Albert, one wonders? We are not told.

We are more precisely informed of Elizabeth Barrett Browning's enraptured discovery of Sand. She declared her to be "as large as a Welsh mountain, . . . [as] eloquent as a fallen angel." While courted by her future husband, she succeeded in converting Robert Browning to her admiration for an author superior to "all other women of genius who are or have ever been." She composed two sonnets in praise of the "large-brained woman and large-hearted man / self-called George Sand!" Her husband agreed to accompany her on two visits to the French writer, and both of them, even Robert, who was somewhat concerned with respectability, found Sand restrained in her manners and surprisingly discreet in her attire. The date was 1851. A few years later, the American Walt Whitman, himself an admirer of Pierre Leroux and open to Saint-Simonian ideas, loudly proclaimed his preference for Sand's fiction over the "frightful and tedious novels of Victor Hugo." Unlike Hugo, who was "continually putting crises in novels, with her, when crises do come, they invariably go to the heart." The 1855 preface to *Leaves of Grass* defines the authentic poet in Sandian terms, as one whom his or her country "absorbs as affectionately as he [or she] has absorbed it." Some reminiscence of the French author may have come into that: the huge Sandian fare, like that of Whitman himself, has perhaps not been indiscriminately "absorbed" by either country.

The tributes paid to Sand by a very different craftsman, Henry James, are not indiscriminate, but are still surprising. We would hardly expect James to have been insensitive to a certain looseness of texture in Sand's novels. Still, having first read some of her later works, he was drawn to some of the early writings, which in their way were perhaps more passionate and often more expert at contriving suspense than even Balzac's stories. James remarked on "her unequalled faculty of improvisation," particularly in her autobiographical writings, and wished that she had provided more details about her methods. However, he admitted that "she never postured as a woman of letters." He gave her generous credit for her courage in depicting passion, an enterprise at which, in his opinion, Jane Austen, Walter Scott, and Charles Dickens had balked. Curiously, when pondering on her biography and her letters, the American novelist failed to find her feminine enough to please him. "She was too imperious a machine to make the limits of her activity coincide with those of wifely submissiveness," he explained somewhat pontifically. The inveterate bachelor in James ponderously proclaimed his verdict (in his essay on Sand in *French Poets and Novelists*), "She was more masculine than any man she might have married." As an inveterate scion of New England, he deplored some "want of moral taste" in her intellectual makeup. In another volume published only in 1914, a little before his death, meditating, wistfully perhaps, on the Venetian episode of George Sand's life, he gravely concluded that "love is a temple built to the lover as an object more or less worthy of his worship, and what is grand in the thing is not so much the god as the altar. George Sand erected 'a beautiful shrine.' "

We may wish, of course, that James had strained his imagination a little more and been able to raise "an altar" to the dead, and that he could have found room in one of his stories for a character fashioned after the extraordinary Sand. One of the participants in the gatherings at Hofstra, Alex Szogyi, has brought her to life in a play; others have composed sketches and drawings of her. Not only among critics and researchers into the past, but also among many scholars of contemporary issues, George Sand continues to be an inspiring, kindred soul in our endless search for freedom and its expression.

NOTES

Most of the relevant information on George Sand and her English readers is to be found in an excellent volume by Patricia Thomson, *George Sand and the Victorians* (New York: Columbia University Press, 1977). See also Paul G. Blount, *George Sand and the Victorian World* (Athens, Ga.: University of Georgia Press, 1979). For Henry James, see his *Notes on Novelists* (New York: Scribner's Sons, 1914) and his *French Poets and Novelists* (1884; reprint, New York: Grosset and Dunlap, 1964). Walt Whitman's remarks on George Sand are reported in his posthumous volume, *Uncollected Poetry and Prose*, vol. 2 (New York: Doubleday, 1921). They date from 1874. See also a learned essay by Henri Roddier, "P. Leroux, G. Sand et W. Whitman, ou l'éveil d'un poète," in *Revue de Littérature Comparée* 31 (January–March 1957): 5-33.

Special Address: The Great Chain

Marilyn French,
Joseph G. Astman Distinguished Conference Scholar

The European intelligentsia of the mid-nineteenth century probably never imagined such an oddity as a literary society devoted to an author; but if they had, they would have been astonished to discover that a hundred years would have to pass before such a society was founded to celebrate their beloved George. It is true that George Sand was not a popular writer; she was read mainly by other writers and intellectuals. Nonetheless, she was a major figure throughout nineteenth-century Europe. In 1842, George Henry Lewes wrote that Sand was "the most remarkable writer of the present century," and when she died in 1876, Matthew Arnold predicted that "the immense vibration of George Sand's voice upon the ear of Europe will not soon die away." In fact, George Sand was forgotten within twenty-five years of her death, and she remained forgotten, by all but a few, for a century. Even now, her life and work are known mainly by scholars.

Like other women writers—Edith Wharton, for example—Sand may not have seen herself as a great writer, the literary hero who transcends other humans. She had a running epistolary feud with Gustave Flaubert on the purpose of art and the position of the artist. It was a good-tempered, even loving, argument—Flaubert was a bit of a misanthrope, but he revered Sand, and addressed her as "chère Maître." Flaubert thought the artist as hero would be a monster, and believed art should be—could be—scientific and impersonal, omitting the artist's opinions: *objective*. Sand felt art existed to nourish a society, that it was a kind of food; and she was passionately committed to social change.

Whatever Sand's expectations for her future reputation, she did believe her life and work would make a difference, at least for women. In reply to her critics, some of whom could read only through spectacles tinted by the prejudices of the period and who excoriated her as scandalous, she wrote, "The world will know and understand me someday. But if that day does not arrive, it does not greatly matter. I shall have opened the way for other women."

These are the words of the best type of revolutionary, one who subsumes herself within a larger purpose and whose motivation is not self-aggrandizement, but participation in creating beneficial change. Her words should have been prophetic, for she was—and remains—a dauntingly large figure. However, she was forgotten, although she had a significant impact on the literature, the thought, and the life of her own and succeeding generations.

She lived with an energy and thoroughness that may be unique. She married; she raised children and helped to raise her grandchildren. She lived in the country and was familiar with its plants, trees, and waters, with the habits of animals and birds, with the work of farms and the people who did it. She also lived in the city and had a sophisticated understanding of the workings of society, its pretensions and customs, its language, and its fascination with power. Indeed, she knew the most powerful people of her age *and* those who challenged them in the name of a different power base—Giuseppe Mazzini, Karl Gutzkow, and Mikhail Bakunin, for instance. She knew major artists, composers, writers, poets, actors, and thinkers of both sexes—Alfred Vigny, Frédéric Chopin, Marie d'Agoult (Daniel Stern), and Eugène Delacroix are only the most famous. She befriended hosts of them, loved many, and made love with enough of them that we can say with assurance that she explored her own sexuality widely and deeply.

She was herself an artist: She wrote sketches, stories, novels, plays, and autobiography, turning out several volumes a year. Her fiction is notable on many counts. Most important, it must have been great fun to read because it still is, even though her allusions have lost the piquancy of the contemporaneous. Her descriptions of nature remain unequalled because they are based in such careful observation, such intimate knowledge. She knew too the life of country people, who are uneducated in letters but not in their work and that of nature. She had great insight into the intersection of psychology and manners; her analyses of the behavior of people in society always go deeper than comedy of manners to examine its roots: she saw that dishonesty about feeling arises from concern with image; that striving to impress is based in a sense of personal worthlessness. She was an expert in the ways power infects love, transforming it into self-sacrifice or domination.

Beyond this, she was a thinker. She probed the sources of conflict and injustice, and isolated one: the need of an elite class of males to dominate all other humans. Far in advance of her age, she recognized that this need was based in infantile emptiness, and she dramatized this perception in novel after novel. She created images new to literature, of love between people of different classes and backgrounds, of worthiness in the poor; she vividly depicted the oppression of women in marriage and the cruelty and absurdity of religious authority and class-domination. She was probably the first European writer to portray the poor with sympathy and respect in a period during which industrialization was further impoverishing them while enriching the wealthy, and when tiny children were hung from straps for fourteen hours a day so they could use both their hands and feet to work the looms. She went further yet: She was deeply involved with the men who incited the Revolution of 1848; and as its (unofficial) propagandist, she produced essays and position papers dealing with socialism, the prejudices and fears of the rich, and the need for a complete democracy.

Her work extended beyond her life. The list of those she influenced is staggering. It includes novelists—Honoré de Balzac, Stendhal, Ivan Turgenev, Fyodor Dostoevski, William Thackeray, George Eliot, Emily and Charlotte Brontë, and Henry James, as well as Gustave Flaubert. She influenced poets as well—Heinrich Heine, Oscar Wilde, and both the Brownings, and, preeminently, Walt Whitman, who took from her work not only the ideas that inspired *Leaves of Grass*, but his dress, his role, and his manner as the poet of democracy. Moreover, social and political thinkers like Ernest Renan, Thomas and Jane Carlyle, John Stuart Mill, John Ruskin, Hippolyte Taine, Ralph Waldo Emerson, Matthew Arnold, Margaret Fuller, Charles-Augustin Sainte-Beuve, and even Karl Marx, who may, like Arnold, have heard in her work "the cry of agony and revolt."

She was, literally, stupendous. Nonetheless, she was forgotten, or if not, remembered as a sexual legend, a pipe-smoking transvestite, a lesbian, a nymphomaniac, a man-eater, a virago. Like Jezebel, the Queen of Sheba, Catherine the Great, Cleopatra, and other powerful women, she was shrunk by history to the size of a vagina.

Not to be surprised: This is not unusual with women. Consider another woman of great stature and accomplishment who was important in her own time but immediately forgotten—Christine de Pisan. Earl Jeffrey Richards wrote, "Christine de Pisan is at once one of the outstanding writers of world literature and one of the most neglected." She was born in 1365 in Venice; when her father was appointed court astrologer to Charles V, the family moved to France. Pisan was educated by her father over her mother's objections; however, she was married at fifteen, and widowed at twenty-five. Impoverished, with three children and a mother to support, she began to write. She wrote lyric poetry, moral verse, and political essays, and became one of the most important writers of her time, publishing twenty-one books in all. She was also deeply involved in the political life of the French court, and counted as her patrons John, duke of Berry; Philip the Bold; John the Fearless; Louis of Orleans and his wife Valentina Visconti; and Charles VI and his wife, Isabella of Bavaria.

Among her books are a volume of lyric poems; a set of teachings and proverbs written for her son; an account of a visit to her daughter, who was at the time living in a convent; *The Book of Peace*, a moral manual for the guidance of the dauphin; *L'Epistre du chemin de long estude*, a design and program for achieving a reasonable world; and a book of feats of arms and chivalry. She was the official biographer of Charles V, and wrote the only work honoring Joan of Arc in her lifetime, *Le Ditié de Jehanne d'Arc*.

Most important for us are her contributions to what became known as the *querelle des femmes*, a quarrel begun by Jean deMeung's completion of *Le Roman de la rose*, a highly misogynistic verse treatise on love, the most popular book and the best seller of the late Middle Ages. Christine de Pisan wrote several works countering Meung's traditional and unthinking but vicious denunciation of women. The most famous and the finest of these is *The Book of the City of Ladies*. Having received some education—unlike most women of her time—Pisan knew what men wrote about them. She was thoroughly familiar with Ovid, Boethius, Valerius Maximus, John of Salisbury, Vincent de Beauvais, and Boccaccio; even if she indeed had read nothing more, some of these men's works provide a powerful introduction to misogyny. Boccaccio, moreover, had written *De mulieribus claris*, a history of famous women—the only previous major literary work on women—and had included any woman who was remembered, whether as an upright or a pernicious force.

Christine de Pisan set out, in *The Book of the City of Ladies*, to revise and rearrange received thought on women. Modeling her work on Saint Augustine's *City of God*, she tried to write a universal history of women within the framework of Christian values, which would emphasize the virtues of women and the social injustices that oppressed them. Pisan had utter clarity about women's suffering throughout history, and raised three main protests: She deplored the fact that women lacked access to education even though, she asserted, their minds were "freer and sharper" than men's; she strongly denied that women invite their own rape, as men claimed; and she denounced men's treatment of their wives—their drunken beatings, and their selfish spendthrift ways, which deprived women not just of their support and support for the children, but even of their own property, which men legally controlled. Moreover, she crossed class lines, which was unusual in her time; although she retained her period's distinction between women and ladies (women of propertied families), she admitted virtuous low-born women into her City of Ladies.

Pisan was revolutionary: No one before her had ever called men to account for their treatment of women. In work after work, she refuted the usual traducements of women, not just by denying them and citing examples to prove her point, but by approaching the charges from a woman's point of view. In this sense, she was the first writer to interpose a female voice into the universally male public world. She countered male assertions that women were incompetent and stupid, not by denials or explicit refutations, but by writing an "astonishingly learned and cultivated prose" herself. She was a brilliant writer, and was much read. Her feminist books laid the groundwork for a literary debate between women and men that would continue for several centuries. *The Book of the City of Ladies* was translated into English in 1521, over a century after it was written; and then, she was forgotten, in France and in England. A new translation of *The City of Ladies* did not appear until four years ago.

Not only was Christine de Pisan forgotten, but so were her arguments, although they were repeated and added to by feminist writers over the centuries. Three hundred years later, George Sand was informing readers to whom the argument was new that women should be educated, that male prerogatives made marriage a hell for women, and that, if women were underhanded and conniving, the flaw lay in a system that made slaves of them, and that, by inhibiting "truthfulness, spontaneity, and passion in women," left them only cunning, the weapon of slaves. Both Pisan and Sand opposed violence, and projected designs or visions of a more just and decent world.

Here are two passages, one from Pisan and one from Sand, that demonstrate the similarity in their positions on one matter. Pisan's Lady Rectitude says:

> I have not the slightest doubt that whoever cared to investigate the debate on marriage in order to write a new book in accordance with the truth would uncover other data. How many women are there actually, dear friend—and you yourself know—who because of their husbands' harshness spend their weary lives in the bond of marriage in greater suffering than if they were slaves among the Saracens? My God! How many harsh beatings—without cause and without reason—how many injuries, how many cruelties, insults, humiliations, and outrages have so many upright women suffered, none of whom cried out for help? And consider all the women who die of hunger and grief with a home full of children, while their husbands carouse dissolutely or go on binges in every tavern all over town, and still the poor women are beaten by their husbands when they return, and *that* is their supper! What do you say to that? Am I lying? Have you never seen any of your women neighbors so decked out?

Pisan replies, "Certainly, my lady, I have seen many, and I feel very sorry for them."

This is George Sand, in a letter to the Central Committee of the Left, of April 1848:

> Our legislation places woman under the covetous domination of man and transforms a married woman into an eternal minor; marriage totally destroys the property rights of one whole sex. . . .
>
> The despotic powers attributed to the husband give him the right to refuse to provide for the material welfare of his wife and children; the right to commit adultery outside the home; the right to control alone, without his wife, the education of their children; a right to corrupt the latter through bad examples or principles—for instance, by giving them his mistresses as governesses as has been known in illustrious families; the right to command the household and give orders to servants and maids; especially the right to insult his wife; the right to turn out the wife's parents while imposing on her his own; the right to reduce her to the hardships of poverty while squandering away her rightful income or capital on prostitutes; the right to beat her and have her complaints rejected by a court of law if she fails to produce witnesses or recoils in the face of scandal; finally, the right to dishonor her by unjust suspicions as well as to have her punished for misbehavior. All these rights are barbarous, abominable, and inhumane.

She adds that, until these rights are abolished, "women will always have the vices of the oppressed, that is to say, the cunning ruses of slaves."

Here we are, 140 years later, having only in this century, and only in certain Western nations, emancipated women from the legal oppression of marriage, but still struggling with its inequities and those of the workplace; having only within the past decade achieved relatively equal access to education; and still campaigning to teach men that women are not responsible for their own rape. Some of us have tried to write universal histories of women; many of us are still trying to achieve enough of a voice in the public world to influence its decisions, to insist that the human race does not have to live in contention and struggle, if it will give up its idolatry of power.

Years ago, a great scholar named Arthur Lovejoy wrote a famous book, *The Great Chain of Being*. Lovejoy liked to trace the course of an idea through history rather than to concentrate on a single period. In this book, he focused on the notion, which he traced back to Plato, of a rational and therefore comprehensible cosmos. This notion was given graphic form in the Middle Ages, when men saw the cosmos as a huge hierarchy in which the power of God was transmitted through ranks: through the various classes of angels and the planets they controlled, through earthly rulers and classes of men, through women and classes of animals, through everything that exists. Each entity—creature or clod, lion or lily—had a stated, fixed place in the scheme of things, and everything was linked—in form, purpose, or similitude—to everything else. Every entity had a purpose, and the whole of creation testified to the glory of deity. This vision of the universe dominated men's minds for hundreds of years, and died out completely only in the eighteenth century. Lovejoy commented that the idea "constitutes one of the most grandiose enterprises of the human intellect," and that it failed—not because people no longer believed in this scheme, but because they were not able to demonstrate that rationality, in the human sense, governed the universe.

When I was asked to speak at this tenth anniversary of the founding of the Friends of George Sand, it occurred to me that there was another great chain—not at all grandiose, but rather, grand; not quite as encompassing, but far more visible and palpable—that runs through human history. It is the chain of women who for hundreds of years—perhaps even thousands—have worked and struggled and written in an attempt to heal the world's sickness. That illness, we now see, may be fatal: nuclear power, chemical emissions, and the increasing incidence of war and lethal accident appear to be carrying our race and our planet to the brink of extinction. Nonetheless, the voice of women still goes unheeded.

What were they saying, our foremothers? "Men, be kinder to women"? Nonsense! They were tougher-minded than that. Christine de Pisan and George Sand were only two among thousands of women who have urged the human race to entertain an alternate vision of life and society, one in which power is not the highest value. If power were not the highest value, the concrete, palpable emblems of superiority would not be necessary. That is, if men did not feel they had to be in control simply in order to call themselves men, they would not so unalterably demand a class of inferiors—women, and men of nondominant groups; they would not so unremittingly seek symbols of status, wealth, and power. Instead of contending against each other interminably, they, and all of us, would find a common ground in which we could respect and live with each other. Not only would material goods be distributed more fairly, but people would be happier—all people. I am, of course, grossly simplifying very sophisticated feminist thinking; but it was with such a sense of things that George Sand wrote her political pamphlets and her novels, and that Pisan wrote her histories, her outlines of a better world, her counsel to the dauphin, and her debates with misogynists.

The root of injustice in this world is the need to dominate; and that need is directed first and foremost at women. Attempts to redress the evils that fall upon women always entail efforts to redress the evils done the poor and the despised (every society has a despised group, different from the dominant group in color, ethnic background, religion, or class), and the harm done to nature itself. *There are no "women's issues"*: problems specific to women affect children, the future generation of humans; and the causes of women's problems are the causes of men's problems too.

To whatever degree they could, our female forebears addressed this basic fact: That the deification of domination—the belief that God is power—is harmful to the human race. Although she herself lived as an autonomous being, Pisan could not suggest revolt against the established order, and therefore could not suggest that women remain single or divorce abusive husbands, acts that were seen as revolt in a society in which women were forced to be dependent on men. In the final paragraphs of *The City of Ladies*, she somewhat sadly advises women to make the best of their circumstances, whatever they may be. Although George Sand had many women friends and lived in relative sexual freedom she could not imagine women supporting women in a sisterhood that constituted a political base, and therefore could not describe such a situation in her fiction; nor could she depict women with sexual autonomy and still find publishers for her work. Neither could women writers of much later times—Edith Wharton, for instance, or Virginia Woolf. Nonetheless, all of these women perceived that oppression of women was fundamental to the man-made miseries of the human condition.

This is a literary and not a political forum, and it may seem I am emphasizing the political aspect of literature to the detriment of matters of style and structure. However, I believe that all literature is political, even literature that does not touch apparent political issues, and that style and form as well as content reflect political thinking—that they are all connected, inextricable even. I believe in a great chain of being—a chain reaching back to the moment power became God (or God became power) and man began to be defined as the controller—of writers, thinkers, artists, and ordinary people who urged a different view of humanity and the purposes of life. Moreover, a major part of that great chain is the work of women pioneers, women of courage and originality, who dared to utter what few wanted but everyone needed to hear. I salute one of the greatest of these women—George Sand.

Part I

RUSTIC NOVELS

1

Apprenticeship According to George Sand

Anne Berger

George Sand wrote her autobiography and a series of novels of country life during the same period. Having gone through the double apprenticeship of the art of living and writing, she decided in the late 1840s to tell the story of her life. She no longer needed, at that point, to learn in order to live. She had "reached an age of tranquillity when her personality had nothing to gain by displaying itself." She no longer "sought the key words."[1] It was when she ceased to believe that the subject could be grasped through speculation that she undertook to "communicate herself" to others in a pedagogical and maternal gesture. At this moment, she definitively assumed the position of the artist, identifying herself with a destiny that she neither foresaw nor wanted, and typing the thread of her life to the thread of the text. It was as an artist that she proceeded to reveal a reality without which the teaching provided by fiction remained, according to her, incomplete. However, she said, "It is costly for an artist to touch on this reality . . . : it is not without a great effort that *I will descend into the prose of my subject*."[2] Thus, the novels of country life coincide with her accession to the peak of art. From this point, the artist will undertake a difficult descent in order to once again touch the reality of his or her subject, indeed of *the* subject.

George Sand's aesthetic concerns in the prefaces of her rustic novels seem to display the success of her ascent. Indeed, she comes close to formulating an aesthetic theory when she examines the complex connections between art and nature, on the one hand, and art and history, on the other. The degree to which she idealizes her rustic characters adds further evidence. Idealization is an essential part of artistic representation and activity, as she repeatedly stresses.[3] Finally, the

I would like to thank James R. Siegel for his assistance in translating this chapter.

apparent lack of autobiographical concern in her rustic novels at the moment when *Histoire de ma vie* (The Story of My Life) was written contrasts with the extensive use of personal material in her other novels. (The personal stance in the prefaces to her other novels accounts for their ideological cast as well as for their tone, which is either apologetic or polemic.)

If the novels of country life seem to assume a stance at odds with the prosaic reality of her subject, they are at the same time the most singular and most accomplished expression of her artistic language. Whereas George Sand often indulges in the novelistic conventions of her time by offering the reader a mixture of realistic description and *rocambolesque* adventures, she has an entirely different purpose in her *études champêtres*.[4] Condemning the novelistic production of her time as an unfortunate offspring of bourgeois ideology, she presents the rustic novel as a reversal of the contemporary novel, which delights in the disfiguration of reality,[5] and uses the pen as a "dagger" in the services of a "brutal and fiery art."

George Sand opposes the study of the quiet "mystery of primitive simplicity" to the violence of bourgeois representation. Indeed, she wrote most of her rustic novels in Nohant, her native village, far from the tumults of history and the seductions of society. She was to return there more and more often in the second and nonwritten part of her life. In this sense, she departs from the implacable law, epitomized in Honoré de Balzac's novels, that governs the course of all social and artistic education. This law commands the break with native land and attachments. It demands that artistic success be defined through social accomplishment, the symbol of which is the conquest of Paris.[6] On the contrary, artistic maturation seems to coincide for George Sand with a return to an original location. I would also like to read this return as an attempt to recover her own language. George Sand did not intend to revive the aristocratic tradition of the "pastoral" whose idyllic representations are obviously part of an idealistic denial, if not a refusal, of history.[7] She dismisses both the parricidal dagger of the bourgeoisie and the shepherd's crook of Marie Antoinette. Indeed, her rustic novels, with the exception of *Jeanne*, have some features in common with fairy tales: All's well that ends well. Obstacles, such as the money problems that threaten the stories with the phantom of bourgeois society, are magically overcome: Marriage sanctifies the abolition of the contradictions and upheavals imposed by history. However, even if she explicitly resorted to the strategies of fairy tales, George Sand insisted on the truth of her endeavor. François Rollinat, her friend and the interlocutor of her preface to *François le champi*, recalls that the priest's housekeeper and the man who twines hemp told them a "true story":

> "Between the two of them they told us a true story, rather long, which looked like an intimate novel. Do you remember it?"
> "Perfectly, and I could retell it word for word in their language."[8]

At the end of the novel, someone who has just heard the story echoes Rollinat's remark:

"Then the story is completely true?" Sylvie Courtioux asked.

"If it isn't, it could well be," answered the twiner of hemp. "And if you don't believe me, go and see for yourself."[9]

Thus, the "truth" of its narrative conditions guarantees the truthfulness of the rustic tale. It is a true story because it was directly recounted by real peasants. All the difficulty and originality of George Sand's project lies in her desire to make the language of the peasants heard. Ethnographic critics tried to determine the extent to which she was faithful to this project, and she was declared faithful because her tale is studded with regional Berrichon expressions, and unfaithful because she occasionally invented similar phrases.

The contradictory necessity of faithfulness and unfaithfulness to the peasant language is precisely the central issue. The peasant mode of expression is fundamentally oral. The relation of "our literature"—which "only knows how to amplify or disguise"—to "rustic songs, narratives and tales" emblematizes the relation of written to oral language.[10] Since we learn to speak before we learn to read or write, the passage to writing can be experienced as a shift to a second language. In any case, it opens a division internal to linguistic practice: It requires translation, which is inevitably unfaithful. It provokes a defiant distancing, if not the total obliteration, of all traces of an orality improper to the code of writing. Therefore, although George Sand was able to "recount word for word in their language" François le Champi's story as it was told by the peasants, she had to translate it from the moment she wrote it down: "Their language demands to be translated; one has to write in French and not allow oneself any word that is not unless it is so intelligible that a footnote would be useless for the reader."[11] What should then be found in the rustic novels is a way to articulate a language doubly primitive and thus doubly menaced by disappearance: primitive or primary because it is oral, and primitive because it is spoken by the most primitive layer of society.

I should like to list rapidly the linguistic devices that, by emphasizing the primacy of the oral, enabled George Sand to be faithful to peasant language. She particularly liked to place the narration in the mouths of peasants; she generally has her characters tell the story. Even in the case of *Jeanne*, the first and least strictly rustic of her rustic novels, where the sad fate of the heroine could be linked to the failure of restoring an original language, she invented the following dedication:[12]

To Françoise Meillant

You cannot read, my quiet friend. But your daughter and mine have been to school. Some day, at a gathering on a winter evening, while you spin, they will tell you the story which will become much prettier by passing through their mouths.[13]

Despite the denaturing quality of writing, the possibility of passing the tale through the mouths of the daughters to the mother might save, if not Jeanne, at least her story. The great importance granted to dialogue in George Sand's novels as well as in all her writings—for example, her insistence on considering written correspondence as "chatter"—seems to me another indication of her desire to inscribe or represent orality.[14]

Dialogue represents the simplest form of oral communication. It also functions as a main diegetic tool in the novels. Whether we think of the dialogue between the narrator and "his" friend in the prefaces of *François le champi* and *La Petite Fadette* or of the dialogues between François and Madeleine, Landry and Fadette, Bernard and Edmée, or even between She and He (*Elle et lui*), in every case their maieutic virtue is essential to the development of the story. Every time women speak, with the exception of the prefaces where the male friend plays the role of initiator and maieutician, it allows that other to give birth to his own speech. The dialogue guarantees his coming into the world; introspection is practically nonexistent in the rustic novels. When it does occur, it involves the interiorization of received speech. Above all, dialogue is the royal path of love; through it, the essence of love manifests itself. Landry falls in love with the speech of little Fadette at a moment when the two find themselves outside the social scene. It is just at the point in Fadette's speech when she tells him that she takes care of her little brother as though she were his mother (thus revealing the maternal figure hidden under her rags and her boyishness) that Landry falls madly in love with her.[15] In a similar way, one could read the story of François the waif as another instance of love at first speech. It tells of the coming to speech, thanks to Madeleine, of a poor, nameless child who "did not know how to say a word." By addressing herself to him and by loving him, Madeleine literally gives him speech.

In *The Story of My Life*, George Sand associates the moment when she was forced by her paternal grandmother to stop speaking the Berrichon patois with her mother's departure. The grandmother forced the mother to leave after the death of their common love, Maurice Dupin, George Sand's father. She provided her granddaughter with a second upbringing (succeeding the original upbringing under the mother's guidance) which George Sand describes as an attempt to break original ties. Thus began a period of suppression that she evoked in these terms: "She [the grandmother] was eager to cast off my inveterate sloppiness which my mother had never bothered to correct. I wasn't to roll on the ground any more, or to laugh so loud, or to talk our broad Berrichon dialect."[16] The repression of the mother coincides with the prohibition of Berrichon.

The distance between the "base" and the "summit" between *The Story of My Life* and the Berrichon novels, between "the reality of the subject" and the artistic ideal, is clearly marked. However, perhaps one could say that in reaching the summit of art, George Sand directed herself toward her mother's tongue as though it were the living source of her artistic language.

The statement that opens the actual narrative of *The Story of My Life* is often forgotten: "One is not only one's father's child, *one is also a bit, I believe, one's mother's*. It seems to me one is even more so; we are held to the womb which bore us in the most immediate, powerful and sacred way."[17] This statement is forgotten because it emerges with such pain and comes with such reticence before it affirms itself. By contrast, one does not forget, particularly if one is a critic by profession, this other sentence, which is so assertive: "I will go on with my father's story since he is, without punning, the real author of the story of my life."[18] It resonates all the more in memory since *The Story of My Life* indeed begins with the story of George Sand's father. Moreover, the word "author" seems to clearly establish the symbolic affiliation between "the author of life" ("l'auteur de ses jours") and the author of novels. It has always been easier, and this was even more true in Sand's time, to have oneself recognized as the child of one's father.

Were we to look more closely, however, we could avoid a precipitous interpretation that would make George Sand, a writer with a masculine pseudonym, the worthy daughter, if not the son, of her father, Maurice. For the story of the father that George Sand recounts so ardently is in fact the marvelous story of a mother and a son and their reciprocal passion. Maurice, the beloved and loving son, will then display these treasures of love transmitted to him by his mother for Sophie-Victoire, the mother of George Sand. A woman of the people, and older than he, Sophie-Victoire could have matched the revolutionary ideals of his mother if the latter had not been jealous of her. Maurice remained faithful to the mother, and was thereafter torn between two loyalties that were one in their origin. I would like to recall two important moments in George Sand's narrative. In the first, she evokes Maurice's voluntary enlistment in the service of the Revolution while his mother was in jail during the Terror: "Although suffering from the Revolution in his very entrails because he felt his adored mother under the knife, I never see him curse the Mother-ideas ["les Idées mères"] of the Revolution."[19] Maurice Dupin is faithful to the maternal principle even when it entails contradiction.

The second moment seems to me even more significant. It follows the recounting of a heart-rending separation, again provoked by revolutionary events:

> This poor child had never left his mother, he had never known, never foreseen pain. *He was as beautiful as a flower and as chaste as a maid.* He was sixteen. . . . *At that age, a boy raised by a tender mother is an exceptional being in creation. He belongs, so to speak, to no gender. He loves his mother in a way a daughter does not love her* and will never be able to love her. Drowned in the bliss of being exclusively loved and adoringly cherished, this mother is the object of a kind of cult for him. This is love without the storms and the faults he will be dragged into later by love for another woman. Yes, this is ideal love, and it lasts only a moment in a man's life.[20]

Thus, the ideal son is indeed a daughter; the loving son represents the ideal daughter of the mother, the one George Sand did not have but was herself. It is in this way that George Sand identifies herself with her father: not with a paternal father-figure, but with the son of the mother, or even of two mothers. George Sand adds, if a man is "capable of ardently and nobly loving a new idol" (his wife), it is because "he will have gone through the sacred apprenticeship of true love with his mother." Was not George Sand the adored and adoring daughter of her own mother and the "son" of her grandmother, who recognized in her the living image of her late son? After a few sentences, the story that George Sand tells us ceases to be strictly biographical and turns into a subjectless reverie, a prelude to a novelistic creation.[21] Can one not recognize in this narrative the very story of *François le champi* that George Sand started to write in 1847, the year she started to put down her own story? Does not François, with his "mother" Madeleine, experience the sacred apprenticeship of a true and ideal love? Nothing is more sublime, indeed more sublimated, than this novel of love, the most perfect and the least erotic of all romantic novels. It tells the story of a son "as well behaved as a good girl," endowed with the extraordinary capacity to act also as the mother.[22] He, in turn, takes care of Madeleine in all the ways she took care of him; he looks after the house, and he cures and feeds her. One could well consider this story the original scene of George Sand's fantasy since this term relates the realm of the poetic to the unconscious. In *François le champi* one finds the system of her identifications as well as the source of her romantic imagination. "In my opinion," she wrote as a conclusion to her description of this sacred apprenticeship, "poets and novelists have not sufficiently recognized this observable topic, this swift and unique moment in the life of a man, which is a source of poetry." Then she interrupts the dream-story of a father eternally kept by death in the guise of a young man, a faithful lover and faithfully loved, with the exclamation: "This existence would have made such a beautiful topic for a novel, had not the principal characters been my father, my mother and my grandmother!"[23] I leave George Sand with her paraliptical statement. I will only note that it could lead us to rethink the connections between the biographical and the novelistic in her work. Whether it concerns Maurice Dupin, George Sand herself, or Maurice Sand, the son who took his mother's name, what she tells is indeed the story of the mother's child. For the first two characters of this intimate novel, it is a story about the restoration of ties upset by history. Is not history itself the sad account of innumerable separations?

George Sand describes the catastrophic separation that initiates the historical process precisely as a separation from original language. In the passage that concerns us she engages in a diatribe against the damage of the second education, the education the boy gets no longer from his mother but at school. The school boy becomes ugly, he begins to fear women, "his mother's caresses make him blush," "the most beautiful languages of the world," those of the poets, disgust him. George Sand concludes:

> It will take him years to lose the fruit of his detestable education, *to learn his own language* forgetting the Latin he hardly knows and the Greek he does not know at all, so he can form his taste, and have the right idea of history. . . . *Only then will he love his mother.* But the passions instantly seize him and he will never have known this heavenly love I was talking about, which is like a pause for a man's soul in the bosom of an enchanting oasis.[24]

Thus, the writer advocates a third moment of apprenticeship aimed at unlearning the lessons of society in order to recover the taste of one's own tongue. In my opinion, this educational project is the most subtle and the most revolutionary aspect of George Sand's thought. She does not conceive of the return to the mother as a regression to a state of nature, a recrossing of the threshold of language acquisition. Rather, she thinks of it as a passage beyond divisions (nature/culture, body/language) created precisely by placing the mother outside the sociocultural order.

Contrary to what a Lacanian or Kristevan analysis would have us believe, in George Sand's life and work it is the mother who guarantees access to the symbolic order and the maintenance of meaning through the gift of speech made to the child. As evidence, I refer the reader to the many anecdotes of language acquisition told by George Sand in *Story of My Life*. They are all connected with the mother, whether they concern the first utterance of the verb "to love" or the endless fairy tales little Aurore invents for her mother. The latter, "a natural artist," helps her daughter keep hold of the thread of her speech. I would add to these examples the reading lessons which constitute a privileged topos in her novels. In *Mauprat*, for instance, Patience learns how to read poetry under the direction of the maternal Edmée. Madeleine teaches François how to read in *François le champi*; the fact that she can read is considered her most striking feature by the peasant narrators. The scene always shows two people reading aloud, such as when the mother tells her child a bedtime story. It is precisely the story of François the waif that Proust's mother tells him in a voice that penetrates him forever. Thus, the dimension of speech is maintained and creates the pleasure of consuming the book in the union of mouths and ears. Through speech, the primitive maternal and cultural pleasure is linked to the production of meaning. Thus, the "problem" Lacan evokes for us might be resolved. "The problem is that of the relationship in the subject between speech and language": "speech" by which the subject believes he or she expresses him- or herself as the subject of his or her desire, and "language," which, by separating the subject from his or her own body, abolishes desire as it sanctions it.[25] "Speech indeed is a gift of language," Lacan wrote. However, if "in the gift of speech resides all the reality of its effects," still Lacan gives us nothing to think of in regard to the gift.[26] He does not qualify the gift; he does not say "who" gives. Rather, he suggests that language gives itself, that the word, in enunciating itself, makes a present of itself, just as the law, God, or the analyst according to Lacan do. However, if Lacan is right to say that the gift of speech, by generating transference, establishes the "efficacy of linguistic symbols" is not what gives, what provokes giving, or what is given, under the name of transference, love? Moreover, if this gift of speech was the gift of the mother's love, it would give, as to George Sand or François, the gift of love as well as the gift of speech.

It is in this perspective that I would read the thematic of the promise (*parole donnée*) in George Sand's work. The promise inaugurates many love stories. Even before being acknowledged as a gift or a bond of love, the gift of a word unites Landry and Fadette as well as Bernard and Edmée, and guarantees their everlasting fidelity. I would say that George Sand conceives of language not as Verbum but as Fides, as oath ("foi jurée"), binding speech, responsible for repairing the upheavals of history, which inscribes the subject in the social at the expense of the body. This is why the nuptials at the end of the rustic narratives coincide with reunion; the wedding ceremony celebrates the return of the hero who for a while has lived in an unfamiliar social scene. It consecrates the victory of the original love bond, the end of separation and its threats, and the retaking of the first paths. This last issue is underlined by the Sandian topology of lost paths, paths leading astray or straight to their goal: to the point of departure. In *François le champi*, *La Petite Fadette*, and *La Mare au diable*, all these paths lead back to the mother.

One can always find one's way back to the mother. Such, too, is the lesson of *Mauprat*. That life offers more than one path, that education can always modify tendencies and allow "a soul plunged in the depths of an unclean mire as it emerges from the cradle" nonetheless to develop, illustrates the good as well as the orientation of a particular apprenticeship: Bernard Mauprat, removed early from the maternal cradle and left to the feudal and masculine barbarity of his uncles, will find in Edmée the educating mother who will help him to unlearn the lessons of his caste in order to learn how to speak and how to love well.[27]

The direct connection between the maternal tongue and the poetic tongue can be attributed to George Sand's own mother's predispositions. She was the daughter of a bird seller and a "singing bird" herself. A "bird song" that "his mother Zabelle used to tell him to put him to sleep, in the parlance of the old days of our country" comes to François on his way back to his "second mother," Madeleine (actually the fourth "mother" according to the plot), whom he has decided to marry.[28]

> Une pive
> cortive,
> Anc ses piviots,
> Cortiviots,
> Livardiots,
> S'en va pivant
> Livardiant
> Cortiviant.[29]

It is also in relation to the mother's desire—at least George Sand's—that I would interpret the writer's characterization of the road to creation: the path of idealization, which she represents as an ascent toward the summit. Here is what she says about it in a letter to her friend Gustave Flaubert at the moment when she reaches the summit, some months before her death: "As for me I want to gravitate right up to my last breath, not with the certitude nor the need of finding elsewhere a good place, but because my sole joy is in keeping myself and mine on an upward road. In other words *I flee the sewer and I seek the dry and the clean*, certain that it is the law of my existence."[30] Is not the learning of the dry and the (neat and) clean (*propre*) the paradigm of all first education and the indication of the child's submission to the mother's desire which, in matters of cleanliness, has the force of law? We can confirm this by referring to the scene George Sand describes as a traumatic memory of her early childhood, when her mother snatched her from the pleasure of splashing about in an imaginary river that she called a sewer. We should no longer be surprised by the story George Sand addresses to "those interested in the making of works of art" in the foreword of *François le champi*.[31] Here she describes how she took a path "no one is ever likely to take" which led to a muddy pond she again calls a sewer. Suddenly a wild child springs over the sewer as if to illustrate Freud's remarks on children's theories of birth. The narrator helps him across the sewer and begins to ask him questions, as Madeleine did in the first conversation she had with François, when she finds him on the bank of the river. The child, who has no name and no parents, does not know how to answer. George Sand concludes with the necessity for education, recalling that she herself had "had several Champi of both sexes brought up."[32]

Does not the law of existence of George Sand's characters consist in having them march in the direction of the dry and the clean (propre)? Is not learning to speak well a way of pleasing the mother by sublimating the erotic impulses and displacing them from the anal-genital zone to the mouth? Under the benevolent protection of the first god of George Sand's first religion, Corambé, the mouth tells stories that are so clean that the body is nearly absent from them. "Let's make a novel which would be a religion, or a religion which would be a novel."[33] Thus was born Corambé, about whom George Sand tells us that she imagined him sometimes with the features of her mother, and sometimes with those of a swineherd named Pleasure!

Education, according to George Sand, begins and ends near the river. "Let's go to the fountain. Maybe I will find my tongue there," François says at the end of the novel.[34] This is where he first met Madeleine; where he was born, so to speak. In the meantime he has learned not to throw himself into the river, not to plunge back into it in a gesture of deadly regression. François and Françoise the Fadette, or even Bernard Mauprat, dirty children of the river, the sewer, and the swamp, thus learn, through love, to live, to speak, to wash themselves, and to become well-behaved (propres)—as well-behaved and pure as François Rollinat, George Sand's devoted friend who was her favorite interlocutor in the rustic novels, the co-singer of a long, amebean song, the ultimate addressee of *Story of My Life*, the representative of an asexual love, and the most faithful and perfect friend of George Sand's life.[35] Indeed George Sand may have taken him for the mother's intermediary; was he not charged with watching over the realization of a desire that had become the law of her existence, the desire transmitted by the mother for a *proper* tongue?[36]

NOTES

1. *Histoire de ma vie* (Paris: Gallimard, Pléiade, 1970), 1:8. Only certain sections have been translated. This and all subsequent translations are those of the author unless otherwise indicated.

2. Ibid., 1:7; author's emphasis.

3. "I must confess that I felt a deathly disgust at imposing my personality on the audience . . . when I felt my heart and my head filled with personalities stronger than myself, more logical, more complete, more ideal, types superior to myself, in a word, characters from a novel"; ibid., 1:6.

4. This is the name she gave to this new literary exercise in her preface to *François le champi* (Paris: Gallimard, Folio, 1976), 50.

5. Ibid., 50.

6. It is still the case today for those who dream not so much of writing as of becoming a writer.

7. George Sand called it "bergeries littéraires."

8. Sand, *François le champi*, 52.

9. Ibid., 251.

10. Ibid., 47.

11. Ibid., 52.

12. "My own style, my phrasing, stood in my way. . . . It seemed to me that I daubed the dry, shiny, naive and flat paintings of the primitive masters with oil and tar." *Jeanne* (Paris: Nelson and Calmann-Lévy), 8.

13. Ibid., 9.

14. See, for instance, *The George Sand–Gustave Flaubert Letters*, trans. Aimée McKenzie (London: Duckworth and Co., 1922).

15. "When I was only ten years old, my mother left to my care the poor ugly child. . . . I cure him when he is ill, whereas my grandmother would kill him, for she does not know how to take care of children; so I preserve this poor little wretch's life. . . . And when I think of going out to service, Landry, so as to have some money of my own, and to escape my present poverty, my heart is ready to burst with pity, and accuses me *as if I were my little Grasshopper's mother*, and were letting him die by some fault of mine. . . . Landry had listened to little Fadette. . . . At last the way in which he spoke of her little brother, the Grasshopper, greatly affected him, and he suddenly felt such a liking for her that he would have defended her against all the world." (*La Petite Fadette*, trans. Jane Minot Sedgwick [New York: George H. Richmond, 1893], 152–154; author's emphasis).

16. Excerpts from *Histoire de ma vie*, translated and adapted under the title *My Life* by Dan Hofstadter (New York: Harper and Row, 1979), 81. Translation modified. For the French, see *Histoire de ma vie*, 1:638.

17. *Histoire de ma vie,* 1:15; author's emphasis.

18. Ibid., 1:157.

19. Ibid., 1:421.

20. Ibid., 1:76; author's emphasis.

21. The narration shifts abruptly from the historical past ("He was sixteen") to an indeterminate present whose generality is emphasized by the use of the indefinite article: "At that age, a boy, raised by a tender mother is an exceptional being in creation."

22. Sand, *François le champi*, 123.

23. Sand, *Histoire de ma vie*, 1:77.

24. Ibid., author's emphasis.

25. Lacan, "Fonction et champ de la parole et du langage," in Lacan, *Ecrits* (Paris: Seuil, 1966), 59.

26. Ibid., 183.

27. George Sand, *Mauprat* (Paris: Gallimard, Folio, 1981), 53.

28 Sand, *François le champi*, 236.

29. This song of a mother bird and her young is a mixture of Berrichon dialect and literary invention. It is virtually a nonsense rhyme and is untranslatable.

30. McKenzie, *Sand–Flaubert Letters*, Jan. 12, 1876.

31. Sand, *François le champi*, 38.

32. Ibid., 39.

33. *Histoire de ma vie*, 1:812; Corambé or Corps-en-B (Body-at-B). George Sand

recounts that the little Aurore obstinately refused to pronounce the letter *B* when her mother was teaching her to read, thus resisting learning the written code, even when taught by her mother, by a single letter. Are we to understand that at *B* the body escapes linguistic discipline?

34. Sand, *François le champi*, 250.

35. Sand dedicated *Histoire de ma vie* to him in 1875, twenty-five years after she completed the book and one year before her death. See the passages that evoke this relationship: 2:122–125, 758.

36. *Propre* means both "own" (one's own) and "clean." Cleanliness is the root of propriety.

2

La Petite Fadette: A Pre-Feminist Dialectic of Tradition

Brigitte Lane

In her 1848 preface to *La Petite Fadette*, George Sand establishes from the very start, and not without irony, a relationship between her novel and the folktale tradition, by declaring: "We dedicate this work to our friends in prison; since we are forbidden to discuss politics with them, we can only create *tales* to entertain them or put them to sleep."[1]

Thus, the novelist, whose declared goal is to create "a series of village tales," returns to the familiar style of *François le champi* (1846) and, as in the earlier work, hides behind a male narrator: the traditional hemp-beater (*chanvreur* or *chanvreux*) of the Berry region, through whom she expresses herself throughout the narrative.[2]

From this beginning, one could therefore expect a very ordinary story dominated by the conventions of the popular tale. This is not the case, however, for beyond the staged figure of her male narrator, the author (an invisible female presence) performs, throughout the work, a subtle manipulation of the usual traditional elements to establish as part of her discourse a subversive (almost feminist) dialectic of the conventions of the traditional folktale and of oral tradition in general.

This chapter will therefore attempt to show how the novel *La Petite Fadette*, which came to be considered as children's literature, especially in the eyes of the French public, is in fact a deeply modern and original work that presented a somewhat revolutionary view of life and society for its time, for beyond the narration (and even beyond the action), George Sand repeatedly counters the accepted male conventions of the traditional folktale. She does so at three different levels.

THE CONCEPTUAL LEVEL

At the conceptual level, the novelist deals first with the notion of "metamorphosis"—a notion that is usually associated, in the realm of traditional literature, with the concept of magic or the idea of "divine" (supernatural) intervention.

One of the best examples of the use of this concept is the well-known story of "Beauty and the Beast," as well as its seventeenth-century literary variants which (for the most part) are mere copies or offshoots of the traditional tale classified as Type 425 by Aarne-Thompson. All of these narratives are more or less derived from the very ancient story of "Amor and Psyche," related by Apuleïus in *The Golden Ass* as early as the middle of the second century.[3]

La Petite Fadette, like the traditional tale, narrates the story of a "monstrous" being (or rather of a being perceived as "monstrous" by others, because of its dual nature: half-human, half-animal). However, the "monster's" inner, spiritual beauty and thoroughly human nature are ultimately revealed through the generous and redeeming love of a human being of the opposite sex. This redemption is usually accompanied by a physical transformation that finally allows physical appearances and spiritual reality to coincide. Meanwhile, the character involved has gone through a physical mutation which has brought him from the animal (and supernatural) realm to a purely human realm.

A similar ambiguity of nature is found in *La Petite Fadette*, for Fanchon Fadet and her little brother, *le sauteriot* (the little grasshopper) are viewed, all the way through the first part of the book, through animal (or even "sub-animal") metaphors, given the fact that they are usually associated with insect imagery or compared with other small animals. George Sand writes, when Fanchon Fadet first appears: "Whether 'Fadette' means a little fairy or the female of the elf . . . she was thin and tiny, dishevelled and bold. She was a highly talkative and mocking child, as lively as a butterfly, as inquisitive as a red-robin and as black as a cricket."[4] She further adds: "And when I compare Little Fadette to a cricket, it amounts to saying that she was no beauty, for that poor little cricket of the fields is even uglier than that of the chimney-corner."[5]

Later, when the Saint-Andoche dance takes place, Sand stresses again the physical ugliness of Fadette, "the little cricket" (*grelet* or *grillon*). She writes: "Poor Cricket was so badly dressed that she seemed ten times uglier than usual. Landry . . . thought her far uglier than in her everyday rags. She had meant to make herself pretty but her efforts to tame her wild appearance only served to provoke laughter."[6]

Here Fanchon Fadet's ugliness touches on the ridiculous and the author concludes her description by stating that the girl "looked like a little old woman in her Sunday best."[7] Moreover, the term *dressage* (taming) stresses Fadette's almost savage, antisocial dimension, bring out again her animal attributes. However, in some respect, the so-called "ugliness" of Fanchon is associated in the villagers' eyes with her daring nonconformism and her boyish manners, which were obviously unacceptable in the nineteenth century. "She always behaved like a boy," writes Sand.[8]

Landry himself, in one of his first surges of sympathy toward Fadette, evokes the contradiction between her physical appearance and her "soul" (if it is true that the eyes are the mirror of the soul), by telling her:

> If your nose were not so short, your mouth so large and your complexion so dark, you would not be bad looking at all. For people also say that, in the country hereabouts, there is not a pair of eyes equal to yours, and if you didn't have that bold and derisive look, many would like to be viewed kindly by those eyes.[9]

Similar to the metamorphosis of the Beast, in the well-known folktale, Fanchon Fadet's metamorphosis corresponds both to a spectacular physical change and to a general change in attitude—to a "humanization" of the character.[10]

It is the love Landry feels for Fadette, as well as her secret love for him, that bring Fadette to this utter transformation in "dress as well as manners." So great is the change that Landry himself, astonished, attributes this phenomenon to witchcraft: "She is a witch, he says. She has wanted to become beautiful instead of ugly as she used to be; and here she is, beautiful by a miracle."[11]

Fadette's newly acquired beauty is also viewed as a form of socialization since she is described as having become "pleasant in her speech and dress, and her bearing towards people."[12] This double metamorphosis, which causes the villagers great astonishment, nevertheless gains her their general favor.

Unlike the metamorphosis of the Beast in the popular tale (and although this latter is partly due to "the magic of love"), Fadette's metamorphosis is not instantaneous, but rather takes place in several phases. The first phase (as mentioned earlier) is provoked by Landry's generous love, which happens to be shared by Fadette; the second phase results from the willed and essentially initiatory journey (and one-year stay) that the girl makes to Château-Meillant. To that must be added the unexpected (and almost miraculous) discovery of the treasure left by old grandmother Fadet. All this contributes to the fact that, when Fanchon returns to the village, she is perceived by the community as a totally different person and even as "the best match in the region." George Sand writes: "Two days afterwards, Little Fadette dressed very neatly, for she was no longer poor and wretched and her mourning was made of fine cloth. She walked through La Cosse and, as she had grown a good deal, those who saw her did not recognize her at first. She had become considerably lovelier during her stay in town."[13] However, eager to make it clear that this incredible transformation had nothing to do with magic or witchcraft, the novelist explains right away: "Being better lodged and fed, she had gained color and flesh as much as was suitable for her age, and she could no longer be taken for a boy in disguise, so handsome and pleasant to look at was her figure. Love and happiness, too, had given her face and person something which is at once perceived but not so easily described."[14]

The hypothesis of a magical intervention is therefore totally eliminated by Sand and, magic being excluded in favor of realism, the extraordinary changes witnessed in Fadette are attributed to highly practical causes: social acceptance, the love of another being (who is socially integrated), unexpected material wealth, better living conditions, and a better diet.[15] The universe of the folktale, which implies magic and supernatural intervention, is therefore subsumed under the rules of the rustic novel which, for its part, relies on daily life and the reality of the peasant world.

One can wonder, moreover, whether the subtitle of the novel should not be "Beauty" (here, in the masculine) and "the Beast" (in the feminine), for the truth is that the basic dynamics of the book depend on female (rather than male) action, and on the central character of Fadette whose outer transformation, indirectly symbolic of her new social acceptance and, therefore, of her entry into collective life, forms the basis of the story. On the other hand are the twins (male characters); Landry plays a relatively passive role while Sylvinet assumes a totally paralyzing function in relation to the plot and the triangle of influence formed by the three main characters.

In *La Petite Fadette*, therefore, the nineteenth-century middle-class male/female stereotypes are not only questioned, but the male/female roles are also somewhat reversed in relation to tradition.[16]

THE THEMATIC LEVEL

On the thematic level, George Sand simultaneously plays with the themes of magic, religion, and even magic as the opposite of religion.

At the beginning of the novel, if one takes into account the superstitions of the Berry region, Fadette is perceived by the village community as an ambivalent being having ties with both the animal and supernatural worlds.[17] A number of metaphors (previously cited) define her "animal" dimension, but her name (*la Fadette*) links her even more to the supernatural world, on the one hand with the *fadets*, *farfadets*, or *follets*, defined by Sand as "sweet but rather malicious elves," and on the other hand, with the *fades* (or fairies) in whom "around here," writes Sand, "nobody much believes any more."[18] The novelist herself insists on the double meaning of the name "Fadette" which (at the supernatural level) can equally mean "little elf" (in the feminine) and "little fairy" and, therefore, can designate a beneficial as well as a malefic being at the level of the conventional role.[19] Mother Fadet (Little Fadette's grandmother) is also well known in the area for her skills as a healer and perhaps a sorceress. The tradition from the Berry region requires that secrets of witchcraft be transmitted orally, from generation to generation. Fadette can therefore be viewed as a potential witch.[20]

Furthermore, her social marginality; her poverty; the fact that, as a child, she was abandoned by her mother (who was considered by the village as far from respectable); her premature role as a substitute mother to her little brother Jeanet; and finally her physical ugliness are so many elements that seem to justify the villagers' prejudices, along with the suspicion and scorn they display toward her.[21]

Moreover, by means of the revelations she makes to Landry regarding her healing talents, Fadette (and with her, George Sand) demystifies all belief in magic (or sorcery), presenting her botanical knowledge as a form of science: "As for me, she says, without being a sorceress, I know the properties of the least herbs you crush beneath your feet."[22] She later adds:

> It is true that God has made me curious, if that means wanting to know things that are hidden. But if people had been good and humane to me, I would never have dreamed of satisfying my curiosity at their expense. I would have confined my amusement to the knowledge of the secrets my grandmother teaches me for the healing of the human body.[23]

It is also Fadette who tells about her inventiveness in the art of healing. She seems indeed to have an even greater knowledge of the subject than her grandmother, since she states: "I find virtues in herbs myself which she [Mother Fadet] does not know they have, and she is quite astonished when I make drugs and she subsequently sees their good effect."[24]

George Sand insists several times on the fact that the knowledge and the use of plants for healing the human body (or even animals) is a kind of science and not magic. She had already stated earlier, wishing to denounce peasant superstitions: "In the countryside, one is never knowledgeable without being some kind of witch." By that, she means, without being *considered* a witch.

Little Fadette obviously is *not* a witch, as Sand reiterates at the end of the novel: "It [her knowledge] did not make her a witch, and she was right in denying the charge; but she had an observant mind, one that made comparisons, notes, trials, and that is undeniably a natural gift."[25]

Fanchon's great curiosity of mind, her early maturity (acquired through suffering), her keen sense of observation, and even her desire to help others, constitute what would be called, in the twentieth century, an innate scientific mind.

To the knowledge acquired in the countryside due to her great freedom will be added another type of knowledge, acquired during her stay at Château-Meillant. Religion will then complement, or rather be superimposed, on magic, for Fanchon's mistress and friend, a former nun, will teach her "a number of fine [medical] secrets which [she] had learned in her convent, in the days before the Revolution."[26]

Since this ex-nun also depicts Fanchon as a "perfect Christian," and therefore the best one can find in terms of religion, all uncertainty is removed regarding the source of the "talents" and "powers" of the young woman. The city (removed from peasant superstitions) has played, at the same time, an initiatory and liberating role for Fadette. It has made it possible for her to create a new social image of herself: an image reflecting her true nature and drawing both from science and religion, while excluding magic.[27]

A healer of the body, Fadette will soon reveal herself as also being able to heal the mind. Sylvinet's first recovery (from "delirium and fever") is accomplished thanks to her medical knowledge but also through religious techniques (imposition of hands and prayers) practiced in a total spirit of self-sacrifice.[28] Another technique she uses is a process close to hypnosis: "His body is not very ill; it is with his mind that I need to deal; I am going to try to make mine enter it," she says to Mother Barbeau.[29]

Science and religion having replaced magic in Sand's dialectical system, the witch has become a saint and the elf both a fairy and a princess, since the reader is told at the very end of the novel that Fadette "had a pretty house built . . . in order to gather in all the distressed children of the commune for four hours every weekday."[30]

As for traditional beliefs regarding twins, they are similarly demystified by George Sand (through Fadette herself, and in the name of religion) when Fanchon says to Sylvinet:

> Don't you fall back on the fact of your being a twin. There's been far too much said around you about this fondness of twins being a law of nature and how you would die, if it were thwarted. So you thought you were obeying your destiny by carrying this fondness to extremes; but God is not so unjust as to mark us for a bad fate when we still are in our mother's womb. He is not so evil as to give us ideas that we can never overcome, and you insult him, superstitious man that you are, by believing that the blood in your body contains more strength and evil destiny than there is power of resistance and reason in your mind.[31]

Fanchon Fadet (and, with her, George Sand) is thus attacking the superstitions of the Berry region, as well as popular traditional philosophy in general and the belief in fate in particular. She indirectly asserts that every human being (man or woman) can (and must) take his life into his hands and shape it himself. Here, the novel (unlike the popular folktale) denies the mythology of evil usually embodied, in oral tradition, by negative creatures such as Georgeon, the devil figure of the Berry region.[32] Thus, if the rustic novel goes against the conventions of the folktale, it also goes against its ideology.

THE STRUCTURAL LEVEL

At the structural level, it is most revealing that the character of Fadette (which gives the novel its title) only appears in the eighth chapter of the book and disappears again (or rather fades into the background) at the end of the narrative. Drawing from a well-known narrative device, which is often used in traditional literature, George Sand uses the male storyteller figure as intermediary and inserts the story of Fadette within a broader story which provides, at the same time, a frame and a context. It is the story of the Barbeau twins and of their excessive attachment to each other—according to the superstitions of Berry—that functions as a framing story. In her article "Métamorphoses du conte, du conteur et du conté, dans 'La fleur sacrée' de George Sand," Edith Jonsson-Devillers refers to it as "metanarrative" (*méta-récit*).[33] Actually, the narrative frame here reflects the contribution (as well as the ideological perspective) of the hemp-beater narrator, whereas the invisible female author surreptitiously enters the novel with the Fadette character. This framing process, which consists of inserting one narrative within another, is very old. It can be found in *The Thousand and One Nights* and also (in literary form) in numerous medieval narratives or even in more recent popular tales. What makes Sand's use of this process particularly original is the fact that she draws from it a subplot giving her novel what could be called a double focus.[34]

The action of the inner narrative, which is essentially dynamic in nature (and can be tied up with the heroic narrative tradition, although expressed here in the feminine) demands reflection. According to the folktale type number 425 (to which the story of "Amor and Psyche" belongs), the journey of the female character should be a desperate quest in search of a lost husband. According to the heroic tradition, the journey should be a male initiatory journey in search of a wife (in order to provide descendants who will assume the continuity of the family name), or "wisdom" (which is supposed to be a privilege of adulthood), and of power. From a female point of view, following the model of "Beauty and the Beast," this journey should also be an irresponsible one. What is George Sand's perspective, however? She stages a female initiatory journey by means of which the heroine moves away from the man she loves, in order to protect him and give them both the eventual opportunity to build their future together. It is not a quest for a lost husband; it is not an escape, nor a family visit. It is rather a willed transfer of the heroine into "another world" (the world outside her village), in order to allow a victorious return (as in the case of Ulysses in *The Odyssey*). The goal is to make possible the future union of those who share a common love and have been faithful to one another in order to promote community peace and social harmony around the main protagonists of the story. The only traditional element left out by George Sand is revenge.

In conclusion, the novelist structures her narrative around the feats of a female character who is neither passive nor deceitful; neither a victim nor a fool, as some traditional patterns would require. On the contrary, she is fully aware, in complete control of her life, and able to take action. With this reversal of the male/female values usually present in traditional narratives (and, particularly, in folktales), Sand asserts and demonstrates the equality of men and women along with the possible superiority of the latter. Fadette is, to a point, Landry's teacher: She shares with him her knowledge of "herbal properties" as well as her "recipes for healing people and animals." She is endlessly full of good advice, and frees him from his superstitions, thanks to her positive approach to the world. Having "taught" Landry, she also "liberates" Sylvinet by forcing him to enter life. Fadette completely dominates the action of the novel, whether from a psychological or a dynamic point of view. She is omnipresent; she is an endless source of light. However, once again, her triumph over her life's circumstances is not due to any kind of supernatural intervention but exclusively to her own qualities: her intelligence, sensitivity, awareness, and willpower.[35] Only the discovery of an unexpected fortune (her grandmother's hidden treasure) can be viewed as a providential event.

Subtle manipulator of the conventions of the folktale, Sand uses it as she does folklore in general: She puts it "through the filter of her own imagination and feelings" as writes Nicole Belmont in her article "L'Académie celtique et George Sand."[36] However, the novelist is willing to draw on definite elements of the genre when they fulfill her ideology. For example, the story has a happy ending (as does any genuine folktale) since the heroine finds love, marriage, wealth, and experiences at the same time—social integration and promotion—as would any central character of a folktale who was originally the victim of his community. Moreover, in *La Petite Fadette*, the surrounding community benefits from the girl's social ascension (both in a material and a spiritual sense) since she helps the villagers get rid of some of their superstitions and dedicates part of her newly acquired fortune to the local children in distress.

In the rustic novel, contrary to the folktale, the negative characters (Madelon and Sylvinet) are neither punished nor destroyed, but rather they disappear in the end.[37] As for the positive characters, in agreement with the folktale tradition, they find their reward: Cadet Caillaud (Landry's faithful companion in the days of hardship) marries Nanette (Landry's sister), and the two weddings are symbolically celebrated on the same day. Obviously, Sand has thwarted, twisted, and fragmented the conventions of the popular tale to integrate them in her novel. However, she has done so in order to promote an ideology of good and make possible a generous ending that illustrates her philosophy of life and her idea of an ideal society.

Invisible (but powerful and omnipresent) beyond the voice of her narrator, the hemp-beater, George Sand dismantles the conventions of popular tradition. In *La Petite Fadette*, she presents us with the poetic figure of a young country maiden "liberated" from the superstitions of her time: Fanchon Fadet.

The notion of metamorphosis which is constantly used by the novelist in her narrative can also be viewed as a metaphor describing Fadette's passage from adolescence to adulthood (a particularly original approach, since Marilyn Yalom tells us that there was no such thing as the concept of adolescence in the nineteenth century.[38] However, such a partial interpretation only corresponds to a minor level of the story. The truth is that the main function of the whole dialectical system elaborated by Sand, in the architecture of her novel, is to show us a female character who, once she has overcome social antagonism and assumed a position of power, is able to act in a totally just, positive, and generous way. In the modern literary tale entitled *La Petite Fadette*, "Cinderella" assumes power and liberates herself: due to her intelligence, her wisdom, and her strength of will. She has no need for the protection of a fairy godmother (or any other supernatural creature) in order to establish her life. She is fully conscious that her life is in her hands.

Such a reading of *La Petite Fadette*, derived from the conventional popular folktale elements, first brings to light George Sand's extraordinary knowledge and deeply romantic understanding of the oral tradition of Berry, as well as of the larger popular tradition. If the folklorist Arnold Van Gennep (founder of French ethnography) wrote most surprisingly in 1926 that the one gift George Sand had was to drown the simplest ideas and the simplest facts in an unattractive prolixity, he was nonetheless right when he stated: "George Sand's goal was not to describe local customs for their own sake or for the sake of science; she only saw in these practices a canvas upon which she could weave 'human' as well as 'humanitarian' generalizations."[39]

Foremost among these humanitarian preoccupations was probably, in George Sand's mind, what Hippolyte Taine has called, in a few beautiful lines paying homage to the novelist, her quest for "social truth."[40]

The idealized peasant world depicted for us by George Sand in *La Petite Fadette* seems quite removed from the Berry country world of "misery and feasting" which came out of the hunger riots around the year 1845, as described by Marc Baroli in his work *La Vie quotidienne en Berry au temps de George Sand.*[41] It is not a realistic depiction but rather a mythical context well suited to the folktale genre. However, Fadette is an extremely modern character given the fact that her passage from the state of a frustrated *fadet* (elf) to that of a stereotyped *fade* (good fairy) might easily symbolize the evolution of women in modern society and their craving for benevolent power.[42] If the novel *La Petite Fadette* can be read as a folktale, it is therefore only as a modern, social and prefeminist narrative, since the term *feminism* had already appeared in France in 1837. It may be considered, in that respect, to serve a utopian ideal that has today become an accepted goal. As Victor Hugo stated at George Sand's funeral: "Beings like George Sand are public benefactors. They pass, but hardly have they passed, that in their empty space surges a new form of progress. . . . George Sand has died, but she is leaving behind for us the belief in women's rights which draws its evidence from the genius of women."[43]

NOTES

1. George Sand, *La Petite Fadette* (Paris: Librairie Générale d'Edition, Coll. Livre de Poche, 1984), 13. This and all subsequent translations are those of the author.

2. For further information on the traditional role of the hemp-beater as storyteller, see the appendix by Hugues LaPaire to *La Mare au diable* and *Légendes berrichonnes* (Paris: J. Gamber, 1927), 25–30.

3 Apuleïus, *The Golden Ass* (New York: Collier Books, 1962), 108–148. See also Paul Delarue and Marie-Louise Ténèze, *Le Conte populaire français* (Paris: Maisonneuve et Larose, 1977), 2:73–110.

4. Sand, *La Petite Fadette*, 69.

5. Ibid. One must remember that, in traditional thought, animals are closely linked with the belief in magic and witchcraft.

6. Ibid., 108.

7. Ibid.

8. It is possible to see a parallel between Fadette's "boyish manners" and Sand's male habits, which were atypical of her century.

9. Sand, *La Petite Fadette*, 129.

10. The fundamental pattern of "Beauty and the Beast" seems to appear in several of Sand's novels. See Yvette Bozon-Scalzitti, "*Mauprat*, ou la Belle et la Bête," *Nineteenth Century French Studies* 10, nos. 1 and 2 (Fall-Winter 1981–1982), 1–16. For recurrent connections between Sand's novels and the folktale tradition, see Béatrice Didier, "George Sand et les structures du conte populaire," in Simone Vierne, ed., *George Sand* (SEDES-CDU, 1983), 101–114; and Pierrette Daly, "*Consuelo* et les contes de fées," in Janis Glasgow, ed., *George Sand: Collected Essays* (Troy, N.Y.: Whitson Publishing, 1985), 20–28.

11. Sand, *La Petite Fadette*, 151. Emphasis seems, however, to be put more on male than female sorcerers in the Berry tradition. See Jean Denizet et al., *Berry* (Le Puy-en-Velay, France: Christine Bonneton, 1982), 155–161.

12. Sand, *La Petite Fadette*, 161.

13. Ibid., 207.

14. Ibid.

15. Fanchon's brother, Little Jeanet, in the end also undergoes a positive transformation. According to Sand this is due to "a better diet" and "happiness" (*La Petite Fadette*, 216).

16. On this frequent reversal of male/female roles in Sand's novel, see Bozon-Scalzitti, "*Mauprat*," and Kathryn Crecelius, *Family Romances: George Sand's Early Novels* (Bloomington: Indiana University Press, 1987).

17. Both realms are very closely related in the traditional mind. Elves are sometimes viewed as a form of the Devil in the mythology of the Berry region. See Hugues LaPaire, *Les Légendes berrichonnes* (Paris: Librairie Universitaire J. Gambe, 1927), 65–69, 127–129.

18. For further documentation on the fantastic beings of the Berry tradition, see Marie-Louise Vincent, *Le Berry dans l'oeuvre de George Sand* (Paris: Champion, 1919), 2:208–258; LaPaire, *Légendes berrichonnes*, 9–12; and Laisnel de la Salle, *Le Berry* (Paris: Maisonneuve et Larose, 1969).

19. Sand "de-regionalizes" the traditional beliefs of the Berry, according to which both the *fades* (fairies) and the *follets* (elves) can be either good or bad, in order to fit the stereotypes of the modern French folktale.

20. Here again, Sand puts the popular tradition in the feminine; folklorists remark that oral transmission of the *secret* (secret magical knowledge) usually took place in specialized families, from father to son. Magical knowledge could also be acquired through esoteric books such as *Le Grand Alber*, *Le Dragon rouge*, or *La Poule noire*.

21. Historians and sociologists in numerous cultures have noted the relationship between social marginality and accusations of witchcraft. See, for example, Paul Boyer and Stephen Nissenbaum, *Salem Possessed: The Social Origins of Witchcraft* (Cambridge, Mass.: Harvard University Press, 1974). In fact, had Landry been more aware of witchcraft practices in Berry, he would have known that Fadette was not a witch since she asked him for a white hen and not a black hen. While the black hen is symbolic of pacts with the Devil, the white hen is a symbol of innocence and happiness.

22. Sand, *La Petite Fadette*, 124.

23. Ibid., 126. Various aspects of popular medicine in the Berry region are described in Denizet et al., *Berry*; de la Salle, *Le Berry*; LaPaire, *Légendes*; Claude Seignolle, *Le Berry traditionnel* (Paris: Maisonneuve et Larose, 1969); and Jean-Louis Boncoeur, *Le Village aux sortilèges: Chroniques singulières sur la magie rustique dans les pays du "Coeur de la France"* (Paris: Fayard, 1979), 63–85.

24. Sand, *La Petite Fadette*, 131.

25. Ibid., 170. Father Barbeau attributes this natural gift, the ability to cure animals, to Landry; little does he know that Landry's knowledge comes from Fadette.

26. Ibid., 216.

27. Science and religion seem to be complementary in Sand's mind.

28. This might also reflect a form of spiritualist thought acquired by Sand quite early in life. According to Eve Sourian, "marvellous elements of the folktale tradition and marvellous elements of the Christian tradition were already blended" in the mind of young Sophie Dupin ("Les Opinions religieuses de George Sand: Pourquoi Consuelo a-t-elle perdu sa voix?" in Glasgow, *George Sand*, 127–138). Such a session might also be compared to modern psychoanalysis.

29. Sand, *La Petite Fadette*, 230.

30. Ibid., 245.

31. Ibid., 236.

32. The Devil is the central figure of popular mythology in the Berry region. The fact

that Fadette does not believe in the Devil, unlike Landry, is another example of her intellectual sophistication and nonconformity.

33. In Glasgow, *George Sand*, 29–39.

34. I owe this formula to Kathryn Crecelius.

35. In that respect, Fadette follows but goes beyond the initiatory progression of the male heroic journey. Her little brother, Jeanet, could almost be viewed as her traveling companion.

36. Nicole Belmont, "L'Académie celtique et George Sand: Les Débuts des recherches folkloriques en France," *Romantisme* 9 (1975): 29–38.

37. This supports Fadette's philosophical view that the world is intrinsically good and that evil is only the product of ignorance.

38. Marilyn Yalom, "Towards a History of Female Adolescence: The Contributions of George Sand" in Glasgow, *George Sand*, 204–215.

39. Arnold Van Gennep, "George Sand folkloriste," *Mercure de France*, June 1, 1926, 373.

40. Cited in Edouard Dolléans, *Féminisme et mouvement ouvrier: George Sand* (Paris: Editions Ouvrières, 1951), 16.

41. Marc Baroli, *La Vie quotidienne en Berry au temps de George Sand* (Paris: Hachette, 1982), 173–179. A more precise evaluation of Sand's "peasant realism" would require a closer examination of the language she uses in the novel. See Marie-Louise Vincent, *La Langue et le style rustiques de George Sand dans les romans champêtres* (1916; reprint: Geneva: Slatkine Reprints, 1978), 34–43.

42. For a general appraisal of Sand's "feminist" thought, consult Dolléans, *Féminisme et mouvement ouvrier*, 2–16; and Dennis O'Brien, "George Sand and Feminism," *George Sand Papers: Conference Proceedings*, vol. 1, 1976, ed. Natalie Datlof et al. (New York: AMS Press, 1980), 76–91.

43. Victor Hugo, "Obsèques de George Sand, 10 juin 1876," in Nicole Priollaud, ed., *La Femme au 19ème siècle* (Paris: Liana Levi and Sylvie Messinger, 1983), 136, 138.

3

The Language of Loss in George Sand's *Le Meunier d'Angibault*

Wendell McClendon

The novels of George Sand often include and occasionally feature scenes in which characters get lost. These scenes function in various ways. Sometimes, they evoke clearly metaphorical uses of getting lost, like those in allegorical literature.[1] At other times, they remind the reader of fairy tale scenes, as analyzed by writers such as Bruno Bettelheim and Joseph Campbell. For example, Consuelo's, Laurent's, or even Marcelle's experiences of getting lost[2] evoke, say, the separation anxiety suffered by Hansel and Gretel, the sense of alienation felt by Goldilocks,[3] or the questing that is central not only to many fairy tales, but as well to stories as diverse as Dante's *Divine Comedy* and William Golding's *Lord of the Flies*.[4]

Quite often, though, the lost scenes in Sand's works play less obvious roles than does Little Red Riding Hood's stray in the woods. That is, while Marcelle de Blanchemont of *Le Meunier d'Angibault*, for example, may be seen as passing through the three ritual stages of the quest, lost scenes such as hers are so well integrated into the novel's narrative structure that the reader may not at once see these connections or even regard the scenes as particularly noteworthy.[5] Nevertheless, a closer look at such scenes will, I think, show how important they are to understanding the social, interpersonal, and personal tensions whose resolution so informs Sand's novels.

I have chosen to approach the "dissemination" of these works through their lost scenes for a number of reasons.[6] First and foremost, the scenes are undeniably present and clearly important to the evolution of the story. Second, their presence and importance suggest what I shall call a "language of loss" that offers useful venues into many aspects of the texts, and, third, concentrating on these scenes and listening to their language helps readers avoid giving too much importance to the language of love when other matters may well be at stake.

Such is the case with *Le Meunier d'Angibault*. This novel deals with the loves of Henri Lémor and Marcelle de Blanchemont, and of Grand Louis and Rose Bricolin. In the end, however, these interpersonal relationships are less important than the personal development of the heroine, Marcelle, and the effects of that development on her, her friends, and her larger society. That is to say, this novel is less a love story than a story of education and social progress.[7] While the newly joined relations may become models for the new social order, they have not generated social progress but rather have resulted from the hard work that has made progress possible.

On the other hand, the education of Marcelle (the one who accomplishes that hard work) has everything to do with generating social progress; and the language of loss has a great deal to do with understanding that education. This brings me to the fourth and final reason why I believe that the language of loss may be important to the investigation of Sand's texts: This language has a built-in ambivalence that allows the critic to get at the irony present in much of the work, an irony which is itself a reflection of the ambivalences characteristic of human relations. Indeed, the language of loss may be especially important to the unraveling of social novels, where problems often turn upon differences between the "good guys" and the "bad guys," between who is found and who is lost, or again between who seems to be lost but is truly found, and so on. I have chosen to consider *Le Meunier* as a test case. It is not only a social novel but also one that contains a single lost scene. The investigation of that scene's language will help to elucidate the entire work through its contributions to the reader's understanding of Marcelle de Blanchemont.

In the figurative sense, Marcelle has been lost all her life. Her recently departed husband has kept her in ignorance and inaction, so that she cannot now take care of the simplest business. Moreover, the heroine's radical-minded lover, Henri Lémor, feels that he must abandon her too, lest he lead her still further into ignorance and inaction. However, Marcelle is also lost in her beauty, intelligence, and upbringing, which leave her unaware of the gap between her way of life and that of other people. In fact, her customary patterns of behavior may prevent her from even beginning to look for truth beyond the illusions.

However, since Lémor has at least shown her some alternative visions, and has thus set her on the path to independence, Marcelle can now find herself. Her search will be made easier because she has never been lost in any deep, moral sense—she has not been willfully lost. However, the task will be lightened most of all by her discovery that it is a misfortune "to be born rich" (95) and by her consequent decision "to let herself go in the care-free manner of a young girl . . . in new, more fertile and fanciful designs" (18–20).[8]

At this point, Marcelle gets lost in the literal sense. For a few anxious moments, early in the novel (31–44), as she is on the way to Blanchemont castle with her son, two servants, and a cart driver, all get hopelessly mired in a riverbed in the depths of the Vallée Noire (Black Valley, 31–44). They have been led astray by, or have misunderstood, an old man (who turns out to be Uncle Cadoche). Night has fallen, the maid is terrified, the manservant is useless in the country, the child is a constant source of concern, and the river proves totally unreliable. To complicate matters, shadowy old Uncle Cadoche shows up again and seems to directly threaten them this time. Then, both Marcelle and the old beggar hear the strains of a song that she has heard earlier, and Cadoche moves back into the shadows as Grand Louis, the miller of Angibault, discovers the struck cart, extracts it from the muck, and provides food and shelter for one and all.

The reader senses at once that Marcelle's getting lost in the Black Valley is (1) a sign of her being lost in ways already mentioned, (2) a warning about the difficulty of accomplishing the "more fertile and fanciful designs" she has made, and (3) a ritual passage, necessary before she can arrive at Blanchemont—the castle on the White Hill. However, more than this sign, this warning, and this ritual, the lost scene serves to bring the heroine together with certain other characters who are also lost (or not) in their various ways, and whose being lost and getting found (or not) expand considerably the vocabulary of the language of loss, as they contribute in one way or another to Marcelle's search for herself. These are the characters whose relationships with Marcelle (and hers with them) I wish to look at more closely, from four points of view: temporal (past, present, and future), Christian, secular, and literary. First, I will address the temporal.

Old Uncle Cadoche, by now an octogenarian, is a representative of the past with whom Marcelle must deal if she is to assume her personal and public history, and thus move beyond them. Having helped when he was young, to beat and rob his neighbor, old Bricolin, and having then hidden the spoils for these many years, Cadoche has allowed his guilt to dominate his life and turn him into a roving beggar, an object of scorn and fear.[9] In addition, old Bricolin was once the foreman of Marcelle's grandfather, and a part of the money stolen belonged to the latter. The restoration of that money cannot give back to Cadoche and old Bricolin their wasted lives, which are forever lost in the past. However, it can at least help to avoid the repetition of such horrors as Cadoche and the *chauffeurs* practiced—horrors that will certainly have no place in the future Marcelle imagines.

In order to deal with these figures from the past, Marcelle will have to confront even more difficult characters from the present—that is, those who are lost not in the past but in the present. If the past was brutally violent, the present is equally violent, but in different ways. Old Bricolin's son, "Monsieur" Bricolin as he likes to be called, having watched his father beat servants and employees, has grown into a monster. He and his wife have amassed great wealth in the management of the Blanchemont estate, thanks in part to the profligacy and the foolishness of Marcelle's husband. They now use that wealth to sustain their power and prestige, even at the expense of their daughters' very sanity. However, Marcelle will neither be able to eliminate those people from her future nor fit them into it. Nor will death take them conveniently away, as it will Cadoche and old Bricolin. As she finds ways to settle the family estate with the younger Bricolins, the best she can do is to keep these powers of the present from drawing her and others into their web of greed and violence, and from causing her and her friends to become as lost as they are.

Fortunately, Marcelle will have help in her interactions with the Bricolins and with old Cadoche. Under the heroine's influence, the Bricolins' younger daughter, Rose, will put an end to the heritage of violence by allying herself with the future that Marcelle has shown her, and thus will help find a new social order. Moreover,

Rose's immediate ally in that future will be none other than the *Meunier d'Angibault*, whom we met in the scene where Marcelle got lost and who is by reputation and actions most un-lost. Moreover, Grand Louis, though he will marry Rose, will provide the ultimate and necessary focus for Marcelle's search for herself, which is the ultimate find. As a representative of the wave of the future, Louis stands unswervingly as a model for the good, against which the bourgeois Rose, the socialistic Henri, and the aristocratic heroine, all, will come to measure their actions and their dreams. "Grand Louis, you have the true religion in your heart," says Marcelle (112), and Henri exclaims later, "For you . . . God will perform miracles!" (189).

God does perform miracles, if not for Grand Louis, at least through him. Louis becomes the vehicle for uncomplicating what others have complicated. Through him, Cadoche can return the money he stole, if not to its rightful owners, at least to their descendants. Then, Rose can "buy" from her avaricious father her right to marry the miller, and Marcelle can settle the family estate with the same greedy Monsieur Bricolin. Moreover, through Louis, finally, Marcelle and Henri can get married and begin to put into action the future about which they have dreamed, and that Marcelle has worked so hard to find.

It is of course significant that Marcelle has worked, and has gone beyond mere miracles, to achieve the future that Louis represents. While Henri knows the way to go, and while Louis represents what life may be like at the end of the way, only a determined effort by Marcelle to deal with her past and her present will get any of them there. Louis recognizes this truth when he says, at the end of the novel, "By casting my nets, I fished out . . . a little angel who brought me happiness and . . . an old devil of an uncle whom I shall perhaps manage to get out of purgatory!" (380). This language brings me to the second phase of my analysis: the language of loss in Christian, secular, and literary terms, which intends to show how a proper exploration of that language will yield at least one key to Marcelle's success with her future.

The biblical overtones of the last quotation are apparent. These words evoke something like Christ's behest to the Apostles that they become "fishers of men." Grand Louis thus becomes, if not a Christ figure, at least an Apostle, who, in saving the sinner and the saint, Cadoche and Marcelle, has shown himself to be found in the fullest Christian sense of the word.[10] In the same way, although they were once lost to one extent or another, Marcelle and Rose, and even old Cadoche, are finally found, while Monsieur and Madame Bricolin are forever lost in their rejection of any spiritual values.

However, the true force of this story grows out of the fact that Marcelle, the aristocrat lost in pursuit of worldly pleasures, can recognize the lack in herself, see that she is in sin, and seek and achieve her own redemption by joining her beauty and social advantages to the natural goodness of a Louis and the dogmatic power of an Henri. The struggle to achieve that redemption gives the outcome even greater value, and what could be more striking evidence of the struggle than the trial that took place in the Vallée Noire. Still "young in the faith," Marcelle could easily have allowed herself to get discouraged and turn back when the cart got stuck, but the determined pilgrim chose to press on, past the Rivers of Fear and Delay to the castle on the White Hill.[11] Such a heroine will surely find her reward in Heaven.

In Christian terms, Marcelle is clearly found. However, in secular terms—which is to say in the terms of the societal values dominant in this story—the simple word "found" may not be sufficient. "Found" may well do for Henri's condition, since he has discovered the path to the new society and made a radical change in order to follow it; but inasmuch as Louis is just admired by his neighbors, except for the Bricolins, he is not so much found as simply un-lost. On the other hand, both Henri and Louis are lost, albeit to differing degrees, in their inability to deal with reality as Marcelle does; and of course, as the Bricolins are if not always admired at least envied and respected by their neighbors, and are thus to that extent un-lost, so are both Rose and Marcelle un-lost and perhaps indeed even found in their beauty and goodness. However, in refusing to abide by traditional standards, Rose, and especially Marcelle, will be considered lost by the majority.

As a consequence, even Cadoche (who is clearly lost in the eyes of most of his fellows) and especially Monsieur Bricolin (who is equally un-lost in their eyes) both feel free to condemn Rose and Marcelle. Cadoche's condemnation is the more interesting, not just because he appears in the lost scene, but also because Marcelle is a member of the class that in a manner has contributed to his downfall, and the old beggar may thus have reason to mislead, to threaten, and then to condemn her. Still even more than that, it is somehow fitting that this person who is most lost of all the characters should attempt to drag Marcelle down with him, since only in the struggle against that attempt will the heroine truly discover her heroism: her willingness and ability to overcome all obstacles standing in the way of accomplishing her "more fertile and fanciful designs," and thus to make the world better, even for Uncle Cadoche.[12] However, much of society could, with little provocation, find cause to call Marcelle at best un-lost—perhaps, indeed, even less so that Monsieur and Madame Bricolin—and thus it is that the secular language of loss will not yield the kind of conclusions the reader senses that the text demands.

In fact, a consideration of literary aspects of the language of loss will be necessary to counterbalance such a prejudiced view of Marcelle and her friends and, in the end, to tip the scales in their favor. The literary point of view shows more clearly than any other just how Marcelle is lost, and just how lost she is. Although she remains un-lost in the ways described, she is also more lost than has been supposed: She is most lost, indeed, in her own eyes. Marcelle's realization that it is a misfortune to be born rich recognizes her loss; the struggle to get to Blanchemont, to set matters straight in her life, is certain evidence. Ironically, though, precisely these proofs of her loss first attract the reader's sympathies. Her candor is charming; her willingness to make the trip to Blanchemont, to take charge of her own life, and her ability to persevere, even through the Black Valley in the dead of night, finally capture our sympathies entirely and thus shift our perspective into direct line with hers.

As a result, we work with her through the puzzlement and hurt of dealing with the past as represented by Cadoche. We accept, with her, that while the Bricolins are essentially lost forever in the "middle-classness," they must nonetheless be dealt with, if one is to live in, or with, the present. We perceive the value in Henri's dogmatism as well as in Rose's beauty and Louis's goodness. Most of all, we learn that while the moral, Christian perspective displays a certain purity, and while the secular, social perspective shows us the world the way it really is for most people, there is another, ideal perspective—Marcelle's—which can bring the moral and the secular together in the hope of a better world here on earth, at least for a happy few. As a consequence of seeing this perspective and using it to see Marcelle's world, we come to recognize that what lost and found mean in secular terms or even in Christian terms does not necessarily fit with what these words may mean in literary terms. In literature, although Marcelle can condemn herself as lost, the reader understands that she is quite un-lost, if for no other reason than that she makes the admission; while those whom society may consider un-lost are in fact quite lost, and while even those who are found in religion, as beneficiaries of grace, seem somehow less virtuous, less found, than Marcelle.

In retrospect, the readers know that their sympathy for Marcelle and her way of seeing really goes back to the scene in which she got lost. The novel's Berrichon society may never recognize how lost the Bricolins are, nor how un-lost are Henri, Marcelle, and Louis. The members of that society may indeed continue to accept domination in the present by unjust practices from the past, imposed by the *gros bourgeois* who ape aristocratic manners; and they may render difficult a new society based on right, good, and love. However, someone of heart, courage, and determination can decide to stand against such ignorance and docility, and in favor of a better world. Marcelle so decides in the lost scene, and thus gains strength and confidence, which will translate into imagination and initiative in her struggles with peasant hostility, bourgeois conniving, and general apathy and inertia. We admire her for deciding to fight the good fight, in part because the fight is still ours.

In conclusion, the reader may say: To the extent that Marcelle already possessed strength, confidence, imagination, and initiative; to the extent that she was never willfully wicked; and to the extent that to be truly and finally found is to achieve perfection (that is, to die), Marcelle is neither utterly lost nor completely found, but simply un-lost. However, to the extent that she has put those qualities to work in her willingness to suffer fear, indecision, repulsion, disgust, and so forth, in order to galvanize other un-lost friends and neighbors into concerted action; and to the extent that she was willing to submit to a ritual of initiation, to get lost in order to move beyond being just un-lost, we must say that Marcelle is found indeed—because she has found herself. This much the language of loss has made clear: For George Sand's characters, getting lost may be a way of finding oneself, and thus a way of assuring that individuals, couples, and whole societies have a chance to find a path out of a present-day purgatory—where an old man must invent avuncular relations to find love, and a young girl must buy her right to marry whom she pleases—out of the Black Valley of despair and onto the White Hill of hope, where to find and actively pursue the will to live a good, loving, and virtuous life can lead to a world where "little angels" and "old devils" live together in peace.

NOTES

1. See *La Mare au diable*, for example.

2. See *Consuelo*, *Elle et lui*, and *Le Meunier d'Angibault*.

3. Bruno Bettelheim, *The Uses of Enchantment* (New York: Knopf, 1976), 15, 217ff.

4. For a discussion of the quest, see Joseph Campbell, *The Hero with a Thousand Faces* (Princeton, N.J.: Princeton University Press, 1968), 30ff.

5. Ibid. Marcelle's quest begins with an accident, getting lost (51); she encounters a protective creature, Uncle Cadoche (69); she makes a ritual sacrifice of the self in ridding herself of her fortune (90–91); and at the end of her quest she finds the paragon of all beauties in close friends and an excellent marriage (110–111). See note 8 for full citation for *Le Meunier*.

6. I use here the term that Roland Barthes prefers over "interpretation": "The text is not coexistence of meanings but passage, traversal; thus it answers not to an interpretation, liberal though it may be, but to an explosion, and dissemination," in order to avoid the certitude somehow connected now to the use of the word "interpretation"; Barthes, "From Work to Text," in Josué V. Harari, ed., *Textual Strategies* (Ithaca, N.Y.: Cornell University Press, 1979), 76.

7. Patricia Thompson calls works such as *Le Meunier* "committed" novels from Sand's "second" period in her *George Sand and the Victorians* (London: Macmillan, 1977), 3–6; while Cécile Stolting claims that through her novels, Sand criticized society, whose inequities she discovered in her experiences of and with love; Stolting, "Aspects de critique sociale dans l'oeuvre de George Sand," Dissertation, Friedrich-Alexander Universität, 1979.

8. George Sand, *Le Meunier d'Angibault* (Verviers, Belgium: Les Nouvelles Editions Marabout, 1977); these and all subsequent translations are those of the editors of this volume. Hereafter all page references to *Le Meunier* will be given in the text.

9. Lémor calls Cadoche's life "shameful and stupid, entirely consumed with the trembling contemplation of its flight" (359).

10. Matthew, 10:39, quotes Jesus: "He that findeth his life shall lose it: and he that loseth his life for my sake shall find it."

11. Between the bog where Marcelle gets stuck and the castle lie two rivers, the Couarde and the Tarde. An author's note says, "The river Couarde is so named because its course is hidden everywhere under the bushes, where it seems to be afraid of being found" and "the river Tarde is another listless and lazy river" (35).

12. When they are lost in the bog, Marcelle must take all responsibility, allay the maid's fears, and cradle the child; she is even willing to do battle with old Cadoche: "She was going to jump into the water on the opposite side from where the beggar approached" (41).

4

François Comes of Age: Language, Culture, and the Subject

Jane A. Nicholson

In the *avant-propos* to *François le champi*, the narrator and a friend discuss the difficulties of expressing true art, or the natural, in civilized literary language. The narrator is challenged to retell a story heard the previous evening at a peasant *veillée* as though both a Parisian and a peasant were listening at the same time. The reader recognizes the Romantic project of valorizing a simpler, truer, and more moral world in response to the harsh realism of novels and early modern social forms. I will discuss Sand's execution of this project by analyzing the textual relationship between the avant-propos and the story of François, as well as discussing symbolized materials in Sand's novel that unveil a broader project, which I call a novelistic project. Ultimately, the conflict of the two forms in the work, rustic tale and bourgeois novel, and the two worlds they present, enable a definition of François's relation to the world.

Sand's original plan was to combine the rustic novels into a series entitled *Veillées du chanvreur*. However, these works were published as separate novels and remain as such. *François le champi* was first published in 1848 in *feuilleton* (serial) form and thus reached a large, urban readership. Moreover, the discussion of art in the avant-propos criticizes contemporary realist literature for its representation of brutal passions and demoralizing scenes. Thus, Sand sought another form of expression that would function as an oppositional form of discourse within the novel genre. She accomplished her project simply by letting the avant-propos stand as a formulation of novelistic problems—that is, those of civilized society. Conversely, the story of François might stand on its own, yet must be read as a novel through the filter of the avant-propos. For although the rustic tale of a foundling who finds love and happiness is not completely obliterated by the novelistic project, another reading of the text is imposed because we expect novels to represent authentic or possible lives rather than model lives. Likewise, the novel suggests an entirely different world than does the folktale, one with different possibilities that determine the individual's relation to the world and to him- or herself. François's story ends with his forthcoming marriage to Madeleine, which I claim represents less an ideal union than his acceptance of real social responsibilities.

The setting of the avant-propos is a highly conventionalized romantic one: In a wooded rustic spot on a starlit autumn evening, two friends discuss their shared admiration for peasant life and culture.[1] Indeed, what is most striking is that the language of the avant-propos is highly conventionalized, conveying an incredibly idealized rustic setting. The painstakingly crafted language displays line after line of nouns with three adjective complements and other series of three that embody the linguistic artificiality decried by the interlocutors. Thus, the problematic in the avant-propos is specifically set up to engage the Parisian reader's sympathy for the project by appealing to his *artificial* sense of nature. The opening pages of François's story stand in distinct contrast to the avant-propos because they portray a nonidealized setting conveyed in very simple language. Moreover, the paradigm nature-rustic-tale does not merely harken back to a traditional form because nature is rewritten in relation to its opposing paradigm, the civilization-urban-novel. Nature is not aligned with physical nature but rather with rustic life-styles and peasant culture. The story itself is supposedly narrated by two peasants—a female household servant who has some education and an illiterate male laborer. This indoor/outdoor dichotomy is sustained in Madeleine's domesticity and literacy and in François's nickname of *champi* (foundling) and his illiteracy.

Despite the idyllic foregrounding of peasant forms and primitive values in the avant-propos, the real world is very much present in this work. Beginning with the second library edition in 1852, the text also contains a Notice, which exposes the author's ire at publishing interruptions that delayed the end of *François* for many readers and also inserts a commentary on the real problems of foundlings in the countryside. Sand noted that since the very poorest people took on these charges for the modest fee paid for their upkeep by the state, neglect was inevitable. In the novel, these two sorts of social injustice—the abandoned child and the abused wife—revolve around a central absent figure: the good husband and father. Thus, despite the title of the novel and the notice, children's issues do not form the entire social backdrop of the novel, for Madeleine's marriage is a bad one.

In her 1967 *Origins of the Novel*, Marthe Robert constructed a history of the form based on two possible versions of the family drama.[2] Robert claims that early novels emphasize the foundling, a child who is handicapped by the conditions of his or her birth, while later forms feature the bastard, who by choice rejects his or her parents and creates a new family for him- or herself. While the foundling lacks worldly experience and tends to avoid confrontation, the bastard figure fights all his or her worldly battles head on. Thus, the bastard consciously seeks a heterogeneous world wherein his or her many desires can be realized. Conversely, the foundling inhabits a sparse world, where intensity of desire is valued over multiplicity of desire. For the bastard's ideal of maturity and action, the foundling, then, substitutes the magical power of inward concentration and imagination. In the end, François represents a foundling in a bastard's story, but at the outset, two salient characteristics convey François's world: an unclear sense of time and a minimum of oral discourse. Clearly, the young François fits the earlier model of a hero who creates a world for him- or herself, an ideal world where temporality is not always respected, space is closed, and speech is privatized.

François's limited sense of time is reflected in his first meeting with Madeleine Blanchet. Coming upon him at a fountain, she asks his name and his age. As the narrator says, he responds "textually" as to his age, "two years old." Nearly half-way through the novel we learn that he was six at the time, and at age twelve, age becomes an important factor due to a matter of social sanction. François has passed his first communion, and asks Madeleine why she kisses her son but not him. Madeleine tries to persuade him that it is not, as he imagines, because he is a *champi*, and thus begins to kiss him each day as she does her own child. One day Madeleine's servant says that Madeleine should not kiss him at his age and that she herself would not kiss him because he is a champi. The issue is foreclosed when François responds to the servant by saying that he cares little who else considers him a champi as long as Madeleine does not. However, from that day forward he does not accept her kisses—not because he understands the shame of his own childishness or the import of others' insinuations, but because he does not like to hear Madeleine rebuked. Because François has no understanding of social convention, he is the natural innocent, unaware of sexuality and acting on instinct. Later, when Madeleine's husband begins to frequent a mistress, the household falls into penury and Madeleine says that she can make ends meet as long as she stays as healthy as when she was young. François is astounded to think that she is no longer young, and finds out that she is about twenty-five. François's complete lack of temporal perspective indicates his captivation with the present and with immediate experience.

As François matures to a young man, he poses a threat to Madeleine, who has "adopted" him.[3] Although her husband has left her for a mistress, he still manages the household and their mill. One night, his mistress accuses François of having seduced her—when in fact he had repulsed her advances—and the husband demands that François leave. At this point the idyllic relationship between François and Madeleine is sundered, and François sets out on a typical quest voyage to acquire the things which he lacks. He undergoes several rites of passage: he finds a guiding father figure in his employer; he experiences the admiration of the employer's daughter; and most significantly, he learns of his mother through a blind inheritance.[4] The inheritance carries with it the stipulation that the mother's identity not be revealed and thus, he takes the last name given to him by the state, la Fraise, designating a birthmark he carries. François, who has never been ashamed to be a champi even though he understands that society at large discriminates against them, finally has a worthy identity and money—that is, he has become a member of the community. Thus, François's story is modeled on traditional narrative forms: He conforms to the folk tale hero by his early misfortunes which are righted due to his essential worthiness. However, we shall see that while Sand is interested in traditional materials, she is not interested in treating them "traditionally." While many of her concerns are "timeless," the ahistorical and idyllic nature of traditional tales is absent from her reinscriptions of them.[5]

On the symbolic level which can be identified as that of the novel form, with its self-proclaimed problematics of expression and nature/culture, these narrative materials must be reelaborated. The effect of François's departure is to rupture the dualistic relation that he has enjoyed with Madeleine. He measures all his feelings and understanding through her, and it is as though there were no one else in his world. Although this is represented as an ideal situation for François, it is precisely the one that he must give up. This is primarily figured through his use of language, which is usually considered a social convention linking speakers into a community and binding them to social conventions. For François, speech is a privatized mode of communication, something to be used very discreetly. While Madeleine at first thought François slow-witted, she came to realize that he had a common sense beyond that of his fellows but which he was merely reluctant to express. François states at one point that he is not so bold as to speak—that is, as a champi, he may not have the right to behave as others do; more important, he prefers to express himself only to a kindred soul.

François begins to speak more and more after his first communion, a social ritual that is given a highly personalized value in his life. Much to the astonishment of the community, Madeleine has taught him to read and recite. Madeleine's sharing of literacy with François represents the gift—and not the law—of culture. This textual knowledge allows for a sort of third in their relationship, God, but we see that François frequently puts Madeleine in His place. The interchangeability of God/Madeleine as the source and model of all good renders the dualistic nature of the son-mother relationship all the more significant. Moreover, the socializing power of language intervenes at the point in the narrative when Madeleine is rebuked by her servant for kissing François, who, although young, is described as being physically mature. Such persistent gaps between the social and the private or personal in François's development form the key symbolic material in the novel.

Jacques Lacan's study of the socializing function of the structure of language allows us to reconstruct François's development.[6] The process of socialization may be described as the passage from *moi* to *je*. *Je* is a psycho-socio-linguistic position that has already sacrificed the identification with the primary Other of childhood, the mother, for the identity provided by society through its conventions. According to Lacan, it is autonomy from the immediate real world that permits manifestations of the self. As long as the subject remains a captive of the primary merging of the self with the mother, the subject does not exist as a distinct entity. Early human experience revolves around the presence or absence of the mother, and there is no real disjunction between real and lived experience. Lacan maintains that language as a wholly symbolic form differs absolutely from reality. Because signs most essentially are not that which they represent, the coherence of their relations is purely formal. The order of signifiers relies on a social convention that recognizes the distinctive elements of language whose combination produces signification. The successful accession of the individual subject into society requires a similar sacrifice of immediate, dualistic relations for mediated relations of a differential nature. Because there is a certain comfort in the power of concentration, similar to that described in another fashion by Marthe Robert, the subject's passage into social forms is a painful one. However, the necessity of acting in the surrounding world and accepting one's already prescribed place in society, and the possibilities for realizing one's desires that this transition affords, assuage the subject's pain.

Lacan states that there is a homology between linguistic fact and social fact: that is, the founding conventions of society are present in the structures of the language we use. Thus, Lacan refers to Claude Lévi-Strauss's analysis of the incest taboo—the rejection of the immediate possession of the opposite sex parent for role modeling after the same sex parent. This process is homologous to the distancing that occurs in signs that substitute symbolic relations for real relations. Accordingly, incest functions as the interface of nature and culture. Thus, while sexuality finds its appeal through sensual affects and fantasies, its expression and behavior are controlled by culture. In this way, love and sex are denatured.

Eventually, François returns to Madeleine with money, social experience, and a new identity. However, by rejecting his employer's young daughter, he has failed to execute the final social responsibility required of him, that of a relation by alliance. He finds Madeleine physically and materially depleted, and immediately sets to restoring her well-being. François must turn to very practical matters, and he now inserts himself as the head of the household. From this point on, he fully accepts the Lacanian symbolic order of a mediated social position, that of husband-father. Although these roles are not yet officially or fully actualized, François is inscribed within them because he must fight for Madeleine's lost land through legal procedures, and he must acknowledge the wickedness of others. The final step in his development is for him to recognize, or more appropriately, to express the nature of his love for Madeleine. In fact, it is the jilted young woman who explains to François that he loves Madeleine as a man loves his wife. Therefore, even in recognizing his obligation to form a relation of alliance, François has not sacrificed his "kinship" relations. In the text, the opposition kinship/alliance is ruptured by Sand's suggestion that natural desire need not be sacrificed to the order of the law. However, legally François and Madeleine are not related, an argument that finally wins Madeleine over, for she has always been thoroughly socialized.

Is the union of François and Madeleine therefore an incestuous one? Because François is a completely good and natural hero who recognizes only natural bonds, he is seemingly clear of any possible transgression. However, the best-known literary reinscription of *François le champi* relies on the incest symbolism in telling Marcel's story. Moreover, the relation of nature and culture has been invoked in the avant-propos, and because theories of culture hold that incest represents the interface between the two, the insistence on incest is essential to the novel. In his 1979 *Adultery in the Novel*, Tony Tanner maintains that novels of female adultery nearly always portray their heroines as negligent mothers.[7] Unlike these adulterous heroines, Madeleine is an exemplary mother who upholds the Romantic ideal of the wife-mother-lover trinity in her final apotheosis as François's wife.

It is in the resolution of the novel that one must resolve the conflict of the two forms. Does the marriage of François to Madeleine represent the promised end to

François's idyll or does it represent his obligation to accept another order, that of social law? Although we are concerned with François's childhood values for much of the novel, François does not take the place of a lost or lacking child but rather that of a bad husband. Moreover, he accepts the symbolic order, that of laws and conventions, above that of marriage, by participating in its civil institutions. The mature François chooses the symbolic or social order over the ideal or personal model. Thus, marriage is a fitting end to the story as idyll but also as novel where the everyday world and its obligations prevail. However, there is yet another effect of this narrative that initially appears to be the mere tale of a foundling.

The family drama inscribed in this novel turns on questions of naming, incest, and religion, all orders of patriarchal law, and it is on this level that Sand's novel troubles Lacan's own patriarchal discourse. François does not know his father's name and receives his name from a birthmark he bears; thus, he bears a name given by his mother. Moreover, we have seen that he often substitutes Madeleine, whose overdetermined name suggests the repentant sinner known for her devotion and generosity for God. However, according to Lacan, it is by identifying with the father that the child receives a name and a place in the family.[8]

Moreover, in Lacan's schema the nature/culture interface is an absolute one; thus, the incest taboo must be absolute as well. We have seen that Sand's novel troubles this notion too. According to the Oedipus myth, the child is removed from his mother by paternal interdiction and accepts this limitation upon his desire as the order of the symbolic, or culture. While this paternal metaphor is explained by Anika Lemaire as a symbolization conceptualizing "an essential structural moment of humanization," the choice of metaphor is telling.[9] Sand's valorization of the maternal role of socializing makes the mother the culture-giver. In adopting François, Madeleine sets out to mold not just any male subject, but her own husband. This idealized family scenario is also a symbolization, one that recuperates the place of the mother/goddess for the monotheistic father/God, and thus does not at all constitute a plea for incest as such or for any other cultural disorder. The symbolic gratification represented in Sand's novel is one that recuperates the position of the mother within culture while addressing the subjugation of the wife to the husband at the same time. Thus, the dynamics of the family romance are reinscribed from the perspective of the desiring female subject. In place of the imposition of law by the father, Sand proposes the giving of culture by the mother, a form whose highest good is a good husband.

That love and marriage do not go together is evident from the lone but touching example of Madeleine's marriage. In 1835 Sand suggested that unions of alliance be freely formed and that all children be under the care of the state, whereas in 1861 she stated that friendship and family ties can compensate for lost enthusiasms in marriage. At the time she wrote *François*, she was presumably in between these two positions. Speaking in part from her own experience, both as neglected child and as unsatisfied wife, Sand formulated the relations she sought in real life in the very process of writing out or symbolizing them. Accordingly, her texts continue to provoke us to analyze the conventions that formalize our individual experience. Clearly, for Sand, the desiring female subject sought to obliterate any discrepancy between the private and the public forms of good. A just man would be a just husband, father, and son.

In *François le champi*, primitive values are an authentic countermodel to the novel, and the built-in story-telling situation keeps the reader on the interface of the two forms, story and novel. The avant-propos and François's story are in conflict because they represent two different forms and thus two different worlds. The contrived prose of the former seems deliberately set forth to contrast with the simplicity of the rustic tale (even though Romantic prose is the civilized version of nature opposed to the civilized world). If François's story is proposed as a countermodel to modern literature and society, then this reading engages the necessary and opposite influence of the civilized world of the novel on the rustic world of the tale in such a way that we see François as a possible man rather than an idealized figure.

NOTES

1. The narrator's friend, identified as R***, is commonly held to refer to Sand's friend Rollinat, a lawyer with republican sympathies in 1848, whose first name was François. It should be noted as well that Sand's husband's name was also François, although he went by Casimir.

2. Marthe Robert, *Origins of the Novel*, translated by Sacha Rabinovitch (Bloomington: Indiana University Press, 1980), 37.

3. The story of a woman adopting a male orphan makes an interesting intertext to Michelet's idealized portrait of the good women who adopt female orphans. See Jules Michelet, *La femme* (1859; reprint: Paris: Flammarion, 1981), 343–347.

4. Napoleon's *Code Civil* dictated that natural children had the right to seek out their mothers but not their fathers. See Priscilla Robertson, *An Experience of Women: Pattern and Change in Nineteenth-Century Europe* (Philadelphia: Temple University Press, 1982), 280.

5. For a discussion of the importance of the folktale to Sand's literary production, see Béatrice Didier, "George Sand et les structures du conte populaire," in Simone Vierne, ed., *George Sand* (Paris: SEDES-CDU, 1983), 101–114.

6. Jacques Lacan, *Ecrits* (Paris: Seuil, 1966), 180ff.

7. Tony Tanner, *Adultery in the Novel: Contract and Transgression* (Baltimore: Johns Hopkins University Press, 1979), 87–100.

8. Anika Lemaire, *Jacques Lacan*, translated by David Macey (London: Routledge and Kegan Paul, 1977), 78–92.

9. Ibid., 88.

Part II

LETTRES D'UN VOYAGEUR

5

Imaginary and Symbolic Orders in "Sur Lavater et sur une maison déserte"

Mary Anne Garnett

In recent years, feminist critics such as Naomi Schor have been examining the implications for women of Jacques Lacan's orders of the Imaginary and the Symbolic. In one of her essays in *Breaking the Chain: Women, Theory, and French Realist Fiction*, Naomi Schor notes the need to explore "the specificities—if any—of feminocentric examples" of the autobiography and *Bildungsroman* to determine "the literary consequences of the anatomical differences between the sexes at the point of articulation of the Imaginary and the Symbolic."[1]

The works of George Sand provide a fertile ground for such inquiry. In this chapter I shall examine a small, but significant, part of Sand's literary production that clearly reveals this point of articulation: her letter "A Franz Liszt: Sur Lavater et sur une maison déserte" in the *Lettres d'un voyageur*.

Marie-Jacques Hoog has called these letters a "turning point" in the life and career of George Sand.[2] Written between 1834 and 1836, they mark "a break in Sand's literary production, a change of sign, a transition from the negative to the positive."[3] At the same time, the text is a "*unifying factor*, a bridge reconciling the work of her youth and that of her maturity."[4] It is precisely the transitional character of this text that so clearly reveals the articulation of the Imaginary and Symbolic registers in the creative development of George Sand.

Of the twelve letters comprising this work, it is the seventh, "A Franz Liszt: Sur Lavater et sur une maison déserte," in which the articulation of the Imaginary and Symbolic registers is most evident. Indeed, the registers are already evoked in the title, where the Symbolic order is represented by Jean-Gaspard de Lavater, author of the book that the subject will rediscover in the Imaginary space of the deserted house. Moreover, this text is of particular usefulness in exploring the differences between the sexes at the point of articulation between the Imaginary and the

Symbolic orders because the image of the enclosed space is so widespread in both the male and the female literature of the nineteenth century.

Victor Brombert has analyzed the importance of images of enclosure in his study *La Prison romantique: Essai sur l'imaginaire*. He deals primarily with male authors, but many of the elements he finds in their works are also found, as we shall see, in George Sand's "deserted house," which she describes as "my beloved prison."[5] As Brombert notes, the enclosed space is ambivalent in Western literary tradition: a place of imprisonment, yet one of freedom and intemporality, associated with both spirituality (the monk's cell) and artistic creation. When this image of claustration is interiorized by "the substitution of the brain for the abstract notion of enclosed space," the result is the metaphor of the "skull-dungeon" so prevalent in the Romantic period.[6] Before we equate Sand's *imaginaire* with that of her male contemporaries, however, we must also briefly examine the ways in which women perceived images of confinement.

In their landmark study *The Madwoman in the Attic: The Woman Writer and the Nineteenth-Century Literary Imagination*, Sandra Gilbert and Susan Gubar argue that "the distinction between male and female images of imprisonment is—and always has been—a distinction between, on the one hand, that which is both metaphysical and metaphorical, and on the other hand, that which is social and actual."[7] For a nineteenth-century middle-class woman, enclosure was very much a social reality, whether in convent schools, the domestic space of her husband's house, or the "confinement" of pregnancy. In addition, the woman writer had to confront the prevailing notion that writing itself was a "male" activity outside of woman's proper sphere. Thus, Gilbert and Gubar find that "the imagery of enclosure reflects the woman writer's own discomfort, her sense of powerlessness, her fear that she inhabits alien and incomprehensible places."[8]

In this social context, similar architectural images employed by male and female writers may have different sex-linked values. Commenting on Gaston Bachelard's statement that "the house image would appear to have become the topography of our innermost being," Gilbert and Gubar conclude that "what is significant from our point of view, however, is the extraordinary discrepancy between the almost consistently 'felicitous space' he discusses and the negative space we have found."[9]

George Sand's deserted house is, on the whole, a "felicitous space," but also one that illustrates the ambivalent position of the female subject. Aurore Dupin's creation of the masculine pseudonym and *persona* of George Sand amply demonstrates the alienation experienced in the female writer's insertion into the literary world of the nineteenth century. In the "Lettre sur Lavater et sur une maison déserte," Sand's adoption of the voice of a man approaching "the twilight of life" (2:823) is also symptomatic of this alienation, despite her disclaimer in the introduction that

> by dressing my sorry character, my poor self, in a costume that wasn't usually its own, and by causing, to the greatest extent possible, its physical existence to disappear behind a more truthful and interesting spiritual existence . . . I have done nothing more than depict my soul in the form it was taking at those times. (2:646)

For the feminist critic, it is precisely this choice of a male voice as representing "a more truthful spiritual existence" that is both disturbing and revealing. If the *Lettres d'un voyageur* exemplify what Fredric Jameson has called "the psychic function of narrative and fantasy in the attempts of the subject to reintegrate his or her alienated image," it is clear that for George Sand this integration was complicated by an ambivalence toward the possibilities of the female subject to be fully assumed into the Symbolic—perceived as patriarchal—order.[10] Even a critic like Béatrice Didier, who interprets Sand's adoption of a male pseudonym as a victorious assumption of bisexuality, admits that in the *Lettres d'un voyageur* the doubling of narrative voices is a mark of transition. Didier concludes, "Perhaps this intermediate form of writing between the novel and autobiography was necessary at a moment when, as Sand notes: her 'individuality was being formed' " (2:298).[11]

The narrative sequence of the seventh *Lettre d'un voyageur* begins with the image of an ideal enclosure: "the upper room" of Pentecost in which the Holy Spirit in "tongues of fire" bestowed upon the apostles its "gift of that sacred language which belongs only to the elect" (2:818). In Sand's reconstruction of Pentecost, the gift of tongues is not the gift of the spoken word, but rather that of "divine song" (2:818). Music is the "divine language perfected" which humanity, "once more become godlike," may ultimately recover (2:819). For Sand, music also represents an ideal of solidarity, understanding, and unity among humanity, and the musician has "a sweet and noble vocation" (2:818). Her own art, by comparison, is "arid and tiresome" and must be practiced "in silence and solitude" (2:818). This contrast supports Philippe Berthier's analysis that, for Sand, "entry into the real, fragmented text is felt to be a fall, an experience of limits."[12]

Denied access to the "upper room," Sand finds a substitute in the deserted house which, in the narrative, is loaned to the male narrator, who is recovering from an illness. The house has a difficult access through deserted, dilapidated streets and a series of broken stairways. Upon entering the enclosed courtyard, however, the traveler experiences a "religious" sensation and hesitates to profane its space by trampling the grass to cross to the house (2:822). He first invokes the female spirit who guards it: "Pardon me, sylphid, I said to her, or give me your light step so that I might cross this space without bending under my heavy step your beloved plants" (2:822). Then, by carefully walking on "broken paving stones without crushing the vegetation," the traveler reaches the door only to find it protected by another mass of foliage: "Long branches of vine had intertwined in front of the entry; everywhere they formed curtains of foliage in front of the windows" (2:823). Finally resolving to "lay a profane hand" against them, the traveler raises the curtain of vines to enter the house. Immediately, however, "these vine branches lithely fell back and embraced each other, as if to forbid me from recrossing the sacred enclosure" (2:823). A prisoner, the traveler spends his nights contemplating the moon through the foliage, and dawn sometimes finds him "immobile and silent, like stone" (2:823).

For the reader familiar with Sand's *Histoire de ma vie*, this description of the deserted house inevitably recalls the temple that young Aurore Dupin dedicated to her mythological divinity, Corambé. The temple to Corambé was a "leafy chamber" impenetrable to the eye (1:819). Access to it was "not without difficulty and scratches," for, to protect its secrecy, Aurore took care "not to leave marks by wearing a path and breaking the shrubs" through repeated incursions (2:820). In the middle of the thicket, there were "three beautiful maples growing out of the same crown of the root," (1:820) even as the courtyard of the deserted house is dominated by "three lindens" (2:822).

In the above descriptions, the reader is struck by the images of vegetation traditionally associated with female sexuality. In his analysis of the myth of Corambé, Philippe Berthier notes that "it is striking that, for the child, the order of the imaginary is equated with the order of the mother."[12] Berthier interprets the temple to Corambé as "the image of a primordial happiness . . . harmonious, unassailable, perhaps like a womb" in which the three maples are an emblem of the lost family triad of father, mother, and daughter.[14] However, Corambé, to whom the temple is dedicated, transcends sexual specificity: sexuality "is abolished in synthesis; Corambé represents the symbiosis of the male and female principles, transfused into one another, indeed interchangeable within a higher unity."

In the deserted house, Corambé has been supplanted by another figure: the book. It is a specific book that the traveler finds there: "the works of Jean-Gaspard de Lavater, minister of the holy gospel in Zurich, published in 1781, in three folios, French translation, with engraved plates, etchings, etc." (2:827). Beyond, yet grounded in its physical specificity, this book represents the entire order of the Symbolic, which is also, in Lacanian thought, the order of the Father. For George Sand, however, this book does not imply a rupture in which the "female" Imaginary is suppressed. The ideal book that she discovers integrates the two orders in a delicate balance. As a sign of this balance, it is tempting to decompose the signifier *Lavater* into its morphemes *La* and *vater*, thus revealing an androgynized (and cross-lingual) figure of the father. Even were the author's name different, however, Sand's discovery of this particular book would reveal, as in the creation of Corambé, a desire for integration and transcendence.

Lavater's book is first associated with a time in childhood when the written sign has not yet dominated the image in the book. Sand recalls:

> I had Lavater in my hands during my childhood. Ursule and I would look with curiosity at its illustrations. We barely knew how to read. We would ask ourselves why this collection of various faces, some comical, grotesque, insignificant, hideous, pleasant? We searched eagerly among the sentences and explanations that we couldn't understand for the principal characterization of each type; we found *drunken*, *lazy*, *gourmand*, *irascible*, *diplomatic*, *methodical*. . . . Oh! at that point we didn't understand anymore and we went back to the pictures. (2:826)

Eventually, the book is mislaid. When the traveler comes upon a copy of it years later in the deserted house, the discovery has a power to restore the past that presages Proust. Sand asks the reader:

> Has the cover of a dusty book discovered on the shelves of a forgotten cabinet never evoked for you the gracious scenes of your younger days? Didn't you believe there suddenly appeared before you the large meadow bathed in the reds of twilight when you read it for the first time, the old elm and hedge that sheltered you, the ditch whose sides served as your couch and workdesk, while the thrush called its companions back home and the reed pipe of the cowherd became lost in the distance? (2:825)

The traveler's rediscovery of the book in the vine-covered deserted house thus recaptures a prior, idealized reading in a natural setting, accompanied by the sound of music. There is no apparent conflict between nature and culture, feminine and masculine, Imaginary and Symbolic. This reading, however, cannot endure. The child must return at dusk to the home of the grandmother who awaits, "unyielding on etiquette" (2:825). It is she to whom the child must show the book, fearful lest she confiscate it, and it is she who, with a smile, finally sanctions the child's activity.

The role of the grandmother in Sand's *Histoire de ma vie* has attracted the attention of critics such as Philippe Berthier and Pierrette Daly. The conflict between Sand's mother and paternal grandmother after the death of her father is seen by Berthier as forcing upon Aurore "a crucial choice between mother and grandmother, that is to say, at heart a choice between mother and father."[16] Pierrette Daly also views this as a conflict between the maternal and paternal orders, between "the power of the mother" and the "phallic grandmother."[17] This interpretation of the grandmother as a representative of the paternal order is certainly supported by the above passages from the *Lettres d'un voyageur.*

The delicate balance that Sand seeks to restore through the creation of Corambé or the deserted house is continually threatened with destruction by the triumph of the paternal order. The book of Lavater manages to reconcile both orders: it is a "source work" (literally, a "mother-work") that is "generative, venerable, sacred" (2:827–828). Moreover, Lavater's science of physiognomy offers the possibility of the eventual transcendence of the written text. Sand does not doubt that "one day man will extend the study of the human form so far that he will be able to read the abilities and inclinations of his fellow man like an open book" (2:828). For the moment, however, that potential is unrealized. Lavater's book has been forgotten by the "pragmatic and materialistic" nineteenth century, which prefers phrenology, the system of Franz-Joseph Gall (2:828).

So, too, the traveler becomes aware that the deserted house itself is slowly decomposing in a "continual crumbling of sand" (2:847). This crumbling of "sand" signals the writer's own mortality and the end of all "lovely dreams of perfection" contained in the deserted house (2:848). The writer has come to the end of a "pleasant page of his life," and the very banality of this expression reveals to the reader the metaphorical chain that has been carefully composed, linking house, book, and self, and that must now undergo decomposition (2:848).

The end comes quite abruptly, and in a somewhat comical fashion, through the intrusion of the forces of "law and order." Alerted by suspicious neighbors who suspect the presence of a "conspirator" in the normally deserted house, the local constabulary arrives to the cry of "Open by order of the king!" (2:849). The traveler is hauled off to appear before the magistrates and, during his absence, the owner of the house returns, cuts the grass, trims the vines, and opens the windows. The traveler considers these to be acts of "vandalism," and remarks, "according to him, the house is put in order; according to me, it is ravaged" (2:850).

The house, that felicitous space in which the Imaginary and Symbolic orders were in harmony, is thus destroyed by the dominance of the paternal order which suppresses the female space. Sand, once again in exile, can only take up the pilgrim's staff once more and continue her voyage (2:851).

It would be wrong, however, to conclude that the text thus ends on a negative note. On the contrary, the tone of the closing passage is resolutely positive in the face of adversity. The traveler does not succumb to defeat but rather recognizes that she or he is engaged in an enduring struggle and that "there will be suffering, there will be work to do as long as life goes on" (2:849). Sand will continue the struggle to regain the lost harmony, to restore the delicate balance. Her *Histoire de ma vie*, for which the *Lettres d'un voyageur* will have prepared the way, will be but one testimony to her achievement.

NOTES

1. Naomi Schor, *Breaking the Chain* (New York: Columbia University Press, 1985), 90.

2. Marie-Jacques Hoog, "*Lettres d'un voyageur*, texte initiatique," in Simone Vierne, ed., *George Sand* (Paris: SEDES-CDU, 1983), 138.

3. Ibid.

4. Ibid., 139, author's emphasis.

5. Sand, *Oeuvres autobiographiques* [*OA*], vol. 2, edited by Georges Lubin (Paris: Gallimard, 1970–1971), 823. Hereafter all references to *OA* will be given in the text; this and all subsequent translations are those of the author.

6. Victor Brombert, *La Prison romantique: Essai sur l'imaginaire* (Paris: José Corti, 1975), 20.

7. Sandra Gilbert and Susan Guber, *The Mad Woman in the Attic: The Woman Writer and the Nineteenth-Century Literary Imagination* (New Haven, Conn.: Yale University Press, 1979), 86.

8. Ibid., 84.

9. Ibid., 87–88.

10. Fredric Jameson, "Imaginary and Symbolic in Lacan: Marxism, Psychoanalytic Criticism and the Problem of the Subject," *Yale French Studies* 55/56 (1977): 353.

11. Béatrice Didier, "Femme/Identité/Ecriture: A propos d'*Histoire de ma vie* de George Sand," *Revue des Sciences Humaines* 44, no. 168 (1977): 575.

12. Philippe Berthier, "Corambé: Interprétation d'un Mythe," in Vierne, *George Sand*, 19.

13. Ibid., 8.

14. Ibid., 15.

15. Ibid., 12.

16. Ibid., 16.

17. Pierrette Daly, "De Sand à Cixous: La 'Venue à l'écriture' au féminin," in Vierne, *George Sand*, 152.

6

Lettres d'un voyageur: Traveling with George Sand

Susan H. Léger

Traveling with George Sand is not a simple undertaking. The first of her *Lettres d'un voyageur*, sent on May 1, 1834, from Venice, is not about Venice at all. Moreover, although it is addressed "to a poet," this letter was to appear in print only fifteen days later in the *Revue des Deux Mondes*. Sand avowed privately, in a note to Alfred de Musset, the poet in question, that she had written the letter spontaneously; "I put it down," she said, "as it came to me, without thinking about all the others who were to read it" (*Corr.* 569). There is little doubt, however, that Sand had nonetheless been considering in some way the reactions of all those anticipated readers, for she takes great pains to lead them—along with Musset—through her adventures in the Bassano Valley in Italy.

The events recounted in this traveling letter took place some three weeks earlier, a few days after she bid Musset a fond farewell at Mestre, where he embarked on his journey back to Paris. This recent separation, along with the inclement weather, accounts, we may suppose, for her low spirits as the letter opens: "I had arrived in Bassano at nine o'clock on a cold, wet evening. I had gone to bed sad and weary after silently shaking hands with my companion" (*Lettres*, 39).

Sand's companion is none other than Doctor Pietro Pagello, who had treated both Sand and Musset in Venice. However, his functions here are not those of a physician. He is reduced to: (a) a foil for the narrator (it is against his wishes that she will undertake her journey), and (b) a textual marker. She will be but eighty-eight words into her narrative and have taken about as many steps before she meets the good doctor the next morning: "I hadn't taken a hundred steps before I came upon the doctor sitting on a rock smoking" (*Lettres*, 39 t.m.). Sand places the doctor in her text exactly where he is required, marking by his presence a coincidence of "steps" and "words." Although she will exploit this implicit equivalence between physical movement and textual traveling throughout the *Lettres d'un voyageur*,

Sand is aware that the energy moving her steps and words forward comes from two distinct sources.

Her feet are set in motion by the beauty of the scenery. Sipping her morning coffee with the doctor while the carriage that is to take them back to Venice is being prepared, she looks up to see the flowering peach and almond trees and the snow-capped mountains framing the scene. She decides to stay. When Pagello objects, she insists that she had come to see the Alps: "Do you expect me to return to your swampy city when I have barely set foot on them?" (*Lettres*, 41).

Disdain for that swampy city, however, has next to nothing to do with the force that drives the words on the page. In her private letter to Musset, Sand reveals that the impetus for the writing of the traveling letter is not to be found in the mountain view: "I saw there only a setting and a pretext to speak aloud of my love for you" (*Corr.*, 569).

Following Sand's lead, we can point to other distinctions paralleling that of landscape/love. The feet and the writing are not only separately motivated, they have, as well, different points of departure. Sand's journey begins in the village of Bassano; the letter narrating the events of the trip leaves sometime later from Venice. In addition, the breaks in the progress of the trip and in the writing come at different places and for different reasons; thus, each movement forms a distinct pattern in the reader's mind. The first journey—the mimetic level of the letter—is interrupted, for example, by restful moments in a grotto, an encounter with a stranger, and sleep; the second journey—the one we might call the diegetic level of the letter—is punctuated with memories, reflections, and future plans.

What happens—what sort of text is produced—when Sand weaves her love for Musset into her journey through the Alps? She is first of all setting a known but unassimilated experience (three months with Musset in Venice) against an unknown but assimilable background (the geography of the Bassano Valley) in an attempt to redescribe the events of Venice by reinscribing them in a new landscape and a new narrative. The resulting discourse, however, moves in directions that cannot be accounted for either by the geography or the emotion. The reader is ultimately led to ask two questions of this traveling writer: On what sort of textual journey is the reader being taken, and what is the final destination?

As an approach to these questions, I would like now to consider the seventh of the *Lettres d'un voyageur*. Written to Franz Liszt and published for the first time on September 1, 1835, it occupies, along with the first letter from Venice, a privileged position in the work. Situated at the center of the volume of twelve letters, it does not describe a journey but rather a moment of repose, and thus offers a marked contrast to the journey through the Alps. In addition, the few events recounted are apparently almost entirely imaginary. Sand seems to have spent the summer of 1835 not journeying down the Loire but rather in her Paris apartment. Thus the "setting" and "pretext" are not chosen from experience but instead were apparently invented to fit and accompany the journey of the words: The mimesis dances to the tune, or writes itself in the musical key, of the diegesis.

Sand herself invites this comparison by opening her letter to Liszt, appropriately, with exclamatory praise of his medium. Music, in contrast to writing, Sand notes, does not oblige its practitioners to work in silence and solitude, but instead encourages artists to work together toward a common end. In spite of this opposition between music and writing, Sand will go on in the following paragraphs to bring them together in two very revealing ways. She first associates music with the twelve apostles, whom she describes as travelers who labor continuously and whose lives are full of strife. Now anyone who has just read the first six letters of this volume will not fail to recognize that this summary of the main activities of the apostles brings them close in spirit to the narrator herself. Concluding this opening passage, Sand imagines modern-day apostles emerging from a retreat knowing how to speak a perfect tongue: music in its most eloquent and persuasive form. Music, then, is language in its rhetorical dress—a language whose significance resides precisely in its power to *move* its listeners, to take its readers on a journey.

What seems at first a puzzling introduction to this letter, in which apostles and music are barely mentioned again, turns out to be a clue to what this letter is, in fact, all about: the seductions of traveling in language. The journey that Sand invites us to take with her in Letter Seven moves in the direction of a longed-for but remote location, a place where, paradoxically, language signifies *without* moving forward; where language is, so to speak, music to one's ears. If this is so, then the journey we make in words can only be said to take place to the extent that it turns aside from its proposed destination; to the extent that it refuses to be led down the road prepared for it by the mimesis and attempts, rather, to find the connections (or, more properly, the tropes) that lead it to that other, longed-for, place.

In this light, reading Letter Seven alongside Letter One allows us to make some unexpected and exciting observations. On the mimetic level, the two letters are very different. The first describes a journey through the Alps; the seventh, a few solitary days, or perhaps weeks, spent in a deserted house out of which the narrator never ventures, not even for meals. Nonetheless, the structure of the traveling experience is remarkably similar in the two letters. Consider these examples:

1. Both journeys result from spur-of-the-moment decisions. In Letter One, the mountain view was enough to make the traveler change her mind about returning to Venice. In Letter Seven, a chance encounter with an old friend sets the direction that the rest of the letter will take. The friend was bidding her good-bye and getting into his carriage, Sand tells us, when he turned around to offer her his small house in town, suggesting that she might be more comfortable there than at the inn. She accepts this unexpected invitation at once and sets off for the deserted house.

2. Both adventures take the place of other plans, replacing prescribed or predetermined itineraries. In the first letter, Sand is scheduled to leave for Venice. In the letter to Liszt, Sand writes that she had been on her way to join him in Switzerland the month before when "the wind of fancy, or of fate, blew me off my course" (*Lettres*, 188).

3. In both cases, the traveler must ignore other obligations or refuse other invitations. Pagello is insistent: " 'Let me remind you . . . that you are in poor health, and that I undertook to bring you back to Venice dead or alive' " (*Lettres*, 41). In Letter Seven, Sand was supposed to be on her way to see Liszt, and she refuses, in

addition, the first offer made by her old friend, who had wanted to take her home to meet his new family.

4. While the decision to make the journey seemed in each case to be easy, and in some ways even necessary, for the narrator, the people around her view her as eccentric, and even a bit mad, to embark on such a journey all alone. The doctor chides her for being unreasonable, and the guide accompanying her to the deserted house takes this strange traveler for "a madman, a conspirator or worse" (*Lettres*, 189).

5. Both of the originally planned trips (taking the carriage to Venice and the boat down the Loire) promised at least the prospect of comfort. The journeys undertaken, however, present self-imposed or unexpected difficulties. As she walked through the mountains, Sand tell us, she chose "the hardest and least trodden paths" (*Lettres*, 57–58). The deserted house that she has been offered is far from the center of town and hard to reach: "We had to go up and down narrow, steep, scorching, badly paved streets that grew ever more deserted and dilapidated" (*Lettres*, 189).

In both letters, then, the adventure that Sand relates is essentially that of starting out for one place and ending up in another. It is precisely this unanticipated deviation from an imposed itinerary, in fact, that seems to constitute for Sand the very essence of traveling. Singularity and unpredictability are the two characteristics that distinguish the true "traveler" from that appalling creature, the "tourist." The narrator of the *Lettres d'un voyageur* is, we are told, a "solitary traveler" who goes by "deserted ways" (*Lettres*, 188); in contrast, tourists exist, rather like insects, only in the plural and in the most predictable places. Sand scorns "those insipid and monotonous faces which each summer brings back to intrude upon even the most sacred and solitary places" (*Lettres*, 52).

The unpredictable and unexpected movement we have defined as traveling on the mimetic level finds its diegetic counterpart in the form of digressions. Hayden White tells us, in *Tropics of Discourse*, that moving "*from* one notion of the way things are related *to* another notion" (2) is the essence of discourse, and it is clear that Sand delights as much in her troping as in her tramping. Chance encounters take the traveler-in-words down unexpected paths of associations and call up long-forgotten memories. Digression in writing is no more accepted by one's readers than is setting off on solitary journeys by one's friends, and Sand deviates so often from her announced subject that as early as the second letter she finds it necessary to make a blanket apology: "Once and for all I must beg your indulgence for my digressions" (*Lettres*, 70).

If Sand's travels in these letters resemble more rambling than recreation, we have a right to inquire about the sort of reader that she envisions. An introduction by Henri Bonnet to a recent edition of her work warns those who would venture here that "the transitions are missing, the links are not obvious" (12), a bit like the travel agent who cautions that in the country you are about to visit connections are difficult and there are no guaranteed reservations. Travel at your own risk: Read if you must.

If Sand could have imagined reader-tourists, she would have undoubtedly described such creatures as those sightseers so disconcerted by the prospect of the unfamiliar that they arrive in the foreign land of the text equipped with their own set of codes and contingency plans. If the genuine traveler is for Sand a "contemplative walker" (*Lettres*, 52), then the genuine reader rambles along the word paths, contemplating the text, and becoming a dynamic part of its landscape.

The answer to my first question—On what sort of textual journey is Sand taking us?—is connected to the directions for reading implicitly set forth by Sand's text. Mimetic travel and diegetic digression converge and conspire to displace our habitual notions of reading. If the true traveler rambles alone through the landscape, and the true travel writer deviates from the landscape in a series of digressions, then the appropriate, implied reader of this travel account is the one who will let the detours of the writing determine the paths of reading.

Given this intimate relationship between traveling, digressing, and reading, it is with more than passing interest that we learn, in Letter Seven, that the narrator remained in the deserted house for "the pleasure of reading and solitude" (*Lettres*, 191). This observation serves to launch a long digression on what could most aptly be called the pleasures of texts. Now she turns the tables on Liszt: From the summits of musical talent, he is brought down to the level of a tourist in the library: "You who read widely because you haven't as much respect as I have for books . . . don't know how important careful, slow reading is to a lazy mind like mine" (*Lettres*, 191). The stroller through the landscape of Letter One becomes the stroller through the text of Letter Seven.

The answer to my second question—What is our final destination?—is suggested by a further comparison between these two letters. At the outset of each, the narrator is unhappy, and the decision to make the journey in each case is an immediate source of joy. This feeling of well-being and good spirits accompanies her as she moves forward and opens pathways to desires beyond her immediate reach. In Letter One, this desire is expressed geographically: She would like to travel as far as the Tyrolean Alps. The desire of Letter Seven is translated into architectural terms. Sand finds a retreat, a refuge, and a shelter in the deserted house, and she regrets not having been there before. She addresses the house as a friend: "Oh, you would have satisfied the needs and desires of my entire life" (*Lettres*, 212).

The narrator has discovered by chance in this house the works of the physiognomist Jean-Gaspard de Lavater that she had read as a child. She seems to be particularly enchanted because, like the narrator, Lavater is a reader-traveler. He moves through the landscape of a face and reads in its features qualities of mind and character.

Sand is particularly interested in the significance that Lavater attributes to the slightest difference between two faces. Distinguishing virtuous passion from vicious passion, for example, is a question of only "a hair's breadth, an imperceptible curve, a dimension which is unnoticeable at first glance. It falls short by so little, we say, but that *little* is *everything*" (*Lettres*, 198). The smallest detail in the text of a face has the power to cause the entire text to signify differently. In the same way, chance encounters of the traveler, as they punctuate her journey, have the power to change entirely her reading of memories and events. Through

Lavater's "magic mirror" (*Lettres*, 209), she now sees her whole past in a radically new perspective.

Sand herself, as reader of places and faces, transforms a moment of silence into a volume and an imagined land into a paradise. She tells of meeting by chance a Tyrolean woman who loved her homeland so much that she was unable to speak about it: "I read into this silent stranger's melancholy a complete romance, a whole poem. Hence this Tyrol, so sensitively and tenderly regretted, became for me an enchanted land" (*Lettres*, 45). The Tyrol comes to signify the place she will never reach, as the house represents the life she will never live. The Tyrol is too far and she is too tired; the house, like herself, she imagines, is getting old: "I weep for these walls that crack, and the furrows on my brow are beyond counting" (*Lettres*, 213 t.m.). However, the traveler-writer has found the connections necessary to take her in the direction of these longed-for places.

For the traveler, the chance encounter and the untraveled road constitute the journey; for the writer, the fortuitous association produces the digression, turning the reader from the direct path and opening a circuitous route through the text. If it is true, as White tells us, that "tropics is the process by which all discourse *constitutes* the objects which it pretends only to describe and to analyze objectively" (2), then it is not the trip that generates the writing, but the "turning" in language, or troping, that produces the trip.

Venice, at the opening of Sand's *Lettres d'un voyageur*, is, I would suggest, neither a place to travel in, a place to travel to, nor a place to travel from; it is a place from which to trope. It is the word that sends Sand off seeking, as White would put it, "a connection between things so that they can be expressed in a language that takes account of the possibility of their being expressed otherwise" (2). Troping from Venice, Sand invents the journey that will take her in the direction of her desires. Venice, in Sand's *Lettres d'un voyageur*, is nothing short of a tropical paradise.

WORKS CITED

Quotations in my essay from Sand's *Lettres d'un voyageur* are from the Rabinovitz and Thomson translation. I have altered their translation slightly in two instances (indicated by t.m. after the page number) where my context required closer adherence to the original. Translations from the other French texts cited are those of the author.

Bonnet, Henry. "Introduction." In George Sand, *Lettres d'un voyageur*. Paris: Garnier-Flammarion, 1971, 11–32.

Sand, George. *Lettres d'un voyageur* [*Lettres*], translated by Sacha Rabinovitz and Patricia Thomson. Harmondsworth, Middlesex, England: Penguin, 1987.

———. "To Alfred de Musset," 29 April 1834, letter 768 in George Sand, *Correspondance* [*Corr.*], edited by Georges Lubin. Paris: Garnier Frères, 1966, 2:568–575. 1964–.

White, Hayden. *Tropics of Discourse: Essays in Cultural Criticism*. Baltimore: Johns Hopkins University Press, 1978.

Part III

AUTOBIOGRAPHY

7

Positioning the Self in Autobiographical Writing: George Sand as Model for Marguerite Yourcenar

Peter Christensen

In *Les Yeux ouverts: Entretiens avec Matthieu Galey* (1980), in the chapter on her autobiographies, Marguerite Yourcenar states:

> I struggle against the notion of the family considered as a closed milieu. No family is like this. A royal family, like the house of France, which for the royalists signified France, is completely mixed with foreign blood. Louis XIV was half Spanish and a quarter Italian. Louis XVI was half German and a quarter Polish. George Sand's ancestry was half common and half royal. There was a little bit of the prince in the peasant (in the time when there were peasants) and much of the peasant in the prince.[1]

Although this is Yourcenar's only mention of Sand with respect to her own projected autobiographical project *Le Labyrinthe du monde*, this nod to her indicates a close similarity. Sand's *Histoire de ma vie*, about 1,600 pages in length, begins with over 500 pages about the history of her family. The author starts by telling the story of her family from Fontenoy to Marengo, and only in the second book of her five-book *histoire* does she make her appearance. Over half her family's story consists of letters sent by her father to his mother and later to his wife.

In the two volumes of *Le Labyrinthe du monde*, Marguerite Yourcenar did not reach her own childhood either. The 302 pages of *Souvenirs pieux* (1974) tell the story of Yourcenar's mother, who died giving birth to Marguerite, and her family. *Archives du nord* (1977), an equally long volume, recounts the history of the author's father and his family. *Quoi, l'éternité?*, the third part, was to take Yourcenar only up to 1929, the year of the death of her father and of the publication of her first major work, *Alexis*. At this time, Yourcenar was twenty-six.

Editors' note: Since this paper was presented, Marguerite Yourcenar has died.

Readers of *Les Yeux ouverts* may thus be reminded of a memorable passage on family history from Book 1, Chapter 2, of *Histoire de ma vie*:

> For we all have important and insignificant ancestors, plebeians and patricians. Ancestors means fathers—that is, a succession of fathers. . . . It is amusing that the nobility has taken over this word for the line of fathers behind it, as if one could not carry the sacred title of father without having a standard, as if legitimate fathers were less rare in one class than in another.[2]

Both Sand and Yourcenar did much research into family history in order to be able to write autobiographies. In so doing, they each found that they needed to incorporate social and literary history into their investigations. Although we cannot make a definite comparison between *Le Labyrinthe du monde* and *Histoire de ma vie*, we can still discuss the first third of Sand's autobiography with *Souvenirs pieux* and *Archives du nord*. Since even in our own age, most autobiographies begin with the author's earliest memories and experiences (as in Simone de Beauvoir's autobiography), Sand and Yourcenar can be seen to offer alternatives to the dominant practice.

Yourcenar discussed her autobiography with Matthieu Galey in *Les Yeux ouverts*. Unlike *Histoire de ma vie*, it does not contain its own rationale in its introductory pages. Instead, Yourcenar makes a fleeting appearance (after her birth in 1903 in the first paragraph) as an investigator looking back on herself as a newborn:

> Having thus consigned these few facts which mean nothing in themselves and which, however, for each of us lead further than our own history and History itself, I stop, struck with dizziness before the inextricable confusion of incidents and circumstances which more or less determine us all. This female child, already marked by the coordinates of the Christian Era and the twentieth century, this bit of pink flesh, crying in a blue cradle, forces me to pose myself a series of questions more formidable in that they seem banal, and which persons of letters who know their job keep from formulating. (*SP*, 11)[3]

Yourcenar goes on to speak of how she must recreate herself as a historic personage from second-hand information and from letters and notebooks. She searches for real human dramas in the records of bureaucracies. What she comes up with is like a collage:

> These bits of facts believed known are, however, like this child and I, the only visible footbridge. They are also the only buoy which upholds both of us on the sea of time. It is with curiosity that I put myself here to rejoin them to see what the result will be—the image of a character and of several others, of a milieu, of a site, or a momentary escape from that which is without name and form. (*SP*, 12)

Yourcenar's birth and her mother's death of puerperal fever ten days later are recovered through a sheet of paper on which the mother, Fernande, wrote a dozen lines before dying.

In contrast, in *Histoire de ma vie*, the Sand who has to be positioned in history is not the infant, but the adult writer. The Aurore Dupin who takes on the name of George Sand and the Marguerite de Creyancour who makes herself Marguerite Yourcenar do not see themselves as authors in the same way. For Yourcenar, the fact that she is alive suffices for her life to be interesting. Sand assumes that her life is of interest because of her many works, particularly the ones she discusses (*Indiana*, *Lélia*, and *Lettres d'un voyageur*).

Rather than explore what Sand distorted or concealed from herself about her relationship with her parents as several recent scholars have done, I would like to return to her stated intentions in her autobiography. She is more concerned with positioning her life than in recounting it. What she wants us to do is to see her life in three contexts—family history, literary history, and social history. Sand's creation of a nonlinear text is aimed at decentering herself from her own life, thus making herself less self-centered. Although it can be claimed that Sand simply dictates how we should understand her life, and only deceives us when she claims that she is no longer at the center of events, I think that this viewpoint is extremist. What matters is that she has provided a valid alternative model in autobiography—one that offers a more reasonable attitude toward a person's control of the events in his or her life. Marguerite Yourcenar has followed in Sand's footsteps in using this technique.

Elizabeth W. Bruss, in *Autobiographical Acts: The Changing Situation of a Literary Genre*, raises the question of how autobiographies can even be compared at all. She finds that many critics have made reductive comments about what an autobiography should be. Despite the wide range in autobiographies, Bruss insists that it is still possible to make intelligent generalizations. She finds that we need to assert that there can be both change and continuity in autobiographical writing, and that we do not have to distort individual autobiographies to fit one mold.[4]

Both Yourcenar and Sand use nonlinear narratives that function to decenter the author from her own life. Yourcenar divides *Souvenirs pieux* into four sections. The first, "L'Accouchement," tells of Marguerite's entry into the world and the death of her mother, Fernande. In "La traversée des châteaux," we follow the history of Fernande's family from the 1300s to the 1800s, as best it can be traced. "Deux voyageurs en route vers la région immuable" concentrates on her mother's uncles, particularly Octave Pirmez, an author who was much grieved by the suicide of his brother. With the fourth section, Yourcenar returns to Fernande and tells the story of her life. At the center of the volume is a flashback. It is Marguerite's birth that frames the family history—one that she has had to create through research. Like Sand, as scholars have already observed, Yourcenar is also in quest of a lost mother. The structure of *Archives du nord* is linear, and ends with the life of Michel, Yourcenar's father. It begins in "La Nuit des temps" even before the first man appears. The following four sections trace Michel's family from the sixteenth century to 1903. The father's story is linear; the mother's is part of a circle. These two narrative strategies suggest two ways humans have of understanding experiences in time.

Although Sand lost her father, Maurice Dupin, when she was four and her mother when she was thirty-three, like Yourcenar she sees herself as more her father's child than her mother's. Sand's family history is primarily that of her father and his mother, Marie-Aurore de Saxe, who died when Sand was seventeen. Sand interrupts the story of these figures twice: first for a chapter on her mother's family and later for a chapter on Maurice de Saxe, the father of Marie-Aurore. About Maurice de Saxe's parents, from which Sand's royal blood stems, there are only six paragraphs (1:29–30). Symbolically, the interruption of Marie-Aurore's story for the insert about Sand's maternal ancestors comes when her narrative has reached 1793. Thus, she shows how the Revolution brought together the aristocratic and plebeian strains of society. Maurice de Saxe's story is inserted when the family history has come up to 1797, although Maurice de Saxe died in 1750, when his illegitimate daughter, Sand's grandmother, was only two. He is placed here because "Napoleon's destiny is like a larger-than-life realization of Maurice's dreams" (1:155). Fontenoy (1746), Maurice de Saxe's battle, serves as an analogue for Marengo (1800), Napoleon's battle. Sand's family chronicle is basically the story of a mother and her devoted son at the end of the Old Regime and during the French Revolution. Fontenoy is not the real beginning; Marie-Aurore's birth in 1748 holds this position. The mother-son duo, of course, was of natural interest to Sand, who had such a great attachment for her own son, Maurice.

Whereas Yourcenar's ancestors proceed out of the beginnings of time and go on for generation after generation, Sand's genealogy places her securely as a child under the First Empire, across the Revolution from the Old Regime, under which her grandmother lived for forty years. Sand herself will be in her forties when she writes *Histoire de ma vie*, and she will decide to take political action. In the course of the writing, France is temporarily again a republic. In response to previous critics of Sand's autobiography, we must point out that one of the qualities of Sand's "lost" mother is her "lostness" to visibility in history, unlike Sand's father and his mother. Although Sand does not wish to be remembered for her noble blood, she clearly does wish to be remembered as a historical figure (author), in the tradition of the visible patrilinear family.

For Sand, knowing the story of the family helps a person to understand the sphere of freedom in which he or she can act. We need to have a clear sense of what is determined and what is not:

> So the blood of kings is mixed in the veins of the poor and humble. What we call fatality is the character of the individual, just as this character is a result of organization, itself a result of a mixture of races—the continuation, always modified, of a series of types connected to each other. I have always considered that natural heredity, that of body and soul, establishes a rather important solidarity among each of us and each of these ancestors. (1:23)

Sand recognizes the fact that the rich, privileged, and powerful leave behind more records than the poor and obscure, and thus, to find out about her own ancestors, she risks this bias. Similarly, Yourcenar speaks out on family histories that are only undertaken to discover someone of power or importance in the past. Both women recognize the significance of those who have perished leaving little trace, yet both also take on those who have left the most trace—the autobiographers themselves.

Sand places her autobiography in the tradition of Jean-Jacques Rousseau's *Confessions*, which she both praises and criticizes in her opening pages. In addition, her ten-page digression on *Die Rauber* by Friedrich von Schiller and its popular adaption as *Robert, Chef de brigands* in Paris during the French Revolution serves as an indicator of her understanding of herself as a writer. Yourcenar's *Labyrinthe du monde* takes its name from a satirical allegory written in Czech in the 1630s by Comenius (Jan Comenski), the famous educational reformer. Since Yourcenar's father translated that work into French (from English) about a year after her birth, as she mentions in *Les Yeux ouverts*, the title is a form of homage to him. She points out to Matthieu Galey that Rousseau and Tolstoy serve as inspirations for the autobiographer, but she does not indicate what connections will be made by her *Quoi, l'éternité?* to Arthur Rimbaud's *Les Illuminations*.

As we reflect on these webs of autobiographical intertextuality, we can see that the responses of Sand and Yourcenar to Rousseau's *Confessions* are a useful entry point for understanding where these authors place themselves in relation to literary history. Yourcenar states:

> The story of his childhood and adolescence is staggering. We love this Jean-Jacques, which we might not have done, had we visited him then. What he did was something very rare: he created a genre which today seems less fresh or even dishonest—that of total sincerity or that which believes itself to be so. He wanted to say everything, the moving, the exquisite, and also that which seems ignoble to us. (*YO*, 228–229)

What attracts Yourcenar to Rousseau most of all is his ability to describe his own personal development into an adult. For this reason she is also a fan of the autobiographical novel *David Copperfield*. Apparently, *Quoi, l'éternité?* will force her to confront the same issue of maturation.

Sand has a different attitude toward Rousseau in the nine paragraphs she devotes to him in the first chapter of *Histoire de ma vie*. She loves the *Confessions* for showing Rousseau the philosopher at odds with his contemporaries, but she is upset by his endless, and to her, unnecessary, self-justifications. She writes:

> In the ordinary course of existence, one had to love oneself tenderly or else have some serious project to succeed at, in order to attach oneself passionately at rebuffing the calumny which strikes everyone, even the best. Sometimes this is a necessity of public life, but in private life one can not prove loyalty at all by discussion. And since no one can prove that he has arrived

> at perfection, we must leave to those who know us the care to absolve us of our faults and appreciate our good qualities.
>
> Finally, since we are all dependent on one another, there is no such thing as an isolated fault. There is no error without cause or accomplice. One cannot accuse oneself without accusing one's neighbor, not only the enemy which attacks us but sometimes the friend who defends us. This is what happened to Rousseau, and it is bad. Who can pardon him for confessing Madame de Warens at the same time as himself? (1:12–13)

Since Sand does not believe that her guilt or innocence can be proven by her autobiographical discourse, she is not compelled to justify her existence. Instead, she ties her life to those of others around her. Whereas Yourcenar favors Rousseau as he becomes Rousseau, Sand prefers him as the man of letters fully formed. It is not, therefore, surprising that Sand begins *Histoire de ma vie* by letting us know from the start some of her fully formed ideas. In contrast, Yourcenar effaces herself for the first two volumes, keeping a low profile as an investigator rather than a major literary figure.

A comparison between Sand's use of Schiller and Yourcenar's reference to Comenius is also instructive. Yourcenar tells Matthieu Galey:

> *The Labyrinth of the World* by Comenius is a very beautiful book, bitterly satirical and different by that from the celebrated *Pilgrim's Progress* of John Bunyan, almost contemporary with it and related to it by genre. I am always astonished that comparatists have not discovered this book, which is a sort of Bosch or Breughel in writing. The work concludes with a purely mystical part, or rather pietistic, *The Paradise of the Heart*, which Michael had also translated.
>
> Nevertheless there really is a paradise of the heart, a happiness of a spirit, soul, or body, partially delivered from the useless. And this happiness beyond words survives inexplicably among some people in the middle of despair caused by the sorrow of the world which is also beyond words. (*YO*, 221–222)

It is at first difficult to understand what Yourcenar sees in Comenius's work to connect it with her own project. She is not writing a satire, and although she refers in passing to Bosch and Breughel (*AN*, 37), they do not provide a major frame of reference. It is also hard to imagine *Quoi, l'éternité?* ending with a mystical vision. Instead, we must conclude that life is a labyrinthine journey full of temptations that may seem gruesome under the aspect of eternity. Nonetheless, this life may still lead to personal happiness.

In *Histoire de ma vie*, the individual's timeless search for personal happiness is downplayed as Sand emphasizes throughout that she is a child of her time. Her comments about the legacy of Schiller are instructive in this regard. In 1798, five years after the Reign of Terror, Sand's father acted in a play then six years old, an adaptation of *Die Rauber* which completely changed the moral thrust of the original. By ending with the reconciliation of Robert with society, it justifies his terrorist activities. Sand asks how it is possible that no one could have learned from recent history the stupidity and moral insensitivity of the adaptation:

> Error of the past generations, I deplore you but do not curse you. But here is an even more curious fact. Our ancestors played *Robert, Chef de brigands* in 1798! The Terror had passed. The cloud had burst on their own heads. It had vomited dreadful scourges, and one knew, alas, that the end does not justify the means. Robert's brigands had tried in vain to purify humanity, which awakened in the middle of smoking ruins, quickly wiped the blood which had just been spilled and killed Robert and his accomplices, henceforth loathed and stigmatized as cannibals. (1:170)

Sand's point is that history can make literature reveal its own irresponsibility. Her motto is that the ends must justify the means, and she declares that she believes in the equality of humankind under God's law. She does not stress how much she is at odds with her own age to the extent that she might have, and, indeed, as Rousseau had, in his pre-Revolutionary *Confessions*. Instead, as a post-Revolutionary writer, she spends time telling sympathetic stories of such contemporaries as Marie Dorval and Eugène Delacroix. Sand's father's theatrical career severs her from the past, which is all part of Yourcenar's more expansive labyrinth of the world. Moreover, as Yourcenar notes, this image of the labyrinth goes all the way back to the Cretan Age.

Although both Sand and Yourcenar let their readers know where they are in time as they work on their autobiographies, Sand does not wish for her life's story to be inscribed in the same type of universal history as Yourcenar's. Sand is born in 1804, at the end of Book 2, Chapter 7(1:464), the last year of the First Republic. On the next page we read about the Second Republic:

> Everything up to this point was written under the monarchy of Louis Philippe. I take up this work again on June 1, 1848, reserving for another part of my story what I saw and felt during this gap of time.
>
> If I had finished my book before the Revolution, it would have been different, the work of a well-meaning child, I dare say. For I had only studied humanity through its exceptional individuals and had done even that at leisure. Then I began to use my eye on a campaign in the world of facts, and I did not end up as I began. I lost the illusions of youth, which I had kept longer than reason should dictate due to my life of retreat and contemplation.
>
> Time marches on quickly, and, after all, humanity is not different from me, that is to say, people grow discouraged and become revitalized with great ease. May God keep me from believing like Jean-Jacques Rousseau that I am worth more than my contemporaries and that I have the right to curse them. (1:465–466)

Sand, as a student of the second Revolution and child of the first one, wishes simultaneously to express herself as one person in the sea of humanity and as the person visible in history in the tradition of her father's family. This does not represent hypocrisy on her part, but rather is a not entirely successful attempt to reconcile the patrician and plebeian parts of her heritage.

Yourcenar's frame of reference is not centered on 1914 or 1939, as indeed it might be. Instead, she is an elderly woman looking back over the expanse of her own life and the labyrinth of history. We hear of her in 1956 as she returns to her native region and in 1928 when her father shows her some family documents. There are references to World War II, which are poignant but casual. It is clear that she is writing from the vantage point of 1970; but unlike Sand, she does not explain the specific circumstances under which she is writing. All of the centuries must be considered in judging her life, not just the last century, as in Sand's case.

Through nonlinear narratives both autobiographers offer humanistic perspectives on how we can locate our lives so they can be judged fairly—in terms of universal history in Yourcenar's case, and recent social history in Sand's.

NOTES

1. Marguerite Yourcenar, *Les Yeux ouverts: Entretiens avec Matthieu Galey* [*YO*] (Paris: Le Centurion, 1980, 218; this and all subsequent translations are those of the author.

2. George Sand, *Histoire de ma vie*, edited by Georges Lubin (Paris: Gallimard, 1970–1971), 1:23.

3. Marguerite Yourcenar, *Souvenirs pieux* (Paris: Gallimard, 1974), 11. References to this volume will be marked *SP*.. For *Archives du nord* (Paris: Gallimard, 1977), *AN* will be the abbreviation.

4. Elizabeth W. Bruss, *Autobiographical Acts: The Changing Situation of a Literary Genre* (Baltimore: Johns Hopkins University Press, 1976), 1–2.

8

Histoire de ma vie: George Sand and Autobiography

Gita May

When George Sand undertook to write her autobiography, on April 15, 1847, as a personal notation attests, she had already experienced a great deal, and had achieved fame as well as notoriety as a prolific and controversial author and novelist who did not allow her gender to inhibit either her literary inspiration or her personal life.[1]

The autobiographical impulse in Sand did not wait until then to manifest itself. Aside from the fact that one can recognize significant features of Aurore Dupin in the heroines of her famous novels, one can also recognize personally revealing elements in works such as *Letters of a Voyager* (1834–1836), *Intimate Journal* (1834), and *Winter in Majorca* (1838–1839).

As a woman who had achieved renown and who in the process had boldly challenged the conventional notion of womanhood, George Sand could not but be acutely aware that, largely because of this, she had aroused a great deal of hostility and had made enemies. That she would attempt to seek in a fuller understanding of her inner self some answer to the provocative image she presented to the world is understandable, especially in view of the example that had been set by a writer she particularly admired, Jean-Jacques Rousseau.[2]

George Sand consistently and proudly proclaimed herself the spiritual daughter of Rousseau, in her political and moral philosophy as well as in her religious beliefs. She would hardly ever miss an opportunity to defend him passionately against his posthumous adversaries, who continued to be as numerous and as vociferous as in his own lifetime.[3] When the young Aurore Dupin came across Rousseau's works, this discovery turned out to be the high point of her restless intellectual and spiritual quest, and in her autobiography she compares the overwhelming effect of this reading to that of "magnificent music brightened by intense sunlight" (1:1060). She had at last found her ideal mentor: "What joy for a clumsy but tenacious schoolgirl to succeed at last in opening her eyes fully and in no longer having clouds obscure her view" (1:1061). It is worth pointing out that while the young Aurore Dupin found the reading of Rousseau "intoxicating," she faithfully kept a promise, made to her beloved grandmother, not to read Voltaire until she had reached her thirtieth birthday (1:1061). By that time, however, Voltaire seems to have had little effect on her: "When I read him, I liked him a great deal, indeed, but without being moved by him in any significant way" (1:1061).

Sand liked to identify herself with Rousseau as a sensitive, religious soul and as a passionate lover of nature. As an enthusiastic social reformer and activist, she also subscribed to his political and ideological program of human betterment. Her main criticism of him in this respect was that he was not radical enough and "thought it necessary to dissemble with the powers of his day" (1:44), and that, like Voltaire and Denis Diderot, he treated rather scornfully and unfairly such a sincere humanitarian and utopist as the Abbé de Saint-Pierre, author of an important pacifist treatise (*Project for Perpetual Peace*) merely because he lacked literary talent (1:44). Like Rousseau, Sand deeply believed in the simple pleasures and satisfactions of a rustic life, and derived greater enjoyment from dealing with unsophisticated countryfolk than with the Paris literati. That she also identified herself with Rousseau as an incorrigible dreamer who found far greater satisfaction in roaming the world of imagination than in facing harsh reality may come as a somewhat unexpected self-assessment on the part of one who has consistently been characterized as an indefatigable activist and a phenomenal worker: "No one has dreamed more and acted less than I in this life" (1:27). Whether we should take this assertion at face value is doubtful, for here Sand's self-image probably corresponds more closely with a Rousseauistic and Romantic fantasy of vulnerability and impractical idealism than with the woman of indomitable courage and tireless activity that she was in reality.

Her own plight as a highly touted yet controversial author caused George Sand to be particularly sensitive to Rousseau's painful odyssey of self-discovery. It was no wonder, therefore, that her *Story of My Life* should begin with a theoretical disquisition on autobiography in which Rousseau is prominently featured. In these introductory pages Sand asks and attempts to answer some basic questions regarding the enterprise on which she is about to embark. In seeking to define what in her eyes constitutes autobiography, and in examining Rousseau's *Confessions* more closely than she had ever done before, she ends up disagreeing more often than agreeing with her revered mentor, and ultimately questioning and even rejecting the way in which he had envisioned and put into practice the idea of telling his life's story.

For the first time, Sand, who had always played the part of the dutiful and loyal daughter and who had tirelessly taken up arms to defend Rousseau against the latter's detractors, finds herself at odds with him and acts out the role of the stern critic, and indeed the unforgiving judge. In this respect, her frequently harsh comments on Rousseau as autobiographer might be considered a classical illustration of Harold Bloom's theory of the "anxiety of influence." She takes her spiritual father to task for performing sleights of hand in order to seduce and deceive his readers, and when she tells us how she will write her own autobiography, it is clear that she has decided to part company with her predecessor in several major ways. While acknowledging the exceptional literary and stylistic qualities of the *Confessions*, as a model of autobiographical writing she rejects it on ethical and ideological grounds. Indeed, it is while formulating her objections to those aspects of the *Confessions* that she looks on as flawed that she clarifies in her own mind what she intends to do or refrain from doing in setting down her own reminiscences. However, even in the midst of her criticism, she pays Rousseau a ringing and touching tribute that is obviously meant to show her continuing and undiminished reverence: "Forgive me, Jean-Jacques, for censuring you upon closing your admirable book of *Confessions*! I find fault with you, and it is yet another way of paying you homage, since this reproach does not affect my respect and my enthusiasm for your work as a whole" (1:13).

If George Sand, despite her misgivings about autobiography as a genre, perseveres in her endeavor to tell the story of her life, she does so because she considers it a duty, and a painful one at that:

> I don't think that there is pride and impertinence in writing the story of one's own life, even less so in choosing, among the memories that this life has left in us, those that seem to us worthy of preservation. For my part, I think I accomplish a duty, a rather painful one even, for I don't know anything more difficult than to define and to sum oneself up. (1:5)

As a social activist and a fanatical believer in hard work, Sand had very serious misgivings about the ultimate value of introspection and self-analysis, which she tended to view as a form of complacent narcissism and solipsistic self-indulgence:

> The study of the human heart is such that the more one becomes absorbed in it, the less one sees clearly into it; and for certain active minds, to know oneself is a fastidious and never-ending study. Yet I shall accomplish this duty; I always have it before my eyes; I have always promised myself not to die before having done what I have always advised others to do for themselves: a sincere study of my own nature and an attentive examination of my own existence. (1:5)

However, Sand starts out by revealing her hesitation about such a project because of its narcissistic implications. To write in the first person and constantly speak about oneself is an undertaking fraught with danger. Through a natural law of human nature, it is almost irresistible to "embellish and elevate the object of one's contemplation" (1:6). Pride, vanity, and *amour-propre* soon come into play, and writers as well as poets are particularly vulnerable to the lure of enthusiasm, which in turn causes them to identify with the divine and the ideal. The temptation is strong indeed to wrap oneself in the mantle of one of the sublime heroes of the human imagination. However flattering and exalting to become another Werther, a Manfred, a Faust, or a Hamlet (1:6)! Such grand depictions of powerful human emotions are indeed worthy of veneration, but these idealized models, while inspiring to the poetic imagination, represent the dream but not the reality of human experience. For her part, Sand is determined to cling more modestly to the prosaic exigencies of truth as she sees it and to resist succumbing to the blandishments of a poetically embellished view of life.

Sand fully subscribes to Blaise Pascal's dictum that "le moi est haïssable" ("the self is hateful"). In this respect, she parts company not only with Rousseau, but even more emphatically with his Romantic emulators:

> I have always found it to be in bad taste . . . to speak a great deal about oneself. There are few days, few moments in the life of ordinary beings worthy of interest and introspection. Yet. like everyone else I have found myself in such days and times, and I have taken up the pen to pour out some sharp suffering which overwhelmed me or some violent anxiety which agitated me. (1:7)

For George Sand, however, the autobiographical enterprise has meaning and justification only to the extent that it transcends the experience of one human being. By its very nature, autobiography is an act that involves far more than a single destiny, notwithstanding its singularity. It represents a moment in history and the expression of an individual's vision of life within the broader social, political, and historical context. The purely personal aspect of autobiography must necessarily pale in comparison with the import of this wider perspective. To stress, therefore, as Rousseau did, the subjective at the expense of the collective is wrong: "Everything contributes to history, *everything is history* [Sand's emphasis], even novels which seem in no way to relate to the political situations that witnessed their inception. It is therefore certain that the real details of every human existence are individual brush strokes in the general painting of collective life" (1:78).

Sand's autobiographical enterprise rests on this premise of collective interdependence and especially what she fondly and repeatedly defines as *solidarity* (1:9, 13, 307), and it is in this light that she reexamines Rousseau's *Confessions* and finds it lacking in several important respects. Not only did Rousseau dwell too indulgently on aspects of his life that concerned only himself, in his misguided compulsion to tell all in the name of unqualified sincerity and veracity and in order to forestall accusations of self-aggrandizement and self-embellishment, he went to the other extreme by accusing himself unnecessarily and gratuitously of peccadilloes which under his eloquent pen assumed the dire proportions of real crimes: "I suffer agonizingly when I see the great Rousseau humiliate himself in this way and imagine that by exaggerating, perhaps even inventing these sins, he will exonerate himself of those vices of the heart that his enemies attributed to him. He certainly did not disarm them with his *Confessions*" (1:12).

On the contrary, Rousseau only succeeded in laying himself open to the most violent attacks against his character and morality. For her part, Sand is determined not to expose herself needlessly to calumny, for she knows only too well that her adversaries are lying in wait for the first opportunity to pounce. Unlike Rousseau, Sand is determined to set certain clearly understood limits to her autobiography, and goes to great lengths in marking the boundaries of what she feels is her private, sacred domain and not to be encroached on even in a personal memoir. In this respect, the pact she makes with her reader at the outset of the *Story of My Life* is unequivocal, even if its restrictive character might surprise and disappoint a public by then accustomed to her boldness and willingness to defy convention and tradition.[4] While ironically reassuring her enemies that she will not take advantage of this opportunity to get even with them: "Let none of those who have harmed be frightened; I don't remember them" (1:13), she also warns those of her readers who out of prurient curiosity would seek out her book in order to find in it sensational revelations: "The sufferings I would have to relate about a purely personal situation have no bearing on general usefulness. I shall only relate those that are relevant to all humankind." Therefore, scandalmongers, close my book on the first page, it is not meant for you" (1:15).

Proudly Sand underscores, however, that her reticences should in no way be attributable to repression or pusillanimity: "I believe that my readers know me well enough, as a writer, not to accuse me of cowardliness" (1:11). Here, her rhetoric leads her perhaps to trade on her controversial reputation as one who hardly ever recoiled before any situation that might be deemed compromising.[5] However, feminist criticism has acknowledged this restrictive notion as a problematic one because it tends to characterize women's autobiographies as a whole.[6]

When Sand takes Rousseau to task for turning his *Confessions* into an apologia, she indirectly reveals her own anxiety about turning her *Story of My Life* into an impassioned but single-minded defense of her unorthodox life and career: "He accuses himself in order to have an opportunity of exonerating himself; he reveals hitherto unknown misdeeds in order to have the right to repulse public calumnies" (1:10). To be sure, she sees herself, like Rousseau, as a victim of public incomprehension and, in many instances, even deliberate malevolence. However, she refuses to be constricted to this role. She wants her autobiography to transcend considerations of personal justification and vindication, and she vows to resist the temptation of either excessive humility or pride.

George Sand is equally determined to refuse to turn her life's story into some artificially orderly narrative. Her book, she informs us, will be as inconsistent and unpredictable as human nature and as life itself (1:13). Here she takes her cue from both Montaigne and Rousseau, who had also invoked the privilege of following the vagaries of their idiosyncratic nature in speaking about themselves, rather than trying to impose some preordained pattern to their works. Echoing her two predecessors without naming them, she asserts: "Human nature is but a tissue of inconsistencies, and I absolutely don't agree with those who always find themselves in accord with their selves of yesterday. My work will therefore reflect in its form this 'easygoingness' [*laisser-aller*] of my mind" (1:13).

To attempt to transform life into art at the expense of the kind of spontaneity without which inner truth is impossible would, Sand warns us, constitute a betrayal of her primary purpose: "I would not like to relate my life as though it were a novel. Form would prevail upon content" (1:13)

However, should we take Sand at her word when she rather blithely proclaims that she will steer clear of the realm of fiction? Sand the storyteller is as adept as Rousseau at seizing and retaining the reader's attention through a richly varied narrative in which her novelistic virtuosity is everywhere apparent. To be sure, Sand probably never experienced the agonies of writer's block, and as a prodigiously prolific author, she liked to trust the impulses of her sensibility and uninhibited inspiration. Furthermore, her self-representation is less spontaneous and candid than she would have us believe. There is, as we have seen, her refusal to speak about some of the most intimate aspects of her inner life and her stern caveat to the reader that her "autobiographical pact" does not bind her to indiscriminate and indiscreet revelations. Not to be overlooked, she warns us, is the fact that self-condemnation necessarily implicates others: "There is no error of which someone is not the cause or the accomplice, and it is impossible to accuse oneself without accusing one's fellow human being, not only the enemy who attacks us, but also the friend who defends us. This is what happened to Rousseau, and it is wrong" (1:13).

When George Sand quips that "Rousseau confessed Madame de Warens while confessing himself" (1:13), this is no idle sally for the sake of witty cleverness. She takes with the utmost seriousness the autobiographer's moral responsibility not to hurt contemporaries needlessly. That Rousseau, in his obsessive compulsion to exonerate himself by telling all, ignored the harm his revelations could bring even to those dearest to his heart, constituted in her eyes a particularly reprehensible betrayal of his trust as friend and lover and yet another proof of his narcissistic egotism and total self-absorption.

Sand's reluctance to place the emphasis of her retrospective narrative on the purely personal and subjective and her determination to remain mindful of the broader historical framework are also indicative of a carefully thought out and deliberate reconstruction of the past. Her reminiscences, she is convinced, will only be meaningful to the extent that they remain subordinate to the vast and tumultuous panorama of recent French history, spanning the Old Regime, the Revolution, the Empire, the Restoration, and the July Monarchy. This explains her decision to begin her narrative not with the date of her birth but with a detailed story of her immediate ancestors (especially her parents and grandmother), even if this means that it will take her more than fourteen chapters and approximately five hundred pages in the Pléiade edition of the *Story of My Life* before allowing Aurore Dupin, the future George Sand, to step at last and even then somewhat gingerly and gradually onto the center stage.

Having reached the fourteenth chapter before even being born, Sand becomes understandably aware that even her most loyal readers may be growing restless and impatient: "But if I continue the story of my father, I will probably be told that I am rather long in keeping my promise to relate my own story" (1:307). This affords her an opportunity to reiterate her basic definition of autobiography: "Humanity has its intimate history in every human being. It is therefore necessary that I embrace a period of approximately one hundred years in order to relate forty years of my life. Without that I cannot coordinate my reminiscences" (1:308.

Despite these high-sounding declarations of principle, there is no doubt that Sand was too good a novelist and student of the human heart not to be carried away by the compelling story of the romance between her father and her mother. Her father, Maurice Dupin, a handsome officer in the French army who had distinguished himself on the battlefield, bore the name of his famed grandfather, Maurice, who was Comte de Saxe and, under Louis XV, Maréchal de France, and who was equally renowned for his military and amorous conquests. The Dupins were also descendants of King Augustus II of Poland, one of the most notorious womanizers of his time. In 1800, Maurice Dupin, serving as first lieutenant in Milan under Napoleon, met and fell in love with the vivacious Sophie-Victoire Delaborde, mistress of General Claude-Antoine Collin. That Sophie was the daughter of a bird-seller on the quai de la Mégisserie in Paris, and that she had led a most irregular life and given birth to two illegitimate children of different fathers, did not deter Maurice Dupin from marrying her in a civil ceremony on June 5, 1804. Hardly a month later, on July 1, a daughter, named Amantine-Aurore-Lucile Dupin, the future George Sand, was born in Paris. The father was twenty-six and the mother thirty-one at the time. In her autobiography, Sand makes much of the fact that in her veins coursed the blood of both kings and paupers, patricians and plebeians (1:15–16).

Sand's paternal grandmother, Marie-Aurore Dupin de Francueil (née Saxe), was cultivated and well-read and a disciple of the Encyclopedists as well as a talented singer. Her role in the early chapters of the *Story of My Life* is a large one, understandably so in view of her commanding personality. On the other hand, Sand's mother, in the writer's own words, was "a poor child of the old streets of Paris" about whose ancestry she knew next to nothing. If she did not benefit from any kind of formal education, she was nonetheless far from stupid, and had artistic talents, notably for singing, embroidery, and drawing. Despite or perhaps because of a difficult and unpredictable temperament, and also probably because she was the underdog in her difficult relationship with the aristocratic, imperious Madame Dupin (especially after the tragic and premature death of Sand's father), she became the object of young Aurore's fierce and total devotion.

Sand somewhat defensively invokes history to justify devoting so many chapters of her autobiography to her family background. In actuality, it was probably the novelist in her that ultimately became fascinated by her parents' romantic love story in the midst of the Napoleonic wars and by the imposing figure of her grandmother, a proud and indomitable survivor of pre-Revolutionary France, who steadfastly remained loyal to the great writers of the Enlightenment as well as to the gracious manners from before the Revolution. *Story of My Life* constitutes a new kind of autobiography, for it not only represents an original and personal odyssey of self-discovery in the Rousseau tradition, it also blazes a new trail as a woman writer's quest for her familial, social, and historical roots. That in the process she should have indulged in some myth making of her own is entirely understandable. She was after all, first and foremost, a novelist, and self-representation of the most sincere kind involves fiction, if the latter is to be understood in its broadest sense as an artistic reconstruction of lived experience.

NOTES

1. See her *Oeuvres autobiographiques*, edited by Georges Lubin (Paris: Gallimard, 1970), 1:xv. All references to the *Story of My Life* (*Histoire de ma vie*) are to this edition; this and all subsequent translations are those of the author.

2. For more information about George Sand's indebtedness to Rousseau, see Ute van Runset, "Illuminisme et lumières: Impact sur les idées sociales de George Sand," in Raymond Trousson, ed., *Oeuvres et critiques, la réfraction des lumières au XIX*[e] Siècle (Paris: Jean-Michel Place, 1985), 29–43; and Gita May, "Des *Confessions* à l'*Histoire de ma vie*: Deux auteurs à la recherche de leur moi," *Présence de George Sand* 8 (May 1980): 40–47. Also see Gita May, "George Sand," in Jacques Barzun and George Stade, eds., *European Writers: The Romantic Century* (New York: Scribner's, 1985), 6:813–836.

3. See Raymond Trousson, "Les *Confessions* devant la critique et l'histoire littéraires au XIXe siècle," in Roland Desné, ed., *Oeuvres et critiques* (Paris: Jean-Michel Place, 1978), 51–62.

4. Compare Philippe Lejeune, *Le Pacte autobiographique* (Paris: Editions du Seuil, 1975).

5. Compare Béatrice Didier, "Femme/Identité/Ecriture: A propos de l'*Histoire de ma vie* de George Sand," *Revue des Sciences Humaines* 168 (October-December 1977): 571.

6. Compare Nancy K. Miller, "Women's Autobiography in France: For a Dialectic of Identification," in Sally McConnell-Ginet, Ruth Borker, and Nelly Furman, eds., *Women and Language in Literature and Society* (New York: Praeger, 1980), 258–273.

9

Aurore Inscribing Aurore: A Reading of "La Reine Coax"

Lynn Kettler Penrod

> Aurore est ma passion, passion partagée, car nous vivons constamment ensemble. . . . Elle m'occupe beaucoup.
>
> —George Sand

Many psychologists have observed the close and harmonious relationship often shared by grandparent and grandchild. The child, still close to the beginning of the life cycle, and the grandparent, nearing the end of life's continuum, find themselves able to weave together wonder and experience and to communicate in a language often denied to parent and child because of unresolved conflicts. Indeed, during the final years of George Sand's life, we notice this very phenomenon: Whereas the parent-child relationships between Sand and her children were often stormy and problematic, her relationships with her grandchildren were always warm and relaxed. What we see, in fact, is George Sand, at the end of her life, turning back to a name virtually abandoned in 1832. She returned once again to the name of Aurore, from Aurore Dupin, to G. Sand, to George Sand, to Aurore, to Aurore Sand—the reincorporation, the revitalization, and the reinscription of the name of childhood. As she wrote to Gustave Flaubert in 1868: "This morning I was dreaming, and I awoke repeating this bizarre sentence: 'There is always one great young lead in the drama which is life. Mine is the role of Aurore.' "[1]

The name Aurore here has, of course, a double resonance: for it "names" not only Amandine Aurore Lucile Dupin, born July 1, 1804, but also her namesake Aurore, born January 10, 1866, daughter of Sand's son Maurice and his wife Lina. That the two-and-a-half-year-old Aurore was a source of delight to the sixty-four-year-old Aurore is made quite clear in the Flaubert letter: "The fact is that it's impossible not to idolize this little girl. She is such a treasure—so intelligent and so good—that I feel I am dreaming."[2]

Aurore or "Lolo" (and her younger sister Gabrielle or "Titite"—born in March 1868) would come to be more and more important to Sand as she neared the end of her life and observed the maturation and repetition of cyclical life experiences in two young granddaughters. Her lifelong passion for education—for teaching—was obviously rekindled during Lolo and Titite's early years. By November 1871 she was giving Aurore two hours of daily lessons as well as two further hours of "instruction in the form of games."[3] These tutorials led Sand to write down her ideas on pedagogy in an 1872 essay, *Les Idées d'un maître d'école*, and the following year saw the appearance of the first *Contes d'une grand-mère*, thirteen stories written for Aurore and Gabrielle which appeared serially in *Le Temps* and *La Revue des Deux Mondes* from 1873 to 1876.

The first series, published in 1873 under the title *Le Château de Pictordu*, includes five stories—"La Reine Coax," "Le Nuage rose," "Les Ailes du courage," "Le Géant Yéous," and the title story—all versions of the child's discovery of the self and the self's relation to the natural world. The second series of grandmother stories appeared in 1876 and includes eight stories, two of which—"Le Chêne parlant" and "Le Chien et la fleur sacrée"—belong more properly to the first group, given their emphasis on the identity quest theme. The other six, however—"L'Orgue du titan," "Ce que disent les fleurs," "Le Marteau rouge," "La Fée poussière," "Le Gnome des huîtres," and "La Fée aux gros yeux"—involve a systematic reflection by Sand on the very nature of matter and life forms, which in turn refers us back to the first Aurore's magical-mythical world of Corambé.

All the grandmother stories are intimately concerned with beginnings and endings, with the necessary rites of passage from childhood to adulthood, and with the very nature of the experience of learning—learning about oneself and learning about the natural world. The young Aurore, to whom many of the grandmother stories are dedicated, thus receives the elder Aurore's written legacy of love, common sense, and imaginative strategies for coping with adult life problems (education, work, marriage, and family) while at the same time these very stories recapitulate the grandmother's own, now nearly completed, process of individuation, in Jungian terms. Here is Sand, again writing to Flaubert in an 1872 letter: "Who would believe it—that with my calm demeanor and at my age, I still love *excess*? My overriding passion, indeed, is Aurore. My life is linked [*suspendue*] to hers."[4] With this image of the "suspension" of one life to another, and this link from Aurore to Aurore made clear, the grandmother stories perhaps take on a deeper meaning.

Of the five stories that make up the first series of grandmother tales, "La Reine Coax" is the oldest, having appeared in *La Revue des Deux Mondes* in June 1872. Sand dedicates the story to "Mademoiselle Aurore Sand": "Since you now know how to read, my dearest, I am writing down the stories I used to tell you in order to teach you and entertain you as much as possible."[5] The young Aurore, who has just learned to read, will now see in print the story she has already heard; the elder

Aurore will inscribe that story (which is, in many respects, her own youthful quest for identity) through the written word.

"La Reine Coax" begins in classic fairy-tale style—in a large old château, localized spatially somewhere in Normandy or Picardy and temporally in the not-too-distant past in relation to the life of the young Aurore. The fairy-tale family lacks both father and mother, but the role of the mother is filled by the châtelaine Yolande (one hears the echo of "la bonne dame de Nohant" in the vowel sequence of the name) who is the grandmother of the fifteen-year-old heroine, Marguerite (called Margot by her grandmother, echoing the name Lolo that Sand habitually used for speaking to Aurore). The nameless château is surrounded by a moat filled with rushes, water lilies, and other wild plants, and inhabited, too, by a large colony of frogs, "some so old and fat that one was amazed at their beautiful shape and strong voices" (117).

As in typical fairy-tale structure, this initial natural equilibrium (a château surrounded by harmonious singing nature) is disturbed by the arrival of a drought, a natural disaster that quickly destroys all that is most fundamentally beautiful in the watery kingdom of frogs and lily pads. Indeed, when the plants and water animals begin to die from lack of water, their decaying corpses transform the rich, moist natural world into a viscous morass of poisonous mud which brings a dreaded fever to the château and surrounding area.

Like all fairy-tale heroines, Marguerite, "very sensible, very brave and very obliging" (118), and much loved by all who know her, does have a disability to overcome: She is not at all pretty: "Her nose was too short, her eyes were too round, and her mouth was too big" (118). Even her gentle and kindhearted grandmother Yolande thinks regretfully what a shame it is that "such a sweet and intelligent child should have the face of a frog!" (118).

This perceived resemblance between Marguerite and the world of the frogs proves to be an important narrative motor in "La Reine Coax," for since the fairy-tale protagonist must of necessity attempt to regain control and reestablish the initial equilibrium (here, the natural equilibrium destroyed by the drought), Marguerite's first action, "in spite of her pity for the innocent [frogs]" (118), is to destroy the frog world in order to prevent a recurrence of fever. Like the *petite fille modèle* she is said to be, it is Marguerite who nurses the fever victims back to health. However, too impatient to wait for the next rainy season and the natural return of fresh water to the château's now dried-up moat, Marguerite decides to create a perfectly controlled environment by transforming the moat into a formal garden where disease cannot possibly thrive. Marguerite's miniature Versailles—the result of filling up the moat with sand and fresh soil and planting fruit trees—is complete with marble goldfish ponds, white swans, and haughty peacocks, but totally devoid of wild flowers, rushes, or, indeed, frogs. Marguerite has managed to reestablish equilibrium but in so doing has created a second, and more important, disequilibrium.

Yolande explains to Marguerite that although the new garden is very lovely, she cannot help missing the natural loveliness remembered from her own childhood—when the water was clean and clear, and when indeed the château was "an estate surrounded by its well-stocked moat" rather than a château resembling a "middle-class home" (119). The need to accept the freedom of the natural world and to be patient with its ebb and flow is the lesson Marguerite learns; for although her own memories do not extend back into time as far as do Yolande's, she does of course remember the beautiful singing of the frogs and realizes that what she has created through good intention has perhaps not been an unqualified success: "I've destroyed something which I used to love and which my grandmother misses, something which was once beautiful and which might have become so again this year with the autumn rains" (120).

Marguerite's residual guilt, however, guides her from lesson number one to lesson number two as she follows one small rivulet of water that leads from her elaborately constructed garden literally and figuratively "back to nature," to a new marshy area near the river, filled with reeds, rushes, and a riot of wild plant, animal, and insect life.[6] However, within this luxuriant new growth of nature, one element of the destroyed world is still missing: "Marguerite looked in vain; she saw everything in the water, save any kind of frog, large or small" (121). Guilt, perception of absence/lack, and Marguerite's own "froglike" affinities here combine to bring about the story's first "marvelous" occurrence.

For Sand, of course, the marvelous must never be confused with the supernatural. As she writes in the dedication (again to Aurore) to *Le Château de Pictordu:* "The question is whether or not there are fairies. You are at an age when children like everything that is marvelous, and I should like to think that you found nature marvelous, too, since you like it just as much. *I* think the marvelous is to be found in nature; otherwise, I should not be able to give it to you."[7] Accordingly, Marguerite's first encounter with the fantastic, her meeting with the frog queen Coax, is "marvelous" (Marguerite finds herself in the middle of the marsh standing on a tiny island—and cannot remember how she got there) but is also grounded in the reality of everyday explanations of such occurrences (Marguerite constantly tells herself that these magical moments might be just dreams).

In any case, the appearance of Queen Coax has all the necessary elements of fairy-tale magic:[8] "Then there was a great silence, all the animals stopped moving, the sun disappeared again behind the clouds, and the reeds parted as if someone were walking through them. Marguerite saw before her a superb green and black striped frog, but huge—so huge that she had never seen one like it before; and she was afraid" (121). Marguerite's fear is justified perhaps when the frog queen, sole survivor of the drought and Marguerite's garden project, warns her: "Never think you can dry up my new kingdom the way you dried up the moat of your estate—where I had deigned to take up residence; you should know that if you were to do the same thing to this meadow, you and your family would suffer terribly" (122). However, upon Marguerite's promise of good faith and her willingness to grant a favor to Queen Coax in expiation for the sin of having destroyed the frog kingdom, the frog invites the girl to an underwater crystal palace where she will hear "marvelous things which no human ear has ever heard before" (122).

Totally captivated by the frog queen, Marguerite is ready to plunge headfirst into the dangerous waters of the marsh when she is stopped by Nevé, the largest and tamest of the white swans who now live in the château garden. Nevé tugs at the hem of Marguerite's dress, the marvelous spell is broken, and Marguerite finds herself alone and frightened, and unsure of how to get home safely. It is only through the swan's intervention that she manages to reach land; and when she finally arrives at the haven of Grandmother Yolande's château, she discovers that Nevé is nowhere to be found.

Marguerite is unsure whether her encounter with the frog queen has been real, magical, or simply part of a dream. She tells no one of her mysterious experience, but during the night hears a musical voice that speaks to her during a storm, reassuring her that she is being watched over but warning her not to trust Queen Coax: "A prudent young lady must under no circumstances speak to frogs she does not know" (123).

With the return of Nevé the next morning, Marguerite, sensible as always, is sure that her disturbing experience of the previous afternoon has had its origin not even in a dream per se, but in a story which Yolande used to tell her when she was a little girl. Like the Aurore-*narrataire* of Sand's story, Marguerite "during her childhood had loved listening to the stories her grandmother told her at bedtime," and she recalls that in one of the stories "there was a frog-fairy who did magical things" (124).

This clever use of *mise en abyme*—Yolande's story told to Marguerite inscribed within grandmother Aurore's story told to granddaughter Aurore—offers a mirrored repetition of the story that is esthetically pleasing, didactically appropriate, and further serves to link *narrataire* and *narratrice.*

However, Marguerite's second lesson is not only to be a lesson about the relationship between the natural and the marvelous; it is also to be a lesson intimately concerned with her own development as a woman. This movement from exterior to interior learning is underlined by the arrival of the first male character in "La Reine Coax," Marguerite's cousin, Mélidor Puypercé—a twenty-year-old colonel in the dragoons.

Puypercé, who prefers champagne to country cider and assumes a mocking and patronizing tone as he talks of Parisian fashion and society to Yolande and Marguerite, is finally reprimanded by Yolande for his rudeness; but it is clear that his subsequent politeness is merely dictated by a desire to obtain a wealthy fiancée in the person of Marguerite.

Indeed, when the two young people are left alone to talk, Puypercé can speak only of material things—particularly Marguerite's fortune (which will come to her on Yolande's death) and which he sees her spending on clothes, carriages, and caviar once she has sold "all these fields, all these meadows, and this horrid château" (127). He neither knows nor appreciates the beloved natural world of Yolande and Marguerite; for him, wild plants and flowers are all "tulips," goldfish are worthy of interest only if they are edible, and a swan is nothing more than the hunter's quarry. Nevé does in fact become quite violent toward Puypercé—and Marguerite is obliged to shut the swan outside the garden enclosure in order to protect her insufferable cousin from the bird's nipping and biting.

Although Marguerite's first impressions of Puypercé (that he is unattractive, insipid, and disagreeable) are ultimately shown to be justified, there is nonetheless always "a small bit of vanity even in the most sensible of hearts" (125), and she hopes for a transformation into something other than her natural self. She wishes for beauty and sophistication—for those feminine attributes that might make her desirable as a wife.

As the two stroll in the garden, Puypercé notices a plump green frog basking in the sunshine and wants to kill it ("frogs are good to eat"). However, Marguerite, who immediately recognizes the frog as Queen Coax, saves the animal from death with her impassioned plea to her cousin to respect the life of nature's creatures. Puypercé, who seems to have developed a grudging respect for his naive little country cousin ("you're a nice person, and you would gain a lot if you were to see the world" [128]), from this point in the narrative becomes the focus of Marguerite's indecision as to her future.

The choice presented to her—country, château, simple life, nature, and grandmother versus city, townhouse, sophistication, civilization, and husband—poses such a mental dilemma that the poor girl soon falls asleep, and once again in a "waking dream" is transported to the magical marvelous world of Queen Coax, who in return for Marguerite's having saved her life, tells her story to Marguerite.

Marguerite learns that her affinity with the frogs indeed has a "marvelous" explanation, for as Queen Coax explains: "I am one of your ancestors, although not a direct one; I am the great-great grandmother of the great-great grandmother of your aunt, Madame de Puypercé, the mother of your cousin the colonel. That's why I am interested in the two of you. At the present time I have the honor of being a fairy, but I was once mortal like you; and I was born in this very château" (131). As the mortal Ranaïde, Queen Coax had learned magic from her father, even the art of total metamorphosis, and had thus gained access to all knowledge. She had kept her powers secret, however, to avoid being called a witch.[9]

Within this second *mise en abyme*, Marguerite hears the fairy tale of Ranaïde's marriage to the handsome Prince Rolando and her happy-ever-after life in the château until one day she suspects that the cloaked male figure she has seen walking at twilight with Mélasie, her lady-in-waiting, is none other than her husband. The jealous Ranaïde transforms herself into a frog so that she may hide in the moat and spy on the mysterious couple; but when she discovers that indeed Rolando is innocent, she is so relieved that she forgets to take the magic potion that will undo her metamorphosis. When Mélasie finds a human-sized frog instead of her mistress in bed the next morning, she rushes, terrified, to find Rolando—who returns and attacks the giant frog with his sword, cutting off one leg. Ranaïde in her frog form is, of course, protected from death—but even when she takes the potion to restore her moral appearance, she cannot reproduce a human hand where the frog leg has been severed. She is thus obliged to "show herself" as she is to Rolando; and once he knows of her secret powers, she must transform him into a white swan who will remain under the spell for two hundred years. She herself is forced to marry the frog king Coax and can only be released from her frog existence if she can once again wear her wedding necklace, which is kept in a small jewelry box in Yolande's room.

The reader and Marguerite, too, of course recognize Nevé as Rolando; but Marguerite, although she wishes to help Queen Coax, is reluctant to fetch the jewels, for they belong to her grandmother. The evil frog, however, knows Marguerite's moral weakness and appeals to her vanity: "These magical jewels have the power to transform even the ugliest young women into beautiful ones, and . . . after you have worn them for only an hour, instead of looking like the frog which I now am, you will look as I once did, and as I will again—the most beautiful of women" (134). Forgetting all warnings about the frog queen, Marguerite obeys—and because she "has never told a lie" (134), she easily opens the locked jewel box with the magic words.

The subsequent failed metamorphosis scene—wherein Queen Coax puts on an emerald necklace and earrings and frantically dances, imploring her mirror to show her that she can indeed "re-become" beautiful—is truly frightening to Marguerite until suddenly the extravagant contortions of the frog transform fear into laughter. The healthy, mature sound of Marguerite's laughter, however, provokes Queen Coax—who curses the girl with "froglike" ugliness and with her evil magical powers transforms Marguerite into the real frog she has heretofore been only metaphorically: "Marguerite took the mirror which the frog handed her and gasped in horror at seeing herself with no hair, a green face, and frog-like eyes. 'A frog! A frog!' she cried out in despair. 'I'm turning into a frog—I am a frog. That's done it!' " (136).

At this critical moment Rolando/Nevé appears and for the second time rescues Marguerite from the evil queen. He gives the jewels to the girl, which allow her to regain her original appearance, and he offers her the sage advice not to try to become beautiful, as Queen Coax has, through "enchantment" or artifice: "Stay intelligent and good, and give yourself only to someone who will love you just as you are" (136).

With the evil frog's lies and manipulations exposed, her corpse first bloats and then becomes a hideous black mushroom and finally a heap of dust. Rolando, after promising his protection to Marguerite, flies away (as Nevé) into the sky, where he becomes the morning star (the star, indeed of *aurore*/Aurore).

The spell again broken, Marguerite awakens from her trance in Yolande's room, wearing her grandmother's jewels. Rushing to the mirror, she discovers with relief that she still has her everyday plain face; but her own perception of it has now altered: "For the first time in her life, she thought she was very pretty" (137). The horrific prospect of animal metamorphosis averted, Marguerite reenters the "real world," speaks to the gardener (who tells her that the swan has flown away), and sees her cousin riding off to Paris (with her prospects of marriage, of course, going with him). Finally, she decides to talk to her grandmother.

Marguerite tells Yolande about her strange waking dreams of the past two days, and together the two reconstruct the remembered *mise en abyme* story of Marguerite's childhood—the story of Ranaïde and Prince Rolando. However, granddaughter learns from grandmother that Marguerite's terrifying dénouement is merely the trace memory and confluence of another childhood storytelling experience—the ending of La Fontaine's "La grenouille qui se veut faire aussi grosse que le boeuf." As for the ending or closure of the Ranaïde story, there is none—for in Yolande's words: "I never had to bother finishing my story. You were always asleep before the end" (140).

Thus is Marguerite/Aurore given narrative authority to write her own ending—whether "dreamed" or experienced, marvelous or natural (or, in the best Sand fashion, marvelous within natural, dream within experience). Marguerite has witnessed "things which have taught her a lesson" (140); and the choice between frog (wishing to be what one is not) and swan (remaining true to one's natural self), the heroine's choice is clearly the swan. Grandmother Yolande/Aurore can then repeat and close the circle with her granddaughter Marguerite/Aurore: "There is only one thing which makes you beautiful-happiness which you have earned" (141).

Bruno Bettelheim, in his analysis of "The Three Languages," equates the bird with the child's superego. Birds that fly high symbolize the freedom of the soul to soar, "to rise seemingly free from what binds us to our early existence," and provide a marked contrast to frogs, which, for Bettelheim, symbolize the most ancient part of the self, the id.[10] Thus Marguerite's final choice of the swan and her acceptance of Nevé's moral lesson demonstrate the marked preference in Sand's tale for self-discipline and for the deferral of adult sexuality until we meet the person who will accept us as we are.

For a story to hold the child's attention, it must entertain as well as arouse the child's curiosity. However, to enrich the child's life, the story must also stimulate the imagination, clarify the emotions, be attuned to aspirations as well as anxieties, and, most important, give full recognition to the child-protagonist's difficulties while at the same time suggesting solutions to them.

George Sand would certainly have agreed that a child needs a moral education that subtly and by implication alone conveys the advantages of moral behavior—not through abstract ethical concepts, but through what seems tangibly right, and therefore meaningful. Thus, Marguerite's "moral lesson" in "La Reine Coax"—perhaps most succinctly put as "be yourself"—is learned not only through the mediation of the grandmother-storyteller but also through direct contact with the marvelous as it appears in the natural world. Yolande to Marguerite, Aurore to Aurore, grandmother to granddaughter—the story of "La Reine Coax" is a story hidden in Chinese boxes but one that links generations and gives some final brush strokes to our portrait of George Sand–Aurore Dupin.

What of the young Aurore Sand? Huguette Pirotte tells us that she "would live to be ninety-five. She wrote under a pseudonym, married a painter, Frédéric Lauth, but had no descendants. At Nohant, which she kept up as best she could, she imitated 'le style Sand.' Around 1955 the villagers used to meet the ninety-year-old lady wearing red pants. When she died in 1961, she left the château to the French government."[11] Tenacity, courage, and pluck—these were qualities Aurore inherited and that are inscribed within "La Reine Coax," qualities of the first Aurore which her readers still admire today.

NOTES

1. Letter from George Sand to Gustave Flaubert, October 15, 1868, in Henri Amic, ed., *Correspondance entre George Sand et Gustave Flaubert* (Paris: Calmann-Lévy, 1904), 139–140; this and all subsequent translations are those of the author.

2. Ibid.

3. Pierre Salomon, *George Sand* (Meylan: Editions de l'Aurore, 1984), 218.

4. Letter from George Sand to Gustave Flaubert, August 31, 1872, in Amic, *Correspondance*, 327.

5. George Sand, "La Reine Coax," in her *Contes d'une grand-mère* edited by Philippe Berthier (Meylan: Editions de l'Aurore, 1982), 1:116; all further references to this work appear parenthetically in the text.

6. Berthier notes the accuracy with which Sand describes the marsh world in "La Reine Coax" and quotes Sand's Agenda entry of August 9, 1872, describing a family outing to Villers, in Normandy: "We stopped in a beautiful garden. . . . Lolo saw a very lovely marsh there and some hart's-tongue and reeds with their thyrses, which she did not know but which she recognized in any case, all the while reciting bits from 'La Reine Coax' which she had managed to memorize after hearing it read just once" (*Contes*, 1:302).

7. George Sand, "Le Château de Pictordu," in her *Contes*, 1:32.

8. The name "Coax" is obviously an onomatopoeia.

9. Ranaïde, from *rana* (frog in Latin).

10. Bruno Bettelheim, *The Uses of Enchantment: The Meaning and Importance of Fairy Tales* (New York: Knopf, 1976), 101.

11. Huguette Pirotte, *George Sand* (Paris: Editions Duculot, 1983), 133.

10

George Sand's Poetics of Autobiography

Marilyn Yalom

When, at the age of forty-three, George Sand began *Story of My Life*, she had very clear ideas about the nature of the autobiographical enterprise. She knew a priori what type of work she wanted to create, what pitfalls she wished to avoid, what stylistic stance she planned to adopt, and what personal and social benefits she hoped to acquire from her efforts. She laid out her intentions in the first section of the work, which constitutes a kind of poetics of autobiography. We could speak of a simple "autobiographical pact," in the words of Philippe Lejeune, a pact by which the autobiographer establishes the rules of the game he or she intends to play with the reader—most notably, the use of the author's real name as guarantor for a verifiable referential system.[1] This is the terminology employed by Ank Maas, the Dutch translator of *Story of My Life*.[2] I use the term *poetics* because Sand offers a theory of autobiography that we can apply both to her work and to that of other writers. Her ideas are worth serious consideration especially when we recall Georges May's assessment that there were very few critical studies of autobiography before the second half of the twentieth century.[3]

Sand's poetics of autobiography derive from two fundamental principles: The first posits a personal profit for the author who engages in the act of telling the story of his or her life; the second asserts that both writer and reader engage in a profound social act, which has favorable consequences for each. However, unlike many twentieth-century theorists who value autobiographical writing for its psychological and even therapeutic potential, by the time Sand began *Story of My Life*, she had ceased to believe in purely psychological truths. She took up the autobiographer's vocation as if it were "a duty," to be performed in the spirit of religious self-examination.[4] Choosing Saint Augustine's path rather than Jean-Jacques Rousseau's, Sand undertakes an interior journey in the hope that it will lead to spiritual elevation.

Although inspired by the Christian tradition to which she remained attached, with its belief in a Supreme Deity and the immortality of the soul, and charged by the idealistic current of her century, Sand came to express the universal ideas of more than two millennia in Western culture. To make autobiography a moral duty recalls the Socratic dictum "Know thyself," and points to the mandate for lucidity. Sand reflected on the astonishing fact that "many human beings live without being really aware of their existence" (8), and she presented the autobiographical act as an occasion and a means for correcting this deplorable deficit. From her perspective, *Story of My Life* was to be "a sincere study of my own nature and an attentive examination of my own existence" (3), an act that would have its value as much in the spiritual work-in-progress as in the final written product.

Moreover, the autobiographer, as Sand envisioned her, never writes for herself alone, whatever the personal benefit. Human beings, interdependent rather than independent in Sand's universe—"solidaire" rather than "solitaire" to use the words of Albert Camus—live within the bonds of mutual obligations, where the duty to reveal oneself to another is not negligible.

At the heart of Sand's thinking we discern what she called "the notion of solidarity" (9). The word "solidarity" was used consciously as a privileged signifier in a contemporary vocabulary; "to speak the language of [her] time," Sand was obliged to use a term that was as highly charged politically in the mid-nineteenth century as it has become in the late twentieth. Always sensitive to the historical evolution of language, she added in a footnote: "One would have said *sensibility* in the last century, *charity* before that, *fraternity* fifty years ago" (9).

What does she mean by this word? Certainly the influence of Pierre Leroux, her intellectual and spiritual mentor during the 1840s, is recognizable. He had popularized the word in his book *De l'humanité*, and had encouraged Sand to formulate and enlarge her own vision of a utopian society founded on Christian socialist ideas. Sand's vision of an ideal human community born from the political convictions of a small group of radical thinkers had an undeniable influence on her writing—on her novels and plays, as well as on her autobiography. Autobiography was to be an enterprise that would extend far beyond the solitary exercise of self-analysis into a domain of communal endeavor. It would be a work written "with a view toward brotherly learning," wherein the writer offered "stimulation, encouragement and even counsel and guidance for other spirits caught up in the labyrinth of life" (9). She insists on the affective bonds that unite human beings, on their similarities rather than their differences.

Sand's style aims at a tone of "reciprocity" that will bring the reader into the narrative; as she tells us herself, she hopes to create the impression of "an exchange of confidence and sympathy" (9). To this end, she conceived a poetics that was radically different from the poetics that had motivated Rousseau's *Confessions*, a work she aptly called "a confused monument of pride and humility" (10). She recognized that "the great Rousseau" was hell-bent on differentiating himself from all others and on establishing himself as a standard of misery so that no one could say: "I was better than that man." Nor would she have taken as a model Benjamin Franklin, whose autobiography was in her personal library, along with Rousseau's.[5] In contrast to these two men, Sand situates the locus of autobiographical intent in the human capacity for empathy; fellow creatures experiencing the same wounds feel a need to confide in one another since "we feel that the life of a friend is our own, just as each person's life is everyone's life" (10). As Béatrice Didier notes in her study of the role of the reader in George Sand's works, the use of the collective "we" is a subtle way of inserting the reader into the text and creating the illusion that the reader shares the author's ideas and feelings.[6]

Of course, in the world of texts the idea of an exchange of confidence is a fiction: The one who tells the story and the one who listens are never equals given the fact that the latter never has the possibility of responding to the former. This consideration does not seem to have bothered Sand; she assumes the literary convention of reciprocity, and writes as if the reader were going to have a turn at self-disclosure, as in real life. This is perhaps why she maintains that vestige of oral language to which Didier refers in her article.[7] Sand always writes with an ear toward a reader who is always there at her side, ready to receive her intimate revelations with the attentive concern of a friend. Sand's reader is not Rousseau's, before whom he confessed in order to be judged—and exonerated. In evoking the spirit of Rousseau, Sand understood all too well that his confessions, often exaggerated and sometimes invented, were destined to psychological failure because, as she said, it is always a mistake to try to justify oneself. Sand's reader is less of a judge than an ally who exists to sympathize with the author. Moreover, she reproaches Rousseau for having "confessed" others as well as himself, most notably his mistress, Madame de Warens. In the avowed interest of protecting those who had once been dear to her, Sand avoids compromising them and herself. Thus, she announces from the outset that it will be a waste of time for her readers to look for scandal in her memoirs, particularly if they are interested in her marital history. A dozen years after the notorious separation trial in which Monsieur and Madame Dudevant had exchanged mutually humiliating insults, Sand chose the high road of forgiveness, even defending her husband against those who continued to accuse him of grievances that she herself had long since forgotten. Nor would Frédéric Chopin, her lover from 1838 to 1847, be exposed, despite the rancor surrounding their break-up. Unflattering aspects of the men in her life might be recognized in characters in her novels—for example, Casimir Dudevant was obviously the model for the odious husband in *Indiana*, and Chopin the model for the jealous prince in *Lucrezia Floriani*—but Sand did not consider it honorable to subject them to the naked light of autobiographical truth. Far from the "tell-all" theory of contemporary autobiography, she was bound by a nineteenth-century sense of literary decorum dictating restraint, respect, and silence in recounting her interpersonal relations, especially with men.

Let us consider man and woman, as Sand suggests, "in relation to their individualism as well as their relationship to society" (9). These two theoretical poles are coupled with two areas of inquiry in the work: Either the writer focuses on "the story of the interior life, the life of the soul, that is to say, the history of one's mind and heart . . . or the historical events to which one ha[s] been witness" (9). Here Sand evokes the two great autobiographical traditions that existed long before the creation of the word *autobiography*, a word born in the English language shortly before 1800 and appearing in French and German a few years later.[8] The tradition of "the interior life" goes back to Saint Augustine, passing through Dante, Benvenuto Cellini, Saint Theresa, the English Protestants of the seventeenth and eighteenth centuries, and, of course, Rousseau. This is the tradition that privileges the spiritual, religious, and psychological development of an individual facing the self in the presence of God. The second tradition, more exclusively French, goes back to the Renaissance; it includes several illustrious authors of the seventeenth and eighteenth centuries, such as Madame de Caylus, the Duc de Saint-Simon, and the memorialists, who survived the turbulent years of the Revolution.[9] Here the accent is placed on public events and the exterior personality. Without naming any memorialist in the first part of *Story of My Life*, Sand mentions several on numerous other occasions in the body of her work: the Duchesse d'Abrantès, Madame de Genlis, and the Marquise de la Rochejaquelein, all of whose memoirs were published in the first decades of the nineteenth century.

Writing one's memoirs has a particular significance for women. It is a literary form that allows them to enter into written history by bearing witness to the lives of others, especially at a time when women themselves were rarely creators of public history. Madame de Genlis, in her *Memoirs on the Eighteenth Century and the French Revolution*, legitimized her right to bear witness in the following manner: "I have reason to believe . . . that having spent a large portion of my life at Court and in the highest social circles, I could give a faithful picture of an extinguished society." Like most of the women memorialists of this period, Genlis situated her personal history in the context of the great revolutionary movement that had destroyed the world of her youth. However, as a woman of letters already celebrated for numerous publications, she hastened to recall her fame as an author and the clarifications that fame entails: "In a century where one sees the proliferation of biographies of living people, it has become almost indispensable to publish one's memoirs . . . in order to rectify an infinite number of errors and slanderous statements."[10] One wonders if Sand was thinking of Madame de Genlis's memoirs when she wrote on the first page of her own account: "I have allowed a rather large number of biographies to be published about me that were filled with errors, both in praising and in condemning me. Even my name is incorrect in some of these biographies." In Sand's time, as in our own, celebrities had already adopted the posture of aggrieved victims obliged to defend themselves against nonauthorized biographies.

The contribution of the memorialists was certainly not wasted on Sand. She recognized as one of the two essential poles of autobiography that of public history. She would consider her own history from the retrospective and even revisionist point of view of post-Revolutionary France, and would make an effort to understand how an individual life fits into the history of one's century.

Between the two poles of autobiography—that of the interior life and that of public history—Sand favored the subject of the family. Family history would inspire a good half of her lengthy memoirs (which number 1,600 pages in the Pléïade edition) because she considered it of paramount importance in the development of an individual. The significance she attributes to familial influences predates Freudian psychology by half a century and, as Georges Lubin has pointed out, forecasts the theory of hereditary influence so prominent in the works of Emile Zola.[11]

In this spirit, Sand defends herself against those who criticized the inclusion of her father's numerous letters at the beginning of her autobiography. Let us try to judge their inclusion in relation to the two essential poles of autobiography that we have established. Certainly the idea of consecrating a third of her memoirs to the letters written by her father to his mother before Sand's birth appears unusual and even questionable. We can well understand her temptation to make use of them, since she had them in her possession; and Sand, who always spoke modestly of her writing craft as a money-making matter, would have been the first to admit that the paternal letters offered an easy means of filling up the number of pages stipulated in her publishing contract. However, let us not forget that Sand also had a few of her mother's letters which she chose not to use. One could object that her mother's letters were much less numerous and less elegant than her father's. Only five or six remain in the Bibliothèque Spoelberch de Lovenjoul at Chantilly.[12] Nonetheless, her mother's letters would have added a few more pages. Moreover, as for the objection that her letters were lacking in style, we know that Sand altered her father's to make them more elegant.[13] On the contrary, we must see in her use of the letters motivations that are considerably more complex and overdetermined (in the language of psychoanalysis); indeed, there exists a weave of motives that are firmly entwined with the author's interior life and the epic history of her country.

The letters of Sand's father to his own mother, written between 1794 and 1804, evoke the heroic period of the Revolution and the Consulate. Like many other writers born at the turn of the century—Victor Hugo, Alfred de Musset, and Alfred de Vigny, to mention the most famous—Sand saw herself as the descendant of a race of giants. Granddaughter of a woman with royal blood in her veins (although illegitimate), daughter of a Napoleonic officer, and distant relative of the reigning monarch Louis-Philippe, Sand could make a good case for annexing national destiny to her own. Even if she herself had not been witness to the revolutionary past that had inspired so many illustrious memorialists, she could still bear witness through her father's letters. One pole of her autobiography would be gloriously anchored in history.

At the other pole, that of the inner life, there were also powerful motivations for resurrecting the paternal letters. We should not forget that Aurore Dupin's father was killed by a fall from his horse when his daughter was only four. That death created a psychic wound that never completely healed.[14] For a small child, the loss of a parent is a catastrophic event; we have reason to believe that the loss of a father—the parent who traditionally incarnates familial authority and represents the larger patriarchal order as well—often leaves a residue of anxiety for a lifetime.

The search for the father is one of the most entrenched of the topoi in Western literature. Telemachus, Oedipus, Orestes, Hamlet—all legendary sons of distant or dead fathers—went to great lengths to fill the paternal void. Add to this list the names of modern writers like Jean-Paul Sartre, Albert Camus, and Jean Cocteau, who, having lost their fathers in childhood, experienced throughout their lives what Cocteau called "the difficulty of being." Moreover, what of the female progeny of deceased fathers? Here we find the same search, especially in post-Freudian, twentieth-century women writers like Sylvia Plath, Violette Le Duc, and Marie Cardinal, all of whom created an entire mythology around the fathers they lost early in life. Should we not understand Sand's use of her father's letters, so prominently inserted at the beginning of her memoirs, as a symbolic means of confronting her loss and bringing her father back to life? As the eminent French psychoanalyst Michel de M'Uzan told me in a discussion of his therapy with Marie Cardinal, the daughter of an absent father will try to find him in other forms, even attempting to recreate him on the analyst's couch—and in literary works as well.[15]

In contrast to her father, Sand's mother left her with more than thirty years of memories. She was the passionate love of Aurore's childhood and the despair of her adult years. Sand evoked the presence of her mother in her affective life with an honesty that was perhaps unique in her century. At that time, mothers were rarely very visible in autobiographies—think of John Stuart Mill's account for the ultimate example of maternal absence and paternal dominance in a self-reflexive test, a pattern that may have obtained in Mill's real life but also corresponds to conventional autobiographical and biographical practice throughout the nineteenth century. It is surely with an awareness of the minimal interest generally accorded to mothers that Sand wrote: "One is not only one's father's child, one is also, to some extent, that of one's mother. It seems to me that one is even more her child, and that we cling to the womb that has borne us, in the most direct, most powerful, and most sacred manner."[16] Following this belief, Sand spoke at great length of her mother: of her lower-class origins and nomadic young adulthood, of her premarital liaison, which produced Aurore's half-sister, and of her marriage to Maurice Dupin barely a month before Aurore's birth. She also included her mother's troubled relations with her mother-in-law, her pride in belonging to "the people" and her discomfort in society, her innate capacity for song and storytelling, and her untutored adherence to a creed of the heart. Without ever having read Rousseau (who figures prominently both in the Dupin family history and in Sand's personal intellectual history), Sand's mother is presented as a child of Rousseau: intuitively gifted, naturally good, and prey to the evils of a society in turmoil.

Among the maternal memories that persist most forcefully into adulthood, Sand recalled a drama of separation brought about by the insistence of a grandmother who could never fully accept her plebeian daughter-in-law and who, by a legal contract, took over Aurore's upbringing and education. Remembering the impression produced by her mother's first absence, Sand wrote: "It is true that I was separated from her for only two weeks, but those two weeks are more distinct in my mind than the three years which had preceded them[;] . . . which only goes to prove that it is suffering that makes the deepest impressions in childhood" (637). Sand's evocation of her childhood through memories of her mother have a unique cathexis; the urgency of these memories, linking the adult Sand with herself as a girl, reminds us of Virginia Woolf's assertion that we think back through our mothers. It seems to lend credence to the belief, held by Sand long before Sigmund Freud, that one's relationship with one's mother provides the template for future interpersonal relationships.

Sand's mother, at the heart of the child's private life, was at the same time connected to public history, as Sand conceptualized it. Through her roots in the working class, she bequeathed to her daughter the blood of the people. Sand constructed a personal myth from her "birth astride . . . two classes" (629), offering the fusion of working class and aristocracy as a paradigm for the new social order.

Most of the ideas on autobiography expounded at the beginning of *Story of My Life* were put into practice in the body of the work. Sand penetrated inward by descending the hazardous staircase of memory, and she looked outward toward the great historic movements of her time. Faithful to her principles, she left in silence much that might have injured those who were still alive or might have cast a slur on the memory of the dead. Maintaining her natural style with its trace of oral speech, she succeeded in creating the desired impression of a personal conversation. The only time she is mistaken is when she wrote the following sentences: "I am certainly not creating a work of art; in fact, I would forbid myself from doing so, because these things have a value only if they are written with spontaneity and abandon. I would not like to tell the story of my life as if it were a novel. Form would prevail over content" (13). Here Sand suggests that autobiography and the novel presume two different systems of communication, the one inspired by "real" life and best expressed in a natural artless manner, the other crafted from imaginary material into a work of art; and, as always, she devalues the artistic quality of her own work. If she was able to maintain her spontaneity and a certain abandon in her *Story of My Life*, that does not mean that it is lacking in style. Its success for more than a century and its continued place in the canon of French autobiographical literature derives as much from its style as from its content, and, despite her demurrals, from her art as a storyteller.

Sand certainly told stories. By her own admission she always had a novel churning in her head. She had authored more than thirty novels before *Story of My Life* and could not dismiss her craft easily. She consciously attended to the questions of her relationship with other human beings, the silences that decorum and good faith demanded, the meaning of her memoirs both for herself and for her reader, and the autobiographical dualism of inner and public life. It was the writer's seasoned style and imaginative strategies that gave these questions literary form. As a consummate nineteenth-century storyteller, carried along by the narrative impulse and the textual elaborations mandated by the act of writing, she draws us into a spiritual adventure that is capable of offering, as Sand had hoped, "a brotherly lesson," or, if I may alter her vocabulary slightly in keeping with the times (a practice Sand would have undoubtedly endorsed), let us call it "a sisterly lesson."

NOTES

1. Philippe Lejeune, *Le Pacte autobiographique* (Paris: Editions du Seuil, 1975).

2. Ank Maas, "*Histoire de ma vie*: Choix de l'auteur et scrupules de la traductrice," in Françoise van Rossum-Guyon, ed., *George Sand: Recherches Nouvelles* (Groupe de Recherche sur George Sand l'Université d'Amsterdam, 1983), 175–192.

3. Georges May, *L'Autobiographie* (Paris: Presses Universitaires de France, 1979), 1.

4. George Sand, *Oeuvres autobiographiques*, ed. Georges Lubin (Paris: Gallimard, 1970), 1:6, 8; all citations are from this edition. I wish to thank Georges Lubin for his generous advice and support.

5. See Georges Lubin, "Les auteurs du XVIIIe siècle dans la bibliothèque de George Sand," *Présence de George Sand: George Sand et le dix-huitième siècle* 23 (June 1985), 4–8.

6. Béatrice Didier, "Rôles et figures du lecteur chez George Sand," *Etudes littéraires* 17, no. 2 (Autumn 1984): 239–259.

7. Ibid.

8. Jacques Voisine, "Naissance et évolution du terme 'autobiographie,' " *La Littérature comparée en Europe orientale* (Budapest: Akademia Kiado, 1963), 278–286.

9. See, for example, Jean Tulard, *Bibliographie critique des mémoires sur le Consulat et l'Empire* (Paris: Droz, 1971). For women memorialists, see also Marilyn Yalom, "Women's Autobiography in French, 1793–1939: A Selected Bibliography," *French Literature Series: Autobiography in French Literature*, ed. Mayner Hardee (Columbia: University of South Carolina, 1985), 197–205.

10. Madame de Genlis, *Mémoires sur le dix-huitième siècle et la Révolution française, depuis 1756 jusqu'à nos jours* (Paris: Ladvocat, 1825), 1:3.

11. Sand, *OA*, 1:xxi.

12. Personal communication from Georges Lubin.

13. Sand, *OA*, 1:xxiv-xxv.

14. For a discussion of this subject, see Marilyn Yalom, *Maternity, Mortality, and Madness* (University Park, Pa.: Pennsylvania State University Press, 1985), 64–67.

15. Yalom, *Maternity*, 65.

16. Sand, *OA*, 1:15.

Part IV

TEXT AND IDEOLOGY

11

George Sand and the Romantic Sibyl

Marie-Jacques Hoog

She comes down to us in images and words—noble images, and words at times "sublime." To do her justice, we would need to be inspired from above, as she was, truly possessed, and possessing a parchment that connects primitive times with the end of time.

Such is the figure of the Romantic Sibyl—a prophetess holding a scroll, inspired sister of Sophia, the other face of the Virgin Mary; she, too, is filled with the sacred breath, the virgin mother of Logos. Noble poet, wearing a turbaned diadem, she reigns gravely, a book in hand. Sublime priestess, her eyes raised to the skies, mouth half-opened, she sees and foresees. She proclaims, she speaks, she is the patron saint of the creative feminine word.

I can only trace here the itinerary of a secular myth that goes back to the rock of Delphi, the cave of Cumae, and the round temple of the Tibur, for Logos is also accompanied by Thambos, sacred fear. Her figurative image passes through Pisa, Sienna, Auxerre, the Sistine Chapel, the Santa-Croce, the Borghese Gallery, Aix-en-Provence, the salon of l'Abbaye, and Garnier's Opéra. As legend, she circulates in the texts of Homer, the Greek tragedians, Plato, the two Virgils (the Virgil of the Fourth Eclogue, and the one of the Sixth Book of the *Aeneid*), Plutarch, Saint Jerome, Christine de Pisan, and François Rabelais, and on to the texts of Paul Valéry and the automatic writing of the Surrealists, to mention only the highlights. I leave aside, for example, the dreadful Bernard le Bovier de Fontenelle who, in accordance with the theories of the first Church Fathers, reiterated their accusations of demonic possession. My purpose here is to study the functioning of this myth, which is perhaps a seminal one, in the works of George Sand.

How did such a mythological figure, dating back to early antiquity, come to occupy a privileged position in the Sandian imagination? Sand's early childhood was entirely under the double spell of fairy tales and mythology: the *merveilleux chrétien* cohabitated in the child's imagination with the *merveilleux païen*. Her first impressions can be summed up as: "[this] strange poetic muddle . . . [this] sense of wonder that [my mother] lavished on me . . . speaking to me of the three graces as seriously as she would of the theological virtues or the wise virgins."[1]

Living on Rue Grange-Batelière, even before learning how to read, she was given an old abridged volume of Greek mythology, lavishly illustrated with engravings. The illustrations are comical, of course, but, as she remembered, "they fascinated me." At Nohant, she discovered the fairy tales of Charles Perrault, those of Madame d'Aulnoy, and the same old abridged mythology with which, now, she was to learn to read: "Nymphs, zephyrs, Echo, all those personifications . . . turned my thoughts toward poetry . . . [I hoped] sometimes that I could catch the wood nymphs and dryads unawares in the forest and prairies of the Berry." (*HV* 1:540, 618) To Marie d'Agoult she once confided: "You cannot imagine all the dreams that come to me as I romp in the sun. I imagine myself in the glorious days of Greece."[2] What are those "glorious days of Greece" if not the seasonal pilgrimages when, for a thousand years, thousands of pilgrims walked up the Sacred Way of Delphi in a rare, mystical union in order to consult the Pythia in the Temple of Apollo?

No need, then, for Sand to have read George Grote's scholarly *Histoire de la Grèce* nor even Pouqueville's work of popularization, which is so often cited in the *Magasin pittoresque*. For her, mythology, reinforced by the reading of the *Iliad* when she was eleven, was the natural breathing space of her imagination. She internalized it. She did not *know* it in the same way as did the scholars who embarked on some digs at Delphi in 1838, but she believed in it. Galatea, the Maenads, the Bacchae, the Sibyls—these were not abstract terms but rather integral parts of her earliest cultural landscape.

Who can judge the influence of a child's first primer, of a first toy? In the paraphernalia of her childhood, next to the terrifying Jack-in-the-Box, there was a small statue made of Sèvres china, a tiny Venus holding doves, which she still talks about with delight in *Histoire de ma vie*.[3]

What about the influence of the wallpaper? At first, outside her mother's alcove in the apartment on rue Grange-Batelière, the child Aurore contemplated the flowers of the wallpaper. The room was decorated in the style of Louis XIV—"all those objects are filled with my musings. . . . I have worn them out by looking at them so much" (*HV* 1:538). Later, at Nohant she slept in a room covered with green wallpaper. Can we not see here the Empire style, decorated with garlands, mythological medallions, Sileni, and Bacchae? Over the doors, especially, there were extraordinary figures. In the morning Aurore awoke before a nymph, dressed in blue and crowned with roses, a laughing and dancing Flora. In the evening, the nymph was replaced with a somber looking Bacchante who presided over her prayer, dressed in green and turbaned in purple, her thyrsus still dripping with the blood of Orpheus (*HV* 1:619). The child's imagination balanced on these two poles, in a veritable hallucination that the creation of Corambé would exorcise. Sand's fundamental dualism is illustrated by this elusive mythological couple—adored nymph versus fearsome Maenad, the feminine couple that one finds again, for instance, in *Lélia.* As early as the composition of "Les couperies," the heroine, a scrawny old witch, pale and humped, would be described as an "old sybil," a common expression at the time to designate an elderly female, one of the aspects of her legendary character being her capacity for longevity (*HV* 2:576). One must not neglect, in our appreciation of the sources of the Romantic imagination, this neoclassical revival, the Empire style, fashions according to Johann Joachim Winckelman and Jacques-Louis David, of which Madame Juliette Récamier was the first exemplar, and that ruled at the Opéra, in the city, in fashion, and even in details of everyday life. It is not without reason that chairs had tripods in the Pompeii style and that women wrapped turbans around their heads.

The first modern author to have extracted the Sibyl from her veritable iconographic lineage so as to launch her in Romantic literature a generation before Sand, was, of course, Germaine de Staël. It was a sensational debut. See how her Corinne, the *improvisatrice*, in the opening lines of Book 2, triumphed in the Capitol, a few steps away from the Palazzo dei Conservatori, which houses Domenichino's Sibyl wearing the same turban.[4] Made fashionable by the brilliant court of Naples (not so far from Cumae and its grotto), this turban encouraged the young women of the time to manifest their awareness of their modernity: no more wigs, no more powder. With the softly shaped headdress, made of seamless material wrapped around their heads like a sentence without a structure, shining like a halo worn like a hat, they expressed their right to speech, their own poetic discourse, at times illogical but at the same time inspired and natural. They took up the Word, they took up the pen, in their flowing style—in the Sandian style.

In her notorious appropriation of the Word, Sand orchestrated this Corinne theme, this theme of the inspired, visionary, improvising Sibyl. A close reading of her early works reveals—first in veiled form, and then in clear fashion—the myth that interests me here, modulated in a brilliant series of variations. My thesis is that the Sibyl, a simile of prophetic or poetic improvisation—Longinus in his treatise *On the Sublime* never ceased to speak of the two divination arts as one, both being daughters of Apollo—became very early in Sand's work the emblem of the feminine appropriation of the Word.[5] From Oliero's revelation on (*Lettres d'un voyageur*, I), it presents itself as one of the unifying factors of the Sandian corpus, unifying the marionette theater and the fiction, even unifying Sand's writing style and the fictional basis of her works. It is improvisation, it seems to me, that unites such disparate texts as *Kourrouglou*, *Lélia*, "Myrza," and *La Comtesse de Rudolstadt*, for example.

I will therefore begin with the improvisation and proceed to the improviser: I will closely examine "En Morée"[6] and *Tévérino.*[7] It is in the time span between these two texts, between 1833 and 1845, that the myth of the Sibyl was elaborated and that its most successful variations in the Sandian dynamic can be found. Proceeding from the improviser to the Sibyl, I will touch on a passage of the "Poème de Myrza,"[8] and then will propose a reading of the two versions of *Lélia*,[9] in which the myth of the Sibyl seems, as a last recourse, to organize both text and main character, those two chaotic creations, and to give them meaning. The apocalyptic conclusion of the second *Lélia* would be taken up again and in a major key in the initiatic finale of *La Comtesse de Rudolstadt*.[10] With *Jeanne*, the Sibyl is represented by the old nanny, a venerable type and a sacred being.[11] The following year, in 1845, Sand launched her *Tévérino*. Next to the little *oiselière*, the child Madeleine, who is full of poetry, stands the Neapolitan improviser, the brother of Consuelo just as Jacques was the literary brother of Lélia. The year that *Tévérino* was published in *La Presse*, Gérard de Nerval, that great reader of Sand, celebrated in his *Chimères* the awakening of the Sibyl with a Latin face. Eugène Delacroix, on his return from Nohant, exhibited at the Salon of 1845, next to his "La Madeleine dans le désert" (Magdalene in the Desert) a "Sibylle de Cumes, le rameau d'or à la main" (the Sibyl of Cumea, Golden Bough in Hand). (His "Education de la Vierge" [Education of the Virgin], in which the portrait of Anne was perhaps too reminiscent of Lélia, had been refused by the jury.)[12]

Let us therefore embark for Morea—the most fashionable and talked-about place in the salons of the 1830s. "En Morée" is a short, enigmatic text that Georges Lubin published in the second volume of the *Correspondance*. As we all know, according to the cliché about Sand, writing for her was almost as easy as breathing; her style flowed from its source to wherever her pen took her, in a constant improvisation, that "laisser-aller invincible" to which she repeatedly admitted.[13] Let us not forget that everyone in the small world of the Romantics was prone to a similar impulse. I am referring to Honore de Balzac's reams and to Stendhal's narrative insertions. In this milieu, marked by the intense ferment of transition, one can sense the arduous tension between the *moi haïssable* of the classical canon and the exaltation of that same *moi* in the young movement's credo.

From her earliest letter writing, and continuing through her voluminous correspondence, Sand evolved her famous "style coulant," that inimitable *léger-de-main*, and also a very particular attitude of openness toward the addressee, whether reader or correspondent, whom she invited to follow her at his or her own pace, "à son pas."[14] A book of Sand's is often an excursion, sometimes a voyage of initiation, and always a flight of the imagination. She herself defined her talent as that of an artist, a poet, an *auteur fantasque*: "Novels are always more or less inventions. These fanciful productions [*ces fantaisies*] are like clouds passing overhead. Where do these clouds come from and where are they going?"[15] she wrote in the "Notice" to *La Dernière Aldini*. What breath propels those *merveilleux nuages*?

Thus, the notions of breath and improvisation allow us to decode the text of "En Morée," which has provoked so much controversy. It is a *billet doux* written at the bedside of the delirious Alfred de Musset, at whose side "stupid" Pietro Pagello is also present. Georges Lubin reminds us that Morea, the Peloponnesus in revolt against the Turkish occupation, had just been the stage of heroic acts on the part of the French expeditionary corps. It is there, next to Lord Byron, that a young Prince Bonaparte had just been killed. Attached to the French forces was the young Edgar Quinet, a volunteer in the archeological mission that would bring back from Greece Olympian metopes and a detailed report. The French imagination was very much struck by the expedition, and made Fauriel's scholarly book, *Chants populaires de la Grèce* (published in 1824, the same year as Byron's death) one of the best-sellers of the year.[16]

Fauriel, along with the *rebetika*, talks about the melodies of Greek folklore, songs of farewell improvised by the wife or the mistress of the klepht, that *guérillero*. He talks about *myriologia*, songs of death in which, over the bodies of the partisans, the women express their grief freely, "selon leur naturel," in an improvisation whose words, by their rigor and pathos, provoke them to faint. The klepht, bard, rhapsode, or *griot* preserves but also composes, upon demand, laments or *thrènes*. Quinet confirms that in Morea, on every pier, in Naflio as in Itea, the Greek fishermen, in their *paneghyri*, improvise. "En Morée," therefore, seems to me to be one of those prose poems that fill *Sketches and Hints*, located halfway between a brief letter and one of those lyrical fragments that make up the raw material of *Lélia*. Sand, between Musset's bed and her table, standing before an unpredictable addressee, perhaps allowed the voice of a woman traveler buried within her to speak her passions; she allowed an imaginary young klepht woman in love to articulate her feelings; going against all the rules of Western restraint and decorum, and setting an example for the future Edmée de Mauprat, she dared to improvise an avowal of love.

We must remember that in 1834 the term *improvisation* was rampant. It had been so ever since Staël's Corinne, the improvisatrice who in turn was the contemporary of a court improviser, Gianni, imported by Napoleon from Milan to Paris. Napoleon was an Augustus who did not listen to what the Tiburtin Sibyl Germaine had to say. Stendhal insisted that Dominique, the alter ego of his journals, was only an improviser. Madame de Bargeton in Balzac's *Les Illusions perdues* and Félix de Vandenesse in *Le Lys dans la vallée* both improvised.[17] Delphine Gay, muse and professional improvisatrice, was crowned by the Academy and at the Capitol, just like Corinne and her model, the Florentine improvisatrice la Corilla. The former insisted, under the pen name of Vicomte de Launay, that ballet schools for little girls were being transformed into schools for teaching improvisation.[18] Journalists and memorialists such as Délécluze or Lady Morgan all showed us improvisers. Take, for example, Sgricci, with his *Mort de Charler Premier* in 1824, even improvising tragedies in five acts and indulging, now in the heart of Paris and no longer in Morea, in veritable paneghyri, presided over by Alphonse de Lamartine. One could read in *La Presse* that "the great event of the week was the success of the improvisor Regaldi at the Athénée Royale. It was a triumph. Never had improvisation attracted such a select audience."[19]

Twelve years after "En Morée," this same character of the improviser reappears in the light-hearted *marivaudage* of *Tévérino*. He is the younger brother of the improviser in one of Hans Christian Andersen's tales of 1834, which were translated into French (in two volumes) in 1847 by Madame le Brun. Tévérino, by virtue of his name, is at the same time a son of the river Tevere, a son of the Anio at its source; of the caves and cascades of the Tibur-Tivoli, famous for its Sibyl whose statue had emerged from the river—the Sibyl of the round temple, of the Sibylline books, and of the Vision of Augustus. Fyodor Dostoevski wrote to his brother Michael in October 1845: "Nothing like [*Tévérino*] has yet been written in our century." [20] Henry James, overcome with nostalgia as he gazed at the salmon pink cover of the *Revue des deux mondes*, sometime around 1880, sighed and wondered who still remembered the exquisite *Tévérino*.[21]

The two novelists are right: The pleasure of writing has rarely been so manifest as here when Sand's nimble and witty pen sends a young couple off on the fanciful paths that lead from the Hôtel des Etrangers in Savoy all the way to "la bella Italia," in search of their own identity. The opening of the novel, which contains echoes of the *Barbier de Séville*, announces the plot: Sabina opens the window as the reader opens the book; she accepts Léonce's pact and will lend herself to the whimsy of this "improvised doctor," just as the Sandian reader lends him- or herself to its author.[22] On their excursion a picnic is improvised: The black nanny, compared to a "bustling sibyl" (42) prepares a hammock for beautiful Sabina. Gracefully stretched out amid hummingbird feathers, she listens to Léonce, who declares to her that she would make a perfect Sibyl. Sabina protests: She does not possess an "unrestrained and breathless nature." He answers: "The Sibyls of the Renaissance are solemn and severe. Haven't you seen Raphaël's Sibyls? They represent the grandeur and the majesty of the present age" (55). Although he alludes here as much to Michelangelo's Sistine Chapel as to Raphaël's Santa Maria della Pace, Léonce's words are not enough for Sabina: She needs an enlightened interpreter in order to understand such sibylline language.

It is at this point that a vagabond appears (64), looking like a Fra Diavolo or a Figaro. However, within a very short time this Italian good-for-nothing, who seems by turns to have stepped out of a painting by Michelangelo or Raphaël, or again by Jules Romains, finally stands posing like a Phidias statue, catching the attention of Léonce, who has an artist's eye (68). It also happens that he has the most beautiful voice imaginable, which rises up "by following the virile inspirations of the popular muse" (69). When the aristocratic Léonce asks him about his talent as a *bel canto* singer, he answers that music is inspired by a god, by Apollo lost on the heights of the Apennines, but that the words are composed by him, for, *permesso signor*, I am an *improvisatore*. When Léonce, delighted, asks the singer to dictate the words to him, he refuses absolutely. One might be hearing Sand's own words when the vagabond insists that "my melodies escape from me like the flame from a hearth. I can repeat them, but I cannot retain them" (71). In this fashion naked and inspired, Tévérino is the equal of the most affluent. Disguised hastily by Léonce, under the name of the Marquis de Montefiori, he proves his statement, and for the last one hundred pages of the novel proceeds to reveal Léonce to Sabina as they embark on an improvised and fantastic excursion into Italy. Finally, true to his word and to his love—the bird-girl Madeleine—whose mind "only understands that which flies in the air" (38), he will relinquish his aristocratic costume in order to put on a monk's habit, but only temporarily. As he removes his marquis-like clothes, he gives up any pretense to Sabina's heart. Her character has been transformed from that of a cold woman to a warm-hearted and renewed being, just as Sand hopes to leave her reader, renewed and restored.

Tévérino was published in *La Presse* from August 19 to September 3, 1846. At the same time, Nohant was witnessing the opening show of a series of dramatic spectacles that would become the fictional basis of *Le Château des Désertes*, in which Sand resumed her meditation on improvisation, amplifying it into a theory that had first found its expression in Boccaferri, and that she incorporated in her small company's production of a multiple *Don Juan*, an amalgam of Mozart, Hoffmann, and the troupe's own invention.[23] These concepts, discussed again in *Théâtre et l'acteur*,[24] and the *Théâtre de marionnettes de Nohant*,[25] are the foundation for a theater of free improvisation. The acting proceeds from a skeletal outline that is distributed to the actors just before they go out onto the stage. The company consists of versatile types. Boccaferri's "théâtre vrai" is thus a modernization of the Commedia dell'arte, based entirely on improvisation, and not by one individual but by the troupe as a collective. Sand, by abandoning her Tévérino temporarily in a monastery—as unlikely a place as can be imagined—betrays the fact that she has not finished dealing with the improviser and his or her art. *Tévérino* is much more a beginning than a conclusion.

"Le Poème de Myrza," Sand's first Sibyl, the improvisatrice, was published in 1835 and stands, it seems to me, at the juncture of the two versions of *Lélia*, which date from 1833 and 1836–1839.[26] The poem thus offers insights into what one might call the sibyllization of *Lélia* II, which Sand revised, off and on, for almost four years before its publication in 1839. Myrza, the wandering prophetess or Sibyl—and Sand uses the term in the portrait that she draws of her heroine on the very second page—is, quite evidently, precisely like Lélia, a projection of Sand herself, when the author shows her "speaking to the people under the porticoes of Caesarea"—Caesarea, and its porticoes are the locus of pure wandering in *Bérénice*. Myrza is also an avatar of Lélia, who, in keeping with the fictional formula that Sand has finally found, is being transformed into Sister Annunciata, the messenger of a new Gospel founded on a new cosmology. It may be in order to confirm the innocence of her feminine readers or to liberate herself that Myrza-Lélia-Sand exposes here, poetically, in a Genesis according to Sand, a creation in the feminine from which Adam's rib is carefully excluded, as are the temptation of Satan and the inexorable fall of all humanity due to our mother Eve: Indeed, Eve's name is not even mentioned. The prophetess, inspired by the divine spirit, improvises a description of the Golden Age, fashioned by humanity out of the primordial chaos, and its subsequent deterioration. Myrza prophesies the end of humanity if she cannot again find the text of the primordial Covenant, the one that established the fatality of the relationship between love and death. Finally we see Myrza weeping, threatened by religious fanatics and wandering off in solitude on the road that is a familiar topos in Sandian revery: the road that leads to the desert of Upper Egypt.[27] It is this same road that will tempt Lélia, another "disconsolate Sibyl."

LÉLIA, THE DESOLATE SIBYL, THE MUTE PYTHIA: FROM THE GOTHIC TO THE MYTHIC

Lélia is an "illegible" work, but nonetheless a master work, comparable to a master beam that gives coherence to Sand's entire corpus. With this heroine we leave the charming porticoes of fantasy to enter, dramatically, into the heart of Sandian writing, a heart laid bare.

First of all, let us not forget that *Lélia* is the only novel in which Sand recognized that she had projected herself. If Lélia is not the author herself (*Elle*), bound by her three male companions, Lélia is at least the author's "Muse." After *Indiana* and *Valentine*, fictions that were carefully distanced from their creator, here is a text that is inwardly directed, made up of Sandian cries and fragments improvised during nights of insomnia, written only for their own sake, almost as if by chance, in the image, by their very disorder, of the narrator's dismembered body ("corps démembré"). Using these pieces of text which had been stitched together like a fortuitous patchwork, Gustave Planche attempted to drape this fabric full of contradictions over a fictional armature, by draping over the *Sketch* of *Le Roman du joueur* these patches of *Hints*, this disjointed rhapsody. From his efforts emerged an "affreux crocodile." Nonetheless, Sand's voice can still be heard here, in the act of confession, in the act of proclamation. She finally allows the Great Voice that inhabits all of us to emerge in order to share it with her reader.

The heroine of the first *Lélia*, therefore, is incomplete, impotent, and invisible; it is nothing but old cast-offs, a bundle of nerves that cry out, trapped in the center of an infernal circle, composed of three men who are incapable of bringing her salvation; a Dantean circle worthy of this sorceress. The Vallée Noire is an integral part of Sand; a dark, wicked abyss, in the image of evil; an absence of all goodness just as black is the absence of any color. There exists a Sandian devil, and she is possessed; Baudelaire will throw this accusation at her.

Sorceress, prophetess, Lélia, *Elle Elijah?*—seen by Sténio, in the first pages, as a minister of the Transfiguration. Trenmor depicts her, in the ball scene, exalted above all, in a black on black costume that is an amalgam of all the Romantic shades of darkness. Corinne, mourning for her lost inspiration as she is mourning for Oswald, is justly cited, along with Hamlet, Romeo, Tasso, and Lara. Lélia, therefore, is no one; she is Madame Nemo, an empty space, a lack of destiny, an absence of faith or law. She has no direction; she is going nowhere. She is only the locus of the great Sandian cry, going round in circles without echo. Lélia's verbal powers are unleashed, in order to say nothing except maybe "destroy."

What makes for her credibility is the fact that Lélia resembles the nightmares of Sand's rebellious period, and by extension, she echoes the bad dreams of we who lead incomplete lives. Ultimately, her absurd life will be interrupted by a death no less absurd, even if it brings her closer to her more valorous sisters, to Saint Cecilia, who sang too well and to Corinne, who improvised too well. *Sois belle et tais-toi*: The rosary that Magnus wraps around her neck throttles her, silencing a voice lacking in substance. We are here reminded of the legend of Pythia. Apollo granted her request to live as long as she had grains of sand in her hand—a thousand years. However, as she refused to give herself to the god, he accorded her only that litteral favor: As she grew older through the centuries, she was reduced to the substance of a grasshopper, and soon was no more than a voice. Lélia's transfiguration in the early part of the text conjures up this very same disfiguration. The dénouement is a knot. In this Gothic scene, the feminine word is silenced.

We know that if *Indiana* has a split dénouement, and if *Jacques* rises again with Ralph in *Le Diable aux champs*, *Lélia* was amplified and completely recast, with an urgency and a passion that is evidenced in the *Correspondance*, where the novel was the subject of discourse for several years.[28] Both passion and urgency are easy to understand, for if Lélia is Sand, and if Sand is not the same after the spring of 1834, then Lélia must not be the same either. Since the oracle of Oliero—the words "Walk, come forward, learn!"—Sand's life and works have changed meaning; or rather, from meaningless they have taken on meaning.[29] Thus, Lélia's frigidity, which was only an accident of her amorous life, now becomes the simile of the incompleteness of the human condition. Lélia, this seeker of God, now fashions a destiny for herself, and she takes it by the hand, as she puts on her veil and appropriates power for herself. As an abbess, her costume is no longer theatrical or picturesque, but rather the sign of a true profession, a vocation. Metamorphosis—the new dynamism that will become the great device of Sandian fiction—imbues the text. Black gives over to white, hard to soft. The convent changes its sex and the Camaldules become the breeding-ground for a new feminine order, while Trenmor the wanderer becomes the great Initiator. Even Sténio gives it a try. It is by confronting the great myths, the myths of Prometheus and Don Juan, that the marginal Lélia finally enters the realm of the mythic: Lélia on her rock. She cannot be imagined happy, as was Sisyphus. Nonetheless, she is calm and accomplished, as Christ is accomplished, when on the last page she finally calls herself by her real name, the *Sibylle désolée*, the mute Pythia.[30]

In the great chapter entitled "Délires" she proclaims herself to be a Sibyl, and in so doing, she effectively becomes a Sibyl, as does the author. We have gone from the Gothic to the mythic. Here death is an ultimate raising of voice and consciousness. Lélia has emerged from the infernal Sandian circle. She has scaled the heights, her cave has become an *omphalos* (a navel), and she converses with the universe. Corinne had triumphed prematurely, in the beginning of the text, at the Capitol, among a delirious crowd. Lélia triumphs in the end, in the essential solitude her new title bestows upon her. She coincides with her fiction: From existence she has moved on to essence. She dies as a result, but her death is a noble one.

Plutarch, the mystical Apollonian priest, recounts a similar death in one of his *Pythic Dialogues*. One day the Pythia of Delphi was constrained to appear before some foreign pilgrims; the signs were not propitious. Her raucous voice was silenced: She was unable to deliver an oracle. She walked out on the steep rocks of the Helicon to die.[31]

However, death, even the most beautiful and the most apocalyptic, could not satisfy Sand in the 1840s, as attested by *Mauprat*, *Horace*, and *Spiridion*. Heroes no longer die in her novels. What was now at stake was living, transmitting the Word.

In a dream-like Italy and Bohemia, Consuelo resumes the travels of an outcast. She is very much younger and poorer than Lélia, and she has a direction: She has heard the oracle of Oliero with Sand. In her position of outcast, of Bohemian, she is predestined to function as a Sibyl. (Was it not among the gypsies that Michelangelo da Caravaggio went looking for the subject of his *Fortune Tellers*?) However, she is also an artist; this talent, too, has been bestowed on her. Already in the first volume we see Consuelo with a destiny, a mission that contrasts sharply with the wanderings of Lélia. Lélia did not put her art into practice beyond her costumes, her letters, and her occasional lyrical outbursts. On the other hand, Consuelo starts with hard work, as an apprentice at the lowest rungs of the artistic world: interpretation. Eventually, at the summit of a prestigious career as a *cantatrice*, she attains the status of creator by improvising some musical compositions during her captivity.

The scenario of *Consuelo* is parallel to that of *Lélia.* Thus, as Consuelo approaches her final initiation in the third volume (which will turn out to be another beginning), Sibyls and prophets enter on the scene. The venerable Wanda is first among them. The rites of passage carry the young singer along in her quest for "the word of Hiram, the lost Word." Was it lost by Lélia? Consuelo is soon initiated by the old woman, the Sibyl Wanda: "Speak, priestess of truth."[32] The sibylline word is so enthusiastic that, in turn, the heroine experiences a lightness of being: "overcome with a kind of intoxication . . . as happened to the prophetesses during the paroxysms of their divine seizures, when they surrendered to strange frenzy and cries, [Consuelo] was driven to express her emotion and sang the most beautiful hymn in a radiant voice" (216). This hymn is well-known both to Sand and her heroine: Marcello's *Magnificat.*

Wanda, mother and model of Consuelo, continues the ceremony. Unusually tall in her long white dress, veiled, and standing near the tripod, she is agitated by transports of enthusiasm (218). She prophesies, announcing the Golden Age, the reign of Astraea, which will flower again, as in Virgil's Fourth Eclogue, when human passions resemble the free love that links Consuelo and Livérani. Livérani, who is none other than Albert the Great, will prophesy in turn on his violin in the conclusion.

However, it is Consuelo, the improviser, the gypsy girl, who will have the final word. In the conclusion, she asks her son Zdenko to sing "the ballad to the virtuous goddess of poverty," one of her improvisations. Carrying a child on her back and a guitar slung across her shoulder, alert and poetic, she disappears in search of Adventure, the traveling Sibyl of green Bohemia (332).

NOTES

1. George Sand, *Histoire de ma vie*, in her *Oeuvres autobiographiques*, ed. Georges Lubin (Paris: Gallimard, 1970), 1:541; hereafter *HV*.
2. George Sand, *Correspondance*, ed. Georges Lubin (Paris: Garnier, 1964–), 3:477.
3. Ibid., 1:555.
4. Germaine de Staël, "Corinne au Capitole," in *Corinne ou l'Italie* (Paris: Garnier, n.d.), 20ff.
5. See Longinus, *On the Sublime*, ch. 7.
6. George Sand, "En Morée," in her *Correspondance*, 2:501.
7. George Sand, *Tévérino, Leone Leoni* (Paris: Michel Lévy/Hetzel, 1856).
8. George Sand, "Poème de Myrza," in *La Dernière Aldini* in *Oeuvres de George Sand* (Paris: Michel Lévy, 1857).

9. George Sand, *Lélia*, ed. Pierre Reboul (Paris: Garnier, 1960). The first version of *Lélia*, as is well known, was published in 1833; the second *Lélia* was rewritten from 1836 until 1839, the date of its publication.

10. George Sand, *La Comtesse de Rudolstadt* (Paris: Michel Lévy/Hetzel, 1857).

11. George Sand, *Jeanne*, ed. Simone Vierne (Meylan: Editions de l'Aurore, 1986). See page 53: "This faithful and soothing nanny who presides like a sibyl over the first effort of the imagination, the first friend of life, the wet-nurse . . . the nanny."

12. Charles Baudelaire, *Curiosités esthétiques* (Paris: Garnier, 1962), 14, p. 8n.

13. See Sand, *Histoire de ma vie*: "I have at present, just as I did at the age of four, an unassailable ease for this kind of creation" (1:542).

14. Baudelaire, "Fusées," in his *Curiosités esthétiques*: "She has that famous flowing style, which is so dear to the bourgeoisie" (894).

15. Sand, *La Dernière Aldini*, 4.

16. Fauriel, *Chants populaires de la Grèce* (Paris: Didot, 1824–1825).

17. See Madame de Bargeton, *Illusions perdues* (Paris: Folio, 1966), 71–72. See also Madame de La Baudraye, "La Sapho de Sancerre," in her *La muse du département* (Paris: Folio, 1984), 23; and Felix de Vandenesse, *Le Lys dans la vallée* (Paris: Folio, 1972), 17.

18. Vicomte de Launay (pseudonym of Delphine de Girardin), *Chroniques parisiennes* (Paris: Des Femmes, 1986).

19. Adele Vitagliano, *Storia della poesia estamporanea della letteratura italiana dalle origine di nostri giorni* (Rome: Loescher, 1905), 211.

20. Pierre Pascal, *Dostoïevski, l'homme et l'oeuvre* (Lausanne: L'Age d'Homme, 1970), 90.

21. Cited by Patricia Thomson, *George Sand and the Victorians* (New York: Columbia University Press, 1977), 226: "Are there persons still capable of losing themselves in *Mauprat*? Has *André,* the exquisite, dropped out of knowledge, and is anyone left who remembers *Tévérino*? I ask those questions for the mere sweet sound of them, without the least expectation of an answer" (from Henry James, *Notes on Novelists* [New York: Scribner's, 1914], 148–168).

22. Sand, *Tévérino*, 6.

23. George Sand, *Le Château des Désertes* (Meylan: Editions de l'Aurore, 1985), 118–119.

24. Sand, *Oeuvres autobiographiques*, 2:1235.

25. Ibid., 2:1247ff.

26. See Sand, *La Dernière Aldini*: "One of the prophetesses of the age, a cross between a gypsy and a sibyl," 206.

27. George Sand, "Poème de Myrza," in *La Dernière Aldini*, 235.

28. See especially in George Sand, *Lélia* (Paris: Garnier, 1966, 1985); Pierre Reboul, "D'une *Lélia* à l'autre," 328–344. See also the 1839 Preface and the 1854 Notice, and Reboul's note: "One can consider this preface to be a masterpiece of bad faith," 349. The critical apparatus of this "D'une *Lélia* à l'autre" is in fact a masterpiece of misunderstanding. Sand's great concern, which Reboul does not even suspect, was to situate *Lélia* in a new perspective, a very difficult task for someone who so disliked making corrections and rereading herself, both of which she indeed did off and on for a number of years. It was at Valdemosa, it seems to me, that she must have found the motif of the Sibyl, which immediately organized the chaos surrounding the character and the novel.

29. Sand, *Lettres d'un voyageur*, *Oeuvres autobiographiques*, 2:674.

30. See Sand, *Lélia*, "Délires," chapter 47, 541.
31. Plutarque, *Dialogues pythiques* (Paris: Editions des Belles-Lettres, 1974), 164–165.
32. Sand, *La Comtesse de Rudolstadt*, 213.

12

Consuelo and *La Comtesse de Rudolstadt*: From Gothic Novel to Novel of Initiation

Isabelle Naginski

As Jean Cassou reminds us in an important article on George Sand and her masterpiece *Consuelo*, the early nineteenth century was a fertile period in the development of the novel, an era that gave birth to a number of new novelistic genres. *Consuelo* alone, Cassou points out, incorporates elements drawn from at least four genres: the *roman-feuilleton*, the musical novel, the Gothic novel, and the novel of initiation.[1]

Originally, of course, *Consuelo* did appear as a series of feuilletons, from February 1, 1842, to February 10, 1844, in the *Revue Indépendante*, a journal founded by Pierre Leroux in 1842 in conjunction with Louis Viardot and George Sand herself. Nor can we deny the central presence of music as a subject in *Consuelo*, as the novel is, among other things an exploration of eighteenth-century musical circles in Venice, Vienna, and Berlin, with at least two real musicians of the age—Nicola Porpora and Joseph Haydn—playing major fictional roles.[2] However, neither "roman-feuilleton" nor "musical novel" designates a formal genre. Neither conjures up the constellation of an established set of thematic elements, compounded with a predictable cast of characters, certain formal exigencies, and a traceable tradition, in the way established genres such as the Gothic novel (*roman noir*) and the novel of initiation do.[3]

Sand's triple-decker novel participates mainly in these two latter traditions. In its use of the established narrative of terror, inherited from the eighteenth-century Gothicists, and by the choice of both inner chronology and setting, *Consuelo* belongs to the tradition of the Gothic novel. However, in its attention to the initiation topos and by its innovative concern for the coining of a modern psychological language, it constitutes one of the most remarkable novels of initiation of the Romantic age. This double allegiance or double affiliation is my immediate concern in this chapter.

A privileged theme of Gothic fiction is the fortified castle, in which the underground spaces are equated with terror. Dungeons, labyrinths, subterranean prisons, secret passageways, crypts, and catacombs dominate the Gothic narrative. When such a castle is introduced in *Consuelo*, Sand immediately bares the device by linking her Château des Géants with Ann Radcliffe's Udolpho, the archetypical Gothic edifice.

> If the resourceful and prolific Anne Radcliffe had found herself in the place of the candid and awkward narrator of this very real story she would not have bypassed such a good opportunity to take you, madame reader, through corridors, trapdoors, spiral staircases, shadows and underground passageways during half a dozen volumes, in order to reveal to you only in the seventh all the mysteries of her learned work.[4]

Despite Sand's gently ironic tone in referring to Radcliffe's exploitation of spaces of terror, Gothic edifices occupy large portions of Sand's text, with the Château des Géants being the site of over a third of *Consuelo*, and the events in the Spandaw fortress making up approximately a fifth of *La Comtesse de Rudolstadt*.[5] Both architectural constructions are direct heirs of Radcliffe's Gothic edifice of terror.

Udolpho, with its huge portcullis, back staircases, winding passages, wide chambers, vaulted galleries, underground chapel, and slender watchtowers, is an exquisite mechanical contraption. A fitting embodiment of Edmund Burke's notion of the sublimity found in a terrible object, it lies in wait for its next victim. However, for all its ominous appearance, Udolpho is a static place. Immutable, silent, and ominous, with its mysteries locked up inside it, Udolpho has a menacing grandeur more illusory than actual. When all the mysteries have been elucidated, Udolpho is nothing more than a white, or should I say black, elephant.

Inversion of the natural order in Radcliffe's castle, both temporal and spatial, suggests another level of meaning, however. Time and space appear to be strangely warped. Plot time is invariably at night, with midnight being the favored hour for the heroine to set out on her wanderings and explorations. The reversed time structure is accompanied by a strangely altered allocation of space. The corridors, the passageways, and staircases take up more room than the various chambers, apartments, and reception halls. It is as though the architect—a modern Daedalus—had concentrated his efforts on building a labyrinth inside the castle, and in his single-mindedness, had forgotten to include sufficient living space.

Udolpho provides what Peter Brooks has called an epistemological model of the depths, an architectural approximation of the Freudian structure of the mind.[6] Emily's walks inside the castle are veritable "voyages of the mind." The bedroom doors, which can be locked or unlocked only from the outside and by forces beyond the heroine's control, suggest that Radcliffe's heroine is prey to the intrusion of her unconscious fears and desires. Her alarm at becoming lost "in the intricacies of the castle" articulates her reluctance to make frightening discoveries about her own psyche.[7] Emily's nocturnal dream life, constituting what Gérard de Nerval called "une seconde vie," fills up the major portion of the narrative time spent in Udolpho.

Maurice Lévy, in his authoritative *Roman "Gothique" Anglais*, provides a Bachelardian reading of those "Gothic heroines who at [midnight] come out of the melancholic torpor which weighs them down during the day so as to walk unflaggingly up and down corridors without end and go down interminable staircases."[8] If going up and down the stairs of a house is a metaphor for changing from one level of consciousness to another, Emily's descent into the catacombs of Udolpho can be read as a plunge into the deeper parts of her unconscious. In an archetypical, dream-like sequence, Emily descends into an underground chapel and then farther down into the vaults and through an adjoining passage to a pair of iron gates, which lead to a flight of steps. As Lévy reminds us: "To descend into the subterranean parts of the castle is to descend into ourselves, down into the deepest part of our inner life. It means leaving the level of rational consciousness to become engulfed in the most archaic levels of being" (630). As Emily starts climbing back up, her perceptions of the castle confirm this vision of the archaic self: "As [she] passed up . . . [she] discovered more fully the desolation of the place—the rough stone walls, the spiral stairs, *black with age*, and a suit of *antient* [sic] armour, with an iron visor, that hung upon the walls, and appeared a trophy of some *former* victory" (*U*, 346; author's emphasis).

Emily's escalating sense of dread and her growing claustrophobia as she explores this fantastic architectural structure is symptomatic of her own dangerous inner journey. Gaston Bachelard has brilliantly expressed the relationship between the dreamer's perception of his or her environment and his or her private emotional gyroscope: "It is not because the passage is narrow that the dreamer feels compressed. . . . [It is because] the dreamer is experiencing anguish that he sees the passage becoming narrower."[9]

In a room off one of the landings, Emily comes across a series of instruments of torture—an iron chair, an iron ring hanging from the ceiling, and iron bars and rings to confine the hands and feet: "It occurred to her . . . that she herself might be the next [victim]! An acute pain seized her head, she was scarcely able to hold the lamp, and, looking round for support, was seating herself, unconsciously, in the iron chair itself" (*U*, 348). Emily's willingness, albeit unconscious, to be the next victim by sitting in the iron chair is significant. Her gesture confirms what William Patrick Day has found to be at the crux of Gothic ideology: the fixed presence of a victim and a torturer. In this relationship based on violence, the Gothic character is "defined through conflict, as giver or receiver of pain in a sadomasochistic dynamic."[10] It is the feminine characters who are invariably the victims of male brutality in Gothic fiction. Radcliffe's novel epitomizes the message that good behavior in women is "equated with victimization and obedience to authority."[11]

However, for Emily the worst is still to come. After the instruments of torture come the results of their action, clearly illustrated. Drawing aside a dark curtain, Emily discovers a corpse, bloody and hideously disfigured. Having reached the epitome of what Julia Kristeva calls "abjection," that state in which "the boundaries between the inner and the outer, [the limits] of the Self and the Other" are perturbed, Emily faints and is taken back to her room.[12]

Thus is completed a circular itinerary: from Emily's bedroom, down to a cave (the locus of *l'être obscur* [the dark, mysterious being]), into a chamber of horrors, and back to her room. Such a circular structure is typical of Gothic narrative. "Transformation and metamorphosis," to quote Day, "lead only back to the place from which one started."[13] Such circularity makes increased self-awareness or self-discovery next to impossible. In spite of repeated assaults on her sensibility, Emily's psychological makeup is not altered in any way. This psychic impermeability to potentially traumatic or revelatory events persists throughout Emily's confinement within Udolpho. She simply withstands events; she does not incorporate them into her own mental life. When she escapes from prison, this Gothic heroine is identical to the person she was when she went in. She leaves, taking only "a small package" (*U*, 399), a symbol of how little psychic growth has taken place as a result of her claustration.[14] Furthermore, her incarceration leaves no permanent scars. Once she is beyond the reaches of the dreadful place, Udolpho ceases to play an active role in her imagination. The memory of it simply fades like "a distempered dream."[15]

Sand's reading of Gothic *prosateurs* ("hack writers," Radcliffe foremost among them) provided her with techniques for building narratives of suspense. She learned to place an emphasis on mood building, to deliberately create an aura of mystery, and to make use of a claptrap of Gothic stage sets and props (to use Lowry Nelson's formula). Many Gothic details, such as mysterious voices, uncanny statues, magic portraits, masked messengers, blood stains, and corpses appear in *Consuelo*, and combine with the dominant topos of the menacing castle, with its enticing and terrifying underground galleries, to make this the most Gothic of Sand's novels.[16] However, as we shall see, in *Consuelo* these Gothic motifs are at the service of a different ideology (in the large sense); they serve a different set of narrative priorities.

In the first volume Sand describes her heroine's descent into the castle's underground realm by means of a well that has been temporarily emptied of water. A structure of terror worthy of Radcliffe unfolds as the character, who has taken the wrong passageway, finds herself walking inexorably down a gallery as the water comes rushing up behind her. In true Gothic fashion, escape, here in the form of a foothold leading to a higher landing, is provided only at the very last moment. As Consuelo continues her wandering through a vast cave, she encounters further dangers, notably the threat of being buried alive, a favorite device of terror in Gothic fiction, which emerges as a recurrent motif throughout the text of *Consuelo*. Here, also, the symbolic weight of these various motifs—torrential water, being buried alive—is significant in psychological terms.

However, as the heroine progresses through this labyrinth of fear toward the subterranean retreat of Albert de Rudolstadt (the hero), the narrative tone changes, and the Gothic voice of terror recedes. A different language of solace now dominates. The landscape of terror gives way to one of serenity and harmony: "A path of cool, fine sand ran upstream alongside the limpid and transparent water. . . . This path ran along the top of a raised embankment of fresh and fertile earth; for beautiful aquatic plants . . . in this sheltered place . . . edged the torrent forming a verdant border. . . . It was like a natural, warm greenhouse" (1:322). Inner and outer landscape correspond. The beneficial effect of this site on Consuelo's mood is almost instantaneous: "Consuelo began to feel the beneficial influence exerted on her by the less sinister and already poetic aspect of exterior objects. Her imagination had been prey to cruel terrors. . . . Now she felt herself being reborn" (1:322). On the verge of a "minor initiation," Consuelo reflects on her preinitiatory state of mind: "I have come here with a fervent soul, a resolution full of charity, a peaceful heart, a pure conscience, an unfailing selflessness" (1:323).

In Albert's "melancholy sanctuary," whose access is reached symbolically by opening three doors, they engage in a bizarre dialogue, halfway between madness and revelation. As in *The Mysteries of Udolpho*, the scene ends with the heroine fainting. However, unlike Emily, Consuelo succumbs not to horror but rather to exhaustion and relief. Whereas Udolpho ultimately led its heroine to objects symbolizing pain, death and decay, the Château des Géants take "la Porporina" (Consuelo's nickname) to an innermost sanctum of rebirth, forgiveness, and absolution.

Although in Radcliffe's and Sand's texts the two itineraries are remarkably similar, Consuelo's quest for Albert has quite a different meaning than Emily's search for her aunt. When Radcliffe's heroine finally locates Madame Montoni on her deathbed, the scene only confirms her worst fears. In Sand's novel, however, Consuelo's discovery of Albert resembles a successful quest: The heroine's suffering is given a purpose. Consuelo's search ends in initiation and growth while Emily's finishes in hopelessness and gloom.

However, the crucial difference lies in the opposing consequences of stasis versus change in each heroine after her trial by terror. In *Mysteries of Udolpho*, as Ellen Moers notes, Emily retains her respectability in the worst situations: "Her sensibility and her decorum never falter; and however rapid or perilous her journeys, the *lares* and *penates* of proper English girlhood travel with her."[17] Nonetheless, there is a moment in the novel when this principle of proper behavior is put to the test. After a hurried flight from Udolpho, Emily finds herself without the proper attire: "Her appearance [in the little town] excited some surprise, for she was without a hat" (*U.*, 454). On the very next day Radcliffe has her heroine acquire "a little straw hat, such as was worn by the peasant girls of Tuscany" (*U*, 455), and the awkward situation is thus remedied.

The detail would be merely amusing if it did not elucidate a major component of the Radcliffean heroine. Through attention to the proprieties and an acute sense of good repute, she retains her sense of identity intact. This stability of character allows her to undergo unspeakable ordeals looking none the worse for wear (give or take the loss of a hat). If, as Day suggests, respectability points to the only form of power available to the feminine archetype in the Gothic world, we may marvel at Emily.[18] From our modern perspective, she may well seem an unexciting character because of her static psychology, but ultimately, she displays that steadfast endurance and sheer pluck in the face of danger that are the counterbalancing virtues of such characterization. (We see this model most often in male heroes of the picaresque tradition.) Her hanging on to her hat, then, is more a mark of courage, what Moers calls her "heroinism," than mere passive acceptance of the proprieties of her time.

How different is the aftermath of Consuelo's trial. Back in her room, she collapses in bed with a fever and spends several weeks harboring an illness of the soul (1:357). Displaying many of the symptoms of hysteria—clenched teeth, livid mouth, and alternating moments of fever and pallor (the canoness sees her changing color from"a devouring redness" to "a bluish pallor" (1:360)—she is literally possessed by the need to absorb and make sense of the events she has witnessed in the grotto's mythic decor. "Consuelo, a victim of the most alarming delirium, struggled against the grip of the two strongest servants of the house. . . . Tormented, as is the case in certain instances of cerebral fever, by extraordinary terrors, the unhappy child wanted to flee from the visions which assailed her; she believed that the people struggling to hold her back . . . were monsters furiously trying to kill her" (1:363). In Consuelo's case, the illusory monsters that her feverish state creates are metaphors for her psychic growth. Whereas in *Udolpho* the monsters belong to the castle and thus cease to haunt Emily the minute she steps off the property, Consuelo's visions of the depths of the Château des Géants continue to haunt her until she is able to give them meaning. Significantly, her illness oscillates between gestures of madness and those of religious ecstasy, thus running almost exactly parallel to Albert's own erratic behavior. As a madwoman, she looks like "a ghost back from the tomb" (1:364). As a saint she resembles a feverish mystic in the throes of a passionate communion with God. This opposition of pallor and fever, of spectrality and ecstasy, to describe the process of psychic "digestion" clearly demonstrates Sand's emphasis on the psychological change brought about in her heroine by experience. Consuelo is not only becoming more like Albert, her initiator, she is also becoming a different character for the reader to encounter. In the final stage of growth, Consuelo falls into a state of limp tranquility, "an uneasy calm" (1:370–371), such as normally succeeds a "great crisis" (1:373). At the end of her trial by illness, she is reborn and ready to embark on a new life.

Such a narrative differs fundamentally from the Gothic. To be sure, the Romantic predilection for freneticism—an offshoot of the Gothic sensibility—can clearly be detected in these pages. Consuelo turning blue makes her a sister of the frenetic Lélia in the throes of an attack of cholera in Sand's most melodramatic novel. However, it is also a marker of the initiation narrative. The initiate must travel through nightmarish geographic and mental landscapes before she can be reborn. Illness and fever only verify that the change has indeed taken place.

The heroine's major initiation, in the Château du Graal (the castle's name needs no comment), sends Consuelo down into the catacombs a second time. Here again terror is at the service of initiation. The grand master informs her: "You will be subjected to several moral torments. . . . It is not in the restfulness of serenity, nor in the pleasures of this world, but in suffering and in tears that faith grows and is exalted. Do you feel courageous enough to confront these painful emotions and maybe violent terrors?" (3:379). Alone, with only a silver lamp to guide her and forbidden from looking back, Consuelo proceeds to this last trial in several stages. The word Sand uses is "stations," indicating that, in Christ-like fashion, this is

Consuelo's passion. The various stations, making up a catalogue of "the misfortunes and crimes of humanity," culminate in a chamber of horrors much like the one Emily discovered in Udolpho. It is filled with numerous instruments of torture, yet Consuelo's eye concentrates on a particularly hideous contraption: "She was contemplating a kind of bronze bell which had a monstrous head and a round helmet placed on top of a large, shapeless body. . . . Consuelo . . . understood . . . that the victim was placed under this bell. The weight was so terrible that he could not, despite the greatest of human efforts, lift it" (3:388). It is through the contemplation of this hideous bell—a powerful metaphor for extreme claustration of the body and spirit—that Consuelo literally reaches out of herself, in a moment of identification with the victim. Just as Emily sat in the iron chair, so Consuelo imagines herself under the bell. The result is, once again, abjection. Consuelo ceases to exist as a separate being: "Consuelo saw nothing more and suffered no longer. . . . Her soul and her body existed only in the body and soul of violated and mutilated humanity, she fell straight and stiff on the ground" (3:389). In spite of its evident Gothic tonality, the scene transcends its initial model. Emily was transfixed with horror when she surmised that the tools of torture might be meant for her. Consuelo, on the contrary, experiences abjection because she identifies with all those outside herself who have suffered at the torturer's hands. As Lucienne Frappier-Mazur remarks: "Having merged her existence with that of violated and mutilated humanity, a sublime Consuelo . . . is reborn . . . [who] rejects any thought of happiness on earth."[19] Indeed, Consuelo's initial reaction is to insist on living with the constant reminder of the horrors she has witnessed: "Why do you speak to me of freedom . . . of love and happiness? . . . Didn't you just make me undergo trials which are supposed to leave an eternal pallor on my forehead? . . . What kind of insensitive and cowardly being do you think I am, if you judge me capable of dreaming and seeking personal satisfaction after what I have seen" (3:396). Here again the narrative stresses the changes in the heroine's psychological makeup. Whereas Emily withstands experience, Consuelo understands it.

We can now formulate the crucial difference between Gothic narrative and a novel of initiation based on Gothic discourse. The former "refuses to offer a transcendent vision and empowering mythology, a new cosmogony and an ethical imperative."[20] However, the closed circuit of the Gothic novel is broken in the text of *Consuelo*, where each episode of horror has a particular purpose, leading the heroine and the reader along with her to new heights of reflection.

The opposition between stasis as dominating element in the Gothic novel and movement as primary force in the initiation novel is further articulated by the road motif in the two novels. In *Mysteries of Udolpho*, the road has a double resonance. In the early part of the novel it is perceived by Emily as a pleasurable place as she and her father journey from their family estate in Gascony toward better climates in Provence. In the latter portion of the book, however, the road is a means of getting away from Udolpho and back home to the château at La Vallée (although with quite a few detours). By its circularity, the road motif very much resembles Emily's excursions into the depths of the Gothic castle. The novel, which had begun at La Vallée, also ends there with nothing changed in the surrounding landscapes or in the interiors. "The . . . furniture of the pavilion remained exactly as usual, and Emily thought it looked as if it had not once been moved since she set out for Italy" (*U*, 585). Indeed, it is the very immutability of the place that has the greatest appeal for the heroine. The final lines of the novel insist on the heroes' being "restored to each other" and to "the beloved landscapes of their native country" (*U*, 672), as if happiness and goodness resided specifically in this act of restoration, turning the clock back, denying time, and reaching for what existed before the adventures began. In a word, they are finding stasis again.

By contrast, Consuelo yearns not for paradise regained but for the exhilarating freedom and uncertainty of "the open road." Locked up in her "gloomy fortress" at Riesenburg she muses: "What is more beautiful than a path[?] . . . It is the symbol and the image of an active and varied life" (1:394). While the comfort of domesticity is Emily's ideal, Consuelo prefers "the open road which . . . beckons and calls me to follow its twists and turns and to penetrate its mysteries" (1:394). For her, the house—whether haven or palace—is always a prison ("A wall or a cliff . . . closes off the horizon") while the road is "a land of freedom" (1:394).

The *Mysteries of Udolpho* culminates in the apotheosis of the familial ideal, represented by the symbolic hearth. In *Consuelo* the controlling image is the road, surprisingly identified with the maternal figure:

> [The]poetry, [the] dream, the passion [of the wanderer] will always be the great path. Oh my mother! My mother! . . . I wish you could take me on your strong shoulders and carry me over there, over there where the swallows fly toward the blue hills, where the memory of the past and the yearning for lost happiness cannot follow the light stride of the artist who . . . thus puts . . . a new world between himself and the enemies of his freedom! (1:394)

The nostalgic desire for return to the maternal body is no longer associated with the traditional desire for enclosure. Sand subverts the standard associations to equate the mother with strength and an ideal landscape of art and liberation.

In fact, Sand's entire text can be seen as an apology of the road, since it begins in the streets of Venice where Anzoleto and Consuelo, like two noble savages, lead a life of freedom, outside the confines of house, family, and bourgeois morality. Living, singing, eating, and sleeping on the street, the two children embody Sand's designation of open spaces as the locus of freedom: "They sang in front of chapels . . . unaware of the late hour, and needing until morning no other bed than the white flagstones, still warm from the heat of the day" (1:54–55). At the end of the novel, unlike Emily whose wealth and property are restored to her, Consuelo renounces the aristocratic surname Rudolstadt and all her inheritance rights and material comfort for the life of poverty and wandering with her mad Albert and their three youngest children. As the narrator watches the group disappear from view at the close of the book, the path they tread is freighted with prophetic value—it promises the way to a paradisiacal land based on liberty and equality: "We watched them for a long time, as they went down the path *strewn with gold*, the forest path *that has no master*" (3:467; emphasis in the original). Sand here inverts the traditional allotment of symbolic space according to gender—the open air as the exclusive domain of the male, with the female restricted to interiors. It is as if the writer had provided us with a new Ariadne's thread, leading us out of the great claustrophobic labyrinth of Udolpho for good.

In conclusion, based on the examination of these two novels by Radcliffe and Sand, I would argue that in Gothic fiction and its younger cousin, the initiation novel, two very different views of psychology are expressed, each in harmony with its age. The eighteenth century still viewed the individual as static, and personality as a homogeneous integral whole. Since personality was considered fixed at adulthood, it could not be altered by experience after the formative years. Adult experience simply provided the personality with occasions to manifest itself. Based on such a stable view of psychology, the Gothic novel experimented with how much a hero or heroine could withstand before disintegrating. Horror, torture, fear, and imprisonment were exercised as tests of the personality. The individual—comparable to a manufactured object—was subjected to an experience of "quality testing." Radcliffe's Emily, then, is a later, female version of La Mettrie's "homme machine," a tough, complex, but mechanized being who, when put to the test, does not overheat or crack, to the satisfaction of both narrator and reader.

In *Consuelo* we encounter something quite different, a psychology of metamorphosis through various stages of epistemological development which expresses a Romantic vision of human personality. The machine has been exploded and replaced by a preoccupation with nonmechanical manifestations of psychic life. Sand's novel explores such areas of irrational behavior as madness, genius, artistic inspiration, the dream life, nightmares, visions, extreme fear, and passionate desire; in a word, the workings of the unconscious on reflection and behavior. Since, as Cassou has suggested, the task of the novel of initiation is to "give expression to all things, to make everything speak, to make the Word a living thing," Sand's attempt to translate into narrative the most occulted of the soul's states of being is also her most admirable enterprise.[21]

If the Romantic esthetic is primarily concerned with new definitions of psychology, Romantic discourse is an exploration of character through the use of dominating figures of speech: oxymoron, hyperbole, and antithesis. In this light, Consuelo's ambivalence regarding important issues reflects Sand's interest in constructing an overall coherent and yet strangely dissonant character: Her heroine loves and yet does not love Albert; she considers her art to be at once divine in the abstract and sullied in the theater; her voice is a manifestation of the divine and yet the *cantatrice* loses her capacity to sing soon after her final initiation. When Michel Foucault talks of the mutation of Order into History at the juncture of the eighteenth and nineteenth centuries, he is also referring to this great change in representing character.[22] Movement replaced immobility, and animated sequences superseded fixed images.

Let us be fair to Gothic prose, however. In their castle depictions, the Gothicists developed a catalogue of architectural images that provided a language with which to talk about the dark side of the psyche (albeit indirectly). Gothic heroes and villains were the prototypes for the more complex characters who would inhabit the nineteenth-century novel. Lowry Nelson rightly sees an evolution in Gothic fiction "away from . . . the rigged supernatural toward a recognition of . . . the 'subnatural,' that is, the irrational, the impulse to evil, the uncontrollable unconscious."[23] Viewed from this perspective, Ann Radcliffe provided a model of "prepsychology" which Sand adopted and extended in the creation of one of her most innovative and haunting novels.

In the end, Sand transforms the *roman noir* into a *roman blanc*. Her novel moves from colorful music to ghostly silence, from black terror to limpid serenity, and from the dark abysses of ignorance and fear to the luminescent realm of initiation.

NOTES

1. "Hence the necessity to reconsider the whole of nineteenth-century literature and to emphasize the crucial importance of the 'literary genres': the Gothic novel, the serialized novel, the musical novel, the novel of initiation. All these genres . . . are combined in the extraordinary *Consuelo*" (Jean Cassou, "George Sand et le secret du XIXe siècle," *Mercure de France*, December 1961, 603).

2. See George Sand, *Consuelo*, ed. Simone Vierne and René Bourgeois (Meylan: Editions de l'Aurore, 1983); "Musique et Musiciens dans *Consuelo*. Répertoire Alphabétique," 2:Appendix.

3. Thematic elements: a castle for the Gothic; a descent into hell for the initiation novel. Characters: a virtuous young lady and her male tormentor for the Gothic; an initiate and a guide for the initiation novel. Formal exigencies: the use of a nonlinear narrative structure for the Gothic; the use of a double discourse in which the visible always alludes to the invisible in the initiation novel. A traceable tradition: the eighteenth-century English Gothicists; the nineteenth- and twentieth-century French *roman initiatique*: novels by Honoré de Balzac, Gérard de Nerval, Jules Verne, Théophile Gautier, Henri Alain-Fournier, André Breton, and René Daumal.

4. Sand, *Consuelo*, 2:265; all further references to this work will be indicated in the text. This and all subsequent translations are those of the author.

5. Three hundred ten pages out of 815.

6. Peter Brooks, *The Melodramatic Imagination* (New Haven: Yale University Press, 1976), 19.

7. Ann Radcliffe, *The Mysteries of Udolpho* (New York: Oxford University Press, 1966), 258. All further references to this work will be indicated in the text as *U* and followed by the page number.

8. Maurice Lévy, *Le Roman "Gothique" Anglais, 1764–1824* (Toulouse: Publications de la Faculté des lettres et des sciences humaines de Toulouse, 1968), 621.

9. Gaston Bachelard, *La Terre et les rêveries du repos* (Paris: Corti, 1948), 215.

10. William Patrick Day, *In the Circles of Fear and Desire* (Chicago: Chicago University Press, 1985), 85.

11. Ibid., 103.

12. Lucienne Frappier-Mazur, "Code romantique et résurgences du féminin dans *La Comtesse de Rudolstadt*," in Didier Coste and Michel Zénaffa, eds., *Le Récit amoureux*, Colloque de Cerisy (Paris: Editions du Champ Vallon, 1984), 65. See also Julia Kristeva's

chapter "Approaching Abjection," in her *Powers of Horror: An Essay on Abjection*, trans. Léon S. Roudiez (New York: Columbia University Press, 1982), 1–31.

13. Day, *Circles*, 47.

14. Compare: "Remembering the few books, which even in the hurry of her departure from Udolpho, she had put into her little package" (*U*, 416).

15. Ann Radcliffe, cited in Day, *Circles*, 106.

16. There are also elements of Gothic architecture and mood in other Sand works, most notably in the opening pages of *Mauprat*, in the *Château des Désertes*, in *Spiridion* (especially noteworthy is a descent into the catacombs), and in *Lélia* (especially in the monastery scenes of both the 1833 and 1839 versions).

17. Ellen Moers, *Literary Women* (Garden City. N.Y.: Anchor Press/Doubleday, 1963), 209.

18. Day, *Circles*, 80.

19. Frappier-Mazur, "Code romantique," 65.

20. Day, *Circles*, 73–74.

21. Cassou, "Sand et le secret," 616.

22. Michel Foucault, *Les Mots et les choses* (Paris: Gallimard, 1966), 232.

23. Lowry Nelson, Jr., "Night Thoughts on the Gothic Novel," *Yale Review* 52 (1963): 249.

13

Consuelo and *Porporino*, or the Influence of Change

David A. Powell

Witness a novel that takes place in Italy in the mid-eighteenth century, toward the decline of the Baroque period in music. The author tells the story of a poor child whose natural musical talent is recognized and rewarded with free music training in one of Italy's most musical cities. Frequent allusion to Free-Mason ideals places the young musician in a historical framework and facilitates a discourse in favor of the modest classes. Music functions throughout as a metaphor for a superhuman language and as the vehicle to a higher plane of existence and understanding.

To anyone who knows the works of George Sand, this seems to be an obvious allusion to her 1842 masterpiece, *Consuelo*. However, this synopsis in fact describes a novel written by Dominique Fernandez in 1974, *Porporino, ou les mystères de Naples*. As striking as the likeness might seem to *Consuelo* and its sequel, *La Comtesse de Rudolstadt*, no criticism of Fernandez's novel has touched on its obvious resemblance to Sand's work.[1] Nonetheless, the similarities of plot and setting are clear enough, as are the various musical metaphors. On a deeper level, though, Fernandez adopts, and adapts, Sand's ploy of presenting a distant, musical world for the purpose of social commentary. The particular social phenomenon that haunts both Sand and Fernandez is the slow change in sexual politics. It is, in fact, the very ideology of sexual equality that at once binds and separates these two novels.

The plot of both novels unfolds in the eighteenth century, a time of considerable debate over musical aesthetics. *Consuelo* takes place about 1743, and *Porporino* about 1775. Sand begins her tale in Venice, the city of Claudio Monteverdi and Antonio Vivaldi; Fernandez sets his novel in Naples, the city that gave us Alessandro Scarlatti and *bel canto* opera. Sand and Fernandez both establish historical authenticity by supplying an elaborate musical background. Each author adopts a historical composer as an important character. Sand chooses Joseph

Haydn. We see him first as a fledgling composer, and follow his progress to official composer to the Hapsburg court in Vienna. Fernandez uses two well-known names: first, to parallel Haydn, he paints the emerging genius of Domenico Cimarosa; and, as a variation of Sand's use of Haydn, Fernandez also celebrates the young Amadeus Wolfgang Mozart and his insightful innovations in musical composition.

In addition to these known composers, the other principal characters are also musicians. It is in the context of their profession that the main characters in both novels suffer moral sanctions from society: Consuelo leads her life as a professional woman alone, although she is ethically and morally upright; Porporino is a *castrato* and a homosexual. Their failure to satisfy societal standards involves their private lives and sex or sexuality, as well as their public lives and the questionable morality of their professions.

This juxtaposition of elements readily demonstrates the extent of Sand's influence on Fernandez. However, the 30-year gap that separates the historical narratives of the two novels, even more than the 130 years that separates their publication, represents a period of great change in music history, a change that has much bearing on the perspectives of the two authors. In comparing the novels in this light, several points of discrepancy are historically accurate. There are four such historical elements that actually bind the two novels closely together. First, whereas Venice had been the seat of Italian musical influence since Monteverdi, it was, to some extent, ceding its place to Naples with the rise of Scarlatti. The Neapolitan school, although it set the foundations for eighteenth-century Italian opera, has often been attacked for its decadent use of Baroque operatic style: the excess of embellishments, and the sacrifice of real emotions in favor of putative perfection in poetical and musical effect. Furthermore, musicologists have traditionally set the end of the Baroque period at date of the death of Johann Sebastian Bach, 1750. However, even in Bach's music we witness a major change in aesthetics away from the Baroque style toward what has come to be called the Classical school, and with it, a shift of attention from Italian to German sensibilities. With this change, first Haydn and then Mozart come into the limelight, representing the Classical school, a style that imposes a greater sense of control over musical emotions.

A third historical change emphasized in both novels is that from *opera seria* to *opera buffa*. The former genre takes its inspiration from classical mythology or religious drama and lauds the virtues of heroism and honor. The latter derives from the everyday lives of common people and speaks of the complex emotions of the human heart. The fourth and final historical change has a direct effect on the main character of Fernandez's novel: As the ancient prohibition of women from the stage began to fade, the traditional and historical justification for the *castrato* also disappeared. Consequently, the need and desire for male sopranos plummeted, opening the door to moral attacks on their very existence.[2]

These aesthetic nuances point less to a difference between the worlds of Consuelo and Porporino than to both authors' use of historical, artistic considerations to convey moral issues; namely, tolerance to change and adaptation. Both paint the modernization of musical style in such a way as to fuel commentary on such matters as androgyny, sexism, feminism, and homophobia. In both works social change is portrayed sometimes as progressive and sometimes reactionary. The tone of these commentaries is often comic or even ironic.

Sand displays her artistry as a historic and comic writer in one scene that will well serve to demonstrate her disdain for the out-of-date, bombastic insistence on baroque *fioritura*. Consuelo, in masculine garb, and Haydn are making their way from Bohemia to Vienna. They narrowly escape being kidnapped into military service by the Prussians, and gratefully accept the help of Count Hoditz. The count hides them in a friend's home and asks for music, since Consuelo and Haydn have told him they are musicians. As Consuelo points out to Haydn, they cannot refuse this pleasure to someone who has saved them from hazardous circumstances. However, they cannot risk revealing too much of their musical prowess without divulging Consuelo's sex, their rank, and their destination, so they agree to sing, but not to the count's total satisfaction. Thus, Sand can treat us to the ridiculous anomaly of Hoditz taking it upon himself to make proper musicians out of these two vagabonds.

In Chapter 73 Sand gives a delightful parody of a music lesson. The passage presents a double musical commentary: on the one hand, the humorous aspect of an amateur trying to teach a professional her own art; and, on the other, the very subject matter of Hoditz's "lesson," the production of embellishments. Hoditz starts the lesson by giving an example of a trill that he asks Consuelo to duplicate. She does it backwards. Hoditz flies into a rage, claiming Consuelo is not listening, and they begin again. In this farcical manner the humor increases through repetition until Consuelo gives in and produces the trill correctly. Of course, Hoditz explains this progress entirely in terms of his own great pedagogical powers. Consuelo, a lowborn woman, unintentionally exposes the awkwardly presumptuous side of an aristocratic man, which produces a comedic scene. The same procedure continues with several other embellishments. The accumulation technique produces a good comic effect, and the passage itself is an added parody of the Baroque habit of piling embellishment upon embellishment.

In addition to repetition or variation on a comic situation, Sand enjoins the reader to participate from a superior point of view. We laugh at Hoditz all the more because the narrator invites us to join the ranks of the musical elite in order to denigrate the musical pretensions of this unsuccessful autodidact. Hoditz, unaware and perhaps even fearful of the changes the musical world is undergoing at this time, clings to the style he knows best and attempts, in his pompous manner, to perpetuate it.

Fernandez makes a similar mockery of outdated styles. He pits the fifteen-year-old Mozart against Carlo Farinelli, a famous Neapolitan *castrato* (1705–1782). Farinelli ridicules Mozart's plans for his first opera and informs him of the "rules" for dramatic music writing which Mozart obviously neither knows nor cares to know: He must have no more than five soloists, three principals and two secondaries; the tenor or higher role must not sing in the first scene of the opera as the audience is still coming in and settling down; the plot must already be known to the public; he must include special considerations for the set mechanics so that special effects can be arranged, not only to please the audience but also to placate the mechanics; and so on. The passage serves to display all that was formulaic in

Neapolitan opera and Mozart's refusal to abide by such external, nonmusical constrictions.

In both instances the authors present a duality of aesthetic tastes that can be reformulated as reactionary and revolutionary. The musical metaphor introduces a commentary on the resistance to change. In these passages the struggle between the old and the new is apparent. On a political level, the characters anticipate the fall of the *ancien régime*. Fernandez includes Free-Masons to discuss the importance of this event and their ambivalent attitude toward change. In a discussion about changing operatic style, one Free-Mason character decries opera buffa as lavish and expensive, and often yielding only ridiculous effects. Later, the same style earns praise from another Free-Mason because of the depiction of human emotions on a more realistic level than in opera seria, and because through it the common people rise to recognition.

Sand also makes use of Masonic principles, although more subtly than Fernandez. In the context of her novel, "la Société des Invisibles" lauds the musician as a communicant with God. Consuelo wins the praise of her Free-Mason analogues partly because of her humble origins but mostly because of her love of justice and equality. In Free-Mason tradition, this love is nurtured through concentrated, solitary study, and transformed into a political ideal that seeks to destroy tyranny. Consuelo also transcends the traditional limits of her sex by gaining admission to the fraternal society.

On a human level, the fear of change lends a sad, almost pathetic, tone to the novels. Hoditz, who is actually good-hearted but caught up in a ruthless struggle for power, holds fast to his sense of stability in the Baroque music he has worked hard to master, even though only to an amateur degree. Farinelli, foreshadowing the hero Porporino, lords over the new generation as a fading star, imposing strict adherence to well-established customs for fear of losing rank in a newer system. This is an especially important notion here considering that the Baroque style had been thriving for 150 years. Porporino finds himself, at the end of Fernandez's novel, the last of a dying breed. Having settled in Bonn (once again, in a movement from the Italian to the German), he learns to accept not only that his expertise in *bel canto* no longer interests the public, but that it is now seen as an abomination.

An important deviation in the development of these two heroes now becomes apparent. On the one hand, Consuelo represents a growing hope that progress in aesthetics, as well as in science and technology, will promote progress in society. On the other hand, Porporino symbolizes a permanent change locked in time while aesthetics and society pass him by. Consuelo advocates changing with the times, leading to the more equitable acceptance of women in professional concerns, whereas Porporino suffers from an irreversible change, making him incapable of following the advances in art. He is a victim of change left with only the despair of rejection. Rather than postulating that time should stand still, Fernandez underlines the permanence of change and the need to adapt. The corollary of tolerance for homosexuality necessarily finds its place in this argument.

Thus, the hero and heroine of these two novels embody the notion of change in divergent perspectives. The ritual of naming plays a significant role in this process.

Porporino, in a variation of the tradition of the great singers, adopts the name of the recently deceased Nicola Porporo, the famous Neapolitan music teacher. Taking a name holds a dual importance in the novel: Not only does Porporino inherit musical renown from his namesake, but he also replaces his own given name. An earlier chapter explains how the eponymic character is subjected to the regional custom of assigning Christian names according to the birth order in the family. Thus, neither his surname, del Prato, nor his given name, Vincenzo, defines him; both names belong to others. (Not unimportant is the similarity here with the state of a woman whose married surname is that of her husband and whose maiden name is that of her father.) Porporino is then a name he dons like a mask, trying to forget his origins and to become an individual in his own right.

Consuelo also adopts the name of her teacher, the same Nicola Porporo. She uses this name as an alias while in Bohemia to hide her true identity.[3] Both Consuelo and Vincenzo exploit the system of pseudonyms to dissimulate their identities. This change, however, is only superficial. Porporino's erstwhile rebirth really represents only the rejection of his native land, his family, and ultimately himself. His adoptive family at the Conservatoire des Pauvres de Jesus-Christ does not offer him any more security or individuality in return. As for Consuelo, her subterfuge is only temporary. Albert mystically knows her given name, and when she flees Bohemia, she becomes interchangeably Consuelo or la Porporina. The two facets of her personality meld, replacing the *mulier duplex*, if you will, with a complex, demiurgic entity. In both cases, the assumed identities merely permit the characters to accede to the full capacity of their musical talent. The successful development of their careers was always an integral part of their personalities; there was never any real change, just as the names never really hid anything.[4]

If the change of name is only superficial, there is a much deeper change that the two singers share: their initiation into a closed society. The initiation of Consuelo into the "Société des Invisibles" constitutes one of the most original and most suspenseful segments of Sand's work, if not of the nineteenth-century novel altogether. Consuelo's superior intellect most prominently manifests itself in music, either in production or interpretation, and this earns her a seat alongside the male members of this variant of the Free-Masons.

Porporino's initiation is rather different, being of a primarily physical nature. Castrati in Fernandez's novel combine feelings of inadequacy with haughtiness, both as a group and as individuals. Porporino belongs to a society of misfits that at once receive the praises of their profession and suffer rejection from general society. His initiation, as well as his change, results in an instability that is reflected in the outside world by the decline of opera seria and thus a decline in the usefulness of castrati on the stage.

Fernandez presents castration as a sort of androgynization, but rather than praising pure androgyny, Fernandez presents a group of mutants who suffer from a complex alienation which nonetheless allows them to enjoy a warm reception for their artistic talents. Moreover, while castrati did sometimes sing women's roles, which is the conventional explanation for their existence, they often performed the higher male roles, usually portraying the traditionally virile qualities of the hero.

These physically altered singers embodied the androgynous admixture of feminine sound and appearance with the force and control traditionally held to be masculine.

The initiations of Consuelo and Porporino involve a combination of the sexes: Consuelo and her mother-in-law, Wanda, are the only women in a man's secret society, and Porporino combines the masculine and feminine aspects of human nature. Herein lies the change toward which both novelists tend. The quality of the sexes, a favorite topic of Sand's, finds a new incarnation in Fernandez's work. Whereas Sand's message comments on the acceptance of women in a man's world, Fernandez addresses the acceptance of someone different into the larger society. He develops the character well enough to show the reader that Porporino is human with all the "normal" human feelings and desires. Both authors are working against discrimination based on sex and sexuality. Fernandez goes one step further to comment on sexual orientation, making a thinly veiled case for homosexuality.

How do these two authors resolve the problem of sexual discrimination? Sand introduces, develops, and praises her heroine for nearly a thousand pages; then, in the last fifty pages, Albert receives full attention as the musician-*vates*, and Consuelo is relegated to the role of interpreter. She no longer practices music, she only translates Albert's musical communication into human language. She is still at an intermediary stage between humanity and God, but she is nonetheless subservient to Albert. In the general atmosphere of optimism for the cause of women, feminism does not finish in a very good light in Sand's novel.

Fernandez follows a similar line of attack, even though his definition of the injured party is the castrato, who, he says, represents the androgynous in all of us, especially today's youth. Rather than the equality of different sexes, he concentrates on the acceptance of difference itself. One might even go so far as to compare Porporino's case with the popularity among heterosexuals of the "token gay" in small circles, while on the greater level of society, the exotic object of curiosity turns to one of repulsion. Fernandez's hero is physically incapable of changing in the hope of being accepted under the new standards, thus causing the novel to end with a tone of resigned pessimism in nostalgia for a past era.

Fernandez's debt to Sand can be explained in the terms of Harold Bloom as stated in his *Anxiety of Influence*.[5] Fernandez recognizes the importance of Sand's message and attempts to take it to new heights, to a more general, more universal application. Bloom calls this type of anxiety of influence *daemonization*, which "attempts to expand the precursor's power to a principle larger than his own, but which pragmatically makes the son more of a daemon and the precursor more of a man [read 'human']" (106). Instead of raising Sand's feminist struggle to a more universal level of freedom from sexual constraint, Fernandez actually produces a more particular case, perhaps just as valid as Sand's but less widely applicable.

Fernandez wishes to replace the androgynous mystique of the castrato with that of the modern man, who now must take up the responsibility of displaying both so-called feminine and masculine traits. Similarly, to encompass all of humanity, modern youth must now carry the banner of sexual equality and promote the cause of tolerance; in 1974 Fernandez saw in fact that the peaceful battle had already begun:

> What reader . . . will not immediately think of the most spectacular social phenomenon of our time, conceived in the bosom of industrial empires and by reaction to their tyranny, the pacific revolution of youth, flower power, unisex fashions, child-like wanderings, the love of music, and the love of love? Boys with long hair, girls with narrow hips, as if the search for the old paradise, where only the lack of sexual differentiation and liberty reign, began to show up in their morphology. Yes, it would be tempting to draw comparisons between the hippie movement in our century and the castrato fad in the other! (12)

Sand's public needed perhaps less explicit encouragement to compare the political and social situation of *Consuelo* to their own. The similarities do not, however, elude the circumspect reader, for just as Consuelo makes a progressive foray into a masculine world, so does George Sand.

However, Sand's novel does not advocate the total liberation of woman or complete equality. Consuelo clearly serves Albert at the close of *La Comtesse de Rudolstadt*. In comparison, Sand herself espoused a moderate and not a militant expression of feminism, which she would defend under attack from Flora Tristan and others just after the 1848 revolution.

Fernandez reinvents a similar process. In an attempt to create both an individual and an allegorical figure, he produced a misfit whose melancholy communicates to the reader a general tone of pessimism, and this pessimism, based on alienation, parallels Sand's attenuated feminism. Thus, Fernandez readjusts the original argument in his own terms but fails to break away from Sand's influence. To her Sublime, Fernandez opposes a Counter-Sublime (Bloom's terms), resulting in a social commentary that is at once more general and more specific than the original. He succeeds, perhaps, in enlarging the boundaries of Sand's world, but in so doing he nonetheless admits to the inspiration of her creation. Fernandez's debt to Sand in no way nullifies the world of his novel. On the contrary, viewing it in comparison with its precursor serves to heighten our appreciation of the fundamental issues of tolerance and change.

NOTES

1. Claude Perruz, in his review of *Porporino* for *La Nouvelle Critique* (81 [Feb. 1975], 82), compares Fernandez's novel to Honoré de Balzac's short story *Sarrasine*; none of the other reviews mentions any similarity to another work. See also Claude Bonnefoy, *Nouvelles littéraires* 2451 (Sept. 16, 1974), 4; Alain Clerval, *Nouvelle revue française* (*NRF*) 265 (Jan. 1975), 102–103; Jean-Claude Dietsch, *Etudes* 341 (July–Dec. 1974), 624–625; Jean-Louis Ezine, *Nouvelles littéraires* 2461 (Nov. 25, 1974), 3; Claude Mauriac, *Le Figaro littéraire* 1478 (Sept. 14, 1974), 13; and Schifano, *Quinzaine littéraire* 195 (Oct. 1, 1974), 5–6.

2. Angus Henriot, *The Castrati in Opera* (London: Caldine and Bogars, 1975), 34 and

passim. Fernandez undoubtedly profited from his edition of an eighteenth-century book on castrati by Charles Ancillon, *Le Traité des eunuques*.

3. Note that Consuelo does have a male counterpart in the novel, who is based on the famous Antonio Hubert and takes the name Porporino. However, in the study of musical lineage, there is no question that Fernandez's Porporino is the intended analogue of Sand's Porporina.

4. Claude Mauriac, in his review of *Porporino* in *Le Figaro littéraire*, calls attention to an early book by Fernandez, *L'Arbre jusqu'aux racines* (Paris: Grasset, 1972), in which one chapter is devoted to "la figure du père"; Mauriac proposed a study of "la figure du père dans l'oeuvre de Dominique Fernandez." Handing down a name, and in this instance a literary career, bespeaks an important influence for both the Fernandezes and the Mauriacs.

5. Harold Bloom, *The Anxiety of Influence* (New York: Oxford University Press, 1973).

14

Intertextuality: *Valentine* and *La Princesse de Clèves*

Lucy M. Schwartz

All text is intertext. Every discourse is a restructuring of previous discourses.[1] Imbedded in the structure of *Valentine* are fragments of a previous structure. Hidden under the melodramatic plot and beautiful descriptions of the Berry region are elements of the characters, plot, themes, and logic of Marie de Lafayette's classic *La Princess de Clèves*.

Nancy K. Miller, in her 1981 article, "Writing (from) the Feminine: George Sand and the Novel of Female Pastoral,"[2] examined this intertextuality from the perspective of what she called "the female plot"[3] and concluded that although Sand did not go so far as Lafayette in refusing "male sexuality as a plot," she rewrote the "conventional" marriage night scene to protest against "the hegemony of male desire," and established the pavilion as the locus of desire outside the paternal eye.[4]

I propose to explore the interrelationships between these two novels from a different perspective—that of narrative focus. By examining three sets of parallel texts, I will show how the transformations in the narrative structure of the seventeenth-century novel create a tension in the nineteenth-century novel, which in turn leads to a reorientation of the narrative focus.

At first glance, the two texts of the first meeting of the protagonists appear to be very different. Madame de Clèves meets the Duke de Nemours at a royal ball, while Bénédict meets Valentine at a country dance.[5] One scene takes place inside, at the Louvre palace, and the other outside, on a village green. The common speech of the peasants in *Valentine* contrasts with the elegant speech of the royal court in *La Princesse de Clèves*.[6]

Beyond these superficial differences, however, the two texts have similar structures. Bénédict meets Valentine as Madame de Clèves meets the Duke de Nemours—in a crowded gathering at a dance. In both cases the hero and heroine have no choice; they are commanded by an outside authority to dance with each other without really knowing one another. The results in both instances are public embarrassment that conceals a private nascent passion.

Textual details underline these similarities in concept. In both texts the arrival of one of the protagonists creates a murmur:

> There was a fairly loud noise near the door of the room as if someone was entering and people were clearing the way for him. (*PC*, 24)

> As he heard this name passing from mouth to mouth, Bénédict, impelled by curiosity, followed the throngs of admirers who threw themselves in her path. (*V*, 551)

Both males are forced to climb to reach the women. The Duke de Nemours climbs over some chairs (*PC*, 24), while Bénédict climbs up on a crucifix (*V*, 551). Finally, both couples dance admirably:

> When they began to dance, a murmur of praise arose in the ballroom. (*PC*, 24)

> She danced la bourrée marvelously with all the assurance and nonchalance of a village maid. (*V*, 554).

A close examination of these parallels between the two passages reveals how the patterns from *La Princess de Clèves* change in *Valentine*. The mutual embarrassment is a case in point. The embarrassment in the text from *La Princesse de Clèves* grows from the fact that Madame de Clèves refuses to admit she has guessed the identity of her partner. The mutual embarrassment in *Valentine* has a more complex source—the social inequality between the protagonists, which makes it inappropriate for them to dance together and to kiss as the folk dance requires. The momentary embarrassment brought about in *La Princesse de Clèves* by the teasing of the king and queen becomes a major social dilemma in *Valentine*, where the peasants laugh as Bénédict is forced to kiss a noblewoman, humiliating her family in public.

One further transformation also emphasizes Bénédict's social inferiority. When the Duke de Nemours arrives at the crowded royal ball in *La Princesse de Clèves*, the dancers make a place for him to pass. He steps *over* a chair and finds himself beside Madame de Clèves. The physical elements of his arrival demonstrate concretely that while he is master of the situation, they are equals in beauty and rank, and stand on the same ground before the king. Valentine, however, is metaphorically described as a "star" who comes *down* to the country dance. In order to see her for the first time, Bénédict must fight the crowd and climb *up* on a crucifix. (This symbol may bear some relationship to the sufferings that Bénédict will endure because of his love for Valentine.) The figurative language expressing ascent and descent graphically portrays the social distance that separates Bénédict from Valentine.

Some patterns in *La Princesse de Clèves* are simply reversed in *Valentine*. The homogeneous gathering of brilliant courtiers in *La Princesse de Clèves* becomes a very heterogeneous society in *Valentine*. The court of Henri II in *La Princesse de Clèves* is a closed world. Described by innumerable superlatives, it contains the brightest, best, and most beautiful elements of French society. Madame de Clèves is the most attractive woman at court, and Monsieur de Nemours is not only the most handsome but also the most courageous of the men.

In contrast, the country dance in *Valentine* attracts all the peasants of the region, a few rich farmers like Bénédict's uncle and aunt, who want to pretend that they are bourgeois, and the one noble family, who own the village château. Valentine is not perceived by Bénédict to be attractive. Although the narrator suggests that her blond hair and simple, noble profile may indeed be beautiful, Bénédict, a gangly, homely lad himself, finds her disappointing compared to his ideal of Spanish paleness.

The confession scenes from both novels provide more significant examples of patterns transformed and reversed. The two texts have similar structures.[7] In each, a woman begs her husband to permit her to move to another geographic location—Madame de Clèves wants to retire to the country, and Valentine wants to leave her country home to follow her husband on his diplomatic missions. Both wish to flee from their lovers; both assure their husbands of their innocence. Each husband responds with questions about his wife's relationship with the man she wishes to flee, finally accusing her of misconduct. Monsieur de Clèves accuses his wife of giving away his portrait, and Monsieur de Lansac accuses his wife of lying about her meetings with Bénédict.

In addition to this general structure, the passages have many textual details in common. Both women are upset by the experience of confession and the potential loss of their husbands' trust which it implies:

> She was so terrified about it that she could scarcely imagine that it was true. She found that she herself had caused the loss of her husband's love and esteem. (*PC*, 99)
>
> She could find in her soul only deep consternation when she realized that she was lost beyond reprieve in her husband's opinion. (*V*, 618)

They both see their fate as a trap from which they cannot escape, and use the metaphor of "a pit" into which they may fall or have fallen:

> She herself had dug a pit from which she would never escape. (*PC*, 99)
>
> Everything warned her that it was time to go back, if she did not want to fall into a pit. (*V*, 618)

Both heroines use the same circular reasoning. Because they are pure, they have the courage to make the confession. Therefore, the fact that they have confessed proves their innocence:

> I am going to make a confession to you that no woman has ever made to her husband; but the innocence of my conduct and of my intentions gives me the force. (*PC*, 96)

> Valentine, who felt that she was innocent, felt at the same time her courage rising. (*V*, 618)

> Is it possible, cried the princess, that you can believe that there is dissimulation in a confession like mine, which nothing forced me to make? (*PC*, 98)

> My straying was always involuntary. . . . [Y]ou know very well that if it had been otherwise, I would not have the impudence to ask for your protection. (*V*, 618)

Madame de Clèves makes a distinction between her actions (which are blameless) and her emotions (which are not):

> I have never given any indication of weakness. . . . [I]f I have feelings which displease you, at least I will never displease you by my actions. (*PC*, 96)

> Be satisfied with the assurance which I am giving you again, that none of my actions has revealed my feelings and that no one has ever said anything to me which offended me. (*PC*, 98)

Valentine makes a similar distinction between her involuntary submission to her lover's kiss and the purity and dignity that she has retained by keeping her virtue:

> I know that you despise me . . . but I know that you do not have the right to do so. I swear, Sir, that I am still worthy to be the wife of an honest man. (*V*, 618)

> Haven't you understood that even if I am guilty and hateful in my own eyes, at least my conduct has not been soiled by the stain which no man can ever pardon? (*V*, 618)

Even some of the smallest details of the two texts are the same. Both heroines kneel to beg their husbands' pardon; both are covered with tears; both are beautiful and eloquent.

Despite these striking parallels, there are major differences: Perhaps the most important is the inversion of the opposition unique/commonplace. Madame de Clèves repeatedly underlines the uniqueness of her action of confiding in her husband:

> I am going to make a confession to you that no woman has ever made to her husband. (*PC*, 96)

> The unusualness of such a confession, of which she could not find a single example, made her see all of its danger. (*PC*, 99)

Her husband agrees that her action is exceptional, using superlatives to describe it and her:

> You seem to me to be more worthy of esteem and admiration than any woman who has ever lived on earth. (*PC*, 96)

> Your confidence in me and your sincerity are priceless. . . . You are making me unhappy by the greatest mark of faithfulness that a woman has ever given to her husband. (*PC*, 97)

In contrast, Valentine's action is seen as romanesque but commonplace:

> She gave herself up to a romanesque and sublime project which has tempted more than one woman on the verge of committing her first fault: she resolved to see her husband and to beg for his support. (*V*, 618)

The very same action that seems unique and noble in the sixteenth-century world of *La Princesse de Clèves* seems ordinary in the nineteenth-century world of *Valentine*. The reversal of the opposition unique/commonplace not only devalues Valentine's action; it also lowers Valentine herself to the level of "most women" who appear to commit more than one "fault." She can no longer believe herself to be a noble heroine like Madame de Clèves, who establishes her virtue by standing out from the crowd.

The outcome of the scene in *Valentine* is the antithesis of that of the scene in *La Princesse de Clèves*. Monsieur de Clèves agrees to help protect his wife, while Monsieur de Lansac refuses to accord his wife the protection she implores. George Sand's corrupt ambassador has nothing in common with Madame de Lafayette's unselfish and understanding hero. It seems inconceivable and almost laughable that a husband whose wife begs him to take her away from temptation would refuse because he finds it inconvenient to live with his wife. Monsieur de Clèves reacts to his wife's confession with nobility and jealousy. He says he is tormented both by the jealousy of a husband (who wants to safeguard his wife as his possession) and the jealousy of a lover (who only wants her to love him). Monsieur de Lansac has neither of these causes for jealousy. He has no intention of possessing his wife, only her property; and he has never had any love for her. His ironic rebuke of her for daring to ask for this favor and for being so naive as to believe in "virtue" is the opposite of his speech to her on the previous evening when he had wanted her property and had spoken to her of their "mutual duties." This point does not escape Valentine who, nevertheless, swallows her pride and begs him to change his mind.

The reader is left with a shock of disbelief that Lansac can be so egotistical and cruel. Our analysis of the underlying text in *La Princesse de Clèves* helps us better to appreciate, in comparison, the inconsistency between Monsieur de Lansac's actions and his rhetoric. Further, by making Valentine a victim, Lansac's inconsistent reproach tends to excuse her subsequent submission to the passion of Bénédict.

In both novels, the pavilion in the garden of a country home has a symbolic value as a place of refuge from the court or the city.[8] Describing the role of the pavilion in *Valentine*, Micheline Besnard points out that it begins as a neutral space between the château, which symbolizes the aristocracy, and the farm, which symbolizes the peasant class; and then evolves into a type of Utopia where Valentine establishes a classless society composed of herself, Bénédict, her sister Louise and her son, and Bénédict's cousin Athénaïs.[9] According to Miller, the pavilion mediates the opposition between the château and Bénédict's cottage as well.[10]

The pavilion in *La Princesse de Clèves* does not have this social value. It is simply a retreat from the court where Madame de Clèves can feel safe from the advances of the Duke de Nemours. In the most memorable scene of the novel, Madame de Clèves gives herself over to daydreams about the duke while contemplating his portrait in a large painting of a battle scene and absentmindedly tying ribbons of the colors he wore in the joust around a cane that had once belonged to him. Although her relative state of undress (a low-necked dress) and the unruliness of her hair (which is not tied up) combine with the heat of the evening to underline the eroticism of this scene, there is no real contact between the lovers. When Madame de Clèves thinks she sees the duke, who is in fact watching her through the open window, she retires to another room where her maids are waiting. Sensing that her retreat has been violated, she does not return to the pavilion the following night.

In the pavilion scene in *Valentine*, the retreat is violated by the husband, not by the lover. When the Count de Lansac arrives at the château after a two-year absence, Valentine is happily entertaining her friends in the pavilion. After she hastily sends them away, she is horrified to discover that her husband wishes to sleep in the pavilion, a wish that is not granted. The next night she agrees to meet Bénédict there, but their interview is interrupted by the count, who follows Valentine from the château to the pavilion. Like the Duke de Nemours, who overhears Madame de Clèves's confession, Lansac hides and listens to Valentine and Bénédict share their declarations of love. Announcing his presence by a loud cough, he pretends to have just arrived. Throughout his conversation with his wife, he uses his knowledge of her lover's hiding place to manipulate her into giving him her property. Thus, the sacred space of the classless retreat is desecrated by the economic concerns of the venal nobleman. The reversal of the pattern of the retreat's violation has the value of making the husband into the transgressor, while in *La Princesse de Clèves* it is the lover who violates the heroine's inner space, disturbs her tranquillity, and ultimately causes the death of her husband.

The result of all these transformations is to change the logic of the narrative. In *La Princesse de Clèves*, the careful reader is assured that the heroine has made the proper choice to satisfy moral requirements as well as to guarantee her opinion of herself, for Nemours is shown to be a person who could certainly prove unreliable if not unfaithful.

In *Valentine*, the reader is not so easily assured that the heroine has made the proper choice. The ending of the novel is ambiguous enough to lend itself to several interpretations. The reader may condemn Valentine for being unfaithful to her image of herself, or the reader perhaps may decide that it is Louise who speaks for the narrator and proclaims the ultimate moral of the story when she berates her sister for erecting artificial barriers of hypocritical religiosity which finally make Bénédict suffer and die. Louise feels that if Valentine had known how to love Bénédict, she would have put away her false pride and given in to him without ruining his life. Whatever the reader ultimately decides about the value of Valentine's choices, one must conclude that the moral message of the novel is not as clearly articulated as the moral message of *La Princesse de Clèves*.

In *Valentine*, the transformations of the patterns from *La Princesse de Clèves* bring about the condemnation of Lansac, underline Valentine's state as a victim, and establish the social distance between Valentine and Bénédict. These changes produce a tension between Sand's novel and the intertext, a tension that reorients the logic of the narrative. This logic does not operate on the moral level. It operates on the social level; and on that level, the message is unambiguous. The reader is led to condemn the social system that makes it impossible for the lovers to find happiness. One is also led to rejoice in the marriage of Athénaïs and Valentin, Valentine's nephew, which ultimately brings about the fusion of the social classes and restores Valentine's property to her intimate friends, who recreate her violated Utopia. The changes in the patterns from the earlier novel transform a novel of moral values into a powerful novel of social protest.

NOTES

1. See, for example, the discussion of intertextuality in such works as Harold Bloom, Paul de Man, Jacques Derrida, Geoffrey H. Hartman, and J. Hillis Miller, *Deconstruction and Criticism* (New York: Seabury, 1979), or Jonathan Culler, *On Deconstruction: Theory and Criticism after Structuralism* (Ithaca, N.Y.: Cornell University Press, 1982).

2. In *The Representation of Women in Fiction*, ed. Carolyn G. Heilbrun and Margaret R. Higonnet (Baltimore: Johns Hopkins University Press), 124–151.

3. She defines "female plot" as "that organization of narrative event which delimits a heroine's psychological, moral, and social development within a sexual fate" (125). The reader will also want to consult Miller's *The Heroine's Text: Readings in the French and English Novel, 1722–1782* (New York: Columbia University Press, 1980) and her "Emphasis Added: Plots and Plausibilities in Women's Fiction," *PMLA* 96 (1981): 36–48, which discuss similar concepts.

4. Miller, "Writing (from) the Feminine," 134, 144–145.

5. All references are to the following editions: Madame de Lafayette, *La Princesse de Clèves* [*PC*] (n.p.: Integral Editions, 1961);and George Sand, *Valentine* [*V*] (Paris: n.p., 1852). The ball scenes appear on pages 24–25 of *La Princesse de Clèves* and pages 551–554 of *Valentine*; this and all subsequent translations are those of the author.

6. Even the Marquise in *Valentine* self-consciously degrades her language (552).

7. The confession scenes are on pages 95–99 of *La Princesse de Clèves* and pages 618–619 of *Valentine.*

8. The pavilion scenes are on pages 129–132 of *La Princesse de Clèves* and pages 613–617 of *Valentine.*

9. Micheline Besnard, "Quelque repères structurels, les lieux dans *Valentine,*" *Présence de George Sand* 22 (1985): 42–43.

10. Miller, "Writing (from) the Feminine," 125.

Part V

POLITICAL AFFINITIES

15

Nanon: Novel of Revolution or Revolutionary Novel?

Nancy E. Rogers

Scouring indices for references to George Sand's *Nanon* is scarcely a rewarding task. Patricia Thompson (in *George Sand and the Victorians*) tells us that Henry James mistakenly placed *Nanon* among Sand's earlier works,[1] hardly a tribute to its worth, and André Maurois dismissed most of the later works, saying there "tended to be a sameness about the themes."[2] Emile Zola is one of the few French writers even to have considered *Nanon*, which he described as a "prose poem"; characteristically, he saw the mythic proportions of the work, depicting "the eternal couple" moving into the future.[3] However, *Nanon* is a far more significant work than Zola envisioned. Published in 1872, it yields surprising gifts to the student of the French Revolution as well as to critics interested in Sand's conception of woman, her place in society, and her potential for transcending society's strictures. *Nanon*, like many of Sand's novels, is an important document for historians, sociologists, linguists, anthropologists, and literary critics alike.

The tale of Nanette Surgeon, or Nanon as she is known—the *non* of her name perhaps reflecting her own stance vis-à-vis the status society has decreed for her—is one of revolution. Like *Mauprat*, the Sandian novel that it most closely resembles and that touched on the American Revolution, *Nanon* is a story of adventure and love, uniting an unlikely couple in an enduring marriage. However, the key to *Nanon* is not the evolution and education of a straying male, as it is in *Mauprat*, but the liberation of the two halves of the couple, resulting in the first entrepreneurial matriarchy in French literature.

Like Honoré de Balzac's *Les Chouans* (1829) and the major portion of Victor Hugo's *Quatre-vingt-treize* (1872), Sand's novel chronicling the French Revolution takes place outside Paris. Whereas Balzac and Hugo set their tales in the midst of the guerilla warfare of the Vendée, Sand only touches on that strange, almost mythical, conflict of fierce peasants and gigantic characters to focus on the effects of the Revolution on one very small corner of France. Sand's interest in the Revolution did not lie in the vast social issues examined by Balzac and Hugo, but rather in the personal results of the conflict, and what it meant on both a local level and in the lives of three individuals, one from each of the social classes. There are no generals in Sand's revolution, only humble foot soldiers when the military appears at all; Georges-Jacques Danton, Maximilien de Robespierre, and even the king are absent actors, unreal and poorly understood. In place of Hugo's animistic guillotine, lumbering across France on its fiendish mission, there is the peasant's scythe and other lowly tools used for the daily tasks of survival; and there are no counterparts to Balzac's glamorous Marie and dashing "le Gars," only frightened monks and uncertain small-town mayors. Nonetheless, Sand's conception of revolution is so deep and far-reaching, so much a part of life on every level, that her novel is more radically revolutionary than either Balzac's or Hugo's, for its aim is liberation on every front, for all classes and for both sexes. A study of Sand's personal conception of revolution as modified by the events of the Commune should be applied to the study of *Nanon*; however, I will confine myself here to the concept of revolution in the text itself.

Sand's French Revolution is historically exact, with dates sprinkled throughout the text to orient the reader to such major events as "la Grande Peur" of 1789, "la Fête de la Fédération" of 1790, the flight of the king in 1792, and the guillotining of Robespierre in 1794. However, the disjunction between historical accuracy and the effect of these key events on the peasants of *Nanon*, who are lost in ignorance and without access to accurate news from the capital, creates a distancing, or an ironic stance, on the part of the reader. This is complicated by the reader's knowledge of what these events actually meant in the history of France. The confusion of the peasants as they try to sift through half-truths and rumors, in contrast to the historic consequences wrought by the events, is almost laughable. One of the meanings of the term "revolution" for Sand, then, is "disorientation," for no one in *Nanon* has either accurate knowledge of what is happening or a sense of stability. As Hugo wrote in *Quatre-vingt-treize*: "And what is the Revolution? It is the victory of France over Europe and of Paris over France."[4] If Sand's peasants, struggling to survive in uncertain times, do not even know what the Bastille is, they may well wonder what country is home; "dépaysé" is thus an accurate word to describe this state, and Sand, by keeping her focus squarely on the little people, shows what a revolution really means by what it does, which is alternately to ignore and to use "the people," who are too disoriented to resist. Buffeted by fear, guilt, greed, and love of the land, and manipulated by clergy, lawyers, politicians, and brigands, the peasant has no means of discerning which wave of the revolution is sweeping across the land, leaving the very earth shifting and unstable; bewilderment is total. "That immense improvisation that is the French Revolution,"[5] in Hugo's words, removes any sense of certainty from the entire population, but George Sand, more than Balzac or Hugo, shows us how the winds of war blow dust storms on the peasants, obscuring their vision and leaving them bereft of focus.

In Valcreux, the fictional setting of *Nanon*, the Revolution seems to fill a vacuum for the main characters. Of the key players, only Monsieur Costejoux, the bourgeois lawyer who lives with his mother, has any deep family ties. Nanon, orphaned at five, is being raised by a great-uncle, one of the poorest peasants in the parish, who tells her at the beginning of the novel, "We own nothing."[6] Emilien, the young monk who is the second son of a noble family, has been deprived of both his birthright and the respect and love of his family. Emilien claims not to know his parents or his brother; all his life he has been told: "Don't get involved in anything, don't attach yourself to anything, teach yourself not to care about anything" (19). Bereft of his birthright as well as any access to learning, "he entered life already dead to many things and as naïve at sixteen years as another at eight" (27). Small wonder then that revolutionary fervor soon fills the void left by family and learning. Lack of status is rampant in *Nanon*; of all the characters in the novel, only Monsieur Costejoux has influence, wealth, position, and education. As for the peasants, the narrator (Nanon as an old woman) says: "A peasant of that time period was of such little worth!" (33). This sense of loss and lack of attachment seems to be a precondition for a true revolution in Sand's view.

The coming of the Revolution brings with it additional loss for all sectors of society in Valcreux. The monks soon lose their only possession, the monastery, when the sale of the Church's goods is decreed by the Revolution. They are thus stripped of their sole reason for existence. Soon they either become involved in the intrigue that accompanies civil war or withdraw into a kind of gullible, self-serving senility, like the prior, who is allowed to live on at the monastery after its purchase by Monsieur Costejoux. As we know, the aristocracy suffered the most direct and drastic loss as a result of the Revolution, losing status, possessions, country, and, often, their heads. Sand, however, is clearly not interested in the fortunes of this group, putting none on stage except the rebel Emilien and his empty, uneducated sister Louise. For the peasants, loss at the hands of the Revolution is a spiritual, rather than physical or financial, affair; those in *Nanon* soon lose their innocence, grabbing the land of noble families and ransacking property. As Nanon notes: "People lived openly by pillaging and became of necessity savage, fearful, bad" (31). The bourgeois class, represented by Monsieur Costejoux, seems to have the most to gain from the Revolution. Costejoux, an upwardly mobile lawyer, not only increases his prestige in the community by becoming a deputy to the Convention and a large landowner as well, but also marries into the noble class. However, he is too intelligent to be blissfully unaware of the consequences of the Revolution. His loss is great, for he loses his idealism and faith when "*la Terreur*" is unleashed. Nanon notes the change in his physiognomy and voice; the cause of this alteration is the inner tension he feels between right and country: "He had sincerely adopted a conviction and a role which could correspond to his principles of patriotism, but which were contrary to his confident and generous nature" (150).

The most dramatic and significant loss in *Nanon* occurs near the end of the novel, when Emilien must undergo the amputation of his right arm after being wounded in battle. For Emilien, the "arm" is linked to identity, which, by extension, means patriotism. When this young idealist is betrayed by his father, who has tried to enlist his son in the royalist army, he passionately chooses to work with his arms rather than merely collecting his dues as generations of his family have done: "Very well, it gives me pleasure to choose work that has to be done with the arms and fidelity to my country, because I . . . I am no longer a noble, I am a peasant, a Frenchman!" (128). When he returns from the war minus his right arm, he realizes that he can no longer assume the traditional role of the peasant and that he will have to find "some sedentary trade" (330). He thus offers himself to Nanon as her manager, for Nanon now heads an agricultural empire. The practical consequences of this sacrifice do not overshadow its symbolic importance, however, for Emilien proudly says: "I have given one of my arms to my country . . . I also gave it for the cause of freedom in the world" (332). The loss of his arm has finally allowed Emilien to join the ranks of those he admires most: "I've paid for the right to be a citizen, a laborer, a father. . . . I've expiated my nobility, I've won my place in the sun of civic equality" (332). Losing an arm has thus given Emilien the rights to live as a free man; to work, paradoxically, with his mind; and to find his true identity as a Frenchman, an achievement his noble birth had denied him.

The states of disorientation and loss in *Nanon*, which bring both negative and positive results, are preludes to the real crux of the novel, in which the affirmative values of "work, desire, and love" (337) dominate, turning this novel of revolution from ideology to praxis. The strong hands, arms, and heart of the heroine do not allow for wallowing in confusion, disorientation, and loss, but instead turn to the practical activities of reconstruction and reversal to make the Revolution an optimistic, liberating event. In the process of describing this liberation, Sand depicts people who, instead of being subsumed by the Revolution, rise above it to find success on every level and to become the backbone of the century to follow.

Left to fend for herself after the death of her great-uncle, Nanon finds herself with a single possession, her sheep Rosette. However, her triple strengths—work, will, and love—combine to make her useful, a trait that literary orphans have traditionally embodied. Nanon is capable of reorganizing those around her into a meaningful kind of existence; her first task is to orchestrate life in the monastery into what she terms "the colony," composed of "the good prior," Emilien, Louise, the old servant Dumont, and herself. Like Jean-Jacques Rousseau's Julie, Nanon is determined to gather all her loved ones under one roof and to recreate a family idyll removed from the realities of life (in this case, the vagaries and swift changes of the Revolution). Emilien treats her "as his sister and his equal" (103), and she sees Louise as both her sister and her daughter. By dint of hard work, especially by Nanon and Emilien, the lands of the monastery are reclaimed and the little band survives as a family unit.

This place of refuge is a prelude to the central idyll of the novel, in "an isolated hovel in an out-of-the-way part of the land" (163), where Nanon, Emilien, and Dumont go into hiding after Emilien's escape from prison. Tony Tanner has effectively shown us in his work, *Adultery in the Novel*, how the distinction between "city" and "field" denotes the topographical model for the realms of sexual relationships: "This simple distinction suggests that there is an area that is inside society and one that is outside, where the socially displaced individual or couple may attempt to find or practice a greater freedom."[7] The description of their retreat brings images of Eden: "It was an oasis of granite and greenery, a labyrinth where all was refuge and mystery" (198). The description of this earthly paradise is marvelous, as Sand depicts huge rocks; tiny, winding paths; enormous chestnut trees; and serpent-like roots. The retreat is further removed from reality by its enchanted nature, for it is also "a fairy domain" (201), full of Celtic monuments and feared by the peasants in the area. The three refugees, with Nanon posing as Dumont's nephew, soon divide up tasks; Nanon fashions furniture, gathers and cooks the food, and generally performs woman's work while the men work in the fields. However, we also learn that posing as a boy has developed her masculine talents as well: "I had become, since I became a boy, clever and strong with my hands at doing a boy's work" (202). Hidden in their deserted paradise, "a bit like Robinson Crusoe on his island" (204), the three recreate a family (with shifting roles, a topic too large to consider here), and become a self-contained and self-sufficient community, "outside the law" (221). In their "field," in Tanner's terms, the love between Nanon and Emilien, between peasant and noble, can flourish and deepen when freed from societal pressure and censure.

The resulting couple is a marvel of reconstruction, made up of two newly created people, the resourceful and courageous Nanon, and the mutilated Emilien, whose wholeness is restored through his melding into the perfect couple. "The breath of freedom" has engendered the ideal pair, destined to mate, produce five children, and share a brilliant future.

Nanon is described throughout the novel as "a little prodigy," capable of empowering herself through learning to read at sixteen and of tutoring the neighborhood children. One of the key passages in this novel of alteration and evolution is the one at the end of Chapter 9, in which Nanon addresses the reader directly. Her description of the change that has taken place in her focuses on her new capacity to use the French language, indicative of a rise in status:

> Now, those who will have read my words know that my education is complete enough so that I express myself more easily and understand better the things that strike me. It would have been impossible for me, during the whole story that I have just told, not to speak a little in the way of a peasant; my thoughts could not have found words other than those that were then contained in them, and, by letting myself use other words, I would have lent myself thoughts and feelings that I didn't have. I will now raise myself a bit to the level of language and appreciations of the bourgeoisie, because, from 1792 on, I was no longer a peasant except by clothes and work. (115)

This extraordinary insight into the elevation of mind, thought, and language that is taking place within her is indicative of Nanon's exceptional nature. Others recognize her outstanding and unique character. As Costejoux tells her: "You are an exception, a very remarkable exception. You are neither a woman nor a man, you are both, with the best qualities of the two sexes" (271–272). This talented young woman, combining the best features of both sexes and cultivating her intelligence to the point that her language evolves in a new direction, is thus Sand's choice as the mate of a true Frenchman, whose own evolution parallels hers.

When Emilien proposes marriage, he does so with the blessings of the Revolution, touting his "title of citizen acquired at such expense" (335) as his emblem of freedom, and founding his future hopes on the land, the symbol of both his newfound peasant status and his love of country. Knowing that working the earth requires physical strength, Emilien offers his only remaining "arm," stating that he will give the earth "the arm that I have left, my ability to think, my intelligence" (335). Nanon responds to his contention that he may be a burden to her by saying that the peasants understand "that a good head is more useful than a hundred arms" (336). She continues to laud his qualities of heart, mind, goodness, rationality, and capacity to love. Combined with Nanon's natural instincts to make money, "heroine's nature" (152), passion for hard work, will, patience, debating skills, and ultimate usefulness, the two form the perfect union, as French citizens ready to found a new world. Just as Emilien has become a Frenchman through his sacrifice, so has Nanon now entered that sacred sphere: "Before the great devotion of my fiancé to the country, I had become less of a peasant, that is, more French" (349). Thus Sand envisions the Revolution engendering an ideal son and daughter, united in their patriotism, love of the land, belief in the future, and unshackling of themselves from their origins. Reconstruction—in agricultural, architectural, and familial terms—is thus one of the central concepts of *Nanon*, and one of the features working as an antidote to the disorientation and loss produced by the Revolution.

This success story would be incomplete, however, with a brief accounting of the many reversals that take place in this bold novel. As noted, Nanon moves from total ignorance of intellectual matters to becoming educated in many facets of knowledge: philosophy, geography, history, finance, politics, and agriculture. She also reverses her class status, from peasant, to bourgeoise, to marquise, and then to a kind of nobility of the heart recognizable from her appearance. The second narrator of the novel, who remains unnamed, is brought in to tell Nanon's story after her death. She or he writes: "I once had the occasion to see the Marquise of Franqueville at Bourges, where she had business. She struck me by her distinguished appearance under her peasant coiffure, which she never wanted to stop wearing and which made one think of those royal heads of the Middle Ages" (354). Thus has Nanon become "royal" to those around her. Through *Nanon* George Sand reiterates one of the central points of her philosophy: Titles and status by birth are meaningless abstractions, for true nobility comes from the heart and mind, and genes play a very small role in its creation. The blurring and crossing of class lines, which is a major theme in much of Sand's fiction, here receives a new and deeper twist: In *Nanon*, it is the fact that the hero and heroine have both incorporated all three social classes within themselves and cast them off to become "French" in the truest sense of the word that motivates the novel. In Sand's ideal world, the new France of the Industrial Revolution and the rise of great family financial empires will be led by people such as Nanon and Emilien. Thus, the Revolution will have liberated all classes to allow the best and brightest to rise to the top.

These exciting and striking reversals are accompanied by the radical alteration in the financial status of Nanon, resulting in the establishment of a woman-dominated business dynasty, the first I know of in the French novel. Nanon receives her first economics lesson from her great-uncle, who, having saved enough to buy her one sheep, tells her: "If you make it eat well, if you don't lose it, if you keep its pen well, it will become beautiful, and with the money that it will be worth next year, I will buy you two, and four the next year" (3). This sage advice becomes a model for the young Nanon, who, through shrewd management and an instinct for profit making, carefully lays the foundation for a financial empire. Her skills are sharpened in the management of the monastery and the hideaway retreat. However, her opportunity to become a businesswoman arrives only when she returns to the monastery alone after Emilien has joined the revolutionary forces. She leaves behind "the poem of my first youth" to achieve "a very set goal" (251). That goal is to become rich; she inquires: "Couldn't I become, if not rich, at least assured a small fortune that would allow me to accept Emilien's condition, whether good or bad, without scruples and without humiliation?" (263). She sets about achieving this goal with characteristic determination, beginning by converting the small sum made from the sale of crops to silver because of the rapid devaluation of paper money. She then allows people to work the fields of the monastery for a fee, forming a plan to buy the property from Costejoux, improve it, and make her fortune. Her ascent is rapid, as she learns to buy low and sell high, taking advantage of political events and making a profit in the wool business. She purchases the monastery on time and with interest, but when she expresses her wish to put the property in Emilien's name, Costejoux makes explicit the thrust of the novel: It is the woman who has the business head and hands; he says, "I see the affair as secure only when it is in your hands" (271). Enriched by her inheritance of 25,000 francs from the prior, Nanon founds her financial empire, her gift to her beloved Emilien and their progeny. As the second narrator says: "She had acquired, by her intelligent management and that of her husband and her sons, a rather considerable fortune, which they had always used nobly and which she took pleasure in saying that she had begun with one sheep" (352).

According to Hannah Arendt, "It was necessity, the urgent needs of the people, that unleashed the terror and sent the revolution to its doom,"[8] and Paulo Freire speaks of the awakening of critical consciousness in "the people" as the key to a successful revolution.[9] In George Sand's novel of revolution, however, neither "la Terreur" nor the development of consciousness reaches the peasant to any significant degree. However, Sand saw what few of her contemporaries did; that is, how the triumph of the wretched as a collective unit meant personal triumph for the smart, resourceful peasant, even for a woman. Sand's other heroines—Edmée, who saves a man by the force of her will and love; Consuelo, the apostle of moral dignity; and Tonine (*La Ville noire*), who seems to be an early sketch of Nanon—all offer the reader a vision of the independent Sandian woman, but Nanon goes beyond them to represent the liberation of the social classes, the female gender, and France. Thus, *Nanon* is a quintessential Sandian novel, an argument for both the unity of Sand's vision and the worth of her later works, directly expressing the philosophy of its creator: optimistic, liberating, and—even without battles, generals, and larger-than-life martyrs—profoundly revolutionary.

NOTES

1. Patricia Thompson, *George Sand and the Victorians* (New York: Columbia University Press, 1977), 217.

2. André Maurois, *Lélia: The Life of George Sand*, trans. Gerard Hopkins (New York: Harper and Brothers, 1953), 453.

3. Emile Zola, *Les Oeuvres complètes d'Emile Zola* (Paris: Bernouard, 1927–1929), 123.

4. Victor Hugo, *Quatre-vingt-treize* (Paris: Garnier Frères, 1963), 135; this and all subsequent translations are those of the author.

5. Ibid., 254.

6. George Sand, *Nanon* (Paris: Editions d'Aujourd'hui, 1976), 118. Subsequent quotations are from this edition and are cited in the text by page number.

7. Tony Tanner, *Adultery in the Novel: Contract and Transgression* (Baltimore: Johns Hopkins University Press, 1979), 23.

8. Hannah Arendt, *On Revolution* (New York: Viking Press, 1965), 55.

9. Paulo Freire, *Pedagogy of the Oppressed* (New York: Seabury Press, 1975).

16

Reasons of the Heart: George Sand, Flaubert, and the Commune

Murray Sachs

Nothing inspires greater admiration among readers of the delightful Sand-Flaubert correspondence than the forthright candor with which the two friends managed to express to each other their many disagreements and differences of opinion about life and love, literature and politics, without compromising in the slightest the tone of genuine affection that pervades their ten years of epistolary exchange. In a letter of 1869, George Sand herself suggested, with shrewd insight, why they were able to differ so amicably: "We are, I believe, the two most different workers in existence; but since that is the way we like each other, all is well. Since we think of each other at the same moment, it must be because each of us needs his opposite; we each complete our own self by identifying ourselves at times with what is not our own self."[1]

There is, however, one six-month period during their ten-year correspondence when, in the judgment of some critics at least, the rapport between the two friends was less than perfect, and when the telltale signs of tension between them appeared in their letters. This was the period between March and October 1871, when the violent episode of the abortive revolution called the Commune, and its bitter aftermath, imposed itself so rudely on the attention of both letter-writers, wringing from each expressions of great pain and despair over the ugliness of those public events. Although both were plainly shocked by what was happening, Francis Steegmuller's reading of the letters of that period is that what Flaubert wrote to George Sand was so "harsh and deliberately insensitive toward her and what he well knew her feelings to be" that George Sand was offended by his letters and showed her displeasure by the "unwonted infrequency" of her replies.[2] In the same passage, Steegmuller claims that when, in a September letter, Flaubert ventured the observation that she lacked the capacity to hate the perpetrators of atrocities during the Commune, George Sand "found his call for 'hatred' intolerable," and replied in the form of an impassioned newspaper article called "Réponse à un ami," in which she gave her reasons for rejecting his call. Claude Tricotel, in his book on the Flaubert-Sand friendship, also interprets George Sand's reaction to Flaubert's criticism of her inability to hate as an angry one, "That says a good deal more than George Sand can bear to read on the subject!" Tricotel says of her feelings upon reading Flaubert's letter.[3] He adds that her famous reply to Flaubert's criticism, "Réponse à un ami," cannot be read as an effort to change Flaubert's mind, but only as a public declaration of how irreconcilably far apart the two had become in their opinions: "How would it be possible for George Sand to persuade Flaubert? They are not just different, they are two opposites, two irreconcilable visions of the world, two lives unfolding in two opposing directions!" (164). The same point about irreconcilable differences is made by Gérard Roubichou, who insists that "Réponse à un ami" was written expressly to underline the great distance between their political views, and to emphasize that Flaubert had misconstrued her position. Roubichou correctly points out, however, that a spirit of conciliation, and not anger, animates George Sand's attempt to set the public record straight in "Réponse à un ami," for she was anxious, above all, not to turn their difference of opinion into a dispute.[4] As she remarked in her letter of September 16 to Flaubert, informing him of the article she had just written, "This letter *to a friend* does not specify you even by an initial, for I do not wish to argue with you in public" (Jacobs, 349).

Roubichou is thus in agreement with Tricotel and Steegmuller in finding Flaubert's remarks provocative enough to have threatened the friendship, but credits George Sand with the coolheaded forebearance to have found a way to correct Flaubert's misconstructions while at the same time calming the troubled waters of their relationship. The clear underlying consensus, however, in these three critical judgments of the state of the Sand-Flaubert correspondence during and after the Commune, is that feelings between them were running so high, on the political issues of the day; as to have reached a dangerous state of crisis by September 1871, and that the publication of George Sand's eloquent article, "Réponse à un ami," was, at the least, proof that the crisis was threateningly real, and perhaps was also the means of its resolution.

That critical consensus seems to me, after careful review of the existing documents, to have exaggerated into a crisis what was originally no more than a temporary failure of communication between those two remarkable correspondents, a failure traceable to a difference in temperament rather than to any serious difference of opinion over politics or world views. The often overlooked truth is that, so far as the Commune itself was concerned, the two friends found themselves in a rare state of agreement in their assessment of all the gruesome details as they unfolded. Both were plunged into a deep depression as early as March 1871, when the revolt of the Commune began. In the ensuing two months, both found the behavior of Republicans and Communards alike reprehensible, and both despaired for the future of France. In letter after letter, from March through July, they each expressed essentially the same sense of horror and pain, as the brutal sequence of events developed—with this one difference, that Flaubert tended to rail against the medieval barbarism of all Parisians, while Sand preferred to lament the shattering of her personal ideals and complained of being too depressed to work. Typical of their exchanges that spring and summer is Flaubert's letter to George Sand on June 11, 1871, and George Sand's reply three days later. Flaubert, just back from a visit to Paris, describes his reaction in these terms:

> The smell of the dead bodies disgusts me less than the miasmas of egotism coming out of every mouth. The sight of the ruins is nothing compared to the immense stupidity of the Parisians. With very rare exceptions, *everyone* seemed to me as mad as a hatter. Half of the population wants to strangle the other half, which in turn has the same designs on the first half. . . . I assure you it is enough to make one despair of the human race (Jacobs, 335–336).

A few paragraphs later, he sums up the effect of the whole trip: "My brief trip to Paris has troubled me very deeply. I shall have difficulty settling down to work again" (Jacobs, 336). George Sand replies, expressing just as much pain, but without the universal denunciations favored by Flaubert to relieve his feelings: "What will be the backlash from this infamous Commune? Isidore [i.e., Napoleon III returning to power], or Henry V [i.e., the restoration of the monarchy], or the regime of the incendiaries, brought back by anarchy? I who have so much patience with my own species, and who have for so long taken a rosy view of the world, I no longer see anything but darkness." In a later paragraph, she assesses her own state of mind: "Still, it is not good to despair. I shall make a great effort, and perhaps I shall recover my equitable and patient self. But at the moment I cannot. I am as troubled as you, and I dare not speak, nor think, nor write, so fearful am I of irritating the gaping wounds in every soul" (Jacobs, 337–338). Similar exchanges had occurred in March and April, and another, just as desperate sounding, would occur in July.

In September, they picked up the thread in the same vein, with Flaubert pronouncing global condemnations of everyone, in accordance with his temperament, and Sand sounding discouraged and depressed, in keeping with hers. In their judgment of the Commune, however, both were careful to favor no side, and neither ever wavered from their common opinion that all sides were to be denounced. All their letters of this period reveal the same truth: The horrifying spectacle of the Commune had been a source of profound suffering for both of them. Underlying that suffering was a common but unarticulated cause: For both, the Commune was an especially unbearable nightmare because it resembled so uncannily a reprise of the events of 1848, that moment in French history that, for their entire generation as well as for each of them individually, represented the epitome of withered hopes for the future and the triumph of humanity's basest instincts. The Commune, coming as it did hard on the heels of the humiliations of the Franco-Prussian War, battered their sensibilities with a particularly violent impact precisely because it forced them to relive again the gut-wrenching catastrophe of 1848 which still haunted their memory.

To appreciate fully how the Commune must have affected them, one must recall briefly what 1848 had meant to each separately, because at that time they did not know each other. George Sand, then in her socialist phase, has been exhilarated by the Revolution, which overthrew the July Monarchy and established the Second Republic. She was directly involved and active in Republican decision making in the following weeks. However, exhilaration quickly turned to disillusionment as she saw the Republican leaders fighting among themselves for the spoils of power, and disillusionment turned to horror during the violent June days, when many of her closest friends and allies were killed, jailed, or driven into exile. Numb with pain after those events—as she put it, in a letter to a friend in July of 1848, "I have so black a view of the future that I feel a great urge and a great need to blow my brains out."[5] George Sand retreated that summer to her country home in Nohant to digest the lessons of the bitter political education she had undergone in a few short months. In her depressed state she stayed aloof from politics, and met even the coup d'état of 1851 with silence. It therefore came as a painful shock to her when she was castigated in the press during the 1850s, by friends and foes alike, for turning her back on public life and for cynically abandoning her principles and her friends. Small wonder, then, with such an experience haunting her memory, that in the aftermath of the Commune in 1871, when she learned that Flaubert and other friends were interpreting her denunciation of the Communards as evidence of a change of position away from her humanitarian and democratic ideals, she rushed into print with a reaffirmation of her belief, in spite of the ugliness of the Commune, in the political principle of equality and in the ultimate political triumph of the common people. That was certainly the import and purpose of her impassioned essay, "Réponse à un ami." Replying to Flaubert's charge that she could not hate was no more than a convenient pretext. What she obviously feared was being accused again, as after 1848, of betraying her friends and abandoning the principles and the causes she always claimed to support.

For Flaubert, 1848 had not been so very different, even though he had played no public role in those events as George Sand had. He too had been elated when the barricades went up in February, and rushed to Paris with his friend Louis Bouilhet to witness the triumph of a revolution. He too was soon bitterly disillusioned by the brutal violence of the June days, and was angered even more by Bonaparte's coup d'état in 1851. It is true, however, that in the 1850s, Flaubert's letters seldom spoke of politics. In the immediate wake of his disillusionment in 1848, and because he had suffered grievous personal losses in those same months (the deaths of his best friend and his sister), he seemed to retreat within himself, as George Sand had done. He took to dismissing politics as the enemy of art, and to denouncing all governments and all politicians, whether on the right or on the left, as contemptible. By the 1860s, however, his literary art itself began to manifest the residual fascination that the Revolution of 1848 had left in his memory. Gradually he became obsessed with the idea that 1848 was clearly the decisive and formative event of his generation. That idea emerged plainly in his novel of 1869, *L'Éducation sentimentale*, which devoted its famous climactic segment—nearly a third of the book—to the detailed depiction of the events of 1848. Even earlier, according to recent scholarly studies, he had made a careful study of the pattern of events in that year in order to have a convincing model to follow when describing the revolt of the mercenaries against ancient Carthage in his novel *Salammbô*, which was published in 1862.[6] Later, in the 1870s, still unable to close his personal book on 1848—perhaps because it had come back to haunt him again during the Commune?—he evoked the whole upsetting series of events again in the sixth chapter of his unfinished novel, *Bouvard et Pécuchet*. Most interesting of all, in all three of his fictional treatments of the Revolution of 1848, he invariably depicted both the right and the left with biting political satire, yet always included one character who is imbued with revolutionary idealism, who grows in moral stature, and who protests, by some gesture or statement, against the corruption among all elements of the political spectrum. That corruption, moreover, obscures the Revolution's goals, and ends by submerging everyone in a violent bloodbath. The comportment Flaubert attributes to Mâtho in *Salammbô*, to Dussardier in *L'Éducation sentimentale*, and to Pécuchet in *Bouvard et Pécuchet* during the revolutionary scenes, provides persuasive evidence that Flaubert himself, in spite of his reputed conservatism in politics and his often angry anarchistic rhetoric, must have initially been in genuine sympathy with the revolutionary ideals of 1848. In 1848 he was still that youthful Flaubert who had written to his friend Louise Colet in 1846 a declaration of his personal revolutionary spirit in these words: "In all politics, there is only one thing I can understand, and that is a riot."[7]

To be sure, Flaubert would eventually be appalled by revolutionary behavior and would therefore suffer a personally agonizing disillusionment in 1848 from which he would never completely recover. However, he never abandoned that essentially revolutionary attitude in his own nature that made him the opponent of authority, in all its forms, whether political, religious, social, or philosophical. That is why, even up to the year of his death, he repeatedly proclaimed himself to be "a revolutionary to the core."[8] That is surely also the most plausible explanation for his raging denunciations of the Communards throughout the summer of 1871: It was not so much that he was opposed to their politics as that he could not forgive them for having squandered a new opportunity for revolutionary change by their primitive, medieval behavior: "As for the Commune," he wrote to George Sand in April 1871, "It is the last manifestation of the Middle Ages. The last? Let's hope so!" (Jacobs, 332). A deep, old wound, freshly reopened, made him cry out in pain in every letter in the spring and summer of 1871.

There can be little doubt, therefore, given the history of their separate entanglements with the Revolution of 1848, that George Sand and Flaubert were reacting similarly, with mutual sympathy, to the outbreak of the Commune in March 1871, for each was well aware of the other's lingering pain left over from 1848. They had after all, discussed 1848 together at considerable length only a few years earlier, at Flaubert's request, since Flaubert collected as many personal reminiscences of 1848 as he could while composing *L'Éducation sentimentale*. However, the difference in temperament between them, which made George Sand sink into depression over events while Flaubert raged and denounced the whole human species to relieve his pain, imparted a strange and unaccustomed tone to their correspondence throughout that spring and summer of 1871 and into September, when the sudden tension erupted in their relationship. In every exchange between March and September, side by side with their expressions of warm mutual regard and concern, there occurred passages in which each vented feelings about the Commune that seemed not to be addressed to the other but rather to answer some private need. Nor did those emotional outbursts evoke any response or comment from the other, as though each wished to show, by silence, respect for the other's grief. Whole segments of each letter, in their sporadic correspondence of that period, took on the air of a poignant and oddly affecting dialogue of the deaf, in which neither seemed to take notice of what the other had to say on the politics of the day. The only substantive communications in their letters in that period were on matters of work and family.

It was Flaubert who, early in September, inadvertently breached their tacit agreement to respect by silence each other's pained outcries on political issues. Encouraged to believe, on the evidence of her recently published remarks deploring the behavior of the working class, that George Sand was beginning to change her political views, Flaubert ventured, in a letter of September 6, to express approval of what he thought her article was saying, and went on, in his next letter two days later, to urge her to take the logical step of denouncing the proletariat as just as much the enemy of liberty and justice as the bourgeoisie or the nobility.[9] Flaubert's urging, together with the letters she received from other friends, made George Sand realize that her article on the working class was being widely misinterpreted.[10] George Sand's answer to Flaubert's urging was, of course, her "Réponse à un ami," in which, as she wisely explained to Flaubert in a letter of September 16: "I spell out for you my reasons for *suffering* and for continuing to *desire*. . . . You will see that my grief is a part of me, and that I do not have the option to believe that progress is but a dream" (Jacobs, 349). In that fashion, she gently reminded her friend that her recent political faith in progress, as expressed in "Réponse à un ami," was a reason of the heart and not of the mind. That Pascalian distinction—"the heart has its reasons which reason does not know"—she invoked again soon thereafter, applying it this time to Flaubert's comments as well when Flaubert complained, after "Réponse à un ami" was published in October, that the image of the "friend" discernible in her article was hardly a likeable one, and that it made him out to be an egregiously egocentric person. She knew very well, she reminded him, "that in your case the heart is not always in agreement with the mind, a disagreement into which, for that matter, all of us can be forced to tumble at any instant." In other words, she insisted, they both had their reasons of the heart, distinct from reasons of the mind on all matters, and those reasons of the heart must always be respected and cherished, especially between friends, "since friendship also has its mysteries, without the storms of personality" (Jacobs, 352). With that wise and sensitive formulation, George Sand was able to put to rest the temporary tension that had arisen between them in September, making it possible for the two friends, like the loves in a Molière comedy after their traditional *dépit amoureux*, to go forward in their relationship with renewed and deepened affection, strengthened by their mutual recognition of their very personal "reasons of the heart." Thus it is possible to conclude that the inspiring friendship between George Sand and Gustave Flaubert did not really undergo a crisis in September 1871, but only a brief misunderstanding that paradoxically enough brought to the surface emotional areas of mutual sympathy they had not previously explored, and that served to fortify their friendship even more against future storms.[11] What seemed at the time to be their most dangerous disagreement actually made them closer than ever, in heart if not in mind.

NOTES

1. Gustave Flaubert–George Sand, *Correspondance*. Texte édité, préfacé et annoté par Alphonse Jacobs (Paris: Flammarion, 1981), 213. All subsequent citations from the Flaubert–Sand correspondence will be from this edition, identified as *Jacobs*, and page references will be given within the text, in parentheses, immediately after each citation; this and all subsequent translations are those of the author.

2. See *The Letters of Gustave Flaubert, 1857–1880*. Selected, edited and translated by Francis Steegmuller (Cambridge, Mass.: The Belknap Press of Harvard University Press, 1982), 181.

3. See Claude Tricotel, *Comme deux troubadours: Histoire de l'amitié Flaubert–Sand* (Paris: SEDES, 1978), 163.

4. Gérard Roubichou's description of "Réponse à un ami" runs as follows: "Confronted with Flaubert's sarcasm, . . . George Sand notes the distance between them, underlines their differences ('Oh! we really do differ!'), but makes the effort to keep up the dialogue; the direct tone, the (literally) *ad hominem* argument both indicate a clear desire to define herself, to affirm her own position relative to the other, even while giving him the opportunity to draw nearer, to comprehend." See Roubichou, "Comme c'est triste, l'histoire!" *George Sand Newsletter* (Hofstra University, Hempstead, N.Y.), 3, no. 2 (Fall/Winter 1980), 3.

5. George Sand, *Correspondance*, edited by Georges Lubin (Paris: Garnier, 1964–), 8:532.

6. See especially Anne Green, *Flaubert and the Historical Novel: Salammbô Reassessed* (Cambridge: Cambridge University Press, 1982). Green documents in detail, in chapters 4 and 5, Flaubert's utilization of the events of 1848 to structure his account of the mercenaries' revolt against Carthage, and remarks, on page 74 of her study, that "the revolution of 1848 had the most profound and long-lasting influence on Flaubert in spite of his apparent indifference at the time. The intensity of his reaction to the Commune in 1871, which he saw as a repetition of the bitter fighting of the June days, is a measure of his awareness of the importance of the 'rendez-vous manqué' of 1848."

7. Gustave Flaubert, *Correspondance* (Paris: Conard, 1926–1954), 1:225.

8. Flaubert refers to himself as "a revolutionary to the core" in a letter of 1876 to the Princesse Mathilde (Conard edition of the *Correspondance*, 7:330), and, on his fifty-eighth birthday, not six months before his death, he wrote to his niece Caroline, commenting on an incident in which a priest had been forbidden to lecture on divorce in the following terms: "It is for that reason that authority is detestable in its essence. I ask what good authority has ever done in the world. That's why your good old uncle is a revolutionary to the core" (Conard edition, 8:335).

9. George Sand's article on the deterioration of working class mores, published on September 5, 1871, in *Le Temps*, was actually a piece she had composed, but not published, back in 1860. Flaubert did not know that, and like others of her friends, took it to be a pointed

commentary on, and explanation of, the violent behavior of the Communards the previous spring.

10. For a full account of the misunderstanding that developed over George Sand's September article about the workers in *Le Temps*, see Jacobs, Flaubert–Sand *Correspondance*, 342–349, including the editor's informative commentary and notes.

11. What the two friends learned from each other, as a result of their "misunderstanding" of September 1871, is perhaps best illustrated by George Sand's letter of October 25, 1871, to Flaubert, in which she admitted that the revolutionaries she had known were basically unprincipled types (ibid., 357), and Flaubert's letter of November 14, 1871, to George Sand, in which he took rueful note of the fact that, in contrast to her kind and gentle temperament, he was too often given to irrational anger against the world (ibid., 359). Theirs had perhaps been less a "dialogue of the deaf" than it had seemed at the time.

17

Freedom Smuggler: George Sand and the German Vormärz

Gisela Schlientz

On April 30, 1840, Heinrich Heine, the Paris correspondent for the *Augsburger Allgemeine Zeitung*, reported to Germany from the French capital:

> Last evening George Sand's drama, *Cosima*, had its premiere at the Théâtre Français. One can have no idea of the extent to which the high society of the capital, everyone here who is prominent through rank, birth, wealth or vice, has gone in the past several weeks to attend this performance. The reputation of the author is so great that curiosity has been stretched to the breaking-point. But it is not merely curiosity; every other sort of interest or passion has also come into play. This audacious author should do public penance for her "sacrilegious and immoral precepts."[1]

However, this first attempt at drama by George Sand failed. The piece did not arouse so much as a hint of scandal in Paris. Nevertheless, Heine's report for the *Allgemeine Zeitung*, at that time a very influential paper in Germany, provides a good sketch of the image of George Sand—either monstrous or sublime, depending on one's point of view—that was then held by her contemporaries. Heine, though he himself was on very friendly terms with George Sand, knew just what tone to take to make the strongest impression on his German readers.

George Sand, then just thirty-six years old, was at this time already equally famous and infamous on both sides of the Rhine. Since 1832 she had already published more than a dozen novels, but it was the notoriety of her eccentricities, so disconcerting to her male contemporaries, rather than her novels, that had crossed the border by express mail. The German intelligentsia was well informed about what was going on in Paris.

This German interest in their neighbor to the west was based not only on traditional social concerns but also on current political issues. Following the wars of liberation against Napoleon, Germany, whose thirty-eight principalities were loosely linked in the German Confederation, was dominated by the oppressive Metternich Restoration. In France, however, the July Revolution had given new life to liberal ideas. The political and literary avant-garde of Germany, the "Men of the Movement," now looked toward France. Heine, living in self-imposed exile in Paris since 1831, very quickly became the primary voice in this Franco-German exchange of ideas.

It was in this intellectual climate that the first translation of a work by George Sand appeared in German in 1834. It was *Lélia*, the young author's third novel, which had been published in Paris the previous year.[2] This selection suggests that the laws of the marketplace functioned then pretty much as they do today, for *Lélia* created not only a sensation, as had both earlier novels, it also created a scandal. In *Lélia*, the vague malaise of the era was sharpened into an indictment of marriage, the church, and the whole social order that left women a choice only between marital submission and prostitution. In France, the resulting storm of indignation over the heroine (and her creator), who dared to talk about her feminine needs and experiences in love, was overwhelming.

Amazingly, however, the novel was received in Germany with no noticeable uproar. One young literary critic, Karl Gutzkow, went so far as to quibble over the excess of allegorical references in *Lélia*. This tendency, he thought, often masked "the real carnality" of the novel. He would have preferred a novel written "in stronger tones," but he praised its magnificent style and concluded by asking, "Is it possible that a woman could transplant herself right into the innermost circle of the thought of the movement? I do not know of a single sequence in this novel which betrays the fact that it originates from a person who wears a petticoat."[3]

A few months after the appearance of this article, in which the critic had revealed himself as a very one-sided interpreter of Sand's novels, Gutzkow published a novel of his own, *Wally, die Zweiflerin* (*Wally, the Doubtress*).[4] The title alone, as well as the characteristics of the primary feminine figure, make it clear that Gutzkow had taken his inspiration from *Lélia*. In a later prologue, he himself confirmed the relationship between the two heroines while not actually stating that the two were similar: "Lélia is a beautiful ideal, which, had she been painted by Titian, would have looked magnificent as a painting on the wall. Poor Wally is but a Cinderella of reality."[5]

The comparisons between Wally and Lélia are limited in a basic sense by the different uses of religious criticism, which in Gutzkow is the central theme but in Sand has only incidental meaning. It sufficed, however, to alert those who supported the Metternich system and who thus opposed the new liberal tendencies emanating from France. In September 1835, one of their best-known spokesmen, Wolfgang Menzel, the editor of the very influential literary journal the *Stuttgarter Morgenblatt*, denounced the novel by Gutzkow, and with it the whole group of liberal authors who were later to label themselves Young Germany, as a "school of the most audacious immorality and most infamous lies. . . . Could there be any more arrogant presumption than for these people who have caught the French disease to call themselves Young Germany?"[6]

After these abusive attacks the authorities intervened. First Gutzkow's novel was banned and confiscated; then Gutzkow was sentenced to four weeks imprisonment on the grounds of "Defamation of the Church and of the moral order." Meanwhile, a virtual literary civil war raged in Germany. On one side of the front, representatives of the government and of the clergy thundered against the "rehabilitation of the flesh" as the source of all anarchy; on the other side, the Liberals and the Young Germans returned fire with their protests and apologetics.

The authors Karl Gutzkow, Heinrich Laube, Theodore Mundt, Ludolf Weinbarg, and Heinrich Heine, the last of whom was recognized as the model and leader of Young Germany, wanted the word "young" to be understood not in its biological sense but in the context of a new political and aesthetic program. They called themselves "Zeitschriftsteller" (Authors of [political] journals), and campaigned against the provincialism and philistinism of this Biedermeier era. The editorial offices of the journals they founded now became their fortresses in this battle of ideas.

After her debut with *Lélia*, the new novels of George Sand were appearing in German at an ever-increasing rate, and more and more often, they appeared not only in one edition but in several editions simultaneously. At that time there was no copyright agreement between Germany and France; any German publisher was free to reprint or translate Sand's works.

In spite of the publication prohibition and the censorship, the Young Germans were increasingly able to find legal loopholes for their writing through the existence of the multiplicity of different German principalities, each with its own versions of the laws, for it was in their political interest to continue to foster the reputation of George Sand. Mundt and Laube admired the powerful eloquence in the emancipation literature of the French woman. They understood, however, that morality, regarded as the only true womanly virtue in Germany, could not be touched, even though they themselves ridiculed this view as "sanctimonious." They strove, therefore, to purge from George Sand's reputation the pernicious accusations of immorality, so damaging to their own political position. Instead they tried to emphasize her "fine femininity," and to direct attention to the aesthetic merits and high ideals of her works. Laube, who published a series of portraits of Sand heroines, saw in her "the modern priestess, whom one must revere even if one does not share her views."[7]

The opposition, those upright champions of orthodoxy, was not so lenient. Wolfgang Menzel, whom Ludwig Börne, a very prominent exile living in Paris, called the "devourer of the French," was tireless in his efforts as their spokesman: "We do not share this admiration. We find the unspeakable expletives and pipe smoking in Madame Dudevant's novels nothing but the basest, most despicable vulgarity. Her novels are swarming with filthy offenses and lewdness."[8]

Nothing more than rumors of her notoriety reached George Sand on the other side of the Rhine. She did not know her German public, who translated her books, or even where they were published. She had never traveled to Germany and she spoke no German. Nevertheless, it was easy for her to make the acquaintance of many of the German authors of her time. Either they were already living in Paris as émigrés, like Heine, or they came during the Vormärz (the name given to the period of one or two decades preceding the German revolutions of March 1848) for at least a fairly long visit in the city that the intellectual avant-garde of Germany regarded as "the cradle of the new Europe."

A visit with George Sand was considered an obligatory part of the political tour of Paris for these "People of the Movement." It was usually Heine who presented them to his "chère cousine." August Lewald, the journalist and author, came in 1836, followed four years later by Heinrich Laube, and in 1842 by Karl Gutzkow. Being the object of this rather sensation-seeking sort of travel journalism, however, made Sand increasingly more cautious; it became more and more difficult to gain admission to the "most poignant phenomenon in the broad field of modern French literature."[9] Indeed many "sincere German democrats," such as Georg Herwegh, waited in vain for an introduction.[10]

It was, without a doubt, primarily through Heine that George Sand came to know the literature of this neighboring country, which was still unknown to her. In the 1840s he was a regular visitor to her salon, but the closer the Revolution approached, the more she distanced herself from her commitment to the social question and from her friend Heine, who tended to lean more toward freedom than equality.

Among the women writers of the Vormärz era, many managed to reach Paris but not one succeeded in reaching their famous French colleague. As early as 1836, August Lewald reported that the names of Rahel Varnhagen and Bettina von Arnim, "these new and so brilliant personages," were entirely unknown to George Sand.[11] About Rahel Varnhagen, around whom the Young Germans and even Heine had created a veritable cult, not a trace is to be found in Sand. This was not the case, however, with Bettina von Arnim. Through her books and her courageous defense of the politically maligned and the socially disadvantaged, she had made a name for herself even in France. In her George Sand recognized a kindred spirit for whom she felt respect and sympathy. The mysterious appearance of a letter from Sand to von Arnim in the German press in 1845, however, made it clear that even for a woman like von Arnim, an association with George Sand was not without danger.[12]

This could be one of the reasons why the Young German women writers, in contrast to their male colleagues, hardly ever sided publicly with Sand. At the same time, the influence of Sand on their novels, on their treatment of sexual and marital problems, and later their treatment of social criticism, cannot be overlooked. They constituted the first generation of women writers in Germany who in their works did not merely reflect the social tensions of the time but also spoke out on matters of concern to themselves. This "spring of German women's literature," which appeared about 1840, had complex origins. Quite obvious is their close temporal and thematic relationship with Sand that allows us to speak of them as her successors. The three best-known authors, Ida Gräfin Hahn-Hahn, Fanny Lewald, and Luise Mühlbach, were each apostrophized by their contemporaries as the "German George Sand."[13]

Actually, in this phase of her work, George Sand differed from the Young

German authors in the revolutionary consistency of her thought. Her thinking was not in terms of bourgeois reforms; her thought was more utopian. She was not interested merely in improving bourgeois marriage; rather, she looked for a far-reaching change in the concept of the relationship between husband and wife, with the ultimate goal of a greater equality and justice among all human beings. On this account she was not understood by many of the Young Germans such as, for example, Gutzkow, who saw in her only the "free woman" who celebrated her emancipation of the heart only as an emancipation of the flesh.

For a long time George Sand's literary standing in Germany remained undisputed, and her characterization as the "first living writer of France" was long generally accepted. Theodore Mundt, since 1842 a professor in Berlin, had contributed to this concept in his *History of Contemporary Literature*.[14] Another contributor was Laube, who broadcast his belief that since Jean-Jacques Rousseau and François-Auguste-René de Chateaubriand, nothing had been written in the French language of such truth, of such power, and of such beauty as the novels of George Sand.[15] After the individual editions had appeared (often up to five different translations of any given work), the first collected works of George Sand began to show up on the German book market. For instance, in 1843, the Weigand Press in Leipzig issued a series of French classics in an edition of eighty-seven volumes.

In contrast to the Young Germans, the German Democrats and the Socialists, who had been obliged to withdraw to the more liberal France of the bourgeois-king Louis Philippe during the Vormärz, valued George Sand as a revolutionary writer and her work as the poetry of their movement. Arnold Ruge, the editor of the *Hallische Jahrbücher*, found the "love sophistry" and the "sunstroke of passion" in Sand's novels not to his taste. What was important to him was clearly formulated in his foreword to the Weigand collected works, "the tendencies of Sand are attacked in France as well as in Germany. . . . She cuts sharply into everything, she dares to go right to the bottom of every phenomenon and every issue. . . . Sand has the most complete insight into the political situation."[16]

When Arnold Ruge and Karl Marx lost their permits to publish their journals, they too moved to Paris in the year 1843. They hoped to persuade George Sand to work with them on their newly founded "German-French Yearbooks." Ruge approached her in March 1844, but in vain, for the only volume of the yearbooks appeared without a contribution from Sand, and in fact without a contribution from any of the French Socialists.[17] Whether George Sand and Karl Marx ever met in the circles of the Opposition which they both frequented, we do not know. He was then an unknown young editor from Germany; she was a European celebrity. In the historical library in Moscow there is a copy of his work, *The Poverty of Philosophy*, which appeared in 1847, with a dedication handwritten by Marx himself to George Sand: "Madame George Sand, de la part d'auteur." This work ends with a quotation from George Sand's novel *Jean Ziska*: "Struggle or death, bloody war or nothingness. This is the inexorable question."[18]

The answer, a preliminary one, as indeed are all answers in the history of humankind, came in the year 1848 with the outbreak of revolution, in February in

France and in March in Germany. Fanny Lewald, attracted to Paris, as were so many like-minded Germans, read the "Lettres au peuple" of George Sand and immediately wanted to translate them into German: "But nothing would be gained from it. Our conditions differ so completely from those here that these letters for the masses would remain ineffectual . . . and the powerful, transcendent impression of her prophetic words would be lost."[19]

These "completely different conditions" had the effect that the uprisings in Germany were suppressed even more swiftly than in France. In Germany, the postrevolutionary suppression had a paralyzing effect on public life. The active opposition was expelled from the country; the Young German writers conformed and came around to the support of the establishment; the Young German women writers became either bigoted or domesticated, with Fanny Lewald the single exception. The "Smuggling of Freedom" between the two neighboring countries, in which George Sand had played so active a part, lost its philanthropic impetus: The precious contraband of ideas came to a standstill.[20]

Nonetheless, George Sand's novels continued to be widely read in Germany. A long article, "La France vue à travers l'Allemagne," appeared in the popular Paris journal *Illustration* in August 1858. It stated:

> The two best-known names in contemporary French literature on the other side of the Rhine are without a doubt Victor Hugo and George Sand. The justifiable fame which George Sand has earned here cannot even compare with the enthusiasm she evokes in Berlin, in Weimar, in Heidelberg, in Stuttgart and Frankfurt, and even in the smallest villages in Germany. And what is remarkable about it is the greater enthusiasm of the women readers. . . . For this reason, the illustrious novelist's influence, particularly in Prussia, is a fact of life. This [popularity] derives not so much, as one might believe, from the more or less dubious maxims of domestic emancipation, but rather from her magnanimous ideas of political renewal, on the resolute striving for a freer future.[21]

At no time did George Sand exert a greater weight or influence in Germany than in the Vormärz era and the following decade. This applies to the recognition accorded her literary works as well as to the effect of her political ideas, not to mention the emancipating effect of her personality. All the same, the quotation from *Illustration* is not the only evidence that the public of the German Biedermeier era (whether male or female, conservative or liberal, or even socialist) reacted to the "women's liberation," the key feminist demand in the work and in the person of the author, either with opposition or at least with reservations.

In the second half of the century, George Sand's radiance gradually faded, although her new works were still eagerly translated. Literary historians, and above all Julian Schmidt, although no longer ignoring George Sand, now began the deprecation of her works with the familiar denunciations of the author's morals.[22] In literature, both fictional and biographical, George Sand has long haunted the scene as the synonym for the emancipated woman, the *femme libre*, the evil specter of all honest housewives. This was a specter with which, according to Lange and Bäumer, the German women's movement had to struggle for the next twenty years.[23] This negative image, sharpened by the Franco-Prussian War of 1870, became even more grotesque in the years following the war. When, during the winter of the conflict, an open letter attributed to George Sand concerning the political situation appeared in the French press, Dr. Ferdinand Haas responded to it with a piece entitled *German Reflections*, in which he asserted that George Sand, with her "undermining, desecrating literature," had exerted a pernicious influence on the spirit and character of the French people, and indeed on all civilized peoples, and claimed that the"works resulting from her infernally masterful hand" were in the end responsible for the defeat of her people.[24]

Fortunately, this rampant chauvinism did not completely destroy the refined tradition that had developed among the educated readers of Sand's novels. Shortly before her death, an editor of the *Gartenlaube*, a popular family magazine, visited George Sand and later honored the author and her work in a beautiful eulogy.

NOTES

1. Heinrich Heine, *Lutezia* (Frankfurt: Insel, 1959), 28ff. This and all subsequent translations in this chapter are by Nancy E. Rogers.
2. George Sand, *Lélia*, trans. Adolph Braun (Leipzig: Kayser, 1834).
3. Karl Gutzkow, "Lélia," *Phönix: Frühlingszeitung für Deutschland*, Literaturblatt 174 (May 25, 1835), 695.
4. Karl Gutzkow, *Wally, die Zweiflerin* (Mannheim: C. Löwenthal, 1835).
5. Karl Gutzkow, *Wally, die Zweiflerin*, ed. Günter Heinitz (Stuttgart: Reclam, 1979), preface of the 1852 edition, 144.
6. *Morgenblatt für gebildete Leser* 29 (Stuttgart: Cotta), Literaturblatt 93 and 94 (Sept. 11 and 14, 1835).
7. Heinrich Laube, *George Sands Frauenbilder* (Brussels: Belgische Gesellschaft des Buchhandels, 1845), xv.
8. *Morgenblatt für gebildete Leser* 34, Literaturblatt 31 (March 23, 1840), 34.
9. August Lewald, *Gesammelte Schriften* (Mannheim: Hoff, 1836–1837), 4:5.
10. See Victor Fleury, *Le poète Georges Herwegh* (Paris: E. Cornély, 1911), 74; and *Deutsche Revue* (April 1908), 43ff.
11. Lewald, *Schriften*, 21ff.
12. See George Sand, *Correspondance*, ed. Georges Lubin (Paris: Garnier, 1964–), 6:824ff.; and Ludwig Geiger, *Bettina von Arnim und Friedrich Wilhelm IV*, Ungedruckte Briefe und Aktenstücke (Frankfurt: Rütten und Loening, 1902), 82, 215ff.
13. See Marieluise Steinhauer, *Fanny Lewald, die deutsche George Sand* (Diss., Humboldt University, Berlin, 1837).
14. Theodor Mundt, *Geschichte der Literatur der Gegenwart* (Leipzig: M. Simion, 1853), 404ff.
15. Laube, *Frauenbilder*, 7.
16. Arnold Ruge, *Sämtliche Werke* (Mannheim: Grohe, 1847–1848), 3:358–378.
17. Sand, *Correspondance*, letter from Arnold Ruge to George Sand, March 11, 1844, 6:476ff.
18. George Sand, *Jean Zyska* [sic] (Paris: Michel Lévy Frères, 1884), 6.

19. Fanny Lewald, *Erinnerungen aus dem Jahr 1848* (Braunschweig: Fr. Vieweg, 1850), 1:97ff.

20. Karl Gutzkow, letter to Georg Büchner, March 17, 1835, quoted in Georg Büchner, *Sämtliche Werke und Briefe*, ed. Werner R. Lehmann (Hamburg: Wegner, 1967), 2:476.

21. Frédéric Morin, "La France vue à travers l'Allemagne. L'Opinion des Allemands sur nos poètes et sur nos romanciers. Considérations générales. George Sand." *L'Illustration. Journal Universel* 32 (Aug. 7, 1858), 94ff.

22. See Julian Schmidt, *Geschichte der französischen litteratur seit der Revolution von 1789* (Leipzig: Fr. L. Herbig, 1858), 2:505ff.; and *Portraits aus dem 19. Jahrhundert* (Berlin: Wilhelm Hertz, 1878), 222ff.

23. Helene Lange and Gertrud Bäumer, *Handbuch der Frauenbewegung* (Berlin: W. Moeser, 1901), 1:23ff.

24. Ferdinand Haas, *Französische Stoßseufzer und Deutsche Reflexionen eines Ausgewiesenen. Antwort an George Sand (Aurora Dudevant)* (Mainz: Selbstverlag, 1871), 4ff.

Part VI

SEXUAL POLITICS

18

Elle et lui: Literary Idealization and the Censorship of Female Sexuality

Marie J. Diamond

It is difficult to imagine a writer more reflective of the difficulties of being a creative woman in a society oppressive of female sexuality than George Sand. Finally celebrated as *la mère*, she was more often denigrated during her life as little more than *une fille*. Not only had she left her husband and become an independent writer, but her affairs were public and scandalous, and none more so than her liaison with Alfred de Musset, culminating in the notorious episode in Venice where he fell ill and his physician, Pietro Pagello, became her new lover. On her return to Paris with Pagello, she took desperate—and ultimately fruitless—measures to avoid social censure, and was tormented by the possibility of ridicule and humiliation. She was far from indifferent to her critics. She wrote her autobiography, *Histoire de ma vie* (published between October 1854 and August 1855) in part to explain and justify herself. However, it only provoked more criticism.[1] In 1858, a year after Musset's death and more than twenty years after the end of their affair, she decided to write her version of what had been a harrowing social and moral crisis. The novel *Elle et lui* was published in 1859.[2] Again the critics responded negatively, generally accusing her of writing an indecent polemic against the dead. Paul de Musset immediately rallied to his brother's posthumous defense with his scathing rebuttal of Sand, *Lui et elle*.

Elle et lui is an epistolary novel connected by a third-person narrative. The letters, written by the painters Laurent de Ferval and Thérèse Jacques, express the tensions of an affair heightened by the shadowy presence of Richard Palmer, Thérèse's American admirer and eventual suitor. Received by the public as a roman à clef and largely intended as such by Sand, it nevertheless draws on the genres of romantic confession and the romanesque. The story is essentially told from the perspective of Thérèse, but her fabulous background bears no resemblance to the biographical data of Sand's life, and Richard Palmer, a one-dimensional exemplar of chivalric virtue, bears no resemblance to the earthly and earthy Pagello. However, reading the work as transparently autobiographical, critics of the novel were outraged by what they saw as the representation of Musset as a moral weakling and of Sand as a model of integrity and self-sacrifice. Not only in her life had Sand broken the code forbidding the open expression of female sexuality, she had had the nerve to present herself as pure and noble. Thus, she was indicted not only for promiscuity but for hypocrisy. This continues to be the case presented against her by her prosecuting critics.

For example, Pierre Salomon, in his work *George Sand*, accuses her of being a coquette with the public and of tendentiously fostering the false image of a free but simple, honest, and independent woman.[3] Henri Guillemin, in his *Liaison Musset-Sand*, interprets the virtuous heroine of *Elle et lui* as a calculated and opportunistic idealization aimed at silencing any suggestion that her morals might be loose.[4] However, in this rabid diatribe against Sand, he parenthetically acknowledges that, had she not disavowed and disguised in her work what he calls her promiscuity, she would never have been published or accepted as a writer. Thus, while condemning her as a hypocrite, he points to the social imperative that forbade a woman writer from acknowledging female sexuality. Indeed, the accepted literary convention demanded the sacrifice, or at least the self-condemnation, of the sexually transgressive heroine. In the romantic transformation of the romanesque tradition, Jean-Jacques Rousseau's Julie dies in a self-sacrificial drowning; Chateaubriand's heroine, Atala, kills herself in order to perpetuate Christian virtue, and René's sister forgoes her passions in the name of the greater glory of God and of the brother she illicitly loves; and Benjamin Constant's Eléonore dies of love on the altar of her lover's ambivalence.[5] Not only male writers in this tradition sacrifice their female characters. Madame de Staël's Corinne, the celebrated poet and a model of female independence, languishes away when she is rejected for a more dutiful and virtuous woman by the man she passionately loves. If Sand saves the artist-heroine of *Elle et lui* from her expected literary fate of self-condemnation and death, she nevertheless depicts her as the ideal embodiment of such patriarchally endorsed virtues as maternal devotion, industry, moderation, and self-sacrifice. Similarly, despite her sexual freedom and independence, she claimed for herself the virtues conventionally associated with self-sacrificing motherhood in the context of marriage.[6] It is this paradox that frustrates and enrages her misogynist critics. What they call hypocrisy and calculation is a response to the paradigmatic dilemma of the nineteenth-century woman writer confronted with the severe social repression of both her sexuality and her creativity. Sand's paradoxical idealization of Thérèse can be understood only in the context of this repression and its psycho-aesthetic dynamics.

The daughter of two opposing mothers, Sand experienced the classic opposition between female sexuality and maternity on the deepest psychic level. On the death of her father, the four-year-old Aurore Dupin was brought up by her paternal grandmother, her socially distinguished and upright *bonne maman*. Her mother, a woman of lowly origin and dubious morals, accepted a pension in exchange for giving up custody of her daughter, and lived an independent life in Paris. Visits by this "unacceptable" mother were carefully controlled by the watchful and disapproving eye of the custodial "good mother." One of Aurore's dominant fantasies, which appears in her earliest writings, is of reconciliation with her absent mother. In her autobiography, Sand recalls a critical episode that dramatically reveals her paradigmatic psychic ambivalence toward the figure of the mother, its traumatic effects, and her desperate efforts to resolve it.

The crisis began when her grandmother unceremoniously slammed the door on her half-sister, the ostracized daughter of the barely tolerated mother, who had come to see her. Hearing her rejected sister's cries of pain and humiliation, the young Aurore fell into a paroxysm of grief and demanded to return to her mother. The following morning, and by way of consolation, she received a gift from her grandmother, a doll in the form of a black woman with a laughing face that she had seen on a shopping excursion with her mother and had particularly admired and desired. Her response to the gift was complex and revealing:

> In fact, my first reaction was one of intense pleasure; I took the little creature in my arms, her pretty smile provoked my own, and I kissed her as a young mother kisses her newborn. But, while looking at her and rocking her, my memories of the day before came rushing back. I thought of my mother, of my sister, of the severity of my grandmother, and I flung the doll into the corner. But as she continued to smile, the poor Negress, I picked her back up, I caressed her again, and I bathed her with my tears, giving in to the illusion of maternal love which excited even more intensely my disconsolate feelings of filial love. Then, suddenly, I felt dizzy, dropped the doll on the floor, and vomited bile, which horrified my nurses.[7]

In *Beyond the Pleasure Principle*, Sigmund Freud suggests that through their games, children assert, even in the repetition of originally painful experiences, the priority of the pleasure principle. He establishes a connection between the pleasure deriving from the playful reenactment of such experiences and the artistic play and artistic imitation carried out by adults who do not spare the spectators the most painful experiences (as in tragedy), which can be felt by them as highly enjoyable. Thus, the analysis of children's games "which have a yield of pleasure as their final outcome" should provide a basis for "some system of aesthetics with an economic approach to its subject matter."[8] Freud's insights emerged from his analysis of the proto-play of a one-and-a-half year old boy who cast away his toy with the word "fort" and retrieved it with a satisfied "da." Freud interpreted the game as a major cultural achievement whereby the child, staging the absence/presence of the objects within his reach, renounces the instinctual gratification of his mother's presence. Noticing that the child played the "fort" part of the game more than the "da" part, he concluded that the pleasure in the repetition of the originally painful experience comes from the transformation of passivity into mastery and from the satisfaction of an impulse in the child, suppressed in actual life, to revenge himself on his mother for going away from him. In this case, the throwing away of the toy also has the defiant meaning of casting off the mother: "As the child passes over from the passivity of the experience to the activity of the game, he hands on his disagreeable experience to one of his playmates and in this way revenges himself on a substitute."[9] Freud's association of the genre of tragedy—renunciation and retribution—with the male child's pleasure at mastery and revenge against the absent mother is fascinating in its sociocultural implications. However, Sand's description of Aurore's doll play suggests quite a different paradigm for the nineteenth-century female child and, consequently, for the aesthetic resolutions of the nineteenth-century woman writer.

First seen in the presence of the mother, the black and laughing doll is a transparent figure of outcast sexuality. It is offered as a substitute for the barred half-sister, the mother's surrogate. Thus, when Aurore first takes the doll to her breast, she mothers her rejected mother. However, as a substitute, it reminds her of her grandmother's injustice and efforts to displace her mother, and she rejects it. As if she were then in fact repeating her grandmother's rejection of her mother, she experiences extreme guilt, retrieves the doll, and cries over its abandonment. Alternately identifying with the rejected and rejecting mothers, and alternately identifying the doll with the rejecting mother and the rejected child, her attempts to mother her mother/self fail as every positive projection immediately turns into its negative double. Her efforts to resolve the ambivalence caused by the beloved and socially admired grandmother's rejection of her mother in her sister (and, of course, Sand explicitly points out, of her mother in herself) in order to resolve her anger at both of them, and to recreate an ideally loving relation between mother and child, leads only to the vicious circle of contradictory projections and introjections that builds up into a vertigo of anxiety and the explosion of physical nausea, a paroxysm of disgust.[10] Given this identification with the double image of the mother, the paradigm of mastery and revenge—the resolution of the male child, according to Freud—cannot apply to the quite different psycho-cultural organization of the little girl. Above all, the "fort" gesture, preferred by the mastering and angry little boy, remains the most painful to Aurore, and is the source of overwhelming guilt. Sand's brilliantly nuanced description of her doll play exposes the destructiveness of the social censure, particularly intense in the patriarchal nineteenth century, of female sexuality. For no matter how unconscious it may be in the young Aurore, implicit in every detail of her game is the scarcely veiled sexuality of the socially exiled mother—the unnamed reason for her departure to Paris and for the ostracism of her "illegitimate" daughter—graphically represented in that stereotypical nineteenth-century figure for unbridled sexuality, the laughing Negress.

The unconscious sexuality structuring the traumatic and unresolved game with the doll became vividly conscious a few years later when, at thirteen, Sand decided to leave her increasingly restrictive grandmother to join her mother in Paris. In order to deter her from her plan, her grandmother painted a grim picture of her mother's dubious past before her marriage and led her to believe that her life in Paris was no moral improvement on what it once had been. Aurore was traumatized by this revelation and became physically and emotionally ill: "This was a nightmare for me; I was choked with emotion; every word sickened me; I felt sweat run down my forehead; I wanted to interrupt her, to get up, to go away, to push away this horrible revelation; I could not, I was nailed to the spot, my head down and bent by that voice that hovered over me and withered me like the dry wind of a storm."[11] Identifying with the rejected mother, she fell into emptiness and despair, and gave up her youthful writing and fantasies: "In fact, I could no longer plan anything, I no longer had sweet dreams. No more novels, no more reveries. Corambé was silent. I lived like an automaton."[12] The "good" mother's exposure of the "bad" mother's sexuality did not, Sand writes, significantly change her feelings toward either of them, but it changed her feelings toward herself, ending her escapist fantasies of ideal reunion with her mother, blocking her creativity, and turning her into a barely functioning "automaton." The pleasure principle, both in the game with the doll and in the ideal fictions, was overcome by the power of the censorship of female sexuality. Far more elaborate strategies were needed for its affirmation. A response to the affair that had exposed Sand to the possibility of the most traumatizing social censure, *Elle et lui* offers a fascinating example of a successful literary idealization.

The action of *Elle et lui* begins with a significant misunderstanding. Laurent de Ferval and Thérèse Jacques have long enjoyed an uneventful friendship when Laurent, overhearing Thérèse's passionate words to an unseen interlocutor, becomes jealous and develops an erotic interest in her. What he does not know is that her words—"I have only one love on this earth, and it is you"—are addressed to her mother.[13] Demanding an explanation that finally uncovers her mysterious past, Thérèse's words not only begin the intrigue of the novel but also indicate its reason for being. Laurent should hardly have been relieved to discover the real destination of Thérèse's expression of exclusive love, for her fidelity to her mother, in its obscure metamorphoses, proves stronger than any male rival. Indeed, Thérèse's unambiguous love for her mother is reflected in the narrator's unambiguous love for Thérèse. Unlike the game with the doll, which could not resolve the ambivalence the young Aurore felt toward the figure of the mother, *Elle et lui* frees its two maternal figures, Thérèse and her mother, from any censure that might be attached to their shadowy past.

Thérèse is illegitimate. As a young governess, her mother was seduced and made pregnant by her employer, a rich banker. He married her off to a husband who treated her cruelly, and eventually forced her to give up her devoted daughter who is her only joy to have the girl educated in a convent. Sand transforms the insistent trauma of the sexually transgressive mother by situating her within a romanesque tradition of beleaguered innocence in which her initial lapse is the sign of her emotional vulnerability and sensitivity. In keeping with the exigencies of the tradition, the mother nevertheless has to pay for her one error with a lifetime of suffering through which she proves how capable she is of duty and self-sacrifice. Still within the conventions of the romanesque, Sand presents Thérèse as an innocent victim of adverse fortune. She was married off by her father to a Portuguese count who took her with him to South America. She became a devoted and loving wife and gave birth to a son, only to discover that her husband had deceived her and already had a wife. Overcoming her natural feelings, she left the compromising situation and returned to Europe with her son. Her husband pursued her and finally managed to kidnap the child and take him back to South America where, after the exhausting journey, he was reported to have died. Thérèse's life as an independent and industrious painter is thus contextualized as the consequence of a series of dreadful misfortunes. Far from being the expression of social perversity or the desire for a loose life, it demonstrates a moral purity and strength of character. Through the romanesque convention, Sand situates evil in the realm of contingency or in the desire of the "other," the predatory male or the "other" women, such as the count's first wife and the harlots who pull Laurent de Ferval into a life of debauchery.

Sand inscribes Thérèse's affair with Laurent within the context of her virtue. For a long time she resists his seductions and endeavors to maintain the equilibrium of friendship. When she eventually succumbs, she views her submission to his desire as a self-sacrifice aimed at saving him from the loose women who are debauching him and destroying his art. She is described not only as the model of maternal devotion but as a saint who sacrifices herself to save a soul, John the Baptist baptizing a sinner into renewed spiritual existence: " 'She dipped him again,' he said, 'in his baptismal waters, she erased the memory of his bad days.' "[14] However, Laurent does not long remain the devoted and grateful lover, and the affair turns into a test of Thérèse's own spiritual mettle as he abuses her and compares her sexual skills unfavorably with those of the women he has possessed. During the crucial trip to Italy, he undermines her work, spends nights away in debauchery, and mocks her care and devotion. Still she remains constant. When he finally leaves her and goes to Venice, where he falls gravely ill and becomes deranged, she rushes to his side, nurses him back to health, and gives him her last penny for his return trip to Paris. Finally convinced that she can do no more for him, she agrees to marry Palmer, her faithful confidant and support during the Italian ordeal. However, Laurent returns and, by the constant demonstration of his weakness, undermines her resolution and the possibility of marriage. Her ascesis reaches its climax in one of the most striking scenes of the novel where, impoverished because of her generosity to Laurent and unwilling to call on the help of the ever generous and patient Palmer, she rents a shabby room on a dark and brutal island off the Italian coast and earns a bare subsistence by making lace, a task at which she surpasses the local women. She leaves the island determined to continue what proves to be the hopeless task of Laurent's reform. She finally admits defeat when, at a masked ball in Paris, she overhears him gossiping about her with a group of loose women, the special objects of her condemnation.

Sand's romanesque/Christian idealization of Thérèse neutralizes her sexuality in the name of the conventional patriarchal ideology which valorizes a woman in terms of her self-sacrifice and maternal devotion. Unambivalently loving toward her own mother, whose sexuality was similarly transfigured by virtue, Thérèse nevertheless becomes an object of extreme ambivalence to her lover/son. Her patriarchal idealization of the maternal virtues inevitably demands the censorship of her own sexuality and that of her lover. Thus, Laurent reembodies an ambivalence that had crippled Sand in the traumatic crises of her childhood. Just as wearing men's clothes and assuming a male nom de plume allowed her the psychic and social freedom to be sexually active and creative, situating ambivalence in the male allowed her, no matter how unconsciously, to contest the idealized and paradoxical resolution of her mother's troubling sexuality.

If Thérèse attempts to cure Laurent of the flesh, he resists her efforts to turn him into an icon, an object not of desire but of contemplative admiration. In a significant confrontation, she predicts, as his apotheosis, that just as the young men of Genoa came to gaze at Sir Anthony Vandyke's portrait of a beautiful countess, women will one day come to gaze at Laurent's paintings in a museum. Laurent violently contests this rejection of life and the transformation of art into idealized objects. He tells her the story of a young man who fell in love with the sculpted figure of a beautiful woman on a sarcophagus and, in quest of the real being, finally raised the stone. Horrified at uncovering the mummified corpse, he nevertheless preferred this trace of a life lived to its petrified idealization. An admirer of the old masters, Thérèse as artist is restricted to the respectful and imitative form of painting portraits for the bourgeoisie. She herself bows to the creativity of the disorderly Laurent, who paints disruptive and subversive romantic visions.

As the embodiment of ideal maternal virtue and at the same time as the mistress, Thérèse becomes for Laurent the source of an extreme Oedipal anxiety. The ultimate patriarchal creation, her power is phallic and threatening. Thus, in his mad ravings during his illness in Venice, he graphically imagines that she is thrusting her gold pin into his head. After her endless ministrations, he compares her not to her patron saint, Teresa of Avila, but to another Thérèse, Thérèse Levasseur, Jean-Jacques's companion who, he claims, turned the writer into an idiot and maniac. Laurent's rage and ambivalence toward Thérèse, typical of his generation of disenfranchised aristocrats, masks a rage against the Oedipal father. He is described from a conventional patriarchal perspective as weak, capricious, unreliable, temperamental, sensuous, irrational, and prone to hysterical fits and hallucinations—that is, as feminine and childish. In revolt against patriarchal idealizations, he represents a sexuality and creativity culturally embodied, in the "masculine" world of nineteenth-century capitalism, in the despised figure of the feminized male. However, as such, the real target of his ambivalence is the figure who combines both patriarchal censorship and motherhood. Having circumvented the daughter's ambivalence, Sand comes face to face with the murderous ambivalence of the son.

Romanesque literature abounds in stories of lost and beleaguered heroines whose virtue finally assures a happy ending, usually the restoration of lost family and fortune and an ideal marriage. Realism defines itself against such myths of virtue and perfection. Thus, in Madame de Lafayette's *La Princesse de Clèves,* the interest of the novel begins *after* marriage when virtue encounters illicit desire. In Marivaux's *La Vie de Marianne*, his first nonromanesque novel, Marianne discovers that the fabulous circumstance of her birth and her unswerving virtue do not lead to any ideal resolution. By the end of the eighteenth century, as shown in the Marquis de Sade's grotesque parody *Justine*, subtitled "The Misfortunes of Virtue," the romanesque convention had been thoroughly demystified. Virtue did not lead to marriage, and marriage offered no happiness. Similarly, despite Sand's idealization of Thérèse in *Elle et lui*, she rejects marriage as a possible outcome.[15] However, this is not merely a nod at realism and a recognition that the structure of marriage, particularly in the patriarchal nineteenth century, meant the legal effacement of women. Given the psychic configuration of Thérèse in *Elle et lui*, marriage is an impossibility. The generous and idealized Palmer, the chivalric knight on a white horse, might appropriately save an innocent maiden, but not a woman who above all must identify herself as mother, and Laurent, the lover/son, remains locked in his ambivalence. Nevertheless, Sand devises a happy ending for her long-suffering heroine.

Saving Thérèse from the vice of Laurent's ambivalence, Sand provides her with an ideal love object through which all conflict is resolved: She restores to her the kidnapped son who was long believed to be dead. Through the physical agency of the self-effacing Palmer, she literally deposits the child on Thérèse's doorstep. When Thérèse discovers this miraculous gift, she almost dies of joy and, with scarcely another thought of Laurent, retires with her son to the mystic depths of Germany.

Writing about adolescence in *Histoire de ma vie*, Sand praises as her ideal the adolescent boy brought up by a loving mother. She describes him as a creature apart, who belongs to neither sex and who loves his mother in a way that a girl, the early prey of coquetry and dissemblance, cannot. However, she goes on to acknowledge that "in these times," such an adolescent does not exist, and clear-sightedly draws the portrait of the ill-kempt and ill-taught contemporary student, infected with some ugly vice, who reads dirty books, avoids a woman's eye, fears women, and blushes at his mother's caresses. Deformed by what she calls his atrocious education, he is marked by the patriarchal contempt for female sexuality and hostility toward his mother. The son that Sand returns to Thérèse at the end of *Elle et lui* is, on the contrary, the embodiment of her ideal, a projective fantasy. Brought up in some remote and exotic land, he seems untouched by the distortions of civilization, and remains transparently pure and loving. He is without the marked gender definition that, especially in the nineteenth century, generates contempt for women. He is the final metamorphosis that permits Sand to resolve ambivalence toward the mother figure, a far more effective gift than the black doll her grandmother once gave her, which played such a critical role in the dramatization of her psychic configuration. Replacing the ambivalent son/lover, the boy permits Thérèse to be an ideal mother to an ideal child. A transparent wish fulfillment that belongs as much to the ideal world of romance as Corambé, the mythological bird of the young Aurore's dreams, he is at the same time the result of a series of complex psychic transformations. Unlike Freud's example of the little boy, Aurore could not, through the game with the doll, renounce her mother with satisfaction or escape ambivalence. In the aesthetic play of *Elle et lui*, Sand reveals that even the idealization of the mother which resolves ambivalence for the daughter produces a destructive ambivalence in the lover/son. Once again, the mother becomes the source of conflict. Only the final idealization, the complete transformation of the *mère/fille* into her opposite image as nonsexual *fils*, enables Sand to provide her heroine with a pleasurable outcome to a no-win game.

NOTES

1. Pierre-Joseph Proudhon was one of Sand's more virulent and misogynist critics. At a distribution of school prizes in Auxerre, *Histoire de ma vie* was condemned as scandalous and immoral.

2. Musset had written his version of the affair in *La Confession d'un enfant du siècle* (1836).

3. Pierre Salomon, *George Sand* (Paris: Hatier-Bovin, 1953).

4. Henri Guillemin, *La Liaison Musset-Sand* (Paris: Gallimard, 1972).

5. In *Literary Women* (New York: Doubleday, 1963), Ellen Moers stresses that Jean-Jacques Rousseau, in *La Nouvelle Héloïse*, gave Julie the power of self-expression, beginning the landslide of modern sensibility that is called the Romantic Movement. She calls his project "loving heroinism [*sic*], a woman's heroic resolve to write, as men had for centuries, the love story from her point of view" (147). Letters in particular are the genre in which women have expressed themselves. However, the major epistolary novels have been written by men, and the death of the heroine, as with Julie, is a common ending.

6. Thus, in a letter to Pierre-Jules Hetzel, September 14, 1852, she wrote: "I have nothing in my private life that makes me blush; nothing, nothing from A to Z" (this and all subsequent translations are the editors' of this book). The overemphatic tone of this statement belongs to the rhetoric of self-defense, but in assuming the stance of the absolutely blameless woman, Sand rings in the change from the ashamed and tortured heroines of Romantic fiction.

7. George Sand, *Histoire de ma vie*, in her *Oeuvres autobiographiques* (Paris: Gallimard, 1970), 1:653–654.

8. Sigmund Freud, *Beyond the Pleasure Principle*, trans. James Strachey (New York: Norton, 1975), 18:17.

9. Ibid.

10. In her "De Sand à Cixous: La venue de l'écriture au féminin" (*Colloque de Cérisy*, ed. Simone Vierne [Paris: SEDES, 1983], 149–155), Pierrette Daly, following Hélène Cixous, interprets this explosion of vomiting as the expulsion of terror, the analogue of talking or writing. The context hardly allows for such an interpretation. Rather, the nausea signifies the failure of finding any imaginative or symbolic way out of an impasse.

11. Sand, *Histoire de ma vie*, 1:856–857.

12. Ibid., 858.

13. George Sand, *Elle et lui* (Neuchâtel: Collection du Sablier, 1963), 143.

14. Ibid., 182.

15. In his "High Analytical Romanticism: The Narrative Voice in George Sand's *Lucrezia Floriani*" (*The George Sand Papers*, Hofstra University Proceedings, ed. Natalie Datlof et al. [New York: AMS Press, 1978], 189–198), Alex Szogyi highlights the irony with which Sand dismissed the antediluvian endings of what she called the fiction of the fabulous ages. She concluded her novel with the two lovers caught in a battle to the death in which each tries to absorb the other. Finally, like a flame deprived of oxygen, the heroine (of course) is extinguished.

19

Mademoiselle Merquem: De-Mythifying Woman by Rejecting the Law of the Father

Claude Holland

According to André Maurois, the novels that Sand wrote in the later part of her life "are not very good and she knows it. In these novels, personified doctrines rather than living characters confront each other."[1] To some extent this may be true. However, it is quite remarkable that in *Mademoiselle Merquem*, a novel written just eight years before her death, we find Sand's ideology still full of vigor and rebellion, and characterized by the same biting attacks we encounter in her earlier works. She has not abandoned her fight against social injustice, her dreams of Utopia, her views on education, or her strong opposition to marriages arranged without the partners' free consent.

However, in *Mademoiselle Merquem* there is something more. There is a conscious demythifying of woman, and in the process, a direct attack on the patriarchal system and a complete rejection of the Law of the Father. Deprived of all civil rights in an essentially androcentric society, a woman was kept in total subjugation by first her father's and then her husband's authority. Her destiny was limited to waiting for the two major events of her life: marriage and motherhood. Moreover, the early nineteenth-century fictional heroine, while placed on a pedestal by romantic idealization, found herself entirely immobilized by that very image, wholly paralyzed by the myths of femininity.[2]

Pierre Fauchery, in his *Essai de gynécomythie romanesque*, rightly sees in these myths "a policy function" through which "woman's destiny would only be, all things considered, the hypostatic projection of the collective will, masculine in principle—mystifying or protective according to the concept—and consenting to restrict the female sex to a flatteringly subordinate position."[3]

In fact, as Claudine Herrmann remarked in *Les Voleuses de langue*, woman was trained to become the negative of man.[4] The following table brings to light the traditional separation of roles in which a woman covers the full range of negativity:

Man	Woman
knowledge	ignorance/innocence[5]
power	helplessness
authority	obedience
aggressiveness	passivity
action	abnegation
freedom	servitude/dependence
creativity	repetition
transcendence	immanence

Sand fought this freezing of woman's image into a stance that prevented her from leading an active, fulfilling life that would give meaning to her existence. In *Emile ou de l'éducation*, Rousseau says "Living is not breathing, it is taking action. . . . It is making use of ourselves, of our senses, of our faculties, of all aspects of ourselves, which gives us the feeling of being alive."[6] However, women were not allowed to grow, "to make use of their faculties," or to create their own image. Their role and place was confined to the microcosm of the home, beyond which no future was conceivable.

In *Mademoiselle Merquem*, Sand presents a very different kind of woman. The heroine, Célie Merquem, is not immobilized by the stereotypes of feminine representation. She ignores the traditional postures of fragility, inferiority, and feminine submission. Instead, she offers the possibility of a redistribution of the roles that up to then were immutably attributed to the two sexes. Her independence of thought and action allows her to shape her own life.

Mademoiselle Merquem is introduced to the reader as a free woman, who is unmarried at the age of thirty, a definite disadvantage considering the short-lived desirability of woman in the novelistic tradition. Here tradition is not only disregarded but deliberately rejected: "A thirty-year-old woman who is unmarried and who must be perfection in marriage: no nerves, no silly curiosity, no extravagant demands."[7] Sand also ignores the then rigid code of respectability concerning women. Mademoiselle Merquem "professes an absolute passion for independence. She lives alone and goes wherever she pleases, alone" (17). Célie is free to go wherever she wants and still is a highly respected member of her community.

In addition, Célie's conversation is never banal or frivolous, and she states that she never suffers from ennui, the usual affliction of the idle heroine whose life is spent waiting for a man. She is a woman of action, dividing her time between the administration of her estate, her responsibilities to the people of the nearby village of Canielle, whom she has taken under her protection, and at the same time pursuing her studies of the sciences. Sand refuses the stereotype of the feeble woman whose alleged pervasive emotional susceptibility and instability prevent her from being part of the rational world of men. There is no doubt when we meet Mademoiselle Merquem that she is in full control of her life.

Célie Merquem represents the antithesis of traditional upbringing. Sand expressed contempt for a woman who was socially educated, that is, whose education was limited to social accomplishments, and considered such schooling a hypocritical means of catching a husband. In *Les Lettres à Marcie* she lashes out against men's monopolizing of educational institutions to their exclusive privilege:

> Women receive a deplorable education and this is man's greatest crime against them. They have abused every aspect of life, monopolizing the advantages of the most sacred institutions. They have speculated even on the most naïve and the most legitimate feelings. They have succeeded in perpetrating this slavery and this degradation of woman that they claim today to be of divine institution and of eternal legislation. They would have had to smother her intelligence or else leave her uneducated. The latter is the course they chose.[8]

An orphan raised by her grandfather, an old admiral, Célie was spared the inferior type of education traditionally reserved for girls. Hers was definitely "un-feminine," and could rather be identified with a young man's apprenticeship. When he retired, the admiral had taken her on sea trips with the best seamen around him. There she learned the principles of solidarity and authority which bring men together in the face of danger. Furthermore, her grandfather's founding of the community of Canielle taught her firsthand how to know and understand the real world of people's relationships and responsibilities. It gave her the opportunity of identifying with the outside world and it broadened her horizons.

Although the admiral was enlightened as far as Célie's education was concerned, he became tyrannical on the subject of marriage. In retrospect, Mademoiselle Merquem recalls how her grandfather had been deaf to any suggestion of independence when she refused to marry the man he had selected for her. The Law of the Father is what determines woman's destiny.

Even during Sand's last years, the subject of marriage brought out her most vehement vocabulary. The metaphors of slavery used in her first novels are still present.[9] When faced with the threat of a forced marriage, Célie asks herself whether "daughters were being sold," and she refuses to be pushed "under the conqueror's tent like a Trojan prisoner" (193). A woman has no choice in deciding her own future, Célie complains: "Refrain from having an ideal, or even an inclination, a preference. Woman is nothing: a virtuous girl has no preconceived ideas. . . . She is ever ready to submit to the degree of capacity of her future master and, in the meantime, she must keep herself in the state of tabula rasa" (188).

Sand denounces the state of ignorance in which a young girl is maintained so as to ensure that a man will have full control of her life. She uses the metaphor of sand for the girl's soul, which must be kept free of any trace so that her husband may inscribe on it whatever he pleases. Sarcastically, she adds, "if in fact he can write anything" (196).

Mademoiselle Merquem is tormented and does not understand the apparent contradiction between her grandfather's previous expression of love and his tyrannical attempts to force her to marry his best friend's son. She is made to feel guilty for her decision not to marry by a society that fears individualism (Célie does not fit into the mold of marriage/motherhood) as well as by her grandfather, who cannot accept or even try to understand her refusal. She tries to commit suicide. Death irrevocably abolishes all possibilities of manipulation. In a society in which a woman has no voice in the shaping of her own future, death was the only conceivable expression of self-determination. Only by renouncing life could she affirm her "self" in a dramatization of passive action that defiantly, if negatively, rejected domination.

However, here Sand rebels. She both opposes coercion and rejects a negative death. She is interested in positive action. Thus, Célie is saved from suicide and taken on an eighteen-month journey that amounts to a second apprenticeship. This apprenticeship is crucial: It is a quest for identity. She has to come to terms with her own consciousness and understand that she has been imprisoned by the Law of the Father. She has to break away and find out that she has the right to make her own choices in life.

It is important to realize that the theme of the quest is a rather recent one as far as female characters are concerned. To my knowledge, it had not been taken up by French novelists before Sand herself, who used it in *Consuelo* and *La Comtesse de Rudolstadt*. The quest was reserved for male protagonists: The acquiring of knowledge and experience was man's not woman's domain.[10]

However, Sand boldly upsets this tradition. In order to allow the quest to take place, she resorts to the only possible solution to the heroine's dilemma: She sends the admiral to his grave.[11] Naturally, Mademoiselle Merquem is traumatized by his death, and she feels responsible for it: hence the attempted suicide and the subsequent journey. It is emphasized in the text that it was a matter of immediate mental and physical survival for the heroine to leave the paternal house where, Célie recalls, "I had almost lost my sanity and my life" (198).

Célie comes back free from the guilt she felt for having refused to bow to her grandfather's wishes. The quest has borne fruit, the search for identity is fulfilled, and she is reborn. She congratulates herself for her rebellion, and expresses "her joy at having escaped a brilliant marriage" (195).

While gaining self-confidence, Mademoiselle Merquem has also acquired a social conscience. This is a characteristic of Sand's protagonists, who are often involved in altruistic endeavors. Upon her return, Célie is able to perceive that her position of wealth and freedom gives her a duty to share these advantages with others. This is when she decides to devote herself entirely to helping the people of Canielle and to the study of science. Sand even goes further in setting her heroine apart. She wants to show that woman's intellectual potential is not inferior to man's. On Sunday, Célie gives a science course with an old scientist who lives under her roof, and she is the one who is able to clarify points that he cannot explain.

Célie never questions the propriety of her activities.[12] One of the most obvious crossings over into man's domain (besides the study of science) is her participation in the rescues at sea with the village sailors. Prepared for the dangers of the expeditions, she is an expert and strong swimmer. It must be remembered that a girl's education did not include any sport, and that athletic stamina was not a desirable attribute. Here, on the contrary, the heroine never shows any sign of the fragility expected of woman. Indeed, she likes the challenge of danger.

Rejecting the encumbrance of feminine attire, Mademoiselle Merquem dresses as a sailor when she takes part in the men's work at sea. Whereas wearing masculine clothing is traditionally used in fiction as a protective device against man's scrutiny,

Sand here stresses its practicality and the fusion of roles it makes possible. Célie does not want to escape her femininity, but simply desires to accomplish her task under the best conditions possible, as would a man. Sand criticizes the conventions that condemn women who step out of their prescribed roles. When complimented on her seaman's costume, Célie answers: "There are, however, men who would dislike this kind of beauty. I have heard some say that women should be timid and nervous for fear of losing their charm and looking like a man" (149). She not only stands her own ground, but expresses her satisfaction with her decision: "I have made up my mind, and you would be wrong to believe that I regret it" (151).

Summing up the novel's thesis, one of the male protagonists remarks, "Does not woman claim to have a soul equal to ours, a personality of her own, a freedom of choice which seems sacred to her?" (125). Indeed, with Mademoiselle Merquem, Sand presented a heroine who struggled for the right of individual thought and action, who was able to gain self-identity and autonomy, and who established her independence over societal conventions and acquired a freedom to make her own decisions. Moreover, in doing so, she reached self-fulfillment through incursions into spheres that, up to then, had been out of reach for women.

Why then does Sand, in the last few pages of the novel, reverse her position and affect a new option for her heroine? Mademoiselle Merquem gives up her independence, her studies, and her commitment to the people of Canielle to marry. It is clear in the novel that the marriage did not require her to abandon all past endeavors. She could have shared these activities with her husband, whom she agreed to marry because he showed the same enthusiasm for her commitments. Nonetheless, Célie surrenders in no uncertain terms: "I no longer have any inclination, habits, affections, pleasures, outside of yours. If you want me to forget all I learned, I shall even forget that I knew anything and that I loved studying. . . . Now command me as you wish, since I know only one pleasure in this world: to obey you" (305–306).

There is a sudden reversion to conventional feminine passivity expressed by her desire to obey as well as to forget her past education, a weapon justly considered at the time the strongest in woman's rebellion. Moreover, Célie gives up any personal voice in the raising of her future progeny. She says, "If God gives me children, I shall raise them before your very eyes and according to your tastes" (306).

It is not the fact that the heroine chooses marriage and motherhood that is surprising, but rather the abandonment of her past work and commitments to others, and her total, almost comical, submission to her husband. Sand's heroines are usually strongly bonded to their commitments. The abrupt shift from a position of rebellion to an unconditional renunciation of the heroine's past claims comes as a shock to the reader. Was Sand attempting to comply, although in extremis, with fictional convention? Did she feel the need to reassure her public that societal rules and myths were ultimately left unchallenged? Could Sand have exercised self-censorship to yield to the male-dominated publishing market of the time?[13]

Since the conclusion is such an aberration in relation to the original thesis, one may wonder whether it is meant to be ironic. The heroine's last statements using the clichés of feminine submission seem to ridicule the very ideology they express.

On the other hand, does the contradiction arise from the tension between Sand's desire to create a truly independent woman and her own concept of woman's destiny?

A look at some of the heroine's comments seems to confirm the latter hypothesis. Mademoiselle Merquem may not originally have had any inclination toward marriage, but she longed to have children. We know that Sand's maternal instinct was very strong. This instinct is revealed in many of her writings, and in *Les Lettres à Marcie* she defines motherhood as a "divine mission" because, she says, "Providence has placed man's childhood in her arms and attached it to her bosom. . . . There is her greatness, there is her glory."[14]

If indeed this is Sand's final argument, we can then assume that it is her viewpoint that is expressed when Mademoiselle Merquem reflects on woman's destiny. First, the heroine sadly assesses and deplores woman's lack of education and need of initial freedom of choice. Then, however, she states her belief that nature has assigned woman a very specific role, that of motherhood. It is, she says, "a vow of Nature" because "woman is born to become a mother. . . . It is in vain that she avoids marriage and abstains from creating a family," she contends, for"everything is family for her" (199).

In fact, the maternal instinct is manifested in all of Mademoiselle Merquem's relationships, whether it be with children, friends, or suitors. Furthermore, she is the godmother of every newborn child in Canielle. It is clear that the call for motherhood comes to the heroine before any thought of love and marriage. The usual sequence of love/marriage/family is ignored. In fact, no longing for a man is expressed. On the contrary, for ten years Célie was quite satisfied with the life she had designed for herself, except that she longed to have children. Thus, it is the issue of a child's education that serves as the intermediary between herself and her future husband and becomes an excuse for a first informal meeting. It allows the beginning of a personal relationship that, had it been in the form of a courtship, would have been categorically refused.

Of course the relationship does evolve into a courtship. Without a love interest, the novel would have remained a pure thesis. Mademoiselle Merquem reflects on the changes love has brought into her life, remarks that "to live alone is to vegetate," and defines love as "the complement of life, its apogee" (226).

In the final analysis it is clear that in *Mademoiselle Merquem* there is a strong impulse to fight and overcome some aspects of the myth of femininity (evident in the plea for self-identity and the recognition of equality of rights and potential). However, this urge coexists with a desire to retain some other aspects of the myth—maternity, passivity, and in the end, submission. Through love, Sand reintegrates a liberating vision into the traditional vision of femininity.

Nevertheless, the original thesis has been stated strongly enough to remain valid. Social conventions and prohibitions must be challenged so that a woman may be allowed to find a self-identity before deciding the course of her life. Above all, Mademoiselle Merquem represents a woman's refusal to accept self-sacrifice for the sake of the Law of the Father, and this rejection clearly defines a feminine voice that demanded to be heard.

NOTES

1. André Maurois, *Lélia ou la vie de George Sand* (Paris: Hachette, 1952), 476; this and all subsequent translations are those of the author.

2. The most comprehensive in-depth analysis of the myths and prohibitions surrounding the role and place of woman in society is Simone de Beauvoir's *Le Deuxième sexe*. Describing the position of the idealized woman, Emily Toth writes: "Placing the woman on a pedestal is not a homage, but a deprivation, for it confines her in the sphere of Love. The men who put forth the claims of Love use the words of devotion and the trappings of beauty, without seeing the individual woman's desire for something larger"; "The Independent Woman and Free Love," *Massachusetts Review* 41, no. 4 (Autumn 1975): 657.

3. Pierre Fauchery, *La Destinée féminine dans le roman européen du XVIIIème siècle, 1713–1808: Essai de gynécomythie romanesque* (Paris: A. Colin, 1972), 828.

4. Claudine Herrmann, *Les Voleuses de langue* (Paris: Des Femmes, 1976).

5. In her article "Ev'ry Woman is at Heart a Rake," Patricia Meyer Spacks points out that "innocence, implying ignorance, the virgin mind as well as the virgin body, is the most crucial female attraction, with knowledge of the world almost explicitly equivalent to sexual violation," *Eighteenth-Century Studies* 8, no. 1 (Autumn 1974): 29–30.

6. Jean-Jacques Rousseau, *Emile ou de l'éducation* (Paris: Garnier-Flammarion, 1966), 43.

7. George Sand, *Mademoiselle Merquem* (Paris: Calmann-Lévy, 1888), 233. Subsequent references will be noted in the text.

8. George Sand, *Les Lettres à Marcie* (Paris: Michel-Lévy, 1869), 230–231.

9. For an analysis of Sand's metaphors of slavery, see Nancy Rogers, "Slavery as Metaphor in the Writings of George Sand," *French Review* 53, no. 1 (October 1979), 29–35.

10. In *The Hero with a Thousand Faces*, Joseph Campbell states quite clearly the differences of roles between the hero and the heroine: "Woman in the picture language of mythology represents the totality of what can be known. The hero is the one who comes to know" (Princeton: Princeton University Press, 1949), 116. Diana Trilling describes the role of the fictional heroine as follows: "Heroines are in the first instance women who please, help and wait. They please men and are helpful to them in their undertaking. They wait for men to return from war, from crusades, from dangerous ways of earning a living, from missions in distant lands"; "The Liberated Heroine," *Times Literary Supplement*, October 13, 1978. "The Liberated Heroine" was delivered as a University Lecture in the spring of 1978 at Columbia University in New York.

11. Elucidating on the relationship between the Law of the Father and Freud's theory on the original murder of the father, Jacques Lacan writes in *Ecrits*, vol. 5, that Freud came to tie "the apparition of the signifier to the Father—thus showing that if this murder is the fruitful moment of the debt by which the subject ties himself to the Law for life, then, the symbolic Father, inasmuch as he signifies this Law, is indeed the dead Father" (812). He concludes by quoting Freud's original questions: "What is a Father?—It is the dead Father"; "Fonction et champ de la parole et du langage," *Ecrits* (Paris: Seuil, 1966), 5:812. Freud expounded his theory about the original murder of the father in *Totem and Taboo* (trans. James Strachey [New York: Norton, 1950]), particularly in chapter 6, "The Return of Totemism in Childhood."

12. In *Impressions et souvenirs*, Sand expressed her position on the separation of roles according to sex as follows: "There is no logical classification by which a woman can be placed in a particular sphere . . . [and] any concept of classification which detracts from these

(natural) laws seems arbitrary and artificial to me. I shall not say that I reject it, I go even further, *I ignore it*" (Paris: Michel-Lévy, 1869), 259–260.

13. In 1847, in a letter to her publisher François Buloz, Sand specified the freedom she demanded in opposition to "your bourgeoisie, your serious-minded men, your government, your social inequality. . . . I remain stubborn on this matter . . . and would rather happily ruin myself so long as I can write what I think. . . . I cannot haggle over my freedom, which must be complete or else I shall resign," from a letter to François Buloz, September 15, 1841, quoted in Joseph Barry's *George Sand in Her Own Words* (Garden City, N.Y.: Anchor Books/Doubleday, 1979), 425.

14. Sand, *Lettres à Marcie*, 198, 199.

20

Healers in George Sand's Works

Annabelle M. Rea

> Madame Sand is a better doctor than I and I have used her services.
> Geneviève Bréton, *Journal 1867–1871*

In the century of Louis Pasteur and Claude Bernard, George Sand, like so many of her contemporaries, was fascinated by medicine. Anyone familiar with her correspondence knows of the centrality of health in her preoccupations, both her own health and that of those around her. For someone who says that she never complains or worries about her health (*Corr.*, 7:614–615), Sand provides in her letters an extensive list of maladies.[1] Georges Lubin has attributed some of Sand's apparent health disturbances to what he terms the "social lie" (*Corr.*, 7:253 n.1), a protective device taken much further by Florence Nightingale, who spent years in bed in order to free her time for her writing. Occasionally in her correspondence Sand admits to turning bothersome visitors away with excuses about her health.[2]

Regardless of how many of her maladies were feigned, Sand was an amazingly strong woman for her time. In 1844, for example, she wrote to her friend the worker-poet Charles Poncy (*Corr.*, 6:591) about spending but one day in bed after the birth of Solange and going riding a week later. Basing her conclusion on Henry James's assessment, Ellen Moers, in *Literary Women*, speaks of Sand's "physical robustness."[3] In this, Sand served as a countermodel in her century where, according to Sandra Gilbert and Susan Gubar, "culture seems actually to have admonished women to *be ill*."[4] Many of Sand's characters imitate her in this respect.

The correspondence, as well as *Histoire de ma vie*, also show the importance of healers in Sand's life. We know that her tutor François Deschartres, who had studied medicine but was "largely self-taught," gave young Aurore lessons in medicine and arranged for her to do further study with the medical student Stéphane

Ajasson de Grandsagne.[5] From her letters we know of her friendship with a number of doctors, especially Gustave Papet, the childhood friend whose loyal service continued throughout the writer's life. Of course, one remembers the care our author gave to Maurice and Solange during their various childhood illnesses, and later her devotion to a succession of ailing lovers. The passage of *Histoire de ma vie* where she describes herself as she prepares "ointments and syrups" and states, "I had become a country doctor," serves to summarize this important aspect of her life.[6]

Throughout her writing career Sand used illness in her works. In a 1975 conference paper entitled "La Maladie comme ressort dramatique dans les romans de George Sand," Mireille Bossis surveys the types of illnesses treated in Sand's earlier works.[7] She shows the rarity of infectious diseases and the frequent use of characteristically romantic fainting spells, brain fevers, and general listlessness, all physical manifestations of psychological stress. For Bossis, illness in Sand is never gratuitous; it always has a narrative function. Through it, she concludes, events are prevented or permitted, amorous passions conflicting with social norms are allowed to hide under a care-giving disguise, and a new social order may be established. Although Bossis cuts off her study of Sand's use of illness with the year 1845, many of her findings for the early works hold true for the remaining years of Sand's production.

My focus, therefore, is not on illness but rather on Sand's healers, and their techniques and functions.[8] In order to better understand the question, one author was especially helpful for understanding the historical and political background in nineteenth-century French medical practice. In three volumes Jacques Léonard, the undisputed expert in the field, gives an excellent summary of medical legislation, scientific advancements, and the daily life of nineteenth-century practitioners.[9] Not surprisingly, many of his examples come from literary texts, from Honoré de Balzac—particularly *Le Médecin de campagne*—to Emile Zola, including regional writers like Emile Erckmann, Alexandre Chatrian, Eugène Le Roy, and even Jules Sandeau. One finds, in all, reference to some twenty-two writers and a long list of works by several of them.[10] Sand appears among the twenty-two, but the only work of hers cited is *Histoire de ma vie*. Although the Léonard volumes are extremely useful, one must protest this sin of omission.

The year 1803 is a landmark in French medical history. From that year, specifically 19 Ventôse Year XI, dates the law professionalizing medicine. By creating two categories of medical men, the doctor and the health officer (*l'officier de santé*, of whom, Charles Bovary is, of course, the most famous), the law was to create one kind of medical treatment for the rich and another for the poor. This situation, along with the century's advances in scientific knowledge, would lead to greater specialization. Finally, the law assured the exclusion of women from the medical profession. Through her characters Sand criticizes the principal provisions of the 1803 law.

Among the doctors in Sand's works we find both the good and the bad. Bad doctors may be relatively harmless tricksters, such as those in *Métella* who cure Count Buondelmonte of two illnesses he never had (201). They may, on the other hand, actually worsen the condition of the patient, as in *Les Beaux Messieurs de Bois-Doré*. After Mario is wounded, we learn that "the doctor had applied a healing salve that had the effect of poison on his entire system" (370).

In an 1870 play entitled *L'Autre*, Sand contrasts two doctors to point out good and bad medical care. The poor physician, Dr. Pons, is a materialist, interested only in the physical being. The family and entourage of the countess, whose stroke has rendered her unable to speak for six weeks, criticize Pons also for giving up too easily and not actively working to save his patient; they call him "Doctor Too Bad" (29).[11] In the same play, Dr. Maxwell, once poor and obscure, has become a rich and famous "man of genius" (58) because he takes into consideration the whole being, both the physical and the spiritual states. He puts his philosophy simply: "I believe the soul controls everything" (29).

Sand's good doctors, then, understand the role of nervous and emotional stress in disease, but they also realize their limitations. In *Le Dernier amour* it is the doctor who tells Monsieur Sylvestre: "The doctor's prescriptions will do nothing, or almost nothing, so you must be your wife's doctor. I'm a friend and not a quack" (185). In *Le Meunier d'Angibault*, the doctor realizes that La Bricoline's madness is out of the reach of his skills, and he chastises her family for not making the appropriate financial effort to have her properly cared for: "Your family was wrong not to make the necessary sacrifices to send her to an institution where skilled medical artists deal with exceptional cases" (293). Sand's loyal practitioners tend to be family friends, but they never hesitate to severely reprimand anyone in the family whose behavior has contributed to the illness in question, as we see Dr. Blondeau do with the vicious Nathalie in *Mont Revêche*. Although Sand's doctors often work with wealthy patients, charitable treatment of the less fortunate does exist. In the 1872 *Francia*, Sand gives us the example of Dr. Faure who, although he himself is poor, treats Francia, collects money for her, gives her fatherly advice, and helps her find lodgings and work as well.

A look at another of Sand's doctors who, as narrator, remains with us throughout an entire book, will help us come to a fuller understanding of her assessment of the medical profession. The nameless narrator of the 1862 novel dedicated to Dr. Jean-Hippolyte Vergne, *Tamaris*, proclaims his commitment to medicine: "My dedication was nothing more than the fulfillment of the duty to which I had devoted my life. Had I not pledged my services to the suffering and the endangered of the world by becoming a doctor?" (143). Like several others of Sand's healers, he collects no fees for his services. In the first paragraph of his account, he tells us how he has cared gratis for his family's benefactor, the Baron de La Rive, to repay his family's debt to the nobleman, and in the book's final paragraph he expresses his joy that marriage has allowed him to practice charitably: "If I don't miss my state of meritorious poverty, it's because I've been able to remain industrious and active, caring for my patients with no reward other than their affection" (175). Those around him reciprocate his great devotion through their care for him during his bout with pneumonia.

An outsider to the region, the doctor harshly criticizes certain of its traditions.[12] If other doctors in Sand's works have seemed more tolerant, however, it may be because the doctor-narrator expresses his criticism only to us as readers and not to the people involved. When he visits the young orphan Nama, the doctor rails at the "pestilential lairs" caused by the lack of hygiene in pig keeping because the pens are cleaned only once a year to obtain the fertilizer. He criticizes the bizarre uses of herbal knowledge, combined with superstition, in love potions, for instance, and the deadly results this combination can have in plans for vengeance or suicide.

On the other hand, he treats children with great tenderness. Louise, the battered daughter of la Zinovèse, is bathed, bandaged, and comforted by him. He watches over spoiled little Paul, first because he responds to the maternal concern of the Marquise d'Elmeval and then out of love for both the son and his mother.

Like others of Sand's doctors, he understands the essential role of the mind in the disease of the body: "Is it possible to minister to the body without treating the soul?" (143). His prescriptions at first cure la Zinovèse but later he is helpless when her passions work against his skills: "One cannot easily save those who are bent on destroying their souls, for the soul is the great driving force that our remedies cannot reach" (77). Nonetheless, he struggles to save her from the poison she has taken, despite her threats to destroy those he loves.

His devotion to medicine gives him the strength and courage to go out at night in dangerous terrain, while just recovering from his illness, to look for La Florade, even though the doctor considers la Florade to be his lucky rival for the love of Madame d'Elmeval. La Florade appears dead from drowning but the doctor refuses to give up and works on the unconscious man until he collapses from exhaustion. Of course, his heroic act succeeds in bringing la Florade back to life. The doctor's total commitment to the well-being of others wins him the love of the marquise and the allocation of her fortune to his medical activities.

This happy ending, however, troubles the careful reader. One is disturbed by the doctor's self-sacrifice, self-effacement, and passivity when it comes to his love for Madame d'Elmeval. Madame d'Elmeval's helplessness as she runs to the doctor each time young Paul falls while playing or has a cold or swollen finger is quite unacceptable. According to the marquise, she has been a health-care-giver for many years, first with her ailing father, then with her husband, and now with her son; should she not, then, with such extensive experience, be a little less dependent on the doctor, especially since both the Baron and the doctor speak of her strength? As the narrator describes her, she is "solidly tempered like a strong woman of the Armor region of Brittany" (94). When Paul becomes stronger, she confesses: "I no longer have any patients and I miss them" (96). Would it be too far-fetched to suggest that perhaps she has used her helplessness as a ploy to win the doctor's love so that she could, at least vicariously, participate in his dealings with sick people? Moreover, what of the doctor's self-sacrifice? Could it be that Sand wanted to endow him with certain stereotypically feminine traits to show that no "law of nature" had made medicine a male profession?[13]

Those who have earned the title of doctor perform only part of the health care in Sand's works. We have mentioned as an obstacle for some patients the cost of medical services, but even those who could afford to pay did not always have a doctor nearby. As Jacques Léonard shows, in the nineteenth century, despite the high ratio of doctors in the Paris region—1 for 662 inhabitants in 1844—or in the south of France, the situation in rural areas was quite different. That same year in the Morbihan, for example, there existed 1 doctor for 5,274 inhabitants.[14] On the average, cities had three times more physicians than did the country.[15] Hosts of Sand's characters serve as care-givers. Many remain within family bounds—mothers with sick sons, such as Madame d'Ermeval in *Tamaris* or Marcelle Blanchemont in *Le Meunier d'Angibault* (and through their sick sons, in fact, both come to meet their future loves). Before their marriage, couples often serve as reciprocal care-givers, inspiring Mireille Bossis's comment about their premarital intimacy.[16] We think immediately of Albert and Consuelo in *Consuelo* and Madeleine and François in *François le champi*. With married couples, the illness often signals an ailing marriage; often, only the husbands provide healing, as in *Le Dernier amour*, *Valvèdre* and *Mont Revêche*. All three wives die, however, because the emotional poison, caused by a lack of trust or respect, or by dishonesty or jealousy, has spread too far and done irreversible damage. In such cases, we have further examples of what I have previously pointed out as Sand's encouragement of small-scale, private reform rather than total societal change. It is interesting to note, in passing, that in Sand's works it is rare for such care-giving to be provided for someone of the same sex.[17]

A number of Sand's characters represent superior individuals who, without going through formal medical training, somehow obtain considerable knowledge.[18] Amédée in *Mont Revêche* has set forth to obtain medical knowledge in order to help his uncle's second wife, whom he adores; as a consequence he says: "I believe I know more than the doctors around here about my aunt's condition" (2:139). The scientist Valvèdre, who looks like a physician with his satchel, is able to cure a child of convulsions with products from his bag. We could add many other examples, such as that of the artist Jean Valreg in *La Daniella* who treats la Vicenza, who has been badly beaten and left for dead by her husband; Valreg depends on supplies and techniques left to him by his uncle the curé, a well-known "remégeur"—a natural healer, something like today's chiropractor. This substitution of a naturally superior individual for a social institution is typical of Sand's tactics.

It is not only men, however, who possess such medical knowledge. In *Mont Revêche*, Dr. Martel acclaims Olympe Dutertre as "the best of doctors" (4:153–154). He continues: "Do you realize that she's our rival? Intelligent women really excel at anything they want to do. In the cottages of the poor, I've seen the marvellous acts of foresight and intelligence that she performed while waiting for me to arrive."

In *Le Marquis de Villemer*, Caroline de Sant Geneix has cured the marquis after his attack by reading the recommended treatment written by one of the finest physicians in France. Of the local village doctors, the sick man had said: "There isn't one here who knows my constitution well enough not to risk killing me if he treats me according to his logic" (177). Caroline has, therefore, greater medical skill than these doctors although she refers to herself, modestly, as a "caregiver" (189) and a "nurse" (195). She does, however, have the pride to assert: "I alone know how to care for that patient" (338). Further, while in the Velay, she treats the village children without advice from a physician: "I'm interested in their children. When I find any who are sick I'm happy to be able to point out the basic care to give them" (301).

Many of Sand's women minister occasionally to the poor. We might cite Gilberte de Châteaubrun in *Le Péché de Monsieur Antoine* in her visits to a woman whose two children have typhoid fever, and the title character of *Nanon* who sacrifices her life in her tireless work during an epidemic. One might claim that because at least in the cases of Olympe and Caroline the woman does not act alone, she is therefore rather a nurse supporting a doctor's activities and thus lower in the hierarchy. In the twentieth century we have become very sensitive to such questions of gender, but here we must contend with the legal realities of medicine in nineteenth-century France.

The 1803 law which shaped nineteenth-century French medical history excluded women from the official practice of medicine. Arguments for such exclusion stun us today; even pharmacy was outlawed: "You will note that because pharmacy is not so much a trade as a learned profession it must consequently be outlawed for women."[19] Mary Poovey explains how the climate for this masculinization was created: "Beginning in the early eighteenth century with the disclosure of the Chamberlens' forceps, technology enabled medical men to extend the domain of medicine into what had previously been seen as a 'natural' territory presided over by women"—she speaks, of course, of childbirth.[20] We could also add to the forceps the nineteenth-century use of anesthesia in childbirth. Barbara Ehrenreich and Deirdre English outline the consequences for women of this evolution: "Thus the triumph of the male medical profession is of crucial significance . . . : it involves the destruction of women's networks of mutual help—leaving women in a position of isolation and dependency—and it established a model of expertise as a prerogative of a social elite."[21] Not until 1870 was a woman, in this case a foreigner, awarded the title of medical doctor in France. The first French woman of the century received her degree in Paris in 1875, one year before Sand's death.[22]

However, beyond the familial caretakers and occasional charitable healers mentioned above, women in nineteenth-century France had another way, though not a legal one, to practice some sort of medicine, often as a full-time occupation: through folk healing. The "triumph of the male medical profession" referred to by Ehrenreich and English was not complete. A work by Marcelle Bouteiller, *Médecine populaire d'hier et d'aujourd'hui*, proved the most useful resource in this area.[23] Bouteiller frequently mentions Sand and her interest in legends and traditions, citing particularly her preface to Laisnel de La Salle's *Croyances et légendes du Centre de la France*, and mentioning details from two of Sand's novels, *La Mare au diable* and *La Petite Fadette*.[24]

Sand's respect for traditional medicine did not remain abstract; it extended to her own life. In 1846 she wrote of Solange's treatment for *chlorose*—iron deficiency anemia characteristic of nineteenth-century female adolescents. She extols an "old wives' remedy that . . . worked wonders. The proverbial *rose* of youth returned to my dear little girl's cheeks, the palpitations have stopped, the masses of black bile which *legal* medicine couldn't break down were expelled by the witch's great art and, as if by magic, I swear to you, almost from one day to the next" (*Corr.*, 7:490). Her choice of the terms "legal medicine" and "the witch's great art" are significant. The 1803 law asserted that all medical practice other than that by doctors or health officers would henceforth be prohibited, but in the provinces, where doctors remained scarce and traditional beliefs were deeply entrenched, "the art of the witch," to use Sand's term, continued to flourish. It has been suggested that to eradicate such folk medicine would have been essentially impossible: "to attack the healer is to wound the community in its affectivity."[25]

In medical histories, we read of different types of folk healers, from the healing saints, and the traveling vendors to the local "witches."[26] Sand neglects the first two categories, concentrating on local healers, who were on the fringe of the agricultural society because of their empirical skills, but who, because of their local standing, were generally safe from being reported to the authorities who were charged with enforcing the 1803 law.

Perhaps surprisingly, the first example is the case of a man. Just as those who possess some formal medical knowledge do not all come from the same sex, Sand's "witches" are not all female. Sand describes the vigorous sixty-year-old peasant, a carpenter and something of a Christ figure, Jean Jappeloup of *Le Péché de Monsieur Antoine*, as being ready to stand up for justice whatever the cost.[27] Of him, a young admirer, the page of Antoine de Châteaubrun, says: "When there's suffering anywhere, one can be sure Jean will appear on the scene. In a situation where no one would risk going, he dashes in, even though he has nothing to gain, not even a glass of wine" (72). Although we never actually see Jappeloup perform medical acts, Cardonnet senior, a local entrepreneur who has little respect for him but needs his skills, calls Jean "the village sorcerer, the one who cures sprains with words" (281). The hero, young Emile Cardonnet, explains Jean's talents thus: "There are certain privileged natures in whom observation and logic take the place of knowledge" (280).

Like doctors, local sorcerers of this kind can be evil or good, as Sand points out in *Jeanne* when she discusses Jeanne's mother Tula and Tula's sister Grand' Gothe: "Old Tula and her sister, Grand' Gothe, were reputed to be magicians, with the difference that Jeanne's mother, who was loved and respected by everyone, was seen as a wise matron and her aunt as a wicked witch" (75). The evil eye of Grand' Gothe caused instant fevers in her victims. The worst that could happen, however, would be "to come upon her at night near the druidic stones—on Christmas night—one could be certain to take to bed on returning home, never to get up again" (76).[28] Here, of course, Sand is criticizing such superstitious beliefs; her primary interest, however, lies in showing the positive effects of folk healing.

Les Beaux Messieurs de Bois-Doré, although set in the seventeenth century, could, from the point of view of its medical contents, have referred to Sand's own time, except for the penalty involved. The legal doctor's treatment has made Mario's wound worse; Pilar, the "Morisque"—a Moslem converted to Christianity—with her centuries-old "secrets," has returned him to health. However, because of his shame at being bested by a foreigner, and, worse, a woman, the doctor accuses her of the illegal practice of medicine, "an accusation that could have much more serious consequences at that time than today since the question of sorcery might always be raised. And sorcery, for the most sober of judges, was a serious crime punishable by death" (374).

La Petite Fadette provides a particularly interesting case of folk healing. If there was a scarcity of doctors in rural areas of nineteenth-century France, there were even fewer pharmacists.[29] The herbal knowledge possessed by folk healers like Mère Fadet thus became especially significant. Mère Fadet's skills enabled her to cure sprains, fractures, cuts, burns, fevers, and pleurisy, and, as she was something of a charlatan also, could even cure ailments one never had. Through her work as a healer, Mère Fadet became a relatively wealthy woman.

Her granddaughter, Fadette, with her common sense, natural curiosity, attention to detail, and powers of observation and experimentation, attained an even greater herbal knowledge than her grandmother. She also possessed skills in animal and child care unknown to Mère Fadet, as well as a talent for psychological counseling based on her willingness to listen and her sensitivity to feelings. After going to a nearby town to work for a sister of charity from whom she learned even more to hone her curing skills, Fadette returned to become the almost saintly natural healer of the village. She would accept no payment for her services, thus showing that she "put more religion than devilry into her spells" (184).

The subversive aspect of Sand's thought does not come simply from her portraits of so many women who serve as health-care-givers. Rather, she describes in her works many widely accepted roles for women who were marginalized by the professionalization of medicine, as Ehrenreich and English have put it in *Witches, Midwives and Nurses*.[30] Sand's statement about women in medicine seems to me a stronger one, however. For example, Landry, as Fadette's only true love, has learned from her the properties of various herbs as well as techniques for caring for animal ailments. With these techniques, for example, he is able to cure a cow that has been abandoned by veterinarians as a hopeless case. His master's admiring conclusion is: "Landry has the right touch and that's something one's born with. Either one has it or one doesn't. Even if one went off to study in schools as the *artists* do, it would be to no avail if one weren't born skilled. And I'm telling you that Landry is skilled. His knowledge helps him find what will work. He has a real natural gift and that'll do him more good than money for the proper running of a farm" (137). Knowing the true source of Landry's skill to be Fadette's "natural gift" (138), we recognize the injustice of Père Caillaud's praise. Fadette has the natural gift; women too can be born with medical talent.

With Sand's valorization of women's medical skills, one might expect an accompanying interest in female health issues. We must not forget that nineteenth-century taboos prohibited reference to many bodily functions. Sand, however, broke enough of the moral codes of her time to have books placed on the Index; she might as easily have broken others. Many of Sand's women, like the writer herself, represent strong physical specimens—Edmée of *Mauprat* rides with passion, and Consuelo treks energetically across Europe. Many, of course, suffer from emotional illnesses, and a number succumb to them. Relatively little, however, appears in the novels specifically about female health. Pregnancy is rarely mentioned; in fact, Sand avoids the subject in a number of ways: Women, now widows, have children before the books open, they adopt them, or the books end with the "hope" of a child. *Les Maîtres sonneurs* does leave us with two pregnant women, but we have little precise detail. In *La Petite Fadette*, we read a few vague comments about the birth of the twins, Landry and Sylvain, such as how the midwife, Mère Sagette, received them in her apron and how the father helped his wife regain her strength by offering her a large glass of mulled wine. We also have a discussion of breast-feeding and its fatigues, and of wet nurses. However, details concerning women's health remain extremely rare in Sand's novels.

In Sand's work, those who succeed in healing others are superior individuals—"privileged natures," as Sand says in *Le Péché de Monsieur Antoine*—both male and female. Superior in Sand's terms, of course; Dr. Maxwell of *L'Autre* is an adulterer, the father of an illegitimate child. Fadette is seen by her neighbors as an unattractive, sharp-tongued tomboy who has connections with the devil. Sand's healers care for both body and soul; they realize that specialization and materialization have done much harm. They heal the rich and the poor, the noble and the peasant, without concern for society's hierarchies. When possible, they perform their healing art without charge, counteracting the century's tendency to provide one sort of health care for the rich and another for the poor.

Finally, we must look at the author herself, for she too had healing powers. When she said in *Histoire de ma vie*, "I had become a country doctor," she meant this on the most literal level. Throughout her life, she generously applied her medical knowledge and caretaking skills to her family, her ailing lovers, and her country neighbors. However, through her writings Sand was also a healer on another level. In 1837 she wrote about how she had to "distill the poisons of the human heart to earn a living. As one crushes them, one breathes them in, and one poisons oneself with the remedies prepared for others" (*Corr.*, 3:773). Perhaps this explains to some extent the litany of complaints about her own health found in the correspondence; however, the important point Sand makes here is found in the words, "the remedies prepared for others."

Certain of Sand's readers attained improved emotional health through her texts. The words of one bright and articulate young middle-class Parisian reader opened this paper. As Geneviève Bréton put it in her diary: "Madame Sand is a better doctor than I and I have used her services".[31] Through her "parables," Sand's purpose was to help the individual work toward small-scale, private reform, and, through those individual reforms, to cure society's ills and move toward a new social order. As she expressed it in 1848: "I have tried to raise serious issues in writings whose frivolous and fanciful form allows the imagination to embark on a search for the absolute ideal that has no political disadvantages."[32] It is in *Valvèdre* that we have the clearest and most succinct summing up of the artist's role: "The artist is the physician of the soul" (132).

NOTES

1. Sand texts quoted in this chapter will be followed by the page number in parentheses. Editions used were: *L'Autre* (Paris: Michel Lévy Frères, 1870); *Les Beaux messieurs de Bois-Doré* (Paris: Albin Michel, 1976); *La Correspondance* (abbreviated as *Corr.*) (Paris: Garnier Frères, 1964–); *La Daniella* (Paris: Michel Lévy Frères, 1857); *Le Dernier amour* (Geneva: Slatkine Reprints, 1980); *Francia* (Paris: Michel Lévy Frères, 1872); *Jeanne* (Grenoble: Presses Universitaires de Grenoble, 1978); *Les Maîtres sonneurs* (Paris: Nelson, 1961); *Le Marquis de Villemer* (Paris: Calmann-Lévy, 1861); *Métella* (Paris: Calmann-Lévy, n.d.); *Le Meunier d'Angibault* (Paris: Michel Lévy Frères, 1869); *Mont Revêche* (Paris: Alexandre Cadot, 1853); *Nanon* (New York: William R. Jenkins, 1893); *Le Péché de Monsieur Antoine* (Meylan: Editions de l'Aurore, 1982); *La Petite Fadette* (New York: Henry Holt, 1865); *Tamaris* (Meylan: Editions de l'Aurore, 1984); and *Valvèdre* (Paris: Michel Lévy Frères, 1863). All translations are those of the author.

2. For example, in volume 3 of her correspondence, in a letter to Charlotte Marliani: "From morning till night, the do-nothings, the curiosity-seekers and the literary beggars besiege my door with their letters and their presence. I maintain an inflexible defense. I neither answer letters nor invite anyone in and let it be known that I'm ill" (589–590).

3. Ellen Moers, *Literary Women* (Garden City, N.Y.: Doubleday, 1976), 12.

4. Sandra M. Gilbert and Susan Gubar, *The Madwoman in the Attic: The Woman Writer and Nineteenth Century Literary Imagination* (New Haven: Yale University Press, 1979), 54.

5. Curtis Cate, *George Sand, A Biography* (Boston: Houghton Mifflin, 1975), 73.

6. Sand, 4:63. Quoted by Jacques Leonard in *La Vie quotidienne du médecin de province aux dix-neuvième siècle* (Paris: Hachette, 1977), 156.

7. Mireille Bossis, "La Maladie comme ressort dramatique dans les romans de George Sand," *Revue d'histoire littéraire de France* (special issue devoted to the Sand Conference of November 15, 1975, at the Collège de France) (July/August, 1976): 4:598–613.

8. In the early stages of this project I consulted Georges Lubin concerning the presence of doctors in Sand's work. He sent a list of twelve works dating from 1833 to 1872 that enabled me to locate many of Sand's medically trained men.

9. Jacques Léonard, *La France médicale au dix-neuvième siècle* (Paris: Gallimard/Julliard, 1978); Jacques Léonard, *La Médecine entre les pouvoirs et les savoirs: Histoire intellectuelle et politique de la médecine française au dix-neuvième siècle* (Paris: Aubier Montaigne, 1981); and Jacques Léonard, *La Vie quotidienne du médecin de province au dix-neuvième siècle* (Paris: Hachette, 1977). See also Olivier Faure, "Physicians in Lyon during the Nineteenth Century, an Extraordinary Social Success," in Patricia Branca, ed., *The Medicine Show: Patients, Physicians and the Perplexities of the Health Revolution in Modern Society* (New York: Science History Publications, 1977), 243–253.

10. A list of the twenty-two authors follows. When many works have been cited, that listing has also been included: Aubert, Honoré de Balzac (*César Birotteau, Le Cousin Pons, La Cousine Bette, Le Curé de village, Le Médecin de campagne, La Muse du département, Pierrette, Ursule Mirouët*), Jules Barbey d'Aurevilly, Paul-Charles-Joseph Bourget, Châteaubriand, Alexandre Chatrian (of Erckmann-Chatrian), Alphonse Daudet, Emile Erckmann (of Erckmann-Chatrian), Gustave Flaubert, Anatole France, Fromentin, Albrecht von Haller, Victor-Marie Hugo, Eugène Le Roy, Guy de Maupassant (*L'Angélus, La Bête à Maître Belhomme, Malades et médecins, Mont Oriol, Nos Anglais, Sur l'eau*), Prosper Mérimée, Jules Michelet, George Sand, Jules Sandeau, Augustin-Eugène Scribe, Stendhal,

Emile Zola (*La Débâcle, Le Docteur Pascal, Fécondité, La Joie de vivre, Lourdres, Les Mystères de Marseille, La Terre*).

11. Jacques Léonard discusses the continuation in the nineteenth century of the "molieresque tradition" of criticism of the medical profession (see *La Vie quotidienne*, 217, and *La Médecine entre les pouvoirs et les savoirs*, 109. Several of Sand's characters are representative: see, for example, the Marquis de Boisguibault in *Le Péché de Monsieur Antoine*: "I don't believe in medicine. Up to now it has been able to get rid of the ailment only by attacking the life principle" (212); and Père Cadoche in *Le Meunier d'Angibault*: "I don't believe in doctors. Let them all go to the devil. . . . Ah, ah. Where is the doctor? I need him to finish me off quicker if I have to suffer like this for a long time!" (342).

12. There appear to be certain resemblances between *Tamaris* and Balzac's much earlier *Médecin de campagne* (1831–1832). Balzac's Dr. Benassis also rails against ignorance and superstition, particularly in the case of the cretinism allowed to flourish in the mountain villages. Moreover, Benassis also serves without charge but, in his case, he does so to assuage a guilty conscience. There are, however, many differences; for example, Sand's doctor is not an empire builder. Benassis serves as mayor of a village he molds to resemble Voltaire's Ferney, and Balzac allows his elitist country doctor to manipulate people paternalistically to avoid what Benassis sees as the evil of universal suffrage.

13. Bossis, in "La Maladie," speaks of the doctor in Sand's early works as having qualities of both mother and father: "Perceived as a synthesis of the two images of the father and the mother, he would symbolize the knowledge and power of the father and the love and devotion of the mother" (610).

14. Léonard, *La France médicale*, 13.

15. Jean-Pierre Gaubert, "The Extent of Medical Practice in France around 1780," in Baranca, *The Medicine Show*, 216.

16. Mireille Bossis, "La correspondance comme figure de compromis," in Jean-Louis Bonnat and Mireille Bossis, eds., *Ecrire, publier, lire les correspondances* (Nantes: Université de Nantes, 1982), 229.

17. Mothers treat sons, daughters fathers. Wives treat husbands, or vice versa. A woman cares for her sister's husband. The tenderness of the duke with his ailing brother the marquis in *Le Marquis de Villemer* is extremely rare: "The duke led his brother into his room, settled him into a big armchair. He cared for him as a mother would have cared for her child, and sat near him, holding his brother's hand in his" (179). He is, however, soon replaced by Caroline de Saint Geneix as the primary care-giver.

18. Mireille Bossis mentions Ralph in *Indiana* and Bénédict in *Valentine* as examples of the phenomenon in her "La Maladie."

19. Léonard, *La France médicale*, 103. For a fine study of healers, especially women healers, in William Shakespeare, see Marjorie Garber, "The Healer in Shakespeare," in Enid Rhodes Peschel, ed., *Medicine and Literature* (New York: Neale Watson Academic Publications, 1980), 103–109.

20. Mary Poovey, *Scenes of an Indelicate Character: The Medical "Treatment" of Victorian Women*, Center for Twentieth Century Studies, Working Paper no. 3, University of Wisconsin-Milwaukee (Fall 1985): 2.

21. Barbara Ehrenreich and Deirdre English, *For Her Own Good, 150 Years of the Experts' Advice to Women* (Garden City, N.Y.: Anchor Press/Doubleday, 1978), 34.

22. Léonard, *La Vie quotidienne*, 190–191.

23. Marcelle Bouteiller, *Médecine populaire d'hier et d'aujourd'jui* (Paris: Editions G-P

Maisonneuve et Larose, 1966). Also very useful on the subject is Matthew Ramsey, "Medical Power and Popular Medicine: Illegal Healers in Nineteenth-Century France," in Branca, *The Medicine Show*, 183–210. See also Léonard, *La France médicale*; Léonard, *La Médecine*; and Léonard, *La Vie quotidienne*.

24. She does, however, mistakenly place Grand' Gothe in *La Petite Fadette*, instead of in *Jeanne*, 186.

25. Quoted from Dr. Maurice Igert, in Marcelle Bouteiller, *Médecine populaire*, 331.

26. Sand speaks little of the relationship between religion and medicine, a major component of nineteenth-century beliefs. In *Le Meunier d'Angibault*, the poor family of la Piaulette borrows a horse from Grand-Louis to make a pilgrimage whenever someone is ill (277). The uncle of Jean Valreg in *La Daniella* represents the curé who is skilled as a natural healer; priests often have medical skills, according to Jacques Léonard. See especially his *La France médicale*, 38. See also Bouteiller, *Le Problème*, 26.

27. Jean Jappeloup, the carpenter, himself points out the connection with Christ when he discusses radical Christian social ideas in opposition to Cardonnet senior's aggressive capitalism: "The good Lord himself said the very opposite and he came down to earth in the form of a carpenter for the sole purpose of proving it" (299).

28. As Simone Vierne explains in her edition (Meylan, France: Editions de l'Aurore, 1986), these stones, called *pierres jômatres* in French, have been proven to be natural megaliths but might still have been used by the Druids, as legend has it.

29. Léonard, *La Vie quotidienne*, 71.

30. Barbara Ehrenreich and Deirdre English, *Witches, Midwives and Nurses, A History of Women Healers* (New York: Feminist Press, 1972).

31. Geneviève Bréton, *Journal 1867–1871* (Paris: Editions Ramsay, 1985), 73.

32. *Corr.*, 8:865; quoted in the introduction of *Le Péché de Monsieur Antoine*, 30.

21

The Divided Self in *Lélia*: The Effects of Dualism on the Feminine Psyche

Wendy Ann Ryden

George Sand's *Lélia* is a romantic study of the divided self in which the spiritual heroine unsuccessfully seeks to regain her sensual component. Through this quest for wholeness, the author explores the dualism that elevates the spiritual over the corporeal, as well as the effect of such dualism on the feminine notion of self, by exploring corresponding dichotomies in Catholicism, politicized sexuality, and art. The binaries that reflect the division of the spiritual and the physical, such as madonna/whore, angel/monster, and frigidity/sensuality, function as peculiarly female images that limit the characters' perceptions of themselves and each other. Furthermore, separation occurs not only within the self but externally in the form of the individual's alienation from nature and society. The struggle of civilization against nature, ego against others, and control versus lack of control are the external counterparts of the internal separation. Establishing this link illuminates the paradox of *Lélia*: Integration of the self must take place outside the self.

The connection between Lélia's plight and Catholicism reveals itself through the numerous references linking Lélia's beauty to statues of madonnas and angels. The admiration she inspires hinges on the ethereal aspect of her marble-like coldness. Her spirituality sets her above mere humans, and forms the basis of attraction for her would-be lovers, the poet Sténio and the priest Magnus. However, the same detachment that earns praise also incurs contempt under the label of frigidity. Sténio, tantalized by her spiritual beauty, is appalled at the coldness of Lélia's hands and lips. Couching his fear in religious rhetoric, he declares she must be either "an angel or a demon."[1] The insane priest Magnus also defines Lélia in two mutually exclusive terms by declaring that there are in fact two Lélias: the detached, mocking, angelic being so spiritual that she challenges God, and the demonic, sensual woman that comes to tempt him in his bedchamber. While Sténio associates the demonic with Lélia's frigidity, Magnus compares it to her imagined sensuality. This contradiction heightens the double bind found in a Catholic mysticism that associates the carnal with evil: To be asexual is to be spiritual and thus closer to God, yet to be asexual is to be inhuman and to challenge God. This notion not only precludes wholeness but also disallows any satisfactory classification of the self.

Since Lélia cannot place herself in such a schema, she rebels against idolization.[2] When she says, "I reproach you for continually placing me above and below myself" (8) and "it was not necessary to worship me like a divinity and then ask me to be your slave and Sulamite" (152), she rejects the power that Sténio and Magnus impute to her through their Mariolatrous and Miltonic allusions. Despite her protests, however, Lélia embraces the very philosophy she attempts to circumvent. In her first love affair, Lélia had approached physical love with the hope of fusing it with her higher ideals. Instead, the division between spirit and body allowed her lover to dominate her through physical possession. Her statement that "I sensed one could simultaneously love a man to the point of submitting to him and love oneself to the point of hating him because he subjugates us" (111) reflects her foiled attempt at self-unification through union with a man. As a result, Lélia almost literally becomes a nun by choosing celibacy and immuring herself in an abandoned church. Sténio correctly identifies the reason for Lélia's fear of sex when he says, "Do you fear obeying me if you surrender to me?" (147), and justifies his desire with the question, "Isn't it man's essence to want to possess all he admires?" (142). Lélia becomes the personification of intellect and spirituality in order to preserve some form of freedom, but her efforts are self-defeating since she perpetuates the gap she hopes to close.

Maternal love most closely resembles the unification that Lélia desires. The relationship between Lélia and Sténio conforms to a parent/child paradigm where physical love consists of her protective caresses. While maternal love may be a poor substitute for the passion she craves, it is at least not celestial and, more important, it preserves the power structure in her favor. Furthermore, for Lélia the incestuous nature of the affair implies a solipsistic completion, or reclaiming of self, but through connection with another.[3] Sténio, on the other hand, cannot settle for this affection even though, when Lélia tells him she cannot love him physically, he claims he will accept her elevated love. He complains so bitterly over her coldness—in this case his inability to possess her ("When you see a beautiful flower, don't you want to breathe it, tear it from its stem, hide it in your bosom, so that it belongs to you alone?" [193])—that Lélia invokes her double, her courtesan sister who *is* Lélia's sensuality, to deflower Sténio. The psychic trick of dividing in two allows the Lélia/Pulchérie persona to be both intellectual and corporeal, both free and sexual.

While Pulchérie embodies the lost sensuality of Lélia, Pulchérie herself is a remarkably complete character.[4] The division between the two sisters occurred during adolescence in an incestuous sexual awakening. Prior to this event, Pulchérie found an outlet for her sexual stirrings in her looking glass, which "inspired [her] with a senseless love" (102). However, Pulchérie and Lélia fall asleep in a hot, moist field, and Pulchérie dreams of a black-haired man kissing her with hot, rosy lips. When Pulchérie awakens, she incestuously lusts after Lélia's dark, masculine beauty, but realizes that she "needed to find an object of admiration and love outside [herself]" (103). That the event strengthens Pulchérie's ties to nature reinforces the completeness she achieves by redirecting her solipsistic desires toward an external union. In a sense, Pulchérie absconds with the better half primarily because she gets more than half. Socially, however, the extreme and limiting label of courtesan, evil counterpart of the madonna role, condemns fulfillment through physical pleasure.

Despite her place in society, Pulchérie flouts the label of prostitute by embracing voluptuousness with religiosity. Pulchérie espouses sensualism, not debauchery. Sténio, however, far from reconciling himself with physical pleasure, does precisely the opposite when he commits himself to Pulchérie and her lifestyle; he drinks himself into impotence. His desire to deaden his senses and free his spirit comes to fruition in his suicide. That his act bars him from Catholic burial is ironic since the death worship in Catholic mysticism, itself a direct extension of the condemnation of the flesh, is what has led him to commit his sin. Lélia, in her attempts to purge and redirect her physical desires, shows the absurdity of this glorification of death when, in order to preserve her intellect and spirituality, she falls in love with the corpse of a priest and a painting of a dead man. Perhaps the most perverse manifestation occurs when Magnus relapses into madness from lust inspired by Sténio's corpse. In a further irony, the suicide allows Lélia to love Sténio in the way he desired in life; nowhere in the novel are physical descriptions of his body more complete than when Lélia professes her love over the dead poet.[5]

In one sense, Sténio's death constitutes a misdirected attempt to retrieve, or perhaps establish for the first time, an affinity with nature. In order to heal the boy's ravaged soul, the ascetic Trenmor deposits Sténio in a monastery whose grounds, divided in two by an impenetrable cemetery, consist of the retreat of the monastery itself with its beautiful, cultivated gardens and a wild pond whose surface has never been "rippled by a fisherman's rod" (187). Advised by the clergy to stay away from the temptation of the pond, Sténio drowns himself in it in final protest to Trenmor's conviction that isolation and order will heal the wayward child. ("Aren't you struck by the magnificence displayed here, by the austere knowledge and patriarchal simplicity presiding over the cultivation of these gardens?" [186]). Sténio's burial in unconsecrated grounds is, in part, a triumph over the dogma that plagued him in life.

Poetry likewise afflicts Sténio in the same way that religion does by severing him from nature. Before his bout with libertinage, Sténio seeks nature as a restorative force because nature reflects his notions of spiritual perfection. However, as Lélia senses, this view, rather than bringing him closer, distances Sténio from the natural world. Both Lélia and Sténio appreciate not the sensuous but the ethereal aspects of creation: the sky, the winds, the sounds, the intangible. By diffusing the experience through his poetry, Sténio heightens and beautifies nature, making it palatable to the cultivated mind. He tames the wild through art; he raises nature to the spiritual (and therefore better) level. Referring to a valley, Sténio asks, "Isn't this place sublime and can you think of anything but God?" (67). When he tells Lélia: "These flowers are as uncultivated, wild, and beautiful as you. Don't you understand the passion I have for them?" (68), Lélia understands the connection between Sténio's view of nature and his desire to possess and control her:

> But we wouldn't live here for three days without blighting the vegetation and sullying the air. Man is always disemboweling his nurse and exhausting the soil that produced him. He always wants to rearrange nature and redo the work of God. You wouldn't be here three days, I tell you, without wanting to carry the rocks from the mountain to the bottom of the valley and wanting to cultivate the reeds growing at the humid depths on the arid mountain peaks. You would call that creating a garden. If you had come here fifty years ago you would have put up a statue. (69)

Perhaps Lélia has in mind a statue of the Blessed Virgin Mary.

The blending of isolation and control reaches its apex in the character of Trenmor. Although critics have referred to Lélia herself as the female counterpart to the Byronic or Faustian hero, Trenmor's compulsive gambling renders him the more likely candidate. Lélia's Don Juanic description of the compulsive gambler links him to the power and energy that redeem the evil of the romantic hero: "If in appearance its [gambling's] goal is vile, the passion it inspires is powerful. . . . One must condemn him because the energy he uses this way is profitless to society . . . but in condemning, don't despise him. . . . [O]nly measure his colossal will that struggles for the sole purpose of exercising its strength" (14). She goes on to claim that the gambler is so egocentric that he is incapable of vanity, since to be vain implies a recognition of others. In praising the gambler, Lélia convolutedly reveals the destructiveness of an impulse that admires solipsism and condemns the conception of art that glorifies such a hero.

Trenmor's "cure" for his gambling, however, is at once the same and the opposite of the obsession itself. Sent to prison for stealing money to pay a gambling debt, Trenmor learns through isolation to subjugate every desire to control and order. When Trenmor acknowledges that the happiest time in his life was when he was in solitary confinement because he found "isolation and silence" (26), he shows no change in his egocentric orientation. Only in this state can he appreciate the "poetic . . . true meaning of Christian mythology . . . and spirituality" (26), the beauty of poetry, and nature because it is imagined and not experienced. In romantic fashion, Trenmor laments the degeneration of experience and justifies his egocentric asceticism because reality never equals the expectation of his own imagination.

When Lélia voluntarily exiles herself in the abandoned church, she is attempting the equivalent of Trenmor's rigor. She thought she "had frozen [her] imagination" through purgation. "But as nature came to life again and made herself more beautiful, she made [Lélia] feel her power" (118). Lélia cannot find the solace that Trenmor finds since religion and poetry, as presented in the novel, mirror the lack of integration and community Lélia experiences in sexuality. Unable to accept, as a living being, the limitations of a lifestyle such as Trenmor's, Lélia's conflict is resolved in the allegorical murder of her body by the demented Catholic priest.

Never able to regain her sensuality and unable to accept its absence, the only solution to such tormented division is a death in which the physical self is obliterated. Lélia embraces the spiritual at the expense of the corporeal, and in so doing, acknowledges defeat, allowing the bicameral world to prevail.

NOTES

1. George Sand, *Lélia*, trans. Maria Espinosa (Bloomington: Indiana University Press, 1978), 3; this and all subsequent references are to this edition.

2. Nancy Rogers, "Psychosexual Identity and Erotic Imagination in the Early Novels of George Sand," *Studies in the Literary Imagination* 12, no. 2 (1979): 22.

3. For a discussion of the link between incest and solipsism in Romantic literature, see Sandra Gilbert and Susan Gubar, *The Madwoman in the Attic: The Woman Writer and Nineteenth Century Literary Imagination* (New Haven: Yale University Press, 1979), 207–209.

4. Rogers, "Psychosexual Identity," 22.

5. Béatrice Didier, "Le Corps feminin dans *Lélia*," *Revue d'histoire littéraire de la France* 76, no. 4 (1976): 642.

22

La Petite Fadette: An Epicene Cautionary Tale

Maïr E. Verthuy

> There is nothing like a girl about you, and your manners and appearance are just like a boy's; and then you take no care of your person. . . . Well, do you think it is nice not to look like a girl at sixteen? . . . It is a good thing to be strong and agile; it is a good thing, too, to be afraid of nothing, and it is a natural advantage for a man. But for a woman, there is such a thing as too much.[1]

La Petite Fadette by George Sand is somewhat of a phenomenon in the history of French literature. It is the only work by this author to have consistently survived the vagaries of her literary reputation and has indeed, almost without interruption since the introduction of compulsory schooling, been part and parcel of the cultural baggage of successive generations of French schoolchildren, although in a somewhat edulcorated form. It has naturally been thought particularly useful in the education of little girls, as the epigraph would indicate.

Two main perceptions of this novel have governed the way in which it has generally been presented. It has been variously seen as either a straightforward rustic idyll or as a realistic tableau of the poor but honest French peasant. In reaching either of these conclusions, critics have no doubt been influenced by the fact that the novel was written and published in 1848, after Sand, who had been revolted by the violence that characterized the Revolution of 1848 in Paris, withdrew to her country home in Nohant, taking refuge in the apparent peace of the countryside.

Such interpretations are, however, somewhat reductive, and fail to address a number of important issues. These include Sylvinet's obsessive love for his younger twin, Landry, a love that is categorically condemned in the text, Fadette's late appearance (one third of the way through the book) and the radical change in behavior she undergoes in the final third. Of the three main characters, only Landry, who goes his merry way in spite of all internal and external obstacles, and who, from the age of fourteen on, grows in apparent moral and physical stature, appears not to present any problem. One might well ask why he is so singled out.

Those critics who have looked beyond the rustic explanations have too often chosen to impose their own structure on the novel and have treated each case in isolation. Sylvinet's obsessive love has, for instance, been attributed to his slightly weaker constitution (yet the twins are identical until Landry leaves home), his emotional insecurity (yet he is the one who is kept at home), or some dreadful fate to which identical twins are subject (yet only one of them suffers from it here). In Fadette's case, her late appearance seems not to have been an issue; her transformation has usually been ascribed, according to whether the critic likes Sand, either to the civilizing influence of love or to the incompetence of the author. Landry is merely considered to be a perfect example of the happy peasant.

While his character may indeed require no explanation, it seems clear that the explanations offered for the apparently incoherent behavior of the other two main characters are insufficient. In treating the three protagonists quite separately, most critics fail to see the pattern that emerges when the three are juxtaposed, and to understand that, taken together, they constitute a cautionary tale about acceptable gender behavior. Landry, Sylvinet, and Fadette are either rewarded or not according to their willingness or refusal to comply with sexual norms, a reality that only becomes visible when the three are compared to one another.

There is also another trio of characters, albeit minor, in the novel: Mère Sagette, Mère Fadet, and La Baigneuse. They are "wise women" with whom the early Fadette has much in common. By their very presence, they raise doubts about the moral the book seems to convey, and it may well be George Sand's opinion that, although it may be advisable in a patriarchal society to conform to certain norms, those women who maintain the ancient traditions of herbal lore and folk medicine are closer to the truth and more useful to society than their patriarchal successors. Unfortunately, they are shown as a dying breed.

This chapter can then be divided into three parts: a comparison of the progression of the three main characters that will establish the lesson in morality that is the apparent theme of the novel, a brief look at the role of the three wise women that will help to reveal Sand's own ambiguous attitude to her subject matter, and a tentative conclusion about the true lesson to be learned.

Fadette does not appear until Chapter 8; it is appropriate, therefore, to begin with the twins. Until they reach the age of fourteen, the two boys are indeed presented as identical; only their mother has no difficulty in telling them apart. They are self-sufficient, require no other companions, and are, in fact, two halves of a single being. "In short, it was labor lost to try to separate them in mind or body" (25). However, as they reach puberty, the father suddenly apprentices one of them to a neighboring farmer, because of financial difficulties. Thus, they are separated for the first time.

From that point on, Landry's story is a real *Bildungsroman*. As the action of the novel goes forward, he becomes more and more manly, growing both physically and mentally. When he meets an obstacle, he overcomes it and draws strength from that process. In exchange for Fadette's help, he agrees to dance with her and only with her at the village fête, even though she is the least attractive girl in the village. That is why he also defends her and her reputation against half a dozen young louts who are older and bigger than he: "and a certain feeling of manhood told him that he was doing his duty in saving a woman from ill-treatment, whether she was pretty or ugly, big or little, so long as he had taken her for his partner in the presence of the whole company" (131). Once he has learned to love Fadette, he can, however respectfully, brave his father's displeasure and maintain his decision to marry her. Landry is a real man, endowed with virile qualities. At the end of the novel he has received his reward: a wife, a family, and wealth.

Sylvinet's progress is less straightforward, since he must first fall, and then be redeemed. The first signs appear the minute his brother leaves home, and it is readily apparent that if indeed they had until then formed a single being, that being was androgynous. Sylvinet is devastated by his brother's departure. He hangs onto his mother's skirts like a child (64), and when Landry returns the next day for supper, he "spoiled and petted his brother to his heart's content, giving him the best of his food, the crust of his bread, and the heart of his lettuce; and then he worried over Landry's clothes and his shoes" (43–44). Such behavior is usually attributed to women and, indeed, Sylvinet becomes more and more feminine with every passing page, as his world, like that of most women, becomes restricted to his domestic circle. Later, on learning that his brother has fallen in love, he goes into the traditional decline of the nineteenth-century heroine: "He has an excess of love in his heart, and because he has always directed it toward his twin, he has almost forgotten his sex; and thus he has sinned against that law of God which decrees a man shall cherish a woman above father or mother, sister or brother" (239–240). Sylvinet has just committed a serious fault: He has betrayed his sex by indulging in stereotypical female behavior.

Since the novel was to be serialized in a newspaper as a picture of rural life, this situation was not pursued to its logical conclusion. Through the love of a good woman, Sylvinet is able to redeem himself. As Landry had lectured her on the behavior that is appropriate for a girl, so Fadette, having learned her lesson, will, ironically enough, lecture Sylvinet on the behavior that is appropriate for him. He then emerges from his decline and in turn falls in love with Fadette, but is able to show his manliness by masking his feelings. He goes even further, literally and metaphorically, and leaves home to join Napoleon's army. Sand tells us that he is recklessly brave and that, after "ten years of fatigue, courage, and noble conduct, he became captain, and was even decorated" (294). Only through that most masculine of activities, war, can he hope to compensate for his effeminate behavior.

Fadette's progress is slightly different. There is no fall, because, when the novel opens, she is already settled into error, even if the fault is not entirely hers. Indeed, it is probably because she is supposed to be an unwitting and unwilling victim of her environment that Fadette is allowed redemption at all. A fall, for her, would be more serious than for Sylvinet. Like Sylvinet, she will, however, have to redeem herself because, again as in his case, she is guilty of betraying her sexual destiny, of behaving like a boy. When she first appears, she has nothing to recommend her in the eyes of the village and, therefore, of Landry. Her grandmother is a healer and, therefore, a "witch," her mother was a camp-follower; her little brother is ugly, crippled, and unpleasant; she herself is rather witch-like and lacks the coquettishness that is seen as appropriate in a young girl: "When she is fifteen years old and *begins to feel her own importance*" (90; author's emphasis). Gradually, however, she too is saved by love—a man's love—and learns to conform to the social norms for her sex. In her case, the redemptive process is rather longer than for Sylvinet, as she must not only change her behavior but also convince the villagers that she has done so—reputation being all for a woman. Needless to say, although Fadette too must leave the village, at least for a short time, in order to come back transformed, her apprenticeship for her new life involves not the army but domestic service: She learns to be a maid.

After some considerable effort on her part—and with a little help from her grandmother's legacy—she becomes irresistibly feminine: "In short, though she was not the prettiest girl in the world, as Landry imagined, she was the comeliest, the best made, the freshest, and perhaps the most desirable in the neighborhood" (249). No man could ask for more. On the one hand, she restores Sylvinet to health and encourages him to fulfill his destiny in the army; on the other, by helping Landry with her money and all her folk knowledge, she makes it possible for him to become an extremely successful landowner. She brings their children up to be amiable and compassionate; she herself engages in charitable work. A thoroughly admirable woman, Fadette's transformation is complete at the end of the story. She is no longer the social outcast she once was, although it is worth mentioning here that the very gifts that made her an outcast—her folklore and herbal medicine—become more than acceptable when shared with Landry, who uses them first to impress his employer and then to develop his own property.

When the three trajectories are compared (see below), it becomes clear that what Sand had in mind is a morality tale, although perhaps not the one that is usually taught.

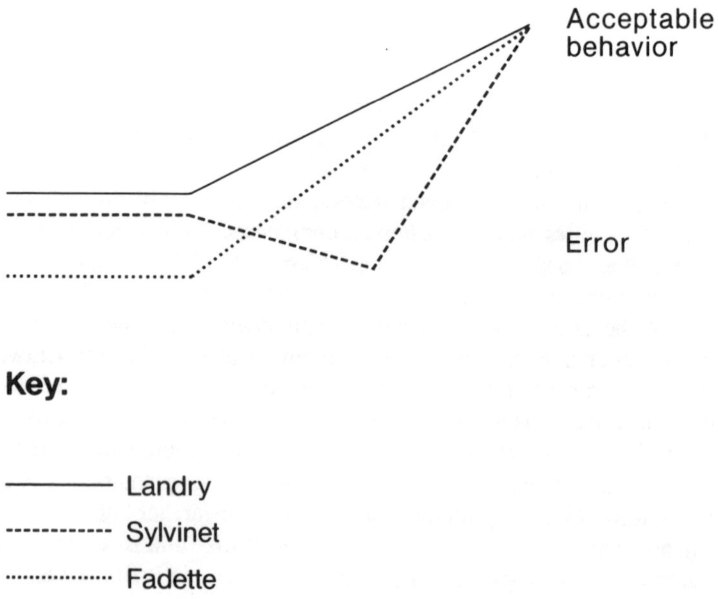

Patriarchal society requires that its members meet certain norms. Landry is the perfect model of truly male behavior; he goes from strength to strength and reward to reward. Sylvinet's lapse into femininity requires that he prove himself by exaggerating his masculinity, namely, by making war. Fadette too has to go to extremes; she must stifle her independence, her audacity, and her boyishness, and become perfect and completely self-effacing in order to erase all memory of her early self.

This is a bitter lesson, drawn perhaps from Sand's own experiences; certainly, Fadette's childhood is reminiscent of Sand's. The lesson is no doubt what explains the novel's continued popularity in the French school system, since it reinforces gender stereotypes in a very agreeable manner.

This may be the overt lesson, but one may well suspect the existence of another more covert lesson to be drawn from the novel based on the role of the other trio, the three wise women. All three are presented as midwives or witches. Mère Sagette is first on the scene. It is she who distinguishes the elder twin from the younger and devises an identifying system, and it is she who provides excellent advice on the proper way to raise identical twins so that they learn to be independent of each other. This advice is not followed, partly because of the parents' own thriftiness and partly because of pressure from the local establishment, in the guise of the village priest. That failure will cause much of the trouble in the book.

When Mère Sagette dies, la Baigneuse de Clavières becomes the foremost wise woman of the area since Mère Fadet is now senile. She diagnoses Sylvinet's problem where others fail, and so prepares the way for his redemption. As for Mère Fadet, the heroine's grandmother, while it is true that she is generally unpleasant during her lifetime, the villagers still make frequent calls on her sorcery. Moreover, it is her money, a considerable sum, left to her granddaughter on her death, that sets the seal on Fadette's transformation. Landry's father may not be won over by the money alone—it would be wrong for him to be so crass—but he clearly adopts a more favorable attitude once he learns of its existence and once Fadette, already transformed to the wiles of a stereotypical woman, consults him about its use.

Fadette herself must also be added to this list, as it is her extraordinary gifts, which verge on the supernatural, that save Landry and Sylvinet from distress or danger on several occasions and that help Landry to become a good, and even inspired, farmer. All these wise women play a very positive role because of their particular skills. They are also the vehicle used by Sand to chart the significant changes that have taken place in society. Mère Sagette's influence is countered by that of the curé, with unfortunate results; Fadette must first repudiate her grandmother, and then transmit her knowledge to Landry. This displacement of the wise woman by the Church and the taking over of women's traditional knowledge by the male power structure are certainly revealing, and lead the reader to conclude that George Sand is describing the tensions between a new, powerful world dominated by patriarchal bourgeois values, and an older, more mediæval, society, in which power was more evenly divided between the sexes, women led more autonomous and more useful lives, and from which natural lore had not disappeared.

If that is so, then the novel is also making a statement about the total disappearance of that older society and all the traditions that went with it. Fadette is the only girl in the village still to possess that ancient motherwit; that folklore or woman's wisdom. When she decides to conform to society's norms—when she turns all her knowledge over to Landry and ceases to exercise it herself, and when she abandons her autonomy—she epitomizes the dispossession that has gradually overtaken women in the modern post-Renaissance world and has here, in post-Napoleonic society, reached even the remote countryside. Fadette is exemplary not because she becomes a "real woman," as defined by her entourage, but because she exemplifies the loss of women's status that society has caused.

By constructing *La Petite Fadette* in this particular manner—by establishing these parallels and convergences, in which each individual's life takes meaning from its relationship to others—George Sand obviously intended that a lesson be drawn from the novel concerning social norms and loss of power and knowledge. This lesson that would apply equally well to girls and boys, since it is no secret that male homosexuals were also victims of those same witch hunts that destroyed women's power for so long. This lesson seems not to have been an article of personal faith; it is a bitter warning to those who live on the margin of society about the heavy penalty the mainstream exacts in modern times from those who would refuse to conform, an acknowledgment that in 1848 there is no escape from patriarchy. A romance with a fairy-tale ending—no; an epicene cautionary tale—yes.

NOTE

1. George Sand, no trans., *Fadette* (New York: H. M. Caldwell, 1893), 140.

Part VII

CONTEMPORARIES

23

George Sand and Alfred de Musset: Absolution Through Art in *La Confession d'un enfant du siècle*

Jeanne Fuchs

The love affair between George Sand and Alfred de Musset is probably the best-documented liaison in nineteenth-century letters. Musset was the first to publish an account of their romance in his novel, *La Confession d'un enfant du siècle*, which appeared in February, 1836—one year after the lovers' final separation. Actually, parts of the novel had been published as early as September 1835 in *La Revue des deux mondes.*[1]

Before turning to the specific analysis of this novel, it would be helpful to recapitulate briefly what had happened between Sand and Musset during the one year and nine months that their relationship lasted. George Sand and Alfred de Musset first met in June 1833 at a dinner party given by François Buloz, publisher of *La Revue des Deux Mondes*. Charles-Augustin Sainte-Beuve introduced them. She was twenty-nine; he was twenty-three. Both were already famous. She had published *Indiana* in 1832; he had published *Contes d'Espagne et d'Italie* in 1829 (at age nineteen), and, at the time they met, his *André del Sarto* and *Les Caprices de Marianne* had just been released.[2]

Both were also notorious: she for her amorous and sartorial eccentricities; he as a dandy, a libertine, and a skeptic. In retrospect, it seems inevitable that this pair of "enfants terribles" of the early nineteenth century should fall in love. Consequently, it should not be surprising that, according to all the most reliable sources, six weeks after the now-famous Buloz dinner party, Sand and Musset were lovers (Adam, 53).

Musset was delicate, gracious, nervous, and effeminate. He felt reinvigorated by Sand, and believed that with her he had found the grand passion of his life (Adam, 57). Sand was the virile one in the relationship; she was charmed by Musset's wit, his manners, his exquisite delicacy, and his freshness (Adam, 59). Most of all, he was what she wanted more than anything else—a child—her "bon enfant" (Adam,

59). She preached the New Testament and wanted him to become a disciple of Jean-Jacques Rousseau. Feeling as if he were reborn, Musset left his debauched companions and let himself be "converted" (Adam, 60).

From August to October, the pair was madly in love; they worked together and were both productive during this period. Musset wrote the masterpiece of nineteenth-century French theater—*Lorenzaccio*; Sand wrote *Lélia*. Because of the lifestyles both had established previously, the lovers had difficulty being alone, and, of course, there was the usual quota of skeptics and scandalmongers who wished the lovers ill. Consequently, they decided to take a trip to escape the troublemakers and be alone. They left Paris for Italy on December 12, 1832.

On January 2, 1833, Sand and Musset arrived in Venice. During the course of what was then a long journey, both had been ill off and on, and soon after their arrival in Venice, Sand became seriously ill. Musset left her alone to go out on the town with the French consul. He began drinking again and frequented the dancers and singers from La Fenice (Adam, 100).

A doctor was finally called to attend to Sand; his name was Pietro Pagello. Thanks to this first innocuous "house call," Pagello was catapulted to a rather dubious fame. Sand recovered, but by February 4, it was Musset who was now desperately ill. He went through what most critics call a "crise de folie," although it was more likely delirium tremens coupled with some sort of viral infection. Once again, Dr. Pagello was summoned. His prognosis was more than gloomy: he told Sand that Musset might die. Sand nursed Musset through weeks of fever, ravings, and illness, but was not faithful. By February 12, she had become Pagello's mistress.

Musset recovered by early March and left Venice alone on March 29 for Paris. He arrived home on April 12 and promptly retreated to his room, where he remained for weeks reading *La Nouvelle Héloïse* and *Werther*.

Sand returned to Paris on August 14 with Pagello. There is much evidence that she was by then already bored with him, for she escaped almost immediately to Berry to see her children, leaving Pagello in Paris. On October 23, Pagello packed and left for Venice; Sand paid the fare. In the interim, Sand and Musset went through a series of violent ruptures and reconciliations. The definitive break came in March 1835.

While Musset's novel does not follow the above events in a factual way, it captures the ecstasy, the tension, the turmoil, the disillusionment, and the ultimate devastation that their love affair encompassed. Written just at the end of the relationship, *La Confession d'un enfant du siècle* emerges as a distillation of the pleasure and pain lovers inflict on one another, transposed into a glorious prose poem by one of the most delicate and graceful writers of the age. Musset's talent as both playwright and poet combined to produce a work at once lyric and dramatic, which possesses much of the force of the many literary confessions that precede his, and to which he was no stranger.

The word "confession" in the title serves to underscore the religious framework within which Musset chose to tell his tale. It is rare to ascribe a religious interpretation to any of Musset's works. As a whole, his oeuvre rests comfortably in the profane category. Nonetheless, even a casual reading of *La Confession d'un enfant du siècle* reveals an intensity of feeling that goes far beyond the simple recounting of a failed love affair. The vocabulary, the imagery, the tone, the structure—in short, all the literary devices used by Musset—point to a profound desire by the author for catharsis, for transcendence, and, to use the religious term, for absolution.

La Confession d'un enfant du siècle remains without doubt its author's *De Profundis Clamavi*; it is masterpiece of its genre, and it was Musset's last major work. Although he lived for twenty-one years more, it is clear he believed that his love affair with George Sand had ruined what was left of his life (*Confession*, 241).

While Sand was also deeply affected by their ruined romance, she was essentially a far more resilient person than Musset. Her life, sustained as always by her work, proved to be long and productive. In the tradition of Romantic poets, Musset died relatively young at forty-seven; Sand lived to the "unromantic" age of seventy-two.

Art as exorcism, confession, or catharsis is not a new idea. Consciously or unconsciously, this beneficent aspect of art is present in most, if not all, works of art. Musset's literary influences in this regard are many; he knew his Rousseau well: In fact, his father, Victor-Donatien Musset-Pathay, had written the standard biography of Rousseau of the period. In addition, Musset had not only read but had also translated Thomas De Quincey's *Confessions of an Opium Eater* into French (*Confession*, xl). However, most important for Musset was Saint Augustine, whom he venerated, and who is mentioned in *La Confession d'un enfant du siècle* itself as "the most manly man who ever was" (*Confession*, 97).

Musset's devotion to St. Augustine is suggested by the religious overtones of the title he chose: "*Confession.*" It is the religious aspect of this work that will be examined in this study. Confession, whether private or public, presupposes private or public absolution, and that is precisely what Musset sought to achieve in this novel through the protagonist, Octave.

Two aesthetic decisions underscore Musset's intentions; each complements the other and enhances Musset's gifts as a dramatist. First is the use of a grandiose historical panorama in which to situate his novel, and second is the complex structure of the work itself.

In general, Musset's work is not characterized by grandness. He was not and did not wish to be a Victor Hugo or an Honoré de Balzac. He never desired to say everything about everybody. In describing his own work, Musset wrote, "My glass is not large but I drink from my glass."[3] Even in *Lorenzaccio*, which is set in Renaissance Florence, Musset concentrates on the individual dilemma of the main character—the political and historical elements become of interest only as they relate to the fate of the protagonist.[4]

It is uncharacteristic, therefore, that Musset begins *La Confession d'un enfant du siècle* on a grand scale. Octave's fate is a metaphor for the moral dilemma of the entire generation of young men that followed the Napoleonic era. The idea of depicting the flaws of an entire generation through one character is clearly announced in the novel's title. It is a confession, yes, but it is the confession of a child of the century, of his own time. The individual and the universal are artfully combined throughout the narration. Therefore, any absolution sought would be for all those who shared the same sins with Octave.

Because of the Napoleonic wars and the promises of glory and empire in which they were enveloped, the fathers of Musset's generation are depicted as perpetually absent. Musset describes the children of this era as having been "conceived between battles"—as remembering their fathers riding off on horseback (*Confession*, 2). He sees Napoleon as "invincible and immortal," and says that "death herself was then, so grand, so magnificent in her smoking purple" (*Confession*, 3). France had become "the widow of Caesar" (*Confession*, 3), and the "children of those absent fathers dreamed of the snows of Moscow, of the sun on the Pyramids" (*Confession*, 4). In the world of disillusionment that followed Napoleon's ignominious defeat, these children would wait in vain; they were left in the ruins. Musset says that if they spoke of glory, ambition, hope, love, or life, they were told, "Become priests" (*Confession*, 5). The immense horizon of the future loomed before them. They were weak, passionate, nervous—figuratively emasculated. An "inexplicable malaise" overcame them, and love became an illusion like glory and religion (*Confession*, 12). There was universal doubt, and French youth believed in nothing. For Musset, the greatest geniuses to come after Napoleon were Goethe and Lord Byron; he calls them"colossuses of sadness."

Musset's analysis of the state of Octave's soul (his *état d'âme*) and that of his contemporaries is meticulous and unsparing—truly Flaubertian in the delight taken in the dissection of feelings. Octave incarnates not the "Everyman" of the Napoleonic era, but rather the "Everychild" as survivor of that era. Although the remainder of the novel is played out in a more private setting, the origin of Octave's malady is never forgotten, and is reintroduced regularly at crucial moments. Society is indicted not just for what it has done to men, but also for ruining women.

The second aesthetic element that stresses Musset's intentions in the novel is its structure. Musset's theatrical gifts and his rich sense of the dramatic come to the fore in the way in which he has constructed the novel. The structure parallels that of classical tragedy. In fact, one critic likened this work to Greek tragedy because of the pity and terror it arouses.[5] It has also been viewed as a decadent *Romeo and Juliet* because of the unbearable intensity of some of the scenes (Rees, 53). Musset divided *La Confession* into five parts or acts. Each part has a varying number of chapters or scenes. Parts 1 and 2 are given over to exposition and the peripeteias of the protagonist. The heroine is not introduced until Part 3, which also contains the climax of the novel. Parts 4 and 5 trace the inevitable destruction of the ideal love so longed for by the protagonist. Furthermore, this destruction is brought about by a flaw in Octave's character—ironically, by his inability to love. By using a classical framework, the author not only highlights the seriousness of the tale for himself, but also reveals that he seeks the catharsis that all tragedy requires.

Thus catharsis is to art what absolution is to religion. By studying Octave's development throughout the work, it becomes apparent that Musset was seeking not just to unburden himself through his confession but also to transcend his experience by receiving absolution.

From the novel's declamatory opening, the reader is whisked into an intimate scene of betrayal. It is a key moment. Seated at an elegant dinner table, Octave gazes dreamily at his beautiful mistress as he contemplates their rendezvous for later that evening. Accidentally, his fork drops from the table and, as he bends to retrieve it, he sees his mistress's leg entwined with that of the young man seated next to her. Neither of their faces reveals the slightest sign of this intimacy; in fact, both are engaged in conversation with others. Stunned, Octave, nonetheless continues to observe the pair with unbearable fascination throughout the remainder of the meal.

The mistress who betrays Octave is never given a name; thus, she becomes the incarnation of the unfaithful and capricious female. She leaves an indelible mark on Octave's soul. The rest of Part 1 traces the stages of jealousy and despair through which the hero passes, and his self-disgust at still being attracted to a woman who could betray him so casually. Octave remains permanently traumatized by her deception.

A literary device often employed by Musset in his poetry and theater is the *Doppelgänger*. In *La Confession d'un enfant du siècle*, the doppelgänger for Octave, who at the outset is idealistic and vulnerable, is a character named Desgenais. He is a bit older than Octave—blasé, skeptical, and cerebral. After Octave's first mistress betrays him, Desgenais, in parts 1 and 2 of the novel, undertakes a kind of sentimental education of his friend.

The concluding chapters of Part 1 and all of Part 2 are given over to long and brilliant, though pessimistic, philosophical discussions about love, virginity, fidelity, marriage, motherhood, and the role of civilization in ruining women. There are successive indictments of literature, the eighteenth century, and society in general. Once again, the narrative alternates between the universal and the particular.

Seeking the absolute is dangerous business, Desgenais informs his friend. Octave has been duped by what poets write about love, which, for Desgenais, has nothing to do with reality. Desgenais uses the example of Praxiteles to make his point: He says that the Greek sculptor created his Venus from a composite of all the beautiful women in Athens, and omitted their faults (*Confession*, 41). He adds, "Wanting to find in real life loves equal to those found in antiquity is like looking for Venus in a public square or wanting nightingales to sing Beethoven symphonies" (*Confession*, 41). Desgenais concludes that human reason can heal illusions but cannot control or stop the torment that one feels because of them (*Confession*, 73). In true Romantic fashion, Desgenais treats love as an illness, and spends all of Part 2 attempting to cure Octave of it. If love is an illusion, one remedy for its loss is debauchery. Part 2 of the novel contains a detailed description of debauchery as well as Octave's personal determination to become a libertine and to develop a blasé attitude toward life in general.

In the culminating scene of Part 2, the course of the novel is abruptly changed by the terrible news of the death of Octave's father. Stricken by this unexpected turn of events, Octave retires to his father's country home—the place where his father had died. In the solitude of this retreat, Octave undertakes an examination of conscience. He compares his father's orderly and virtuous existence with his own dissolute life. He feels remorse and shame, and determines to mend his ways.

Thus has Musset, the master playwright, carefully prepared the moment for the arrival on stage of his heroine. In the George Sand role we have Brigitte Pierson. Up to this point in the novel, the love depicted has been profane. Now, at the very heart of the narration, the first and only example of sacred love is introduced, and seems to have been waiting in this idyllic setting to redeem or, at least, to rehabilitate the deeply scarred protagonist.

Brigitte is a young widow who lives quietly in the country with her aunt. She is ten years older than Octave. The widow is known in the region for her piety and her good works: She has become a sister of mercy in caring for the poor and the ill in the countryside. From the moment she appears in the novel, Brigitte is depicted in intensely religious terms: "ange," "soeur de charité," "rosière," and "Brigitte la rose." In this pure and rarefied atmosphere, Octave sees the chance to lead a virtuous life. That he might achieve his goal through Brigitte's intercession is implied from their first meeting. Octave is impressed with Brigitte's simplicity, her intelligence, and her infectious gaiety. He feels a return to innocence when he walks through the fields with her (*Confession*, 139). Indeed, in this wholesome setting, Octave begins to recuperate and to regain a sense of inner worth. Crediting Brigitte with this change, he says to her, "God sent you like an angel of light to pull me out of the abyss" (*Confession*, 162).

This, of course, is precisely what Sand had done for Musset. Alfred, like Octave, met George after a failed love affair followed by a period of debauchery (Adam, 45–48). Just about everyone who has written about Sand and Musset—both their contemporaries and later critics—agree that she had, at least at first, a salutary effect on him. Henri Lefebvre goes so far as to assert that it was thanks to Sand that Musset became a man and an authentic writer.[6] Lefebvre goes on to analyze the qualities found in Sand that aided Musset in his own development: "George Sand united the contradictory qualities that Musset demanded from a woman and from love. Genial and sensual, amorous and maternal, pure and impure, experienced and naive, George was able for some time to effect a reconciliation between dream and reality, between him and himself" (*Confession*, 62).

By making the age difference between Octave and Brigitte greater than that between him and George (ten years as opposed to six), Musset stresses the feminine qualities cited by Lefebvre, and thus heightens the fatal nature of the couple's love in the novel.

Part 3 of *La Confession* is suffused with a religious aura, and traces the growth of love between Octave and Brigitte. As long as their love for each other stays on a spiritual plane, there is peace. Brigitte seems to intuit this, for, when she realizes that Octave has fallen in love with her and she with him, she runs away. First she leaves the village to visit relatives, and then she persuades Octave to leave the village for several months. Of course, none of these ploys works and, eventually she confesses her love to him in an intensely voluptuous and romantic scene as they are riding horseback through the forest.

The final chapters of Part 3 rise in a magnificent crescendo—an ode to love written with an intensity of passion not found in the earlier descriptions of profane love. Octave feels that "a hymn of grace was coming from his heart and that their love was rising up to God" (*Confession*, 172). The vocabulary is markedly religious: There is a blending of Octave's passionate feelings, which have left him in a state akin to religious ecstasy, and sensual delight. Love becomes "a principle of the universe . . . [a] precious flame which all nature, like an uneasy vestal, surveys incessantly in the temple of God" (*Confession*, 172). He speaks of those who have "blasphemed" using the name of love, and of love finding its true "apostles" united in a kiss; he evokes the first timid signs of love with cherubs hovering above the lovers; and he recalls their "divine dreams," and their "serenity of happiness." He bemoans his own sense of powerlessness to capture his feelings about love when he explains, "What human word can ever describe the weakest caress?" (*Confession*, 173).

Paul de Musset tells us, in his biography of his brother, that Alfred considered ending the novel with Part 3. Indeed, Sainte-Beuve thought that he should indeed have concluded on this delirious note. Sainte-Beuve speaks of the "exquisite and irreproachable voluptuousness" of the last chapter, and compares it with "passionate and intoxicating" passages in *Adolphe* and *Obermann*. He says that Musset's passage is like "a warm breeze in May" or "the first scent of lilacs."[7]

Obviously, however, Musset did not opt for the deliriously harmonious ending that Part 3 would have afforded him. Modern critics celebrate his decision.[8] The exultation of Part 3 is short-lived, and Part 4 shifts to an even more confessional tone as the relationship between the lovers begins to deteriorate. Octave becomes suspicious of Brigitte almost immediately: His suspicion is triggered by a white lie she tells him. Brigitte often plays the piano for her lover. One particular piece that he appreciates was written by Brigitte herself, but she has told Octave that it was composed by the Italian composer Stradella. One day, after she finishes playing it for Octave, she laughs and calls him a "dupe," and says that she has "tricked" him, that he has been "deluded" by her because it is she who has written the piece. This one miscalculation costs Brigitte dearly. It brings back to Octave a flood of unhappy memories of the deceitfulness of women and his betrayal by his first mistress. He sees himself sinking into an abyss of suspicion and jealousy, but he is powerless to stop his descent.

The romance between Octave and Brigitte follows the same downward trajectory as Octave's mood. He begins questioning people about Brigitte's behavior before he knew her. His suspicions drive him to become sadistic toward her. Even though he feels remorse over his actions, he willfully pursues his destructive course. Brigitte's reaction, at first, is one of complete astonishment, but little by little, she realizes that Octave's attitude and the change that has come over him are beyond her powers to reverse. She begins to treat him like a sick child and to resign herself to the pain caused by his illness.

In the meantime, Brigitte's reputation is tainted because it is obvious to all in the village that Octave is her lover. A further blow is dealt when her aunt dies. Shunned and alone, Brigitte resigns herself to her now-unhappy life with her lover. At the same time, she realizes that she can no longer endure life in the village, and so the lovers leave for Paris in a highly charged scene that ends Part 4.

It is clear that once physical possession has occurred, Octave reverts to the

Octave of Paris, the libertine. The suffering caused by unconsummated love is replaced by a cerebral, self-inflicted suffering, rooted in suspicion and jealousy. Happiness eludes Octave, and by extension, Brigitte, because of his own perversity and willfulness. Ultimately incapable of reconciling spiritual and physical love—the sacred and the profane—Octave becomes determined to destroy any relationship between himself and Brigitte.

While the change to Paris in Part 5 has, at first, a positive effect on the couple, their happiness evaporates quickly. Paris, in the novel, recaptures in large part the tension of the real-life drama of Sand and Musset in Venice. The lovers escape the pain of the present by planning trips and projects for the future. Paradoxically, Octave and Brigitte's desire to flee is juxtaposed with their inability to act. On the figurative plane, they cannot depart for the "promised land." In fact, they had left behind any hope of attaining it when they abandoned the original setting in which their love blossomed. Religious imagery abounds in these passages. Octave envisions their trip as containing the "terrors of exile" and "the hopes of a pilgrimage" (*Confession*, 237). When Octave watches Brigitte sleep, he longs for purification through "repentance." He wishes that a temple, consecrated to love, existed where he might be baptized (*Confession*, 233). He compares himself to St. Thomas, doubting and adoring. Curiously, when Octave evokes St. Thomas, it is the St. Thomas in a portrait by Titian that he has in mind. Musset's choice here produces a mirror effect between the Titian portrait and his own work of art, his novel: Just as Musset's portrait of the love affair between Octave and Brigitte has become more intense, and more "real" than the actual love affair between George and Alfred, so too Titian's rendering of St. Thomas had been filtered through that artist's sensibilities and goes beyond whatever reality it originally represented. Because of the immediacy and universality of the work of art, it transcends the moment it depicts, and fixes it on another plane. Musset's choice of St. Thomas is of further interest in that it supports the thesis that the author was seeking absolution for his hero (it also is an oblique reference to Venice). Musset equates Octave with an apostle, a man who overcame his doubts and became a saint.

The catalyst necessary to break the lovers' impasse arrives in the person of a young man, a distant relative of Brigitte. The Pagello character is named Smith in the novel. It seems curious that Musset chose such an innocuous and British Protestant name to designate his rival, Pagello, an Italian Catholic and self-styled Don Juan. The vagueness of the name, as well as the character, reveal Musset's intention in choosing it: He did not blame Pagello for what happened in Venice; he blamed himself. Besides, Pagello had afforded an escape from what had become an intolerable situation. Smith is described in simple, noble terms, and when Brigitte falls ill, he begins to visit the couple daily. Once well, Brigitte hesitates about leaving Paris, and their departure is repeatedly delayed, sometimes by Brigitte and sometimes by Octave.

Octave begins to observe Smith and Brigitte when they are together, and he is struck by their sadness. With no evidence of intimacy, he concludes that they are in love. The only indication he can uncover of a link between them is a single, empty teacup, from which he suspects they both have drunk (*Confession*, 343 n.215).

Octave begins to dwell on his former debauchery; he believes that he is permanently tainted because of it, and decides that he and Brigitte are doomed if they stay together. Even after this insight, he is unable to let go of her, and a series of violent scenes follows. The turning point comes one evening, as he stands over the sleeping Brigitte with a knife in his hand. When he uncovers her bosom and sees a crucifix there, he falls to his knees and repents. During this scene, Octave speaks to Christ, and acknowledges that it was through suffering that Christ became God (*Confession*, 314). At dawn, Octave finally resolves to let Brigitte go. The final chapter depicts Brigitte and Octave exchanging tokens of friendship—rings—just before they part forever. She goes off with Smith, and Octave remains alone.

Musset places the blame for the failed love affair on Octave; he exculpates Brigitte and Smith completely. The text reveals Musset's understanding of himself and a deep sense of guilt about his behavior. The suspicion and jealousy that Octave feels about Brigitte are imaginary, but they were not imaginary in the real-life drama. Sand betrayed Musset in Venice. There was no question about it. By putting all the blame on his protagonist, Musset makes Octave the sacrifice, the victim in the tragedy and its most arresting figure. Octave's flawed character has caused him to lose the woman who might have saved him from himself. Nonetheless, his suffering, coupled with the realization of his faults, ennoble him.

Brigitte emerges as a more mundane figure. She leaves Octave for someone else, while he remains solitary. The heroine echoes the sentiments of George Sand, when she tells Octave that he is not capable of love (*Confession*, 279). Musset reiterates this idea in both the novel and his letters. What he could not attain in his own life, in his relationship with Sand or with any other woman, Musset achieves through art. The difference is that *La Confession d'un enfant du siècle* seeks purification for the protagonist and attains it after a painful examination of conscience and confession.

Musset's novel represents a supreme effort to resolve, on the aesthetic plane, what had become irreconcilable for him in reality. Through confession, the poet seeks, at least, a laicized form of absolution. The reader may serve as the surrogate priest, as the protagonist repents and asks for absolution for his overburdened soul.

NOTES

1. Alfred de Musset, *La Confession d'un enfant du siècle* (Paris: Garnier Frères, 1968); all translations are those of the author.
2. Antoine Adam, *Le Secret de l'aventure vénitienne: La Vérité sur Sand et Musset* (Paris: Librairie Académique Perrin, 1938), 51.
3. In *A Survey of French Literature*, ed. Morris Bishop (New York: Harcourt Brace and World, 1965), 2:61.
4. *Théâtre de Musset*, ed. René Clair (Paris: Gallimard, 1964), 1:347–490.
5. Margaret Rees, *Alfred de Musset* (New York: Twayne, 1971), 23.
6. Henri Lefebvre, *Musset: Essai* (Paris: L'Arche, 1955), 62.

7. Charles-Augustin Sainte-Beuve, *Portraits contemporains* (Paris: Calmann-Lévy, 1891), 2:211.

8. Joachim Merlant, *Le Roman personnel de Rousseau à Fromentin* (Geneva: Slatkine Reprints, 1970), 393.

24

George Sand's Multiple Appearances in Balzac's *La Muse du département*

Janis Glasgow

Anne-Marie Meininger's introduction and notes to the Pléiade edition of Honoré de Balzac's *La Muse du département* are carefully researched and meticulously presented. Regarding one particular conclusion, however—that of the model for Balzac's heroine, Dinah Piédefer—I choose to differ with Meininger: George Sand was far more for Balzac than "a rare example of an indirect model."[1]

Meininger dismisses several theories concerning the identity of the primary model for Dinah Piédefer, Baronne de La Baudraye.[2] She maintains that Rosa de Saint-Surin must be understood as the model for Balzac's heroine, all the while admitting that "we know almost nothing about Balzac's relations" with her (*CH*, 613).[3] It is fitting that we quote from W. P. Trent's translation of the novel, Balzac's witty presentation of *le sandisme*.

> If it were not that the word would, to many readers, seem to imply a degree of blame, it might be said that George Sand created *Sandisme*, so true is it that, morally speaking, all good has a reverse side of evil. This leprosy of sentimentality has spoilt many women, who, but for pretensions to genius, would have been charming. Still, *Sandisme* has its good side, in that the woman attacked by it bases her assumption of superiority on feelings scorned; she is a blue-stocking of sentiment; and she is rather less of a bore, love to some extent neutralizing literature. The most conspicuous result of George Sand's celebrity was to elicit the fact that France has a perfectly enormous number of superior women, who have, however, till now been generous enough to leave the field to the Maréchal de Saxe's granddaughter. (*MD*, 240)[4]

In my opinion, this paragraph was not so much an attempt on Balzac's part to separate Dinah Piédefer from George Sand as it was a monumental spoof. Furthermore, while Balzac's heroine is surely patterned on his observations of many women, Piédefer's adventures, as numerous critics have observed, certainly parallel those of Sand with Jules Sandeau. Moreover, in the pre-original texts, Balzac dubs Dinah's lover, Lousteau, both Jules (like Jules Sandeau) and Emile (like Emile Regnault) (*CH*, 1366, 1371–1375) before finally settling on Etienne.[5] Even though Balzac separates Piédefer from Sand by sending her back to her husband at the conclusion, his heroine was merely conforming to his own beliefs: A woman's revolt against the rules of society and the Code Napoléon was (and should be) doomed to failure.

Our primary reason for terming *La Muse du département* a spoof on George Sand is that Balzac not only presents his character as based on Sand, he also gives us a multiplication of his own Sandian references. Indeed, the book may owe more to the woman novelist than just witty references. Something that no Balzac scholar seems to have imagined is that George Sand was probably the originator of the novel's title. Thierry Bodin states that "Karénine insisted that Sand had lent Balzac her correspondence with her convent friends."[6] In the novel, not only does the relationship between Anna Grossetete (the Baroness of Fontaine) and Dinah Piédefer strikingly resemble the one between Sand and her convent friend Jane Bazouin (the Countess of Fenoyl), but in Aurore's dedicatory letter of 1829 to Bazouin sent with the early fictional creation "La Marraine," she had quipped:

> May God keep me from ever throwing myself into the domain of poetry, even if all the laurels of Pindar should crown my forehead, even if I should be called *the muse of my department*, a title so envied by every provincial woman who knows how to read passably in the Book of Hours of her diocese and who can write an invitational note for her literary evening without making more than three spelling mistakes.[7]

Georges Lubin calls this "the first appearance of the expression which Balzac will make famous fourteen years later" (*Corr.*, 1:563n). Assuming that Karénine was accurate in stating that Balzac used Sand's correspondence with Jane Bazouin, it seems highly improbable that this first literary effort and its preface fit the category, "correspondence with a convent friend."

When it was that Balzac gained access to Sand's material we cannot know, but George Sand was in Paris from January 1 through May 21 of 1843 (*Corr.*, 6:3), while Balzac was writing "Dinah Piédefer". Balzac's novel first appeared under that title in serial form, between March 20 and April 29, 1843, in *Le Messager*. According to Meininger, "On March 12 [Balzac] finds a new title: *La Muse du département*, 'more comical and more explicit' than "Dinah Piédefer", but must renounce it for *Le Messager*, doubtlessly because it is too late" (*CH*, 4:1351). The last segment of "Dinah" appeared several days after the novel had been distributed in volume as *La Muse du département* (*CH*, 4:1352).

George Sand's other recorded statement referring to this novel was written in her *Histoire de ma vie* after Balzac's death. She displays a certain identification with the title: "One of my friends who knew Balzac a little had introduced me to him not as a *muse of the department*, but as a good provincial person very much in awe of his talent."[8] According to Georges Lubin, Sand and Balzac had been introduced either by Sandeau or Regnault (*OA*, 2:1339n).

Jean Gaulmier strongly agrees that Sand was Balzac's model.[9] Also in agreement is Thierry Bodin, who argues, "Certainly Dinah strongly resembles Caroline Marbouty, but, above all, isn't her story George Sand's? Balzac's precautions at the beginning of the work, in his chapter *Sandisme*, continue to be suspicious" (*AB*, 225).

Because aspects of Dinah Piédefer that resemble George Sand have been so well demonstrated both by Gaulmier and Bodin, short examples should be convincing. About Piédefer's musical ability, Balzac had written: "When they heard the fair Dinah playing at sight, without making the smallest demur before seating herself at the piano, the idea they conceived of her superiority assumed vast proportions" (*MD*, 250). Similarly, concerning her life with Lousteau:

> Dinah intended to be indispensable; she wanted to infuse fresh energy into this man, whose weakness smiled upon her, for she thought it a security. She found him subjects, sketched the treatment, and at a pinch, would write whole chapters. She revived the vitality of this dying talent by infusing fresh blood into his veins; she supplied him with ideas and opinions. In short, she produced two books which were a success. (*MD*, 390)

The two books were *Indiana* and *Valentine*. We learn, too, that "more than once she meditated suicide" (*MD*, 401), and that in leaving Lousteau she told him: "For you I will always have . . . the heart of a mother"(*MD*, 407)—a strange statement for Dinah, in her twenties, to tell her lover, who is in his late forties, unless she represents George Sand, for whom it rings true. (Balzac made Lousteau and Bianchon older than Dinah because, having appeared in other novels, they needed to conform to already established birth dates.)

To prove that Balzac was clearly not setting a distance between George Sand and his "muse," it is amusing to note how he multiplies her. First of all, Balzac compares Piédefer to Sand: "in and around Sancerre, Madame de La Baudraye became the rage; she was the future rival of George Sand" (*MD*, 275)[10], as well as in two other such passages: "The young man [Gatien Boirouge], under a genuine illusion, spoke of Madame de La Baudraye [to Lousteau and Bianchon] not only as the handsomest in those parts, a woman so superior that she might give George Sand a qualm, but as a woman who would produce a great sensation in Paris" (*MD*, 280). Similarly, "Of course, Lousteau spoke very ill of the great female celebrity of Le Berry, with the obvious intention of flattering Madame de La Baudraye and leading her into literary confidences, by suggesting that she could rival so great a writer" (*MD*, 316). Elsewhere, when Balzac mixes the names of Dinah and George, he manages to add his avowed Sandian prototype, Camille Maupin (pseudonym of writer Felicité des Touches in *Béatrix*): "When, after the Revolution of 1830, the glory of George Sand was reflected on Le Berry, many a town envied La Châtre the privilege of having given birth to this rival of Madame de Staël and Camille Maupin, and were ready to do homage to minor feminine talent" (*MD*, 273). Moreover, he manages to use Camille Maupin's real name when his narrator mentions Horace Bianchon having recited *La Grande Bretèche* for the first time at Mademoiselle des Touches's supper party (*MD*, 301–302). Moreover, Camille Maupin surely derived her name from Théophile Gautier's androgynous heroine of the novel *Mademoiselle de Maupin*, whereas the name Camille, with the same sexual ambiguity, also suggested Camille Andriani, the real name of the hermaphrodite heroine Fragoletta of the Henri de Latouche novel of the same name.[11] Although Dinah is a purely heterosexual heroine, this fact, coupled with her being dubbed "the Sappho of Saint-Sur" (*MD*, 252), surely reinforces the argument that his model was probably Sand, at least as Balzac imagined her.

My next observation is found in Piédefer's literary output. Until now, no critic of Balzac has been able to identify the source of Dinah's poem, which was written under her pseudonym, Jan Diaz.[12] I contend that "Paquita la Sévillane" alludes to Sand's little-known text "Le Toast," published in December 1832 in *Soirées littéraires de Paris*.[13] Paquita is the heroine in Dinah's poem, where she gives vent to her marital unhappiness. Balzac underlines the parallels between Dinah and her heroine when he calls Dinah "Paquita of Sancerre" (*MD*, 316). A key element is the fact that Balzac created another heroine named Paquita, Paquita Valdès in *La Fille aux yeux d'or*. By extension, his well-informed reader can equate the two.[14] Furthermore, Pierre-Georges Castex, in his introduction to Balzac's *Histoire des treize*, implies that the adventures of Paquita Valdès were inspired by those of Sand and Marie Dorval.[15] Balzac's suggestion seems to be: George Sand/Camille Maupin/the Sappho of Saint-Sur/Paquita.

Before presenting Dinah's poem, here is Balzac's explanation:

> *Paquita la Sévillane*, by Jan Diaz, was published in the *Echo du Morvan*, a review which for eighteen months maintained its existence in spite of provincial indifference. Some knowing persons at Nevers declared that Jan Diaz was making fun of the new school, just then bringing out its eccentric verse, full of vitality and imagery, and of brilliant effects produced by defying the muse under pretext of adapting German, English, and Romanesque mannerisms. (*MD*, 269)

No critic has ever located the mediocre journal Balzac satirized; we wonder if Balzac may have created the name to contrast it with *L'Echo de la Jeune France*, where an article about George Sand had appeared on July 15, 1835 (*Corr.*, 3:3).[16] Advancing to Dinah's dreadful opus (four pages in the Pléiade edition), he intersperses it with witty asides. We learn Paquita is from warm and sunny Spain, where she danced in satin slippers "from eve till dawn" (*MD*, 269), and that now she is in dark, cold, and noisy Rouen in a "squalid room" (*MD*, 270). Balzac then gives a magnificent description of Rouen, which Dinah had never visited, followed by a criticism of industrial cities as opposed to the poetry of sunny Spain.

Sand never visited the Low Countries. Her heroine Juana of "Le Toast" recalls Dinah's Spanish pseudonym, Jan Diaz. Juana, though not from Seville, is from Andalusia. Like Paquita, she has left her warm, sunny climate for the cold, dark, north—not Rouen, but Holland. Whereas in Dinah's poem Paquita follows a lover during the Napoleonic Wars, in Sand's story Juana has followed her family during the years of the Spanish domination of the Netherlands and Flanders, and was married to the Governor van Sneyders of Berg-op-Zoom.[17] However, her real love is for the young page who joins the French army.

Considering Balzac's information on Paquita, we quote Sand regarding speculation and the climate:

> You often saw the rich families of the Low Countries regild the dusty coat of arms of the old Castillian nobility, or, in other words, the good, and heavy burghers of the Dyle and the Escaut rivers marry these pale, young girls newly arrived from the banks of the Guadiana, beautiful flowers soon withered under the cold, leaden skies of Holland. (*T*, 220)

Similarly:

> Juana, dreamy and sad, hated all these good Dutchmen so thick and so dull; she regretted her lovely [Spanish] sun, her beautiful rivers whose warm and harmonious waves seem to speak of love to the flowers on their banks. The snows and the ice of these swamps knotted her heart, the cold penetrated to the bottom of her soul. Add to the influence of the climate, the company of a husband who was very rich, very down-to-earth, very knowledgeable about everything which concerned his business and government, but, we must admit, very boring, and you will understand why the fair and tender Juana was homesick. (*T*, 221–222)

While the parallels continue, there are also major differences: Paquita performs provocative dances while Juana only listens sensitively to romantic music played on the guitar by Ramire, the Spanish page. These differences derived more from Balzac's susceptibility to gossip about Sand than from "Le Toast." Sand's lifestyle held an obvious fascination for him: In all his creations of her, whether Camille or Paquita Valdès, he observes her like a judgmental voyeur. Was Balzac thinking of the duel fought by Gustave Planche with Capo de Feuillide in defense of *Lélia*, and of Sand's string of lovers after Sandeau, as well as her notorious "mésaventure" with Prosper Mérimée? Was he remembering her in relation to the author of the *Théâtre de Clara Gazul*?

Another fictional parallel appears in Balzac's commentary: "Nothing could be more dainty than the description of the parting between the Spanish girl and the

Normandy Captain of Artillery" (*MD* 271). Sand had Ramire sent to the Governor of Antwerp by the jealous Sneyders, who resembles in husbandly traits both Casimir Dudevant and Colonel Delmare in *Indiana*. Ramire bears a message inciting revolt against Spain, and Sneyders has added a note for Ramire to be taken hostage. Several paragraphs describe Juana's sadness and feelings of hostility toward her husband.

We learn from Balzac that much of Dinah's poem told of Paquita's suffering alone in Rouen awaiting the end of the campaign. In Sand's text, Sneyders tries to force Juana to drink a toast to his colleague in Antwerp, but just as Juana rephrases it more acceptably, she hears a guitar in the distance and a sad voice singing one of her favorite Spanish romances. With joy, she clinks the glasses. Juana's husband dies in the wars and, still young and beautiful, she becomes free to find happiness.

On the contrary, however, Balzac gives Dinah's heroine a miserable ending in a house of ill repute, where she ends repeating the song of the opening lines. Maliciously, Balzac terms Dinah's final pages "rather too like the flayed anatomical figures known to artists as *écorchés*" adding that "Dinah shuddered with shame at having made 'copy' of some of her woes" (*MD*, 272).

Another amusing aspect concerns Monsieur de Clagny, Dinah's ever-faithful admirer, for he composes a pseudo-biography of Jan Diaz. Similarly, Balzac had asked Jules Sandeau to write a biography for the *Oeuvres complètes d'Horace de Saint-Aubin*, a creation of Balzac himself (*CH*, 1,401 n. 4). Sand and Sandeau created a Horace in *Rose et Blanche*, and Sand carried the joke even further with her own Sandeau character Horace, in the 1841 novel of that name.

The reactions of Dinah's husband to her literature are amusing. Had Balzac recreated the Baron Dudevant's reaction to *Indiana*? About Baron Polydore de La Baudraye, Balzac had written: " 'Little La Baudraye' dealt her glory a mortal blow. He alone knew the secret source of *Paquita la Sévillane*. . . . Dinah sometimes detected in his eyes, as he looked at her, a sort of icy venom which gave lie to his increased politeness and gentleness" (*MD*, 276). Jan Diaz's collected works are an elegy "Tristesse," "Chène de la masse," three sonnets, and a description of the Cathedral of Bourges and the Hôtel Jacques Coeur, plus a tale called *Carola*, published as "the work he was engaged in at the time of his death" (*MD*, 274). Scholars have tried to identify *Carola* as the *Cora* of Caroline Marbouty, while Meininger sees the text on the Hôtel Jacques Coeur as Rosa de Saint-Surin's work on the Hôtel de Cluny (*CH*, 1401–1402 n. 4). We speculate that while *Carola* could be George Sand's story "Cora," more probably it is the text that George Sand had just published in January 1843 in the *Revue et Gazette Musicale de Paris: Carl* (*Corr.*, 6:3). Balzac would have had access to that text, which deals with a dream world of musical hallucinations and death. As for the Cathedral of Bourges and the Hôtel Jacques Coeur, Sand had ample reason to know them thanks to Michel de Bourges, as they are the sites of her legal separation. Her letters of July 1836 mention the beauty of the cathedral (*Corr.*, 3:486), and the Hôtel Jacques Coeur is in *Mauprat*.[18] "Tristesse" recalls for us only Musset's poem, and *Chène de la messe* remains unidentifiable, unless it was suggested by the lost manuscript, "Engelwald," on which Sand was still working when Balzac visited her in 1838 (*Corr.*, 4:937).

Some of Sand's works are referred to by title in *Le Muse du département*. In one quotation, where Balzac juxtaposed Camille, Dinah, and Paquita, he avoided her name but mentioned *Leone Leoni* (*CH*, 4:718). The translator, however, added it:

> "I say," replied the Public Prosecutor [Clagny], "that the romance [*Olympia, ou les vengeances romaines*] is not by a Councillor of State, but by a woman. For extravagant inventions, the imagination of women far outdoes that of men: witness *Frankenstein* by Mrs. Shelley, *Leone Leoni* by George Sand, the works of Anne Radcliffe, and *Le Nouveau Prométhée (New Prometheus) of Camille de [sic]* Maupin."[19]
>
> Dinah looked steadily at Monsieur de Clagny, making him feel, by an expression that gave him a chill, that in spite of the illustrious examples he had quoted, she regarded this a reflection on *Paquita la Sévillane*. (*MD*, 336)

Another, more subtle, allusion to Sand's fiction is the following sentence: "Madame de La Baudraye, accustomed to take the stage, acquired an indefinable theatrical and domineering manner, the air of a [*P*]*rima donna* coming forward on the boards, of which ironical smiles would soon have cured her in the capital" (*MD*, 267). The allusion is also a contestable one, since such a work by Augustin-Eugène Scribe and Melesville was actually performed, but its power of suggestion may have amused Balzac: "The doctor [Bianchon] chose . . . *La Grande Bretèche* . . . that . . . was put on the stage under the title of *Valentine*" (*MD*, 301–302). Last is an allusion that appeared only in the pre-original texts: Polydore de La Baudraye was first named Melchior (*CH*, 1390 n. a), the title of Sand's 1832 short story.

We hope, therefore, despite Meininger's argument to the contrary, that George Sand's place in this novel will be reevaluated. Of all of Balzac's texts dealing with Sand, this one is perhaps the most entertaining. His vision of her is actually more flattering here than in *Béatrix*. While the reader gains better insight into Balzac's psyche than into Sand's in *Le Muse du département*, we discover the fascination she held for him. His closest colleagues undoubtedly savored the piquancy or aspects that we are only now reconstructing. Certainly, George Sand, alias Dinah Piédefer/Jan Diaz/Paquita la Sancerroise/Paquita la Sévillane, and then, by extension, Paquita Valdès/Felicité des Touches/Camille Maupin, proves herself a major force in Balzac's literary creation. As he affirmed the greatness of the Berrichon celebrity under all eight names, and *le sandisme*, using not just her life but also her literature, what can we conclude but that he heartily enjoyed his clever game? George Sand was apparently amused, too, for after Balzac's death, she fulfilled his wish and wrote the preface to the 1853 Houssiaux edition of *La Comédie humaine*.

NOTES

1. Honoré de Balzac, *La Comédie humaine*, intro. and notes by Anne-Marie Meininger (Paris: Gallimard, Pléiade, 1976), 4:616; hereafter referred to in the text as *CH*. All

translations are those of the author except those from Balzac's *Muse of the Department*, trans. W. P. Trent, vols. 29–30 of *The Works of Honoré de Balzac* (New York: Chesterfield Society, 1900); hereafter referred to in the text as *MD*.

2. These theories include those of Jean Savant, who suggests Louise Breugniot; and Bernard Guyon, who discusses Zulma Carraud, George Sand, and Caroline Marbouty in his introduction to Balzac's novel, *La Muse du département* (Paris: Garnier, 1970). Meininger states that because Caroline Marbouty tried so desperately to imitate George Sand, it is difficult to distinguish "the imitator from the one she was imitating" (*CH*, 613).

3. While Rosa de Saint-Surin may have contributed something to Balzac's creation, she also may be just another muse aptly fitting Balzac's generalities. For Meininger's full discussion of Rosa de Saint-Surin, see *CH*, 616–623.

4. Balzac was mistaken: George Sand was the great-granddaughter of the Maréchal de Saxe. Georges Lubin believes Balzac coined the expression *le sandisme*; see Meininger (CH, 139 n. 1) and Guyon in Balzac, *La Muse* (458).

5. Thierry Bodin in his article "Du Côté de George Sand" in *L'Année Balzacienne* (Paris: Garnier, 1972), 256 (hereafter referred in the text as *AB*), cites Wladimir Karénine, *George Sand, sa vie et ses oeuvres, 1804–1876* (Paris: Plon, 1899–1926), 2:137.

6. For additional material on the relations of the quartet Balzac, Regnault, Sandeau, and Sand, see Jean Gaulmier, "George Sand, Balzac et Emile Regnault," *Hommage à George Sand: 1804–1876* (Strasbourg: Faculté des Lettres de Strasbourg, 1954), 11–49.

7. George Sand, *Correspondance*, ed. Georges Lubin (Paris; Garnier, 1964–), 1:563 (emphasis added); hereafter referred to in the text as *Corr*.

8. George Sand, *Oeuvres autobiographiques*, ed. Georges Lubin (Paris, Gallimard, Pléiade, 1970), 2:1339 (emphasis added); hereafter referred to in the text as *OA*.

9. Jean Gaulmier writes: "In spite of the thesis which tries to make of Madame de La Baudraye a reminiscence of Madame Marbouty, I am convinced that Balzac took as the point of departure for his novel the liaison of George Sand with Sandeau"; see Gaulmier, "George Sand," 13, n.2.

10. Emile Regnault furnished Balzac his information on Sancerre; see Gaulmier, "George Sand," 12–14 n.8.

11. Rose Fortassier mentions the name of the heroine of *Fragoletta* and gives details concerning Balzac's use of the Latouche novel for *Séraphita*: see her introduction to *La Fille aux yeux d'or* in *La Comédie humaine* 5:774–775. Joseph Barry confirms our own interpretation in *George Sand, ou le scandale de la liberté* (Paris: Seuil, 1982), 242.

12. Patrick Berthier, in his edition of Balzac's *La Muse du département* (Paris: Gallimard-Folio, 1984) writes: "The subject itself, around 1830, was as overworked as the Romantic style could bear, Seville ceding only to Grenada, from Victor Hugo with his *Orientales* to Gautier with his *España* (331 n.2).

13. *Corr.* 2:7: "Le Toast" was reprinted in *La Coupe* (Paris: Calmann Lévy, 1876), 219–232; hereafter referred to in the text as *T*. In that publication there also appeared one of Sand's only poems, "La Reine Mab." Did the poem inspire Balzac to make Dinah Piédefer a poet?

14. Paquita Valdès's physical appearance and exotic origins recall those of Indiana's double, Noun.

15. Honoré de Balzac, *Histoire des treize* (Paris: Garnier, 1956), 259–261.

16. Meininger equates it with *La Revue de l'Est* while Patrick Berthier in his edition of *La Muse* calls it "a trail to follow more carefully, but which just stops" (331 n.2). Sand had

published no fiction in these journals, but had sent a letter and an article on Jules Néraud to the *Journal de l'Indre* in 1835 and 1836 (*Corr.*, 3:5) and had also written "De Madame Dorval" for the *Journal de Toulouse* in January 1837 (*Corr.*, 3:637).

17. Another trail to explore: Prosper Mérimée used Berg-op-Zoom for the location of a play, *Théâtre de Clara Gazul* (preface by Pierre Salomon [Paris: Garnier-Flammarion, 1968], 21).

18. After Balzac's death Sand also mentioned the Hôtel Jacques Coeur in connection with Michel in *Histoire de ma vie*, *OA*, 2:318.

19. Paul de Musset named George Sand "Olympia" in his *Lui et elle*, 1859.

25

George Sand's Reception in Russia: The Case of Elena Gan

Kevin J. McKenna

There is a tendency, when describing George Sand's literary reception in nineteenth-century Russia, to focus exclusively on the many prominent literary figures who gratefully acknowledged their debt to the French author. The list of names includes some of the most esteemed writers and thinkers of the century, almost all of whom had different and often personal reasons for bestowing their praise on her. For example, Vissarion Belinsky, the well-known social-utilitarian critic of the time, understandably hailed Sand as a beacon of social protest and an enemy of class prejudice. In one of his many review articles on the contemporary Russian scene, he went so far as to refer to Sand as the "Joan of Arc" of the time.[1] What appealed to him most of all, of course, were Sand's humanitarian ideals and persistent belief in the social mission of the artist.

The appearance of Sand's first novels in the early 1830s served to infect an already analytic new breed of young Russian intellectuals with an absorbing interest in French Utopian Socialism. The aspects of her novels that they found particularly compelling were Sand's religious doubts and misgivings and her quest for political and social justice. This fascination with the French writer came at a time when the hold of German abstract idealism had begun to loosen its grip on the minds of Russia's leading thinkers. Mikhail Bakunin, one of the founders of modern political anarchism, stated that as a result of Sand's influence, many Russian intellectuals realized that the time for philosophic theorizing had passed. Like many of his comrades, Alexander Herzen, a leading Russian revolutionary thinker and philosopher of the mid-nineteenth century, saw in Sand's novels a model for humanitarian idealism. This passion for ideals, as we recall, was to become the hallmark of Russian social and literary preoccupations for the remainder of the century.

Ivan Turgenev and Fyodor Dostoevski also acknowledged their esteem for Sand in their respective eulogies on the occasion of her death. Turgenev in particular had cause to lament her passing. Not only were Sand's sentimental and idealized peasant tales an important source of inspiration for his first literary success, *Sketches from a Hunter's Notebook*, but Sand herself was a personal friend who on several occasions had graciously shared her home with the Russian writer.

Fyodor Dostoevski offers perhaps one of the most florid testimonials to the memory of George Sand in a nine-page entry in his 1876 *Diary of a Writer*. He states:

> I believe I do not err when I write that George Sand promptly assumed in Russia virtually the first place among a whole Pleiad of new writers who at that period suddenly rose to fame and won renown all over Europe. Even Dickens, who appeared in Russia about the same time as she, was less popular with our public.[2]

Later in his account, Dostoevski also notes Sand's importance as a transmitter of Western ideas that managed to get by the strict Russian censorship. He writes:

> In those days fiction was the only thing permitted, whereas the rest, virtually every thought, especially coming from France, was strictly forbidden. Nevertheless, novels were permitted in that period. And precisely here, in the case of George Sand, the censors committed a grave error. That which in those days burst into Russia in the form of novels proved the most dangerous form; there arose thousands of lovers of George Sand.[3]

Although there are numerous accounts such as these that document Sand's impact on Russian social thought, far less consideration has been given to questions of her literary influence on Russian writers.[4] What little research exists has focused primarily on the idealized peasant tales in Sand's and Turgenev's short stories.[5] The purpose of this chapter is to discuss the least investigated area of Sand and Russian literature—that is, the issue of her influence on women writers in nineteenth-century Russia. The novels of one woman in particular, Elena Gan, one of the first female prose writers in Russia, demonstrate certain similarities with Sand's early writings, that is, the period of her feminist novels *Indiana*, *Valentine*, and *Lélia*.[6] Similar to the fate of George Sand's works, Gan's stories and novellas hold little but historical interest for today's readers. In mid-nineteenth-century Russia, however, Gan enjoyed a good reputation among literary critics and social commentators alike. Using the pen name "Zeneida R-va," she wrote eleven short stories and novellas whose central theme always served to reveal the frustrated lives of talented women trapped in a patriarchal Russian society.

A discussion of literary influence of course poses a number of formidable barriers, not the least of which is a definition of the term itself. For the task at hand—that is, of showing the relationship between Elena Gan's and George Sand's novels—I will discuss, first of all, the extraliterary or "ideational" consequences of pertinent social, intellectual, and cultural factors, and second, the internal, artistic issues of form and content.

Relevant biographic data concerning Sand and Gan provide considerable insight into their similar choice of themes, characters, and plots: that is, presentation of the plight of the gifted and sensual woman at odds with her oppressive and stifling environment. Both women shared the experience of being raised and educated in family surroundings that were highly conducive to the development of finely tuned independent minds. Gan, born in 1814, was the first child of an unusually well-educated mother who was to share with her daughter her knowledge of French, history, and botany, and to infect her with a keen mind and a sharp sense of inquisitiveness.

In addition to similar upbringing and education, Sand and her Russian disciple shared the unfortunate experience of early and highly disappointing marriages: Sand to an army officer when she was eighteen, and Gan to a cavalry officer when she had just turned sixteen. Their husbands were considerably older than the child spouses, and soon displayed cold, rational approaches to the highly romantic notions of their wives. From their diaries and later accounts, we know that the attempts of these two women to inspire in their husbands their fondness of books, poetry, and intellectual companionship met with utter failure. Finally, in spite of the glaring incompatibility that characterized their married lives, both women soon gave birth to children who were to provide them with the happiness and spiritual bonds of which they were deprived by their husbands.

Given the circumstances of their incomplete and frustrated married lives, as well as their highly romantic and idealistic natures, it comes as little surprise that both women turned to writing careers. Chronologically, of course, Sand was the first to publish her novel, in 1832. Both Sand and Gan established themselves as literary figures at the age of twenty-eight.

For both women, high romanticism was the dominant literary force of the period, and their novels reflected the demise of patriarchal values that had so plagued their respective environments, this being more the case, of course, in provincial Russia. The time was ripe for their messages of personal understanding and greater humanity among all people, based on the doctrine of sublime feeling and the liberation of previously subdued emotions.

In view of the similar formative influences in their education and upbringing by gifted, poetic-minded mothers; their disastrous marriages to cold, insensitive military men; and the cult of Romanticism that held sway during the early years of their careers, we can better understand the mutual concern of both women for portraying the lamentable plight of gifted, noble-minded heroines stuck in the mire of provincial indifference toward the lot of women. That Sand's depictions of the rebellious women were well received in Russia is amply documented by personal diaries and critical reviews. We also know that her novels were read enthusiastically, French being the common language of the educated populace in Russia. Furthermore, the novels were almost immediately translated into the Russian language. For example, Sand's first novel, *Indiana*, which was published in Paris in 1832, was translated into Russian and released in 1833. Gan, of course, was capable of reading them in the original French.

In an examination of Gan's novels, one notes many familiar themes reminiscent of *Indiana* and *Lélia*. The first of these is the lyrical plea for a woman's right to emotional freedom: the right to be more fully human and to follow the dictates of the heart; in a word, to love. In the preface of her 1832 edition of *Indiana*, Sand, for example, writes that her heroine is a type, "a woman, the feeble being whose mission it is to represent passions repressed . . . or suppressed by the law; she is desire at odds with necessity; she is love dashing her head blindly against all the obstacles of Civilization."[7] The heroines of Gan's novels equated love with the aim of their entire existence, and found in it their only retreat from harsh reality. Gan's first novella, *The Ideal*, is the story of Olga Holtzberg, a romantic and intelligent young Russian girl, who is sold by her parents into a miserable marriage to a provincial military man nearly twice her age. In an attempt to save herself from the tedious existence of an officer's wife confined to a dreary military outpost, the heroine immerses herself in the verse of a popular poet, Anatoly T. In time, Olga manages to meet her ideal, whose initial interest in her soon wanes when she effectively resists his efforts at seduction. Following a difficult and long separation, Olga returns to his apartment only to find it vacated. There remains a letter, however, in which Anatoly has described to a friend the indifference he feels for Olga. The despair of her situation brings on a prolonged illness and the realization that she will never find happiness. On the other hand, at the close of the novel, Anatoly remains carefree and happy. In typically Sandian fashion, Olga states her views on the injustice a woman suffers for the man she loves:

> A man deprives a woman of the most important capability of her soul—the ability to love passionately, constantly, unconditionally with total selflessness, knowing no obstacles nor fears; he deprives her of the capability to concentrate all of her emotional and intellectual energies in one feeling—to unite her being with love.[8]

She later refers to this ability to love as a woman's being, strength, and genius.

The capacity of women to devote themselves to love, even to the extent of self-sacrifice and death, is another familiar theme from Sand's early novels, *Indiana* in particular. Zeneida, the heroine of Gan's novella *Society's Judgment*, describes her notion of true love as being the *only* inspiration that sustained her in her existence as a social outcast. In a letter discovered by her doubting and weak-willed lover following her death, Zeneida states that she has based all her existence on the possibility of real love, that she trusted in the possibility of achieving her own form of utopia, and that she was willing to end her life rather than be untrue to her ideal.[9]

Still another frequent theme in Sand's novels and correspondence is the capricious way in which a woman's role in society has been assigned merely by being born a woman. If Sand was able to make such a statement, based on her experience as a woman in generally liberal-minded France, Gan had all the more reason to feel this way in backward, provincial, and patriarchal Russia. Gan's heroine Olga, in *The Ideal*, angrily evokes this protest, asking:

> What evil genius has so distorted woman's destiny? She exists to please and entice, to amuse men in their leisure hours, to dress herself up, to dance and hold sway over society. But in point of fact she is a paper idol before whom the clown bows in the presence of an audience, but whom he flings into a corner when he is alone. In society, men raise us up on thrones and our vanity adorns them. We fail to notice that these thrones are made of paper and stand on three legs. All we have to do is lose our balance ever so slightly, and we tumble for the indiscriminating crowd to trample us underfoot. It seems sometimes that the world is created only for men.[10]

Although the world of Sand and Gan may have been created only for men, the male figures who populate their novels rarely prove worthy of the women who love them. Even in Gan's *Society's Judgment*, the only one of her novels in which a man is portrayed as being capable of love, the male hero shows a lack of faith in the woman he loves, succumbs to jealousy, and eventually contributes to her death. The husband in *The Ideal* is typical of the men who dominate the world of Gan's novels. He is cold, ill-mannered, and totally unresponsive to his wife's needs. We learn at one point in the story that he considers the essence of a woman to be an impenetrable mystery and not worth the time, which he would rather devote to his fellow officers, drunken parties, and horse breeding.[11]

From these brief glimpses into Gan's stories, we hear the echo of Sand's impassioned protest against the inequalities of marriage. In one of the less veiled criticisms of a woman's fate in marriage, the narrator in *The Ideal* protests that in the "lottery of marriage the odds are a thousand to one that the extraordinary woman will cast her lot with the most ordinary and vulgar member of the opposite sex."[12] In characteristically rhetorical and florid prose, the narrator continues to overstate her case, much in the fashion of Sand's frequent declamations: "Only this yoke (that is, marriage) could harness a sluggish bull, with all the sensibility of the hay he feeds on, to a noble and passionate Arabian mare. And these two are destined to pull the plough of marriage through the boggy soil of life."[13]

In addition to the insensitivity of their dull-witted husbands, the heroines in Gan's and Sand's novels must fortify themselves against the petty prejudices of the patriarchal societies in which they live. One of the many obstacles confronting Sand's heroines, for example, is society's inability to forgive them their exaltedness, and especially their open love and admiration for the men of their choice. As a heroine of a new order, Indiana is a good example of a woman who believes in the primacy of love over the moral strictures of society. She rebels against these bonds first by refusing to submit to her husband's will, then by giving herself to Raymon, and last by living with Sir Ralph without the sanction of marriage.

Reminiscent of these same strictures against the social mores of her time, the heroines in Gan's novellas frequently complain that their sufferings result from the conflict between their emotions and the laws of nature and society. Like her French mentor, Gan repeatedly chastises society for its shallowness and refusal to acknowledge the basic human needs of its women. Characteristic of the fashionable circles of Sand's novels, these social conventions, be they in Petersburg or in the provinces, serve to constrain women, punishing them not only for deviance from accepted norms but also for following the dictates of their emotions. In a story appropriately entitled "The Futile Gift," a talented daughter of a simple steward is forbidden to exercise her skills at writing poetry, and as a result she grows insane and dies at the young age of eighteen.[14] In addition to the rigorous existence of self-denial that married women must face, the lot of the unmarried woman is a frequent theme treated by both authors. In the novella *Society's Judgment*, a provincial society condemns a noble-minded woman as immoral because she is unmarried, but accepts her when she weds a repulsive, domineering colonel in return for his sparing her younger brother's life.

As was often the case in Sand's novels, the plea for equality frequently takes on an indignant tone. Olga in the novella *The Ideal* angrily notes that the world must have been created only for men. In her opinion, only men have access to the secrets of the universe, and the enjoyment of fame, art, and knowledge. "A woman," she continues, "from the time of her birth is fettered by the chains of respectability, enmeshed by the awesome question of what society will think. And if her hopes for a family are not realized, she has little else to sustain her life, for her narrow education prevents her from devoting herself to meaningful work."[15] Similarly, the heroine of "The Futile Gift" objects that the gifted woman is doomed "to vegetate in the desert, in anonymity away from the world, from all the great models, from all opportunities to satisfy her soul's thirst for knowledge, and only because she is a woman."[16]

If a case is to be made for literary influence, attention must be given as well to those areas where the authors and their works depart from the literary model. Thus far we have noted the numerous correspondences between the heroines and themes of Sand's novels and those of Gan. Let us now turn to some of the differences in their works.

One of the most prominent differences is the greater range of themes in Sand's works. Gan's stories reflect only the themes of a woman's instinctive passion for life and the obstacles she encounters because of her sex. Sand's heroines, on the other hand, although appearing to be in constant search of an ideal love, in fact choose freedom over confinement to love's sphere. In comparison to Sand's characters and plots, Gan's stories are less skillfully developed. Instead, one feels that more attention has been given to the thinly veiled message that the stories were designed to purvey.

Also important in noting contrasts between Sand's heroines and those of Gan is that the latter's heroines, although sharing the passionate nature of Sand's women, are often pathetically naive and helpless, and invariably fall victim to the pettiness and slander of provincial gossip.

Finally, in comparing the authors' personal lives and the impact they made in their respective societies, we note the greatest difference in Sand's position as a monumental persona of the century who played an important role not only in literature, but also in social and political affairs, and who succeeded in leaving her stamp on the consciousness and lives of many prominent thinkers in a large number of countries.

Gan never achieved a similar position in Russia. Her accomplishment, however, was nonetheless significant in that for the first time, the thoughts and feelings of Russian women were being evoked in an authentic feminine voice.

NOTES

1. V. G. Belinsky, *Polnoe sobranie sochinenii* (Moscow: Izdatel'stvo Akademii Nauk, 1953–59), 12:115.
2. F. M. Dostoevski, *Diary of a Writer*, trans. Boris Brasol (New York: Octagon Books, 1973), 1:346.
3. Ibid., 344–345.
4. One of the most recent studies on Sand's influence on Russian social thought is Carole Karp's "George Sand and the 'Men of the Forties'," in Natalie Datlof et al., eds., *The George Sand Papers, Conference Proceedings*, vol. 2, 1978 (New York: AMS Press, 1982), 180–188.
5. For a recent monograph devoted to a study of this literary relationship, see Patrick Waddington, *Turgenev and George Sand: An Improbable Entente* (Totowa, N.J.: Barnes and Noble, 1981).
6. While Gan was the subject of a number of scholarly articles in late nineteenth-century Russia, there are only two English-language studies devoted to her writing: Marit B. Neilsen, "The Concept of Love and the Conflict of the Individual versus Society in Elena A. Gan's *Sud Sveta*," *Scando-Slavica* 24 (1978): 125–138; and my article: Kevin J. McKenna, "Gan, Elena Andreevna," in Harry B. Weber, ed., *The Modern Encyclopedia of Russian and Soviet Literatures* (Gulf Breeze, Fla.: Academic International Press, 1986), 101–105.
7. George Sand, *Indiana*, trans. George Burnham Ives (Chicago: Academy Press Limited, 1978).
8. Z. R-va, "Ideal," *Biblioteka dlia chteniia* (Readers' Library) 21 (1837): 137.
9. R-va, "Sud sveta" (Society's judgment), *Biblioteka dlia chteniia* 38 (1840): 99.
10. R-va, "Idea," 144.
11. Ibid., 128–129.
12. Ibid., 128.
13. Ibid., 129.
14 Z. R-va, "Naprasnyi dar" (The futile gift), *Otechestvennye zapiski* (Notes of the fatherland), 25 (1842).
15. "Ideal," 144.
16. "Naprasnyi dar," 38–39.

26

George Sand and Flaubert: Inspiration and Divergence

Mary Rice

After George Sand's death in June 1876, Gustave Flaubert expressed his regret that his "chère Maître," as he called her, would never read the finished version of "Un Coeur simple," the story that she had inspired and that he had written for her. Certainly there are marked affinities between this story and Sand's own works. Flaubert's main character, Félicité, recalls the Berrichon peasants who people Sand's *romans champêtres*. Both Sand and Flaubert portray a world whose vision and language lie for the most part outside literary tradition, yet each writer resolves the problematics of this representation in accordance with his or her own style, be it Romantic or Realist. The resemblance between "Un Coeur simple" and Sand's novel, *François le champi*, as well as the stylistic differences between the two works, illuminate George Sand's influence on Flaubert and his divergence from that inspiration.

George Sand's brand of realism differs from the kind of Balzacian realism of detail to which Flaubert is most often considered heir. Sand's intent in the romans champêtres was specifically to capture in narrative form the reality of a dying pastoral culture, a project evident in *François le champi*, her account of Berrichon marriage customs which follows *La Mare au diable*. However, Sand's vision of this—or any—reality includes a moral side as well as a descriptive one. In this vein, Sand wrote to Flaubert critiquing Emile Zola's *Rougon-Macquart* novels: "Art must be the search for truth and . . . truth is not the painting of evil. It must be the painting of evil and of good. A painter who sees only one is as false as he who sees only the other."[1] About two months later, Flaubert replied: "You will see by my story of a simple heart, where you will recognize your immediate influence, that I am not as stubborn as you believe. I believe that the moral tendencies or rather the human underside of this little work will be agreeable to you!" (*C*, 533). Thus, Flaubert too intends to present the moral side of humanity, or rather the underside, as he redefines it, but of course he must do it in his own style, that of the impartial, objective author of *Madame Bovary* and *L'Éducation sentimentale*. Sand had approved of Flaubert's first novel because of what she judged to be its clear message regarding Emma's adulterous illusions, but she felt Flaubert's impartiality weakened *L'Éducation sentimentale*:

> You have excessive prejudice for words. . . . Nourish yourself with the ideas and feelings amassed in your head and in your heart; the words and sentences, the *form* of which you make an issue, will come out all by itself from your digestion. You consider it [form] a goal, it is nothing but an effect. Happy manifestations only come from an emotion, and an emotion only comes from a conviction. (*C*, 517)

Sand thus admonished her friend to give voice to his own heart and soul in his writing rather than to concentrate only on the form of his writing, his style.

In the *avant propos* to *François le champi*, George Sand directly addresses the question of narrative voice in the novel. In a dialogue between the author and a good friend, this prelude exposes the gap that exists between the realm of art, science, and knowledge, on the one hand, and the peasant's realm of sensation on the other. In theoretical terms Sand would bridge this gap with feeling; in more concrete, formalistic terms, she chooses a narrative stance that enables her to present the story of François in a peasant voice, for she recounts a tale she has ostensibly heard from a traditional storyteller while her own role is that of listener. Her work is therefore colored with words she takes from the local patois, usually modified for "French" readers. Archaic expressions as well as earthy ones also lend the text a flavor of peasant speech. However, despite all these stylistic techniques, Sand's hero, François, is ironically unable to express himself even in this peasant world. François is a *champi*, a foundling with no knowledge of his natural parents, an outcast or "foreigner" even in this simple society.[2] Ridicule is directed not only at the circumstances of his birth, but also at his silence and seeming stupidity. He appears dumb in both senses of the term, for he seems like an animal, incapable of human speech or reasoning.[3] Indeed when his benefactress, Madeleine, the miller's wife, comes upon him in the fields, the child cannot even tell her his correct age. It is soon clear to those closest to him, however, that François is more apt to express himself in deeds than in words, and that he lacks neither intelligence nor heart. He can even speak his piece when necessary, as the miller's old servant, Catherine, acerbically remarks: "So you know how to put three words one in front of the other, François? Well then!" (*F*, 259). François nonetheless remains an essentially non-verbal character who expresses his love and devotion through hard work and even through the sacrifice of his earnings and later his small inheritance. Reciprocally, he is sorely grieved when he matures to the point where he is no longer permitted, for propriety's sake, to share the maternal embraces that Madeleine lavishes on her young son, Jeannie. When action no longer suffices, it is the narrator's task to explain François's state of heart and mind, as in the following: "The *champi*, as simple in heart as he was, was not so simple of mind, that he did not finish by understanding that which they insinuated to him, and what he said here he did not say unintentionally" (*F*, 316). Finally, when François's devotion changes from filial love to a deeper sexual passion, he must rely on Jeannette, his former master's daughter, to speak for him. Even at this, the most important point in his life, François lacks adequate words. Fortunately, Jeannette conveys the message well, and François and Madeleine are united at last, with no further need for discussion. Thus, Sand's novel draws to its close.

A similar drama of voice and silence is played out in Flaubert's story "Un Coeur simple," although in its own unique way. Flaubert's main character, Félicité, she of the simple heart, is an outsider like François. Abandoned by her first lover, the desolate peasant girl flees to another village in provincial Normandy and there becomes the devoted servant of the impoverished widow Aubain and her two young children. As her story unfolds, Félicité is repeatedly abandoned, often through death, by those she has come to love: her cherished nephew Victor, the Aubain children, and Madame Aubain herself. From the first line of the story, Félicité appears as an object rather than a member of the provincial community: We are told that for half a century the bourgeois of Pont-l'Evêque have envied Madame Aubain her servant. The narrative goes on to describe the Aubain household, Félicité's immediate surroundings, and finally her appearance, culminating in her characteristic silence: "Always silent, back straight and gestures measured, she seemed a wooden woman, functioning in an automatic manner."[4] All that follows quickly belies the superficial judgment that Félicité is the unfeeling, uncaring automaton implied in this description, and thus undermines the Realism of the story's opening paragraphs.

Flaubert's free indirect style makes it impossible to attribute this sort of judgment to any one particular narrative voice. When we read in the next part of the work that Félicité, "like any other, had her own love story" (*CS*, 166), we cannot be certain if it is the woman herself who feels this way or if this springs from the hearsay knowledge of some other narrator. Félicité's actions, on the other hand, are clear indications of her capacity for deep emotions, as she throws herself to the ground sobbing at the news that her lover, Théodore, has married; as she literally knocks herself unconscious in her race to bid her nephew goodbye before his ship sails; and as she tenderly lays out the little body of the dead Virginie Aubain. The text underscores the inconsonance of words and actions, the same inconsonance embodied in *François le champi*. The narrative of the character's actions exhibits the same terse immediacy that Walter Benjamin ascribes to the traditional story form, where the object is the transmission of experience, not information; the storyteller passes on an experience without analyzing it.[5] Ironically, when Félicité risks her life to save the Aubain family from an enraged bull, her heroism becomes a subject of village conversation for years thereafter, but it is conversation in which the heroine herself takes no part, for she does not realize that she has done anything extraordinary.

In addition to Félicité's exclusion from the spoken word, Flaubert's text also encodes her ignorance of the written word, since she is far less socialized than François and completely illiterate. Other sorts of "reading" are likewise foreign to her, so that when a neighbor brings out an atlas in order to show the woman where her nephew has gone, she can make no sense of its lines of longitude and latitude or their connection to Victor; she wants to see his picture instead. She is fully able, however, to apprehend the illustrations of exotic animals and cannibals that adorn the atlas because she sees in them enough resemblance to the people and animals in her own corner of Normandy to understand such representations. This is the same process that enabled her to understand her lover's desires, for like any farm girl, she had observed barnyard animals from childhood, and this had constituted her education in love. While George Sand peppers her narrative with earthy metaphoric expressions and proverbs in order to give it the flavor of peasant speech, Flaubert's style remains a Realist one, highly objective and devoid of rhetoric. He instead reveals the workings of the peasant's metaphoric vision, grounded in the resemblance of like to like.

Flaubert himself signalled the difference in style to Sand, writing:

> You, from the first bound, in all things, you climb to the sky and from there you descend to earth. You depart from the *a priori*, the theory, the ideal. . . . Me, poor devil, I am stuck on earth as if by leaden heels; everything troubles me, tears me up, ravages me and I make efforts to climb upwards. If I wanted to take your manner of seeing the whole of the world, I would become laughable, that's all. (*C*, 521)

True to this assessment, in *François le champi* Sand departs from a theoretical avant propos in which she justifies the stylistic techniques she uses in her novel. In comparison, Flaubert presents the same problematics indirectly, encoded within his text. Sand likewise makes no secret of her socialist ideas or convictions, for in true Romantic fashion, her art is highly personal and expressive of its author's individual emotions. Not so Flaubert, who attempted to purge himself of his early Romantic tendencies; his goal, as ever, is to disappear, opinions and all, from his story. When George Sand writes of one of her protagonists, Madeleine, that "she knew that her mother-in-law and her husband had little pity, and that they loved money more than the next person" (*F*, 225), and then has the miller's wife go off to right the wrongs caused by this lack of charity, the author leaves no doubt as to whose attitude she finds more commendable, that of Madeleine or the others in her family. In "Un Coeur simple," the situation is not as clear. When Monsieur Bourais, the neighbor with the atlas, laughs at Félicité and her "limited . . . intelligence" (*CS*, 171) when she cannot read a map, there are two sides to the question. It is understandable that Bourais is surprised at the servant's ignorance, but it is also foolish of him to expect someone who has never seen a map to be able to use it. He confuses ignorance with a lack of intelligence, and is himself ignorant because of it. At the same time, Félicité's hope that she will see Victor's image before her is not so strange after all, given the development of travel photography in Flaubert's own time. Her desire unwittingly shows common sense.

Flaubert further problematizes the value of words and reading—as well as "dumbness"—in Loulou, the parrot Madame Aubain hands down to her servant.

Unlike Félicité, Loulou is vociferous, but his words consist of nothing but formulaic clichés: "Charming boy! Your servant, sir! Hail, Mary!" (*CS*, 174). These are phrases that have long lost their feeling and meaning through overuse, and only sound all the more hollow coming from a bird. As Félicité grows increasingly deaf and blind with the passing years, however, Loulou's is the only voice that remains accessible to her; as it pierces the silence and replaces all other forms of verbal communication once open to her, it puts the value of such dialogue into question and accentuates yet again the woman's already established isolation from the community. Her separation seems still more complete after the parrot's death: "Communicating with no one, she lived in the torpor of a sleepwalker" (*CS*, 176).

It is in this dreamlike state that the metaphoric process quickens, as Félicité notes the now-stuffed parrot's likeness to images she has seen of the Holy Spirit. It seems only natural that at her own death the ever-dedicated and devout old woman believes she sees, in the open heaven, a giant parrot above her. Flaubert's objective style, as always, allows no narrative intervention or interpretation on the author's part at this, the story's close. Instead, Félicité's final vision is merely relayed to the reader.

Sand has her traditional storyteller end *François le champi* in a similarly terse vein, despite previous comments in the text, made by the narrator or some other character, about society's mistreatment of its *enfants champis* or the poor in general. We see François and Madeleine retreat to the fountain where the young man hopes to find his tongue at last ("maybe I'll find my tongue there" [*F*, 403]), but no dialogue ensues in the text. Instead, the storyteller depicts a scene, viewed from the exterior, in which Madeleine cries tears of joy while François sinks to his knees before his beloved in gratitude at her response. We are only certain of what has happened when the narrator next reports that he attended their wedding shortly thereafter, but otherwise he refuses to comment on the finished story: "If it [the story] isn't [true], it could be . . . and if you don't believe me, go see" (*F*, 403). His admonition not only implies that his listener might witness the truth in a visual sense, but might "see for himself"—or herself—and actually live it as well.

The emphasis on sight rather than speech is crucial in the final scenes of both *François le champi* and "Un Coeur simple." Each ending translates an immediate visual perception with little attention to the detail of this image; only its broad outlines appear. The vision is thus centered in silence rather than in words, a fitting close as the central drama of the "dumb" main character's life is played out. In the absence of any analysis, it is left to the listener or reader to assimilate the experience and so establish his or her own sense of it. Such writing approaches what is for Benjamin the essence of the storyteller's art: the transmission of an integral piece of human experience, unadulterated and whole.

Because Sand and Flaubert have grounded the works in question in the lives of essentially nonverbal characters, the result extends far beyond the type of information characteristically found in a detailed Realist account of a particular social milieu. Sand the Romantic and revolutionary openly declares her intent to break new ground outside the domain of science, art, and knowledge, the three terms tellingly lumped together in her *avant propos* just as they are interconnected in

Realist doctrine. Flaubert handles the problem less overtly, choosing a Realist framework that is ultimately subverted from within, as we have seen. The significance of Félicité's story does not arise from the sum of its parts—the fragmentary details of the servant's appearance, routine and background—nor is her stalwart devotion the logical outcome of repeated abandonment (the same can be said of François's unwavering loyalty). The part-to-part relationships that define meaningful metonymy are here frustrated, just as metaphoric vision, with its comparisons of whole-to-whole, is privileged.[6] Nothing "follows" merely on account of contiguity or causality. This is why Félicité's story, much like the tale of the *champi* that Sand has ostensibly borrowed from oral tradition, must be taken as an integral whole if its meaning is to become clear. Moreover, because each of these texts foregrounds metaphor at the expanse of metonymy, it represents a radical departure from the predominant mode of nineteenth-century Realism.[7]

These works are doubly radical in that this modal change also entails a marked shift in content as action supersedes narrative's more "passive" elements, descriptive detail and analysis. Because François and Félicité express themselves through acts, acts become the principal focus in their life stories. A single deed can be delineated in a few swift motions (its simplicity and cohesion even more pronounced in the French *passé simple*, which is used with some frequency by both authors in these two works), hence producing a seemingly visual effect. Moreover, their potential for action distinguishes the "speechless" as capable, vital, even powerful.[8] The writers' ability to create literary expressions for voices traditionally excluded from literature—to write silence, as it were—allows them to transcend the limitations of milieu and moment in order to translate the profound essence of human experience. In so doing, they renew language itself. The precise debt Flaubert owes his "chère Maître" would surely be impossible to ascertain. Nonetheless, "Un Coeur simple" bears the traces of the innovative example set by George Sand despite the acknowledged differences in temperament and style that ensure Flaubert's own artistic singularity.

NOTES

1. Gustave Flaubert and George Sand, *Correspondance*, ed. Alphonse Jacobs (Paris: Flammarion, 1981), 528; this and all subsequent translations are those of the author. Further references will be indicated in the text as *C*.

2. George Sand, *La Mare au diable, François le champi*, ed. Pierre Salomon and Jean Mallion (Paris: Garnier Frères, 1962), 263; further references will be indicated in the text as *F*.

3. It should be noted that the French word *bête* connotes the words mute or dumb, stupid, and beast; for this reason it resembles the English phrase "dumb animal" but is far more heavily charged.

4. Gustave Flaubert, "Un Coeur simple," *Oeuvres complètes* (Paris: Seuil, 1964), 2:166; all further references will be indicated in the text as *CS*.

5. Walter Benjamin, "The Storyteller," in his *Illuminations*, trans. Harry Zohn and ed. Hannah Arendt (New York: Harcourt Brace and World, 1968), 83–109.

6. For a more complete definition of these tropes, see Pierre Fontanier, *Les Figures du*

discours, intro. Gérard Genette (Paris: Flammarion, 1977). For a study of tropes as they inform narrative, see Hayden White, *Tropics of Discourse: Essays in Culture Criticism* (Baltimore: Johns Hopkins University Press, 1978).

7. Metonymy, the trope of contiguity and causality, is associated with the empirical side of Realism, including inference from detail, sequential chains of cause and effect, and so on. Because narrative itself consists of a sequence of contiguous sentences, metonymy is also said to underpin all narrative texts, including the novel and short story in question. Their differences from Realist texts is therefore relative.

8. The subtle political and social implications of this potential for action depend on the historical context: Sand completed *François le champi* just prior to the 1848 Revolution in hope of social change; Flaubert, on the other hand, wrote "Un Coeur simple" in 1876, well after the failure of 1848 and while he was still ambivalent about the class struggles of 1871.

27

The Important, Little-Known Friendship of George Sand and Alexandre Dumas fils

Eve Sourian

Because most of the letters of Alexandre Dumas fils remain unpublished, the great friendship between him and George Sand is, even today, little recognized. It began in 1851 and was never disavowed. Sand referred to him as "my dear Son," while he called her "my dear Mama." A son and a mother of choice: chosen affinities. Who would have imagined it? If, to quote Professor Murray Sachs, George Sand and Flaubert were "a wildly improbable and ill-suited pair," what can we say of the deep friendship linking Indiana-Lélia and the author of *L'Ami des femmes*, considered by many to be an enemy of women?[1] Though he thought of himself as sympathetic to women, Dumas wrote:

> Woman is a circumscribed, passive, instrumental, available being, in a perpetual state of expectation. She is the only unfinished work which God permitted man to take and to complete. She is an angel rejected. . . . Nature and society have made a pact and will do so eternally, whatever the demands of women may be, so that women may be subjected to men.[2]

The friendship between George Sand and this tall man with steel-blue eyes twenty years younger than she was certainly a strange one. It began in 1851 when Alexandre Dumas fils discovered, near the Polish border at the home of a friend who was lodging him, the letters from George Sand to Frédéric Chopin. In May 1851, he wrote his father:

> While you were dining with Madame Sand, dear Father, I, too, was concerned with her. Can you now deny our kindred spirits? Imagine that I have in my hands all the correspondence from ten years with Chopin. You can well imagine how many of these letters I have copied. They are so much more

charming than the proverbial letters of Madame de Sévigné. I am bringing you back a notebook filled with them, for, unfortunately, these letters were only lent to me.[3]

As a good friend, Dumas père warned George Sand of his son's discovery, and when, panic-stricken, she answered that she wanted the letters, he reassured her: "Now everything has gone to Mystowitz where Alexandre will still spend two more weeks, and I have every hope that he will bring back to you those precious pieces of your heart."[4] Dumas fils brought the letters back and wrote to George Sand:

> But, do believe me, Madame, there has been no profanation of them. My heart which found itself so far away and so indiscreetly the confidant of yours, had already belonged to you for a very long time, and its great admiration had existed for as long a time as the oldest of devotions. Will you please believe this and pardon me?[5]

On August 20, 1851, Alexandre Dumas fils therefore sent her the notorious packet of letters, which he had placed, as a further measure of security, in a box covered with paper and then oilcloth, which was sewed together. Finally, on October 7, the novelist sent him a long letter of thanks from Nohant, in which she requested his absolute discretion:

> Certainly, there is no secret there, and I would rather have to glorify myself than to be embarrassed for having cared for and consoled, like my child, that noble and incurable heart. But now you know the secret side of our correspondence. It is not a very serious thing, but it would have been painful for me to see it commented on and exaggerated. . . . I would have suffered a great deal if this mysterious book of my private life, the pages where—amidst both smiles and tears—I had inscribed my daughter, had been opened to the whole world.[6]

Later in the same letter, she asked the young man to forget everything he had read: "If you were to remember it, moreover, you would tell yourself: 'It is the secret of a mother that I came upon by chance; it is sacred in a quite different way from a woman's secret! I would bury it in my heart as in a sanctuary.' " The secret was well kept, alas, and the letters were destroyed. A long friendship developed, based on the gratitude that George Sand felt toward the young man and on the admiration he felt for her.

In 1854 he wrote a beautiful review praising her play *Flaminio*. Touched, she responded: "I have just read your excellent and charming article. It comes from a good son and I thank you from the bottom of my heart. . . . Remember that I have adopted *you* as *my* son!" (*Corr.*, 12:611). From that time on, Dumas fils began to call her "Dear Mama," and sometimes even "Dear Master." He read and reread *Elle et lui* three times. In February 1861, while traveling to Genoa, sick and depressed, he read *Lettres d'un voyageur*, and wrote:

> Oh yes, my dear Mama, I would like to be near you even though it has already been nearly two months that I have been living with you intellectually. . . . In the letters of little Zorzi I have rediscovered my own soul. . . . If you only knew what solace and what hope weakened souls can find in the confessions and effusions of a soul as strong as yours. . . . I have never told you my opinion about you, because in placing you so high, you hold a position surpassing all good or bad evaluations, but you are a good fellow, and the chap who will have to replace you hasn't yet been conceived.[7]

His admiration extended to *Jacques*, *La Mare au diable*, to *Le Marquis de Villemer*, and *Flavie*, which he also read three times. This intellectual and artistic admiration was accompanied by a deep tenderness; he developed a very strong need for her. On June 15, 1861, he decided to go to Nohant, and wrote:

> I am going to barge in on you and ask you what only you can give me now, rest and peace of mind, confidence in life, because, even when I try to read you from morning 'til night, it's still yourself I need. . . . Only you can accomplish this miracle. . . . I have spent my life seeking someone whom I could love and admire without reservation and when all is said and done, I can see only you.[8]

In spite of all this, he felt upset and intimated in her presence:

> You are such a good woman that people don't dare tell you that you are a great man. Unless they call you "my cousin" like Marchal and make a plaything of your individuality without realizing too well what they are doing, people are so bothered when they love you that those who respect and admire you without limits are unable to take an intelligent and comfortable attitude with you.[9]

He felt awkward. Evidently Alexandre Dumas père did not have these problems with Sand, whom he called his "Dear and Illustrious Friend" or "Our Lady of Nohant." Sand used the informal *tu* with Charles Marchal and Gustave Flaubert, but always used *vous* with Dumas fils, thereby maintaining a certain distance between them. He wrote:

> If you yourself are nothing, it's easy, you just gape, in open-mouthed admiration . . . but if you have an awareness of your personal worth and yet your relative inferiority, you feel awkward. You can't place yourself among the humble and at the same time you don't want to place yourself among equals. Those who are used to expressing their feelings, who have been brought up that way, who know how to give easily of themselves, immediately find the right tone with you and put themselves in tune with you through that admirable quality, but I, who am constipated concerning feelings, and who don't even know how to cry when I feel like it and need to,

> have the passionate desire to throw myself at your feet, but then I stop, restrained by my upbringing.[10]

Half joking, half serious, he told her: "What bad luck that I am not your real son with the father that I have, for I would have made you a pretty product all the same!"[11] It was in this mother-son relationship that he felt the most at ease. It was, moreover, the only possible one for this misogynist, who scorned all women except for mothers. He declared:

> The man who most scorns women never scorns his mother, whatever may have been the errors that she committed as a woman: for, as a woman, she doesn't exist for him. . . . [A] mother doesn't have any sex in the thought of Man; she is of a divine sort. . . . We kneel before Mothers, but we don't fall at Woman's feet for that reason.[12]

Thus, Dumas fils could kneel before Madame Sand, George Sand (whom he never called George), Indiana, Lélia, and his dear Mama. As for Sand herself, we know her predilection for mother-son relationships. Pessimistic, doubting the world and himself, he needed the optimism and the idealism of his mother of choice: "I prefer, I would rather, above all, do what you do than what I do. It is nobler, higher, calmer, more consoling. That is the book that one should always present to humanity little by little to make it better, nobler and more divine-like."[13] Moreover, he recognized the limitations that resulted from his character:

> I do not have that chord in me which responds with indulgence, pity, pardon, understanding to the weaknesses of the heart. I am implacable. . . . That is why I can only do a book from time to time, or a play once in a while. My brutal approach would be immediately unbearable. I don't have any tenderness, alas, no tenderness at all. No generosity, no Christian philosophy.[14]

Actually, George Sand tended to accept the judgment of her "dear son" regarding himself and his work. However much she praised his skill and the didacticism of his plays (for she too adored instructing the public), she still wished for him to show more heart. Consequently, writing to him after having attended *Le Demi-monde*, she said: "It is a masterpiece of skill, of mind, of observation. It shows progress in the science of the theater and in life; nevertheless I liked Diane and Marguerite better because I like plays where I cry" (*Corr.*, 13:410–411). She had the same reproach upon reading *Le Supplice d' une femme*:

> It is in fact a masterpiece of skill to have known how to catch hold of the heart with a terrible, even odious subject, which, on reflection, revolts our conscience. Oh, the nasty woman and the nasty lover. . . . Faced with a similar novel, I would have fled to the end of the world. . . . You have made a triumph with what would have been for anyone else a shameful defeat. (*Corr.*, 19:215)

It is true that when she saw the play on October 5, 1865, she admitted to having cried a great deal. She did not change her opinion, however; she did not like the play. Nor did she like *La Visite de noces*, seeing in it "always more talent and still as much spirit" but reproaching the author for having sacrificed too much to create an effect.[15]

In fact, for George Sand, the goal of theater was to introduce the mind of the spectator into a world more pure and inspiring than the sad and hard realities of daily life. She would like this diversion to be "an inspiration toward higher things, a poetical mirage in the desert of reality."[16]

She went on to deplore the fact that materialism and the positivist school had invaded the theater. Too many dramatists only succeed "in showing ugliness and rendering the public blasé in a sad confrontation with it."[17] Pushed by a spirit of reaction against the ugly, the low-level, and the false, she declared: "I, given my temperament, have taken the opposite track."[18] Her dreams were of heroes, of divinities speaking a sublime language, of enchanting backgrounds and inebriating harmonies.

It was not surprising that she should have felt ill at ease in this period when all the old values seemed out-dated. She wrote to Dumas fils: "I consider you first among the dramatic authors in the new style of today's manner, as your father is the best of yesterday's. As for me, I am of the style of the day before yesterday or of the day after tomorrow, I don't know which, and I don't much care! (*Corr.*, 13:411).

In the same letter, full of nostalgia for the style of yesterday, she asked: "Why don't we see anything of A. Dumas père? . . . We need him; heroic drama has only ended because the masters have abandoned it."[19] The unfeeling skill of the present did not suit her.

Dumas père, in an acute analysis of *Mauprat*, said: "George Sand, with great difficulty and by means of art, succeeds in making theater."[20] First she would write her novel, then adapt it for a play, and thus, since she was above all philosopher, dreamer, and painter, the action in her plays would suffer. Besides this, she began her novels or her plays without knowing where her characters would lead her, a procedure at odds with the architecture of the well-made play. For Dumas père, George Sand, like Alfred de Musset, staged things not made for the theater. He was quick, moreover, to observe: "That doesn't mean we should not put such productions on the stage; they may not be object-lessons for their own authors who can't judge their own work, but they are admirable objects of study for others."[21] Dumas fils agreed:

> It is quite true that she lacks ingenuity and related skills, and perhaps also that sense of development, so crucially principal to dramatic art; yet by gaining these, she would lose that naïveté which accounts for the charm in her work and which makes for a theater that is not everybody's theater, something notable in itself.[22]

Conscious of her own lack of skill, and an admirer of the technique of Dumas fils, she appealed to his consummate experience. During his stay at Nohant with her, from July 12 to August 10, 1861, he read *Le Marquis de Villemer* and exclaimed that in it she had a highly successful play. She proposed that he write the script; he accepted. On August 15, 1861, he wrote: "I am working as much as I can at *Villemer* but I can't work much."[23] George Sand replied:

> I am very curious about what is going to come of *Villemer*. It amuses me a bit to think that the marrow of it is to be extracted without my having had to do a thing and that upon awakening one of these mornings, I shall see the result—a delicious morsel at which I haven't had a hand. (*Corr.*, 16:532)

She invited him to come and work at Nohant where she could spur him on and where every day he could read her his morning's work. Nevertheless, she realized through his letters how he was suffering at the task, and suggested that he abandon it: "I know very well that I can't just summon up zest and enthusiasm on demand, and that sometimes it's a bore to be pushed" (*Corr.*, 16:551). However, she knew very well he was not going to drop it. He was concerned because the audience would realize from the first scene that the young man was going to marry the girl. She did not understand his "misgivings about an outcome known in advance. Does it really matter?" (*Corr.*, 16:669). Finally, on December 15, 1861, he found "some original things for putting *Villemer* into action. . . . I count absolutely on you," he wrote, "to cut, pare down, and especially to sentimentalize."[24] She hesitated, hardly sure of herself. "Do you believe me capable, with your beginning and your advice, of doing the rest of the play?" (*Corr.*, 17:649). The play, presented at the Odéon Theater on February 29, 1864, was an immense success. Dumas fils had refused to place his name on it, but George Sand insisted that they share the profits.

In 1865, she put together a new play, *La Dernière Aldini*, and asked him to read it. The verdict of Dumas fils was clear: The play had to be redone from beginning to end. Again he advised her and she rewrote, but this time La Rounat, the Odéon's director, did not like the play. Dumas thought he was right, and the play was not produced.

Dumas suggested adapting *Mont Revêche* for the theater. "The whole play is in the book," he wrote. "Even the dialogue is done." However, this time the dear son was less enthusiastic. He lacked the time. George Sand needed a precise, clear scenario, but Dumas fils felt unable to write it; it would be an endless task. However, he would be happy to come and talk with her about it. After the failure of *La Dernière Aldini*, he was pessimistic. "The fruit of this incestuous joining of mother and son has been obscurity," he wrote. Besides, he felt uneasy. It was she who had written the novel, and she was not "a person whom one displaces or whose work one distorts without emotion and without remorse."[25] Nevertheless, he finally did accept, and on February 15, 1867, she expressed her great joy at the news.

However, Dumas fils was not very happy. "I have the same scorn for collaborative work as you do. It can only be an amusement, a necessity, a business venture; it will never be art."[26] He constantly repeated:

> I only want to be agreeable and useful to you, if I can, and help you earn money without you having to struggle. During that time you can write a good novel, to add to your reputation and I, I hope, will compose you a good "pièce de résistance" to add to your assets, but which, done by me or by both of us, will never be more than a business arrangement. It is the book which is the lasting work; the play drawn from the book is only the exploitation and the outgrowth of it.[27]

George Sand's answers indicated that she did not share his scruples. Perhaps she hurt him, for by insisting on the collaboration she seemed not to appreciate him at his full artistic worth. She, for example, would never have had the idea of accepting anyone's collaboration in writing one of her novels. She never discussed them with anyone in her letters. Dumas pulled out. The play was never produced. George Sand, however, continued to ask Dumas fils for advice. He lavished her with advice for *L'Autre*, which was a success. She wrote him: "We have had a number one success. I say *we*, because you are responsible for a good part of it. You made me see clearly."[28] A professional, he advised her also on the choice of theaters, recommended actors, and helped her with contracts; it was he who drew up for her the agreement with the Vaudeville Theater for *Les Don Juan de village*. He also served as an intermediary between her and Adolphe Lemoine-Montigny, the director of the Gymnase, whom she found stingy and unscrupulous. Dumas went to verify the accounts from *La Petite Fadette* at the Opéra Comique since she felt she had been cheated, and showed her that it was not the case. He found for her a German, Mr. Hirsch, who bought her books to translate and publish in Germany, and once again he served as the intermediary. His devotion was steadfast, and so it was he whom she asked to supervise the publication of her correspondence with Alfred de Musset, in the event that Emile Aucante, to whom she had given that task, were to die before her. She knew she could count on her "cherished son."

For one thing, the issues obsessing Dumas fils were not foreign to her: the issues of women, marriage, prostitution, proof of paternity, and divorce. In 1845, she had written her own *Dame aux camélias*, entitled *Isidora*, three years before his. Although they had the same model, the two works differ. The courtesan of Dumas fils is regenerated by a man's love, but at the price of her love and her life. George Sand, more realistic and more optimistic, knew very well that neither marriage nor love could save Isidora; what saves her is friendship and the maternity she has chosen, for she adopts a little girl. "For me," Dumas fils declared, "with my feeble capacities, I shall pursue, as long as I can, these two articles of the [Napoleonic] Code: seeking proof of paternity is forbidden and marriage is indissoluble."[29] The problem of natural children never ceased to trouble him, it was an obsession. He treated the matter in *L'Affaire Clémenceau*, in *Les Idées de Madame Aubray*, and in the preface of *La Dame aux camélias*. George Sand had the same concerns. As Gay Manifold has noted, she wrote *Claudie* long before he wrote *Le fils naturel*.[30] It is therefore not surprising that Alexandre Dumas fils wrote to George Sand: "*Madame Aubray* [the play] is getting bigger and bigger and will say papa about the fifteenth. Will you be there, godmother?"[31] For his work she wrote a beautiful review. George Sand also had very precise ideas about the upbringing of girls and about their ignorance on the eve of marriage. She confided these thoughts to Dumas fils, who used them for the theme of *L'Ami des femmes.*

The novel *L'Affaire Clémenceau* and the play *La Femme de Claude* both ended with the murder of the perfidious and adulterous wife. George Sand approved of the creation of Césarine, the feminine monster, saying: "If she were not capable of everything, she would be a failure. Why should there be all this fury over such a successful literary type?"[32] Nevertheless, George Sand wanted a counterpart for *L'Affaire Clémenceau*; she wanted Dumas to create a play where the situation would be reversed and where the wife—pure, charming, and naive—would be in the clutches of a husband who needs courtesans:

> What can she do! She can't kill him. She feels disgust for him; his homecomings nauseate her. If she wants to refuse him, she doesn't have the right to do so. Ah, what will she do? . . . Hunt a solution! *I*'m hunting one. . . . We have made the wife jealous, loving, furious, or moaning, never proud and daring to say to herself . . . "my body, that is to say my modesty belongs to me, and I can't let myself be raped by one who is repugnant to me." *I* can't perhaps show that page of human life . . . but *you* can do a lot of things that I cannot. (*Corr.*, 20:46–47)

Dumas fils had thought about such a theme too, but in his opinion, the wife in such a situation would be led to take a lover and to attack the institutions of marriage and society. He did not want such an outcome. Nevertheless, he wrote *La Princesse Georges*. George Sand liked the play, but the outcome left her perplexed because the princess forgives. "She is good and loyal, she will pay for that dearly. . . . The husband will start all over again, she will be forced to hate him and to leave him if she has children, because he would ruin them financially and lose them. But what does that do to the play which is the first act of the drama of that ill-starred life?"[33]

Alexandre Dumas fils was certainly a misogynist. In his preface to *L'Ami des Femmes*, he established himself as the emblematic male chauvinist, attacking the feminists of the period: "Emancipation of Women by Women is one of the most hilarious pieces of drollery ever born under the sun. It is pure nitrous oxide. . . . When women revolt, they immediately pass on to a state of craziness."[34] However, George Sand never fought at the side of Jeanne Deroin, Flora Tristan, or her sisters of *La Voix des femmes*. For her, only the change in the civil rights of the married woman counted, and she reproached feminists for having retarded the freedom of women by preaching without better perception, without good taste, and without enlightenment. The reactions of Dumas fils, therefore, did not particularly shock her.

It was in the fight for divorce that she wished for him to be most active and involved. In a brochure entitled "L'Homme-femme," he responded to a Monsieur d'Ideville who had asked whether one should kill an adulterous wife or pardon her. While d'Ideville had opted for forgiveness, Dumas fils concluded: "Kill her!"

George Sand did not approve the set-up of that pamphlet; she wanted the conclusion to serve as a point of departure: "I would have made the final point the base of the edifice, and starting from this fact, that the subject of my drama is a husband who kills his wife, I would have beamed all the causes of conjugal despair toward the reforms which I wanted and which you would have had in mind."[35] Dumas fils went on to try to show that:

> "Kill her!" was only the mathematical consequence of that stupid law which condemns whoever absolves and which absolves whoever punishes, a law which weighed on your own whole life and which chained you socially, you, a value of the first order, to that eternal non-value, the contaminated and cumbersome Mr. Dudevant.[36]

Thus, he made a demonstration by the absurd of the necessity for divorce. George Sand, moreover, was not offended by the misogynist attacks of her "dear son." First of all, she was firmly convinced that men and women are not beings of a different sort, and that their inequality is due to laws on the one hand, and to the lack of education of women on the other. In any case, these attacks really did not concern her. Had he not written her the following? "You are you, unique among the women of all times, past, present and future. For you to be superior even to the most eminent men, you lacked only the right and the means to act."[37] At the death of his father, in a very beautiful letter, he wrote to her: "There are three of you in this century, you, Balzac and he, and then afterward, good night, there are no more and there will not be anyone else."[38]

During the terrible years of the Commune, the bonds between George Sand and Dumas fils were strengthened.[39] George Sand saw in Dumas fils the moralist the nation needed in order to be reborn. When she received his *Lettre de Junius*, she exclaimed: "It is a masterpiece! . . . I am quite happy to have felt and thought like you on all points, as if with only a word we understand each other completely." She was very proud of her "son," so it was with admiration and emotion that she declared to him:

> You have entered a period of admirable knowledge and lucidity. . . . Do you remember that I told you after *Diane de Lys* that you would bury everyone? *I* remember, because my impression was of a complete strength and certainty. You appeared to be not aware of it. You were so young! It was perhaps I who revealed you to yourself, and that is one of the good things I have done in my life.[40]

She thus fully accepted her "chosen maternity," and recognized him as her spiritual son. For his part, the lines that follow are the most beautiful homage he ever offered to his "Dear Mama":

> It is noon, the time when one sees everything! Notice this woman descending her flight of stairs. She has graying hair under her little straw hat; she is all

alone; she walks in the sun, quietly contemplating her everyday horizon; she listens to the vague sounds of nature; with her eyes, she enjoys following these storm clouds which you don't want. She chats with the gardener, she bends down to smell the flowers which she refrains from picking, she stops, she listens! To whom? She herself doesn't know! To something which still doesn't exist and which one day will be. She sits down on her stone bench. She doesn't move. There she becomes one with the immensity; there she is a plant, star, blade of grass, ocean, soul! She remembers, she divines! Everything you hear in the midst of the waves, she hears too, just as well as you hear it, under her dome of lilacs: the birds and the storms, and everything that sings, and all that cries, and all that laughs. She wanders, observes, listens in this fashion, without knowing very well what she is accomplishing, a somnambulist by day, and as the shadow covers the plain, as these plants which are impregnated from morning to evening by dew and by rain and sun, and which only open and emit their perfumes at night, at night this woman will restore to the world of the soul and of the spirit everything she has received from the material and visible world; for this woman thinks like Montaigne, dreams like Ossian, writes like Jean-Jacques. Leonardo sketches her phrases and Mozart sings them, Madame de Sévigné kisses her hands, and Madame de Staël kneels when she passes.[41]

NOTES

1. Murray Sachs, "George Sand and Gustave Flaubert: French Literature's Odd Couple," *George Sand Newsletter* 5, no. 2 (Fall/Winter 1982), 20.
2. Alexandre Dumas fils, *Théâtre Complet* (Paris: Michel Lévy frères, 1870), 4:43–44; this and all subsequent translations are those of the author.
3. Most of Alexandre Dumas fils's letters have not been published. This and many subsequent citations are drawn from copies I found in dossier E882 of the Spoelberch de Lovenjoul Collection, Institut de France, Paris (hereafter cited as Lovenjoul); other letters cited are from the Christiane Smeets–Sand Collection, Bibliothèque Municipale, La Châtre, France (hereafter cited as Smeets–Sand).
4. Alexandre Dumas père, Lovenjoul, May 30, 1851.
5. Dumas fils, Lovenjoul, June 3, 1851.
6. George Sand, *Correspondance*, ed. Georges Lubin (Paris: Garnier, 1964–), 10:455; hereafter referred to in the text as *Corr*.
7. Dumas fils, Lovenjoul, February 1861.
8. Ibid., June 8, 1861.
9. Ibid., October 31, 1861.
10. Ibid., October 31, 1861.
11. Ibid., December 15, 1861.
12. Dumas fils, *Théâtre Complet*, 4:7.
13. Dumas fils, Smeets–Sand, August 1866.
14. Dumas fils, Smeets–Sand, February 1861.
15. George Sand, Smeets–Sand, November 3, 1861.
16. George Sand, *Souvenirs et impressions littéraires* (Paris: E. Dentu, 1861), 183.

17. Ibid.
18. Ibid., 184.
19. Ibid.
20. Alexandre Dumas père, *Souvenirs dramatiques* (Paris: Calmann Lévy, 1881), 311.
21. Ibid.
22. Alexandre Dumas fils, *Entr-actes* (Paris: Calmann Lévy, 1878), 1:299–300.
23. Dumas fils, Lovenjoul, August 15, 1861.
24. Ibid., December 15, 1861.
25. Dumas fils, Smeets–Sand, January 22, 1867.
26. Ibid., June 1, 1867.
27. Ibid., January, 1867.
28. George Sand, Smeets–Sand, February 26, 1870.
29. Ibid., July 6, 1866.
30. Gay Manifold, *George Sand's Theatre Career* (Ann Arbor, Michigan: UMI Research Press), 60.
31. Dumas fils, Smeets–Sand, February 26, 1867.
32. George Sand, Smeets–Sand, April 10, 1873.
33. Ibid., December 21, 1871.
34. Dumas fils, *Théâtre Complet*, 4:27–28.
35. George Sand, Smeets–Sand, December 29, 1872.
36. Annarosa Poli, *George Sand et les années terribles* (Paris: A. G. Nizet, 1975), 278.
37. Dumas fils, Smeets–Sand, March 10, 1869.
38. Ibid., April 19, 1871.
39. See Poli, passim.
40. George Sand, Smeets–Sand, May 23, 1871.
41. Dumas fils, *Théâtre Complet*, 3:14–15.

28

Two Monologues from *Dialectic of the Heart*

Alex Szogyi

Dialectic of the Heart was written especially for the Seventh International George Sand Conference held at Hofstra University in 1986, which also celebrated the tenth anniversary of the founding of the Friends of George Sand.

The purpose of the work was to elucidate and dramatize the relationship between George Sand and Frédéric Chopin. Almost all previous works devoted to this fascinating subject were overly romanticized. Doubtless, the influence of the Romantic era caused writers to treat their relationship in this manner. My work as a Sand scholar coupled with my professional experience in the theater, along with a grant from the City University of New York to do research in France, enabled me to undertake this project. I am also grateful to Christiane Sand and the books she placed at my disposal at her home in Gargilesse and in the library at La Châtre. I would like to acknowledge Gisela Schlientz, who kindly sent me a German play about the relationship between Sand and Chopin.

Working with the pianist Byron Janis was most illuminating. As president of the Chopin Society in France, he was privy to many letters and documents relating to George Sand and Frédéric Chopin. He helped me to understand Chopin and to balance the ledger of their relationship. The play I wrote was shocking to Sand scholars because it did not spare Sand; her destruction of their relationship was totally understandable in the context of events. I have tried to give all the reasons and make what occurred between them explicit.

The monologues presented here were written with the conviction that only a Shavian experience, such as the one in *Don Juan in Hell*, would adequately sum up the complete experience of Sand and Chopin's complicated relationship. This is the first form of the work, which is still evolving and will one day be in its final form. I have since rewritten the play in French and reduced the monologues, which are now more manageable on stage. I am pleased that the original monologues will be preserved in this volume.

I shall always be grateful for the deep understanding and support of those who felt there was something genuine and valuable in this work. My deepest thanks go to James M. Shuart, president of Hofstra University; Natalie Datlof, Director of Liaison and Creative Development of the Hofstra Cultural Center and founder of the Friends of George Sand; and Françoise Gilot, international artist and *sandiste*, for their understanding of what I tried to do.

GEORGE SAND

Chopin was perhaps the greatest love of my life. I was certainly his. I had lived so much before. I was adequately prepared. He was not. When I met him, he enchanted me. He was for me the quintessence of artistry. All my life, music was for me the ultimate art. I surrounded myself with it in huge doses. When I sat under Liszt's piano, I was in heaven. With Chopin, I also loved the man who made the music. At first, he refused me his body. I was too overwhelming, too much an earth creature to enchant him. I used every wile at my disposal. I wrote to his friend, Grzymala, and would gladly have consulted everyone in his entourage. When he finally succumbed, I learned once more in my difficult erotic life that the sexual act was but a symbol. I was overjoyed to possess him, to be for him the ultimate woman. . . . Once again, illness played tricks on me. It caused me to be lucid. I was fascinated by knowledge. Doctors seemed to possess that knowledge. When my lovers fell ill, I consulted the doctors for an answer to their distress. And the doctors became part of our life. Penetrating the wisdom of the doctor became as important as anything else. This was especially true with Musset. If Musset had been a composer, he might have been my last great love. But it was Chopin who held the key to my happiness. It became my goal to minimize the illness, to master it and preserve the creator. Any means of doing that was valid. I did not need Chopin in bed to make all this possible. Devotion was all. As long as we shared our devotion, as long as we were both able to create, nothing else mattered. Creation enveloped all other experience.

When a man and a woman are linked in love-making, that is their form of expression. They can sacrifice the rest because their physical liaison is total. They join physically and that is the meaning of their lives. We all know this rarely lasts. Why should it? Perfection is not of this world. When, however, one perfection dies, we must replace it with many others. All relationships are in danger when the sexual aspect dies. But it is then that the other elements take over and these rarely die unless they are betrayed. Loyalty, the joys of daily communion, the building of a shared existence, children—all these make for more of a marriage than sexuality. Children, our posterity, there we must be fortunate. Our children are our emblem, our pride, we must never allow them to destroy our lives. They must be for us like the living of a second existence. They are sometimes even our spiritual lovers. My son, Maurice, was that for me. He was the man I never had and he stood steadfast at my side as no one else ever did.

God gave me Solange to torment me. She took it upon herself to torment me. She could never bear my happiness. I tried to inculcate in her all the good that life ever taught me but she needed allies to oppose me. Destiny would have it that she enlisted Chopin as her leading ally. That I could not bear. Her father, Dudevant, was bad enough. I would not allow anyone else to betray me in this fashion. I had devoted a decade to Chopin. I had neglected too much for his sake. I needed his loyalty. I would not allow him to become Solange's plaything. Nor could he become her surrogate parent. I would not allow Solange to possess Chopin. That was the one thing I could never permit. We all have our own rules. We are inexorable in certain parts of our lives. Otherwise, all is chaos.

Whether he slept with her or not, I shall never know. Of what importance is it? He did worse. He preferred her welfare to my own. He preferred to come to her defense instead of to mine. He humiliated me with my worst enemy. Can that ever be forgiven? No, dear Lord, not by a woman who *is* a woman. One doesn't give up a decade of one's life to an ideal just to be tarnished by that ideal. What a silly little man lived inside that genius! I have never known a more atheistic poet or a more poetic atheist. He believed that he believed in a sort of divinity. It was nothing more than the waves of his genius. I protected him from all of his insufficiencies. I never complained. Genius was all. After all, his greatest works of art were conceived with me nearby. I allowed that genius to flourish. I watered and cultivated it and preferred it to my own. What more can one human being do for another? I killed off Lucrezia Floriani so that he, the egotist, would never realize that I was revealing him to the world in all his egotism. And he was such an egotist that he never even noticed. And I would never have allowed him to notice. I preserved his immunity. I gave him the best that can be had. And at what a cost! How disciplined can one human being be! God made me forbearing. I have borne the stupidities and cruelties of every man I have known until I could bear them no longer. And then devil take the hindmost.

George Sand loved exclusively until she could love no more. And then she went on to another life. We all live many lives in one carapace. We sometimes live them simultaneously, if one has a gift for such a thing. We may stop living with the men we love and yet we may love them forever. They will certainly haunt us forever. My absolute rule has been never to return to those I leave. Let us say it has been my habit. Once it is over, it is over. They must take the consequences. If they cannot live without me, they should have known better.

I have always given the best of myself. I put their need before mine. But they must not trespass on my heart forever. I lost my father when I was only a child. I played his role for the women in my life. I learned to play the man early in my existence and relished the role. I played the woman and I played the man and I played them supremely well. I gave myself as a votive gift to the world and was never afraid to play the laughing stock. I was trained perfectly by my mother and my grandmother. They made me into the creature I became. They needed the man in me. We all have both in us, but how few are called upon to play both roles simultaneously. How good an actress I became. I am the grand chameleon of the Romantic age, all things to all men and all things to some women. And what a risk it was to be adored and disdained by so many, always hoping my lovers would prize me sufficiently. For survival was all.

I did not use illness as so many others did. My creations were sane and I had to preserve myself for my work as well as for my life. Only my nervous stomach betrayed me in the end and only very late. We are none of us, after all, immortal. But in that fantastic chess game of life, one must preserve one's dignity. And so I wrote to Chopin to break our contract. I might never have been able to do it had he been at my side at Nohant at the time. He had gone too far. He had betrayed me with my own daughter. Chopin was certainly the greatest love of my life but also my greatest trial. I gave up more for him than for any other lover. And he appreciated it less. He gave his genius to no one else but himself. He kept it for the world. He fed it to the piano. But not to anyone else. He never dedicated anything to me. Not one of his creations bears my name. Yet the world knows and always will that I gave him the last decade of his life as a grand gift. I allowed him to perfect his genius and I took care of him as if he were my third child. I preserved him for himself. Let him wherever he is now deny that. My dignity is intact. I respect myself. I banished him from my life when he deserved me no longer.

And, of course, he died. No one else could preserve that vain creature as I did. No one else could give him any more than the adulation which was his daily bread. Not one of those grand ladies and Polish patriots could given him what the heathen Sand could give him out of the warmth of her heart. He learned his lesson.Creativity lives on gratitude, not ingratitude. Solange never inspired anything but lowly incense. She was not worthy to be my daughter as he was not worthy to be my love. But do we know this in the beginning? No, we fall in love desperately with an ideal. We capture it like an elusive butterfly. We enchant ourselves into believing that love is the answer to life. We romanticize our existence. And then we learn, suddenly, that we were never prized, never sufficiently loved, never for more than a moment for which we fought gallantly.

We have our talent, we have our genius, we have our work. We have our duty and our destiny to work out and we are betrayed, sooner or later. Thank God we have the strength to live beyond each experience, to press into another part of our existence. If we died physically with every love, we could never progress. We are the keyboard of destiny. Life plays upon us and creates its themes and variations to which we must vibrate. God at least gave me an existence which went further than most of the others I witnessed. I was given a multifarious destiny and I lived it to the hilt. I was given Chopin, I conquered him and we may yet meet again in some other existence. Then he will have to live with his karma, indeed, and expiate more than he did in his life for the way in which he sacrificed me. He will need more than a little student, a Jane Stirling to take him away to a better clime. I loved him more than myself. I gave myself to him. No one can ever blame me for giving him up when he betrayed me. Solange was with him at the end. I hope he was satisfied!

FRÉDÉRIC CHOPIN

(Playing the Funeral March)

George Sand was the longest love of my life, perhaps because she was not really my type. I loved Maria Wodzinska and could not have her. I loved Delphine Potocka, yes. Women in the abstract, yes. I loved them all. I loved their beauty, their elegance, their nobility of spirit. I loved the way they made me feel . . . inside of myself. I have listened to the music within me. My heart has danced the mazurkas and the polonaises within me. My whole life has been the struggle to exteriorize the music I have heard inside of myself. I have been maddened by the inability to perfect what I have heard. It was revealed to me in all its perfection and then I have agonized to set it down, to relive every nuance and perfect every harmony. Sometimes it has taken days and weeks to get back to what I first heard in the depths of my being. No one ever fully understood that struggle even if they witnessed it in mute admiration. Could they ever have comprehended the struggle of creation, the unearthing of depths within our souls? Living only for that and nothing else. I have loved my heritage. My mother, my father, my friends. I would have died for my friend, Titus. He was my ideal. His body attained a perfection I had not been given. If only I had been given a stronger frame, I might have composed the entire canon of nineteenth-century music better than Bellini. I could have conquered the world at the piano, as Liszt did, relying mostly on pyrotechnics. There are three *fortissimi* in me for every two of his. But I was given the fragility of genius without its ultimate strength. I was created a Pole and that provided dignity forever. I was given friends and the adulation of the aristocracy. I was befriended by the best, always. But I was fragile.

God gave me George Sand when I began to suffer and although I would never have chosen her, she chose me. What does it matter who does the choosing and who is chosen? She also disdainfully let me go when I most needed her. She made me pay for everything she ever gave me. And I never understood why. I did not ask for her love. She poured it over me like honey. She was not my ideal. She lived for the people, she was a democratic woman who never understood the meaning of aristocracy. Though she was descended from Polish royalty on the one hand—surely we were destined to meet—she was also the daughter of a common woman, and she loved the people and their ambitions more than she cared for one man. She was of the moment, a bourgeois daughter of her time. She loved me and what was inside of me but she loved it as an outsider. I fascinated her. I was her little Chopin, her aristocratic doll, and she pitied me as much as she loved me. I brought out her maternal spirit. Her son was her protector. Her daughter was her rival, her enemy. Who could deal with George Sand once she had conquered Paris and the world of writers and artists? Only I was her true child. Only I could behave to her like a needful child. She turned me into that role, rehearsed me, perfected my role and never let me forget that I was her creation. She disdained me later as I had disdained her at first. She always took revenge and hers was the worst kind—one never knew it was happening. When she threw me out of her life, I could not believe it. I had never done anything to harm her. I put up with her political notions and her heretic creativity. I lived with her ideals and did what best I could to rival all her other heroes. Pity Liszt never took to her physically. He would have been her ideal, and it would have been he who finally left her. But Liszt was a compassionate fool who allowed himself to get into the clutches of inferior women. At least George was superior and I adored her for it. I tried to share her ideals and her artistic theories though I cared nothing for anything but friendship, love and the demon within me.

I could forego the world for a salon. I didn't need to play for the multitude if I could exist in the hearts of the few. I could live in exile in Paris while Poland remained imbedded in my heart. I had my beliefs which transcended all banal religion and nothing could crush them. I only needed the happiness of my childhood and my heritage to remind me of it. I knew only loyalty and gratitude. When I fell in love with Madame Sand, it was forever. She helped to cure me, she made me not afraid to die while she was with me. She was my guardian angel. She allowed me to create and she created, as well. We were good for one another, mostly. We had a life together. And even when we were separated by the distance of Nohant and Paris, my happiest moments were spent fetching and carrying so that she might be spared some errand I might do for her.

I loved her daughter. I could not love her son. We were like oil and water. Solange needed me. I was for her like the real father she had never had, not like the brute Dudevant. I watched her flower into womanhood. I was the first to see her elegance, a spirit much more female than her mother, a fragility her mother never possessed. I felt close to her. I could be for her a surrogate parent. Was I wrong? Is it never possible to have a pure relationship with anyone? Is even purity just the tarnishing of the soul without the outward turmoil? She enchanted me because she was the finer side of her mother. She had none of her qualities except that she was a woman. She did not look upon me as if I were sick little Chopin. She did not pity me. She took to me. She grew up near me. When she became a woman, she felt my manhood. She tried out her womanhood on anyone that would taste it. She opposed her mother as any daughter would. With all her goodness, George was so self-righteous and dominating. She hadn't a flaw and flawed people always resent that. Nothing is more in danger than a graven image. We all soil the good. Solange made me feel like a man. She asked for my protection. What passed between us will always be a secret. It doesn't matter whether we slept together. The most intimate moments between a man and a woman are not always physical, Lord knows. Intimacy is not always a sexual recognition. Intimacy is the work of the soul. George and I were intimate for a decade and I cannot believe we will not continue to be for all eternity.

Despite Solange, we will still love one another forever. One cannot stop loving for paltry reasons. What is vanity one hundred years later? True pride lies elsewhere, does it not? Solange gave herself to that lout, Clésinger. She was no less charmed by him than her mother. There they were on common ground. George could have slept with him, as well. Men like that are never refused in the imagination. Lord only knows how far it went. Solange might have as much to reproach her mother with as what she was accused of. Clésinger would have coupled with the devil himself and stolen all his possessions. They didn't tell me that they were to be married. Sand kept it from her Chopin, knowing I could never approve. To soil everything that was fine in Solange by associating herself with that ruffian? There are some abominable acts in life! But she did it and her mother approved and I was not consulted. And when Maurice finally threatened him and was attacked by the monster gigolo, George finally understood what had happened to her daughter. But it was too late. Solange came to me for help. She ran to me. For her mother's sake, I came to her rescue. Who could fault me for that? Should

I have rejected her? Should one reject the person one loves? Not if one loves. I helped her despite her mother as any gentleman would have. I helped her when she needed it. I was not her father, but her surrogate father and surrogate parents play a role in life even if they have no legitimate name.

When a mother and a daughter cannot understand one another, they must have help. I gave it and paid dearly. Sand rejected me. She left me to die. She once promised me I would die only in her arms. She gave me to my destiny, and even if she was in the right, her coldness was the ultimate punishment. Perhaps there was nothing left in me anymore. Perhaps my illness was timed to take hold of me once and for all. I could not exist only as a creator. I had grown used to the love of a good woman and I had a surrogate family of my own. I would not beg for what I no longer seemingly deserved. I would go away. England would give me what France could no longer. All that I ever needed was a helping hand, the adulation of a few worthy ladies, a few well-placed friends. Sand had taken her toll. She had abandoned me at the worst moment. She was vindictive and cruel. I would not accept that. I would love her even though I was deprived of her. I would love her through all eternity. Solange would replace her in my heart. She would watch over my last days intently and be there for me while I endured. She would give me what her mother no longer could and her brother never could. She would be my family for a short while. She would not abandon me. She would make George take notice and regret her bad behavior. I would yet live to have a better day.

But it was not meant to be. We were separated forever by a whim, by a moment's inadvertence. By stupid, unconquerable pride. We will live forever beside our great creations as the most important lovers of our time. Liszt was ultimately alone. Marie d'Agoult was too proud to share herself with anyone. But Sand and Chopin will always be synonymous with a certain devotion. I loved her almost as much as I loved my parents, my country, my heritage, my music. She wanted more than anyone could give. That is the price of generosity. For no one was ever as generous as she. None of her rationalizations, her divine white lies could ever deny that. That great man was a great woman. She must always be treasured. Always be loved throughout eternity.

We met only once more. Chez la Comtesse Marliani. I was leaving the soirée when she arrived. . . . We met on the staircase. . . .

29

Fanny Lewald and George Sand: *Eine Lebensfrage* and *Indiana*

Margaret E. Ward and Karen Storz

By the time the German writer Fanny Lewald (1811–1889) wrote her autobiography in the late 1850s, she had been compared so often to George Sand that she found it necessary to distance herself rather peevishly from the French writer. Although she uses the masculine pronoun, she clearly knew that George was a woman. "As often as people—who must not have known George Sand's or my work very well—have been fond of comparing me to him and of calling me his follower, I have never been this and could not have been (*Lebensgeschichte* 3:306).[1] Despite her disclaimer, the identification of Fanny Lewald with George Sand continued to be made. In a 1937 dissertation, Marieluise Steinhauer explored in great detail the reasons for, and the legitimacy of, this comparison.[2]

More recently, Renate Moehrmann has shown that George Sand's reception by German writers of the *Vormärz* was mixed. By contrast to the men of Young Germany, who saw in Sand and her early heroines their ideal of the "femme libre," women like Fanny Lewald and Louise Otto-Peters were more ambivalent.[3] However, Moehrmann stresses Lewald's interest in Sand's political and social activism on behalf of women, thereby obscuring the way in which George Sand's early novels actually sparked Lewald's imagination at a time when she was just emerging as a writer.

Fanny Lewald may very well have first read Sand at the time of her stay with relatives in Breslau in the fall and winter of 1832–1833, when *Indiana* was published, for here she had access to her uncle's library and greater freedom in her choice of reading matter than under the watchful eye of her father, who detested novels. Lewald was introduced by her cousin, Heinrich Simon, to the works of the Romantics and the Young Germans. Moreover, it was her unrequited love for Simon, from which she suffered for almost a decade thereafter, that made her particularly susceptible to Sand's heroines. As she admits in her autobiography:

> There was something unexpected, something powerful in the ardent and audaciously outspoken passion, with which France's foremost living author, George Sand, presented women characters to us, figures whose great hearts men were unable to treasure, and who were unable to find peace or happiness, because no man was in a position to cherish or merit such a heart. (3:305)

Lewald even praises Sand for the truthfulness of certain female characters who are shown to be hard-working, for she could identify with this "good middle-class element," in contrast to the idle aristocrats of similar novels written by German women (Ida Hahn-Hahn in particular, whom she considers boring). The way in which Moehrmann quotes selectively from Lewald makes it seem as if the accusation were leveled directly at the French writer.[4] However, Lewald actually praises Sand wherever her novels are based on "truth and reality."[5] Lewald specifically mentions *Lélia*, *Leo* [*sic*] *Leoni*, and *Le Compagnons* [*sic*] *du tour de France*.

Lewald published a scathing parody of the Hahn-Hahn style novel with her *Diogena* in 1847, but she by no means put George Sand into the same category. Instead, she continued to hold the French writer in high esteem. When Lewald first went to France in March 1848, she wanted above all to meet Sand personally. In her published reminiscences she rather bluntly asserts that since she was unable to meet Sand—who had temporarily left Paris for Nohant—she would at least make sure to seek out Heinrich Heine. In several of her conversations with him, George Sand was mentioned.[6] Lewald had read Sand's *Lettres au peuple*, and was so impressed that she even toyed with the idea of translating them into German.[7]

Again in 1850, Lewald hoped but failed to make George Sand's acquaintance in Paris. This time she carried a letter of introduction from the Italian revolutionary, Giuseppe Mazzini, whom she had just met in England. In a passage from her British travelogue, Lewald expounds on the novel *Mary Barton* by Mrs. Gaskell. What appeals to her—in specific contrast with Sand's work—is the novel's foundation in reality. The French novelist is closer to the Romantic tradition, Lewald asserts, a tradition toward which she herself felt ambivalent.[8]

Nonetheless, in 1855, after seeing George Sand's "revolutionary idyll," *Maître Favilla* at the Odéon, Lewald wrote to a Berlin theater director praising its "purity of feeling" and the "beauty of its language," and suggested that she could provide a translation in German should he be interested in mounting a production. He evidently was not.[9] Despite Lewald's genuine and lasting admiration for Sand, her autobiography quite correctly emphasizes differences between their familial, social, and religious backgrounds as the source of a basic dissimilarity in their literary works.[10]

Both Fanny Lewald and George Sand were intellectually precocious at a time when this was looked on as unfeminine and impractical. However, Lewald's middle-class Jewish family made her feel more acutely at a young age the disadvantages of being a girl with ambition. She identified with a patriarchal father, whose enlightened convictions about the preeminence of reason led him to educate her at a Pietist private, coeducational school until the age of thirteen. His model of true womanhood was nevertheless her uneducated, submissive, and completely domestic mother. Lewald had to struggle throughout her childhood and young adulthood with contradictory expectations. The power of conventional sex-role stereotypes was enhanced in a home that was a "model of domestic harmony."[11] Although she suffered for years from a sense of uselessness and restriction, she remained an obedient daughter until she was twenty-five.

Aurore Dupin, on the other hand, experienced a relatively tempestuous family life, which undermined the power of traditional family values and sex roles in her development. At an age when Fanny Lewald was well aware of the disadvantages of being a girl in her society but was attempting to adapt to please her father, Aurore Dupin was developing a contempt for the conventions of a society in which aristocratic prejudices worked to separate her from her plebeian mother, whom she loved passionately. The virtues of discipline, self-control, and responsibility, which produced for Lewald a sphere of inner freedom while at the same time binding her to the bourgeois value system, had no comparable meaning for Sand. Her unhappy family situation caused her great suffering, but it also freed her from the tyranny of a model of domestic felicity.

Similarly, Sand's position in the aristocracy ultimately exempted her from some of the pressures and restrictions of Lewald's middle-class background. She experienced the freedom of life on a large estate, where she could escape the strictures of domestic etiquette. Moreover, as the future heiress of Nohant, she was not under quite the same economic pressures as Lewald to become an attractive commodity for the marriage market. Faced with the prospect of independent wealth, Sand could gain a sense of her own power by rejecting inherited privileges. At the age when Lewald was forced to leave school, Sand was sent to a convent school. Instead of encouraging conformity, however, the mystical experience she had there actually enhanced her sense of self.[12]

This brief comparison suggests that conditions were more conducive to rebellion against social conventions in Sand's case. However, contrary to expectations, it was Sand who entered into a conventional marriage at the age of eighteen, whereas Lewald openly resisted this fate even at the age of twenty-five, when her father tried to marry her off to a propertied lawyer—a total stranger to her. She declared that such a marriage would be far worse than prostitution.[13] He refused to allow her to work as a governess or teacher, however, for in his view, a working daughter would signal his inability to provide for her. Lewald's talent for writing was nonetheless recognized and encouraged by her cousin, August Lewald, who began to publish excerpts from her letters in his journal. After the success of her first novels—published anonymously at her father's request—she was able to move to Berlin and start an independent life at the age of thirty-four. She did not marry until a decade later, and then by choice.

For Sand, the early marriage to Casimir Dudevant, which was to provide an escape from her mother's tyrannical love, proved to be a submission to a different kind of tyranny. Although she tried to adapt to the role of wife and mother, she experienced her marriage as a form of slavery. Lewald was spared a similar fate by her father's more reasonable attitude. However, his thwarted attempt to arrange a marriage of convenience had revealed to her the full extent of the contradictions in the bourgeois value system, which stressed the importance of independence and self-sufficiency but enjoined women to relinquish these virtues in order to be supported by their husbands. Since she had not yet fully emancipated herself, these same contradictions are inherent in Lewald's early novels, in which she appealed to positive bourgeois values in her belief that society could be reformed through education and enlightenment.

By contrast, Sand's misery in her nine-year marriage to Dudevant led to a much more radical rejection of the whole social order. Her struggle for independence as a married woman in France—which under the Napoleonic Code did not recognize women as legal persons and which did not permit divorce—required a much more radical rebellion.[14] The way in which these dissimilar backgrounds directly affected the two women's writing can be quite vividly demonstrated by comparing two early novels that both deal with the problem of marriage.

A mixture of radical attack on social and legal injunctions imposed on women and resigned and elevated suffering in the hope of personal liberation pervades Sand's first novel, *Indiana.* The retired colonel, Delmare, is a dull-witted, hot-tempered husband, who insists on his marital rights, while Indiana is confined to isolation and idleness in the domestic sphere. Sand's characterization of Delmare goes beyond an attack on the loveless marriage of convenience. It also indicts society's moral code, under which Delmare is considered to be an honest man. "Provided that he religiously respects the lives and purses of his fellow-citizens, nothing more is demanded of him. He may beat his wife, maltreat his servants, ruin his children, and it is nobody's business."[15]

In the character of Raymon, the cynical and callous but suave and refined opportunist who becomes Indiana's lover, Sand also attacks a social code that not only accepted, but even admired and encouraged, such a lady-killer. Sand also uses Indiana to denounce the Napoleonic legal code: "I know that I am the slave and you the master. The laws of this country make you my master. You can bind my body, tie my hands, govern my acts."[16]

However, the heroine is a more problematic figure. She is neither the poor seduced girl nor the fallen woman who has sacrificed duty to inclination. Her passion is portrayed as positive and her adultery as courageous. With such a heroine, Sand argues not only for the emancipation of women from the legally sanctioned tyranny of their husbands, but also from injunctions of sexual passivity and from the tyranny of the "feminine virtue" of marital fidelity.

In Indiana's relationship with Raymon, however, Sand wavers between portraying her as a tragic victim of the romantic illusions to which social conditions condemn her, and showing her to be the glorified victim of the feminine need and capacity for absolute self-sacrificing love. Indiana suffers repeated humiliation at the hands of a man who is incapable of loving her, and yet she does not give him up until he is married to another, whereupon she resolves to die. This obsessive love is described as inherent in woman's nature, and it is considered her particular virtue: "Love is woman's virtue; it is for love that she glories in her sins, it is from love that she acquires the heroism to defy her remorse."[17]

As Moehrmann has pointed out, Sand only reverses the values given to the feminine half of what is still conceived as a basic dichotomy.[18] Women are considered superior, both in their ability to love and in their capacity for suffering. In her portrayal of Indiana, Sand therefore wavers between images of energetic struggle and resigned passivity. She is saved from martyrdom only by her faithful companion, Ralph, who by declaring his love for her after the death of her husband, restores her to life. The novel's ending, with its romantic idyll on the Ile Bourbon, expresses Sand's sense that an ideal relationship between man and woman cannot exist in society. The boldness of the novel lies not in this conclusion, but rather in Sand's insistence on a woman's need for fulfillment, and her consequent argument for women's emotional and sexual emancipation. However, in the character of Indiana, she also idealizes the passive suffering of a woman awaiting the male liberator who will finally fulfill her need.

By contrast, the main character of Fanny Lewald's third novel, *Eine Lebensfrage*, is a man suffering in a marriage of convenience. The inspiration was provided by the debate in the 1840s about a proposed revision in the relatively liberal divorce laws which existed under the Prussian Allgemeines Landrecht of 1794.[19] Lewald wished to prove that there are cases in which the dissolution of a marriage can be a highly moral act.[20] She was unmarried at the time, so her interest was more dispassionate than the interest that informed Sand's *Indiana*. However, in arguing for the necessity of divorce as a remedy for certain marriages of convenience, and in opposing revisions in the legal code that would restrict the former without disturbing the latter, Lewald speaks from the experience of a woman who has resisted the typical fate of middle-class daughters and is justifying her resistance.

The cause of Alfred's suffering in his marriage is the housewife mentality of his wife, Caroline. Lewald makes it clear that unequal education and lack of opportunity to travel have been the cause of this unhappy alliance. Therese, the woman with whom Alfred falls in love during his separation from Caroline, is educated, and enjoys some freedom and independence living with her brother. While Alfred focuses primarily on the legal obstacles to his desired union with Therese, she is struggling with her belief in the so-called feminine virtues of self-denial and sublimation of desire. Her decision to marry Alfred is Lewald's ultimate refutation of the bourgeois ideal of a woman who sacrifices inclination to duty.

However, Lewald's novel does not contain the same kind of affirmation of passion and rebellion against the very institution of marriage as George Sand's *Indiana*. Alfred considers marriage to be the ideal union of man and woman, which is degraded when it is based upon anything but mutual love. Lewald thus argues through his voice, and that of the narrator, for a reform of the institutions of marriage, and indirectly for the education of women to be equal to that of men.

Throughout the novel Lewald questions many bourgeois ideals of femininity; her array of female characters shows various degrees of submissiveness, ignorance, and dependence, and these characteristics are shown to be weaknesses cultivated for their appeal to men. Julian, Therese's often cynical, epicurean brother, represents the extreme male point of view, in contrast to Alfred. He finds ignorance in women "charming"; female dependence "gives a man the enticing privilege of protecting a woman, of being everything to her."[21] Lewald's exaltation of other so-called feminine virtues, however, shows the extent to which she had internalized certain bourgeois values. Although they do not define her women completely, some of the characteristics that she puts forward as truly feminine are the same as those promulgated by the patriarchal handbooks of family ideology of the time: mildness, forbearance, selfless love, and quiet domesticity.[22]

The one figure in Lewald's novel who stands outside the boundaries of bourgeois morality, and therefore comes closest to being modeled on Sand's heroine, is the French actress Sophie Harcourt. It is not incidental that the passage in Lewald's autobiography about George Sand, to which we have referred above, follows directly after this particular character is mentioned. Harcourt is talented and independent; she loves passionately and scorns marriage as a bond that destroys true love. Lewald's portrayal of Sophie seems to reflect her ambivalent reception of Sand's heroines. Therese deeply admires Sophie's boundless capacity for love, and eventually sympathizes with her rebellion against the laws that would restrict it. However, she rejects such an ideal of free love because of the inevitable suffering it brings women in the form of exploitation by men who are not equal to such a great passion and scorn by society. Sophie's lover, Julian, spurns marriage too, but for him the affair is more a matter of pleasure than love, and he breaks it off out of concern for his reputation.

Although Sophie suffers greatly from this rejection and contemplates suicide, she does not take her life, nor is she saved by another man. Instead, she commits herself to the caring profession of nursing. However, this decision is not idealized. The happiest outcome is still seen as a marriage between equal partners, such as that on which Alfred and Therese embark at the conclusion of the novel. Sophie's new profession is just another self-sacrificing alternative, in which the woman cannot attain the true fulfillment of her desire. Ironically, however, without the model of Sophie's uncompromising love in front of her, Therese would probably not have had the courage to risk social criticism in order to assure her own happiness.[23]

George Sand's and Fanny Lewald's early novels express many of the same concerns. Their different experiences in their respective families and within their societies, however, influenced the way in which they rebelled against the existing definitions of women and the restrictions placed on them. Sand's lack of a positive domestic model in her youth and her early experience in marriage of the extremely oppressive legal and social codes of French society contributed to a more complete rejection of the social and legal order. Lewald escaped the negative marital experience, but she suffered for many years under the restrictions of a patriarchal family, as well as under laws and social prejudices that perpetuated her state of dependency. She also experienced positive aspects of the bourgeois order: a stable family life, parental love, and the benefits of education. Thus, while arguing more realistically for the rational reform of women's social and legal position, Lewald also internalized more of the bourgeois views of women. On the other hand, while George Sand's rejection of the existing order was more radical than Lewald's, her romantic discontent with the world and her longing for a utopian solution, expressed in *Indiana*, caused her at times to glorify resignation and patient suffering as women's virtues. It is this essential difference between her romanticism and Lewald's realism that distinguishes *Indiana* from *Eine Lebensfrage*.

There is little doubt that Lewald was influenced by Sand when she began to write in the 1840s, but she was also justified in insisting in her autobiography that "While I unquestionably recognize his mastery, I am nevertheless entitled to my own insights and my own mistakes, my own success and failure."[24] Lewald quite rightly points to differences in their family, social, and religious backgrounds as the reason she cannot be simply thought of as a German George Sand. A reading of the two early novels shows that despite these differences, in the person of Sophie Harcourt Lewald created a female character who exhibits the same depth of passion and contempt for the social order that she admired in Sand's heroines. Although Sophie is a minor character who does not achieve self-fulfillment, it seems significant that she in turn acts as a source of inspiration to the woman who is ultimately able to reject the old pattern of self-denial. Sand's romantic ideal remains unfulfilled because there is no man who merits Sophie's heart, but in Lewald's realistic world, true love as a partnership of equals is nevertheless seen as possible.

NOTES

1. Fanny Lewald, *Meine Lebensgeschichte*, in her *Gesammelte Werke* (Berlin: Otto Janke, 1871), 3:306; this and all subsequent translations from Fanny Lewald are by Margaret E. Ward.

2. Marieluise Steinhauer, *Fanny Lewald, die deutsche George Sand: Ein Kapitel aus der Geschichte des Frauenromans im 19. Jahrhundert* (Diss., Humbolt University, Berlin, 1837).

3. Renate Moehrmann, *Die andere Frau: Emanzipationsansätze deutscher Schriftstellerinnen im Vorfeld der Achtundvierziger Revolution* (Stuttgart: J. B. Metzlar; 1977), 56.

4. Ibid.

5. Lewald, *Lebensgeschichte*, 3:306–307.

6. Fanny Lewald, *Erinnerungen aus dem Jahre 1848*, ed. Dietrich Schaefer (Frankfurt am Main: Insel, 1969), 35, 69. See also the account in Fanny Lewald, *Zwoelf Bilder nach dem Leben* (Berlin: Otto Janke, 1888), 208.

7. Lewald, *Erinnerungen*, 35.

8. Fanny Lewald, *England und Schottland: Reisetagebuch* (Berlin: Otto Janke, 1864), 1:307–308.

9. Gay Manifold, *George Sand's Theatre Career* (Ann Arbor: UMI Research Press, 1985), 92. Fanny Lewald, letter to a Berlin theater director, Paris, September 28, 1855, letter 3, Lewald Handschriften, Acc. 241, Rep. 324, Landesarchiv, Berlin.

10. Lewald, *Lebensgeschichte*, 3:306.

11. Ibid., 1:22.

12. George Sand, *My Life*, trans. Dan Hofstadter (New York: Harper and Row, 1979), 30. See also Curtis Cate, *George Sand: A Biography* (Boston: Houghton Mifflin, 1975).

13. Lewald, *Lebensgeschichte*, 2:185.

14. For more information on the legal status of women under this code, see Marianne

Weber, *Ehefrau und Mutter in der Rechtsentwicklung* (Tübingen: J.C.B. Mohr, 1907), 319–325, and *The Code Napoléon*, trans. Bryant Barret (London: W. Reed, Law Bookseller, 1811), 50.

15. George Sand, *Indiana*, trans. George Burnham Ives (New York: Howard Fertig, 1975), 96.

16. Ibid., 206.

17. Ibid., 260.

18. Moehrmann, *Die andere Frau*, 54.

19. For more information on the legal status of women under this code, see Weber, *Ehefrau und Mutter*, 331–339; and Ute Gerhard, *Verhaeltnisse und Verhinderungen: Frauenarbeit, Familie und Rechte der Frauen im 19. Jahrhundert* (Frankfurt am Main: Suhrkamp Verlag, 1981), 171, 451.

20. Lewald, *Lebensgeschichte*, 3:299–300.

21. Fanny Lewald, *Eine Lebensfrage*, in her *Gesammelte Werke* (Berlin: Otto Janke, 1872), 10:203.

22. See Gerhard, *Verhaeltnisse*, 126, 363–374.

23. Lewald, *Lebensfrage*, 341–343.

24. Lewald, *Lebensgeschichte*, 3:306.

Selected Bibliography

David A. Powell

BIBLIOGRAPHIES

Brynolfson, Gaylord. "Works on George Sand, 1964–1980: A Bibliography." In *George Sand Papers: Conference Proceedings*, edited by Natalie Datlof, vol. 2, 1978. New York: AMS Press, 1982, 189–233.

Datlof, Natalie. "Bibliographies by or about George Sand in English." In *George Sand: In Her Own Words*, edited by Joseph Barry. Garden City, N.Y.: Doubleday/Anchor, 1979, 452–460.

———. "Bibliography: George Sand in Foreign Languages." *George Sand Newsletter* 1, no. 3 (1978): 14–17.

Keane, Robert A., and Natalie Datlof. "George Sand and the Victorians: Bibliography." *George Sand Newsletter* 1, no. 2 (1978): 5–6.

Poli, Annarosa. *George Sand vue par les Italiens: Essai de bibliographie critique*. Paris: M. Didier, 1965.

Spoelberch de Lovenjoul, Charles. *George Sand: Etude bibliographique sur ses oeuvres*. 1914. Reprint: Bibliography and reference series, 429; Essays in literature and criticism, no. 152. New York: Burt Franklin, 1971, 118 pp.

RECENT EDITIONS OF INDIVIDUAL WORKS

Flaubert, Gustave, and George Sand. *Correspondance*, edited by Alphonse Jacobs. Paris: Flammarion, 1981, 600 pp.

Sand, George. *André*. Présenté par Huguette Burine et Michel Gilot. Meylan, France: Editions de l'Aurore, 1987, 256 pp.

Sand, George. *Le Château des désertes*. Présenté par Joseph-Marc Bailbé. Meylan, France: Editions de l'Aurore, 1985, 192 pp.

Sand, George. *Le Compagnon du Tour de France*. Introduction par René Bourgeois. Grenoble: Presses Universitaires de Grenoble, 1988, 397 pp.

Sand, George. *Consuelo* and *La Comtesse de Rudolstadt*. Introductory essays by Léon Cellier and Léon Guichard. 3 vols. Paris: Garnier, 1959.

Sand, George. *Consuelo* and *La Comtesse de Rudolstadt*. Présenté par Simone Vierne et René Bourgeois. 3 vols. Meylan, France: Editions de l'Aurore, 1983.

Sand, George. *Contes d'une grand'mère*. Présenté par Philippe Berthier. 2 vols. Meylan, France: Editions de l'Aurore, 1982.
Sand, George. *Correspondance*, éditée par Georges Lubin. 24 Vols. Paris: Garnier, 1964– .
Sand, George. *La Daniella*. Présenté par Simone Balayé. Geneva: Slatkine, 1979, 630 pp.
Sand, George. *Elle et lui*. Préface par Joseph Barry, présenté par Thierry Bodin. Meylan, France: Editions de l'Aurore, 1986, 228 pp.
Sand, George. *La Filleule*. Présenté par Marie-Paule Rambeau. Meylan, France: Editions de l'Aurore, 1989.
Sand, George. *François le champi*. Préface par André Femigier. Folio 738. Paris: Gallimard, 1976.
Sand, George. *Gabriel*. Préface par Janis Glasgow. Paris: Des Femmes, 1988, 230 pp.
Sand, George. "Histoire de ma vie." In her *Oeuvres autobiographiques, with other texts*. Introduction et présentation par Georges Lubin. 2 vols. Bibliothèque de la Pléiade 215 et 227. Paris: Gallimard, 1970–1971.
Sand, George. *Un Hiver à Majorque*. Présenté par Jean Maillon et Pierre Salomon. Meylan, France: Editions de l'Aurore, 1985, 215 pp.
Sand, George. *Horace*. Présenté par Nicole Courrier. Meylan, France: Editions de l'Aurore, 1982, 395 pp.
Sand, George. *Indiana*. Présenté par Béatrice Didier. Folio 1604. Paris: Gallimard, 1984, 416 pp.
Sand, George. *Indiana*. Introduction par Pierre Salomon. Paris: Garnier, 1985, 520 pp.
Sand, George. *Jean de la Roche*. Présenté par Claude Tricotel. Meylan, France: Editions de l'Aurore, 1988, 208 pp.
Sand, George. *Jeanne*. Présenté par Simone Vierne. Meylan, France: Editions de l'Aurore, 1986, 320 pp.
Sand, George. *Laura, ou voyage dans le cristal*. Introduction par Gérald Schaeffer. Paris: Nizet, 1947, 158 pp.
Sand, George. *Lélia*. Introduction par Pierre Reboul. Paris: Garnier, 1960. Reprint: 1986, 601 pp.
Sand, George. *Lélia* (1839 edition). Introduction par Béatrice Didier. 2 vols. Meylan, France: Editions de l'Aurore, 1987.
Sand, George. *Lettres d'un voyageur*. Introduction par Henri Bonnet. Paris: Garnier-Flammarion, 1971, 320 pp.
Sand, George. *Mademoiselle La Quintinie*. Présenté par Simone Balayé. Geneva: Slatkine, 1979, 370 pp.
Sand, George. *Les Maîtres sonneurs*. Préface par Marie-Claire Bancquart. Folio 1139. Paris: Gallimard, 1974, 530 pp.
Sand, George. *Les Maîtres sonneurs*. Présentation par Pierre Salomon et Jean Maillon. Paris: Garnier, 1981, 604 pp.
Sand, George. *La Mare au diable*. Préface par Léon Cellier. Folio 892. Paris: Gallimard, 1973, 256 pp.
Sand, George. *La Mare au diable*. Préface par Pierre Reboul. Paris: Garnier-Flammarion, 1975, 190 pp.
Sand, George. *La Mare au diable* and *François le champi*. Présentés par Pierre Salomon et Jean Maillon. Paris: Garnier, 1962, 443 pp. New edition: 1981, 450 pp.
Sand, George. *Le Marquis de Villemer*. Présenté par Jean Courrier. Meylan, France: Editions de l'Aurore, 1988, 286 pp.
Sand, George. *Mauprat*. Présenté par Claude Sicard. G/F 201. Paris: Flammarion, 1969, 314 pp.

Sand, George. *Le Meunier d'Angibault*. Présenté par Béatrice Didier. Paris: Livre de Poche, 1985, 444 pp.
Sand, George. *Le Meunier d'Angibault*. Présenté par Marielle Caors. Meylan, France: Editions d l'Aurore, 1990.
Sand, George. *Nanon*. Introduction par Nicole Mozet. Meylan, France: Editions de l'Aurore, 1987, 258 pp.
Sand, George. *Nouvelles*. Préface par Eve Sourian. Paris: Des Femmes, 1986, 441 pp.
Sand, George. *Le Péché de monsieur Antoine*. Présenté par Jean Courrier et Jean-Hervé Donnard. Meylan, France: Editions de l'Aurore, 1982, 415 pp.
Sand, George. *La Petite Fadette*. Présenté par Pierre Salomon et Jean Maillon. Paris: Garnier, 1969, 319 pp. New edition: 1981, 400 pp.
Sand, George. *Les Sept cordes de la lyre*. Introduction par René Bourgeois. Paris: Flammarion, 1973, 189 pp.
Sand, George. *Tamaris*. Présenté par Georges Lubin. Meylan, France: Editions de l'Aurore, 1984, 214 pp.
Sand, George. *Valentine*. Introduction par Aline Alquier. Meylan, France: Editions de l'Aurore, 1988, 255 pp.
Sand, George. *La Ville noire*. Préface par Jean Courrier. Meylan, France: Editions de l'Aurore, 1989, 176 pp. Reprint: Grenoble: Presses Universitaires de Grenoble, 1978, 203 pp.
Sand, George. *Voyage dans le cristal*. Préface par Francis Lacassin. Paris: Union Générale d'Editions, 1980, 317 pp.
Sand, George, and Gustave Flaubert. *Dialogue des deux troubadours. Correspondance entre George Sand et Gustave Flaubert de 1863 à 1876*. Préface et choix de Georges Lubin. Paris: Les Cent-Une, 1978, 367 pp.

BIOGRAPHIES

Atwood, William G. *The Lioness and the Little One. The Liaison of George Sand and Frederic Chopin*. New York: Columbia University Press, 1980, 316 pp.
Barry, Joseph. *Infamous Woman: The Life of George Sand*. Garden City, N.Y.: Doubleday, 1977, 436 pp.
Cate, Curtis. *George Sand*. Boston: Houghton Mifflin, 1975, 812 pp.
Dickenson, Donna. *George Sand: A Brave Man—The Most Womanly Woman*. Oxford: Berg, 1988, 190 pp.
Jordan, Ruth. *George Sand: A Biography*. London: Constable, 1976, 368 pp.
Karénine, Wladimir. *George Sand: Sa vie et ses oeuvres*. 4 vols. Paris: Ollendorff and Plon, 1899–1926.
Mallet, Francine. *George Sand*. Paris: Grasset, 1976, 449 pp.
Maurois, André. *Lélia, ou la vie de George Sand*. Paris: Hachette, 1952.
Salomon, Pierre. *George Sand*. 1953. Reprint: Meylan, France: Editions de l'Aurore, 1984, 270 pp.
Schleintz, Gisela. *George Sand: Leben und Werk in Texten und Bildern*. Frankfurt: Insel Verlag, 1987, 407 pp.
———. *Ich liebe, also bin ich: Leben und Werk von George Sand*. Munich: Beck, 1989, 311 pp.
Winegarten, Renee. *The Double Life of George Sand, Woman and Writer: A Critical Biography*. New York: Basic Books, 1978, 339 pp.

CRITICAL STUDIES

Special Issues or Collections of Essays

Colloque George Sand. Proceedings from the 27e congrès international de l'association internationale des études françaises, 1975. *CAIEF* 28 (1976).

Colloque sur George Sand de la société des études romantiques (1976), selected papers, *Romantisme* 16 (1977).

Europe 102–103 (June–July 1954).

Europe (March 1978).

George Sand. Colloque de Cerisy, 1981, edited by Simone Vierne. Paris: CDU-SEDES, 1983, 190 pp.

George Sand: Collected Essays, edited by Janis Glasgow. Troy, N.Y.: Whitson Publishing, 1985, 329 pp.

George Sand: Recherches nouvelles, edited by Françoise van Rossum-Guyon. Amsterdam: C.R.I.N., 1983, 264 pp.

George Sand: Some Appreciations of Her Roles as Artist, Feminist, and Political Symbol, edited by Paul Blount. *Studies in the Literary Imagination* 12, no. 2 (1979).

George Sand: Voyage et écriture, edited by Jeanne Goldin. Montreal: Presses de l'Université de Montréal, 1988, 113 pp. *Etudes françaises* 24, no. 1.

George Sand Colloquium. Proceedings of the conference at Amherst College, 1976, edited by T. Goetz, *Nineteenth-Century French Studies* 4, no. 4 (1976).

The George Sand Papers: Conference Proceedings, edited by Natalie Datlof, Edwin L. Dunbaugh, Frank S. Lambasa, Gabrielle Savet, William S. Shiver, and Alex Szogyi, vol. 1, 1976. New York: AMS Press, 1980, 213 pp.

The George Sand Papers: Conference Proceedings, edited by Natalie Datlof, Edwin L. Dunbaugh, Frank S. Lambasa, Gabrielle Savet, William S. Shiver, and Alex Szogyi, vol. 2, 1978. New York: AMS Press, 1982, 241 pp.

Hommage à George Sand, edited by Léon Cellier. Publication de la faculté des lettres et sciences humaines de l'Université de Grenoble, no. 46. Paris, PUF, 1969.

Hommage à George Sand: Pour le 175e anniversaire de sa naissance, 1804–1979. Préparé par Georges Lubin et Alexandre Zviguilsky. Paris: Association des Amis d'Ivan Tourgueniev, Paulin Viardot et Maria Malibran, 1979, 191 pp.

La Porporina. Entretiens sur "Consuelo." Actes du colloque de Grenoble (1974). Présenté par Léon Cellier. Grenoble: Presses Universitaires de Grenoble, 1976, 147 pp.

Revue d'Histoire Littéraire de la France 4 (July–August 1976).

Revue des Sciences Humaines 76 (October–December 1954).

Revue des sciences Humaines 96 (October–December 1959).

West Virginia George Sand Conference Papers, edited by Armand Singer. Morgantown, W.Va.: West Virginia University, 1981, 111 pp.

Critical Books, Parts of Books, and Articles

Bailbé, Joseph-Marc. *Le Roman et la musique en France sous la Monarchie de Juillet.* Paris: Minard/Lettres Modernes, 1969, 446 pp.

Balayé, Simone. "Consuelo:Déesse de la Pauvreté." *Revue d'Histoire Littéraire de la France* 74 (1974): 614–625.

Blount, Paul Groves. *Sand and the Victorian World.* Athens, Ga.: University of Georgia Press, 1979, 190 pp.

Bowman, Frank P. "George Sand, le Christ et le royaume." *Cahiers de l'Association Internationale des Etudes Françaises* 28 (May 1976): 243–262, 374–376.
Brahimi, Denise. "Ecriture/féminité/féminisme: Réflexions sur trois romans de George Sand." *Revue des Sciences Humaines* 168 (1977): 577–588.
Buis, Lucien. *Les Théories sociales de George Sand.* Paris: Pedone, 1910, 250 pp.
Cassou, Jean. "George Sand et le secret du XIXe siècle." *Mercure de France*, December 1961, 601–618.
Cellier, Léon. "L'Occultisme dans *Consuelo* et *La Comtesse de Rudolstadt.*" *Romantisme* 16 (1977): 7–19. (Also in his *Parcours initiatiques.* Neuchâtel: La Baconnière/Presses Universitaires de Grenoble, 1977, 309 pp.
———. "Le Roman initiatique au temps du romantisme." *Cahiers Internationaux de Symbolisme* 4 (1964): 22–40. (Also in his *Parcours initiatiques*, Neuchâtel: La Baconnière/Presses Universitaires de Grenoble, 1977.)
Courtivron, Isabelle de. "Weak Men and Fatal Women: The Sand Image." In *Homosexualities and French Literature: Cultural Contexts, Critical Texts*, edited and with an introduction by George Stambolian and Elaine Marks. Ithaca, N.Y.: Cornell University Press, 1979, 210–227.
Crecelius, Kathryn. *Family Romances: George Sand's Early Novels.* Bloomington: Indiana University Press, 1987, 183 pp.
———. "Writing a Self: From Aurore Dudevant to George Sand." *Tulsa Studies in Women's Literature* 4, no. 1 (Spring 1985): 47–59.
Dauphiné, James. "Ecriture et musique dans *Les Maîtres sonneurs* de George Sand." *Nineteenth-Century French Studies* 9, nos. 3 and 4 (1981): 185–191.
Deutelbaum, Wendy, and Cynthia Huff. "Class, Gender and Family System: The Case of George Sand." In *The (M)other Tongue: Essays in Feminist Psychoanalytic Interpretation*, edited by Shirley N. Garner, Claire Kahane, and Madelon Sprengnether. Ithaca, N.Y.: Cornell University Press, 1985, 260–279.
Didier, Béatrice. *L'Écriture-femme.* Paris:Presses Universitaires de France, 1981.
———. "Femme/identité/écriture: A propos de *l'Histoire de ma vie* de George Sand." *Revue des Sciences Humaines* 168 (October–December 1977): 561–576.
———. "Sexe, société et création: *Consuelo* et *La comtesse de Rudolstadt.*" *Romantisme* 13–14 (1977): 155–166.
———. "Le Souvenir musical dans *Histoire de ma vie* et l'ombre de Rousseau." *Présence de George Sand* 8 (1980): 48–52.
Dolléans, Edouard. *Féminisme et mouvement ouvrier: George Sand.* Préface par Armand Hoog. Paris: Editions Ouvrières, 1951, 179 pp.
Evans, David Owen. *Socialisme romantique: Pierre Leroux et ses contemporains.* Paris: Librairie Marcel Rivière, 1948. Chapter 3: "Pierre Leroux et le roman—George Sand," 105–131.
Fahmy, Dorrey. *George Sand, auteur dramatique.* Paris: Droz, 1934, 506 pp.
Frappier-Mazur, Lucienne. "Code romantique et résurgences du féminin dans *La Comtesse de Rudolstadt.*" In *Le Récit amoureux, Colloque de Cerisy*, edited by Didier Coste and Michel Zénaffa. Paris: Editions du Champ Vallon, 1984.
———. "Desire, Writing and Identity in the Romantic Mystical Novel: Notes for a Definition of the Feminine." *Style* 18, no. 3 (Summer 1984): 328–354.
———. "Nostalgie, dédoublement et écriture dans *Histoire de ma vie.*" *Nineteenth-Century French Studies* 17, nos. 3 and 4 (Spring/Summer 1989): 265–275.
Freadman, Anne. "Of Cats and Companions, and the Name of George Sand." In *Grafts: Feminist Cultural Criticism*, edited by Susan Sheridan. London: Verso, 1988, 125–156.

Frey, Julia Bloch. "Theatre in an Armchair." *George Sand Newsletter* 2, no. 1 (1979): 20–23.

Glasgow, Janis. *Une Esthétique de comparaison: Balzac et George Sand. "La Femme abandonée" et "Métella."* Paris: Nizet, 1978, 218 pp.

Greene, Tatiana. "De J. Sand à George Sand: *Rose et Blanche* de Sand et Sandeau et leur descendance." *Nineteenth-Century French Studies* 4 (1976): 169–182.

Grimm, Reinhold R. "Les Romans champêtres de George Sand: L'Échec du renouvellement d'un genre littéraire." *Romantisme* 16 (1977): 64–70.

Guichard, Léon. *La Musique et les lettres au temps du romantisme.* Paris: Presses Universitaires de France, 1955, 310 pp.

Hirsch, Michèle. "Questions à *Indiana.*" *Revue des Sciences Humaines* 165 (January–March 1977): 117–129.

Hoog, Marie-Jacques. "Du Rêve à l'écriture chez George Sand." *George Sand Newsletter* 5, no. 2 (Fall–Winter 1982): 47–50.

———. "Le Pic, le soc, le burin et le stylet." *George Sand Studies* 8, nos. 1 and 2 (1984/1985): 15–23.

James, Henry. *French Poets and Novelists.* Introduction by Leon Edel. New York: Grosset and Dunlap, 1964, 149–185.

———. "George Sand." In *Notes on Novelists* by Henry James. New York: Scribner's, 1914, 160–186, 187–213, 214–244.

———. *Literary Reviews and Essays by Henry James on American, English, and French Literature,* edited by Albert Mordell. New York: Twayne, 1957.

Karp, Carole. "George Sand, Balzac and the Russian Soul." *Michigan Academician* 10, no. 3 (Winter 1978): 347–359.

L'Hopital, Madeleine. *La Notion d'artiste chez George Sand.* Paris:Boivin, 1946, 310 pp.

Lacassagne, Jean-Pierre. *Histoire d'une amitié: Leroux et Sand. D'après une correspondance inéditée, 1836–1866.* Paris: Klincksieck, 1973, 368 pp.

Laforge, François. "Structure et fonction du mythe d'Orphée dans *Consuelo* de George Sand." *Revue d'Histoire Littéraire de la France* 84 (1984): 53–66.

Lane, Brigitte. "Voyage et initiation dans *La Mare au diable.*" *Etudes françaises* 24, no. 1 (1988): 71–83.

Larnac, Jean. *George Sand révolutionnnaire.* Paris: Editions Hier et Aujourd'hui, Collection Grandes Figures, 1947, 205 pp.

Lubin, Georges. *George Sand en Berry: Albums littéraires de France.* Paris: Hachette, 1967.

Mallet, Francine. "George Sand et la musique." *Présence de George Sand* 10 (February 1981): 32–38.

Manifold, Gay. "George Sand: Mother of Realism." *George Sand Studies* 7, nos. 1 and 2 (1984/1985): 24–29.

———. *George Sand's Theatre Career.* Theater and Dramatic Studies, no. 28. Ann Arbor: UMI, 1985, 188 pp.

Marix-Spire, Thérèse. *Les Romantiques et la musique: Le cas George Sand (1804–1838).* Paris: Nouvelles Editions Latines, 1955, 425 pp.

May, Gita. "Des Confessions à *Histoire de ma vie*: Deux auteurs à la recherche de leur moi." *Présence de George Sand* 8 (May 1980): 40–47.

Michel, Arlette. "Musique et poésie: Sand et Balzac lecteurs des Kreisleriana." *Présence de George Sand* 13 (February 1982): 23–31.

———. "Structures romanesques et problèmes du mariage d'*Indiana* à *La Comtesse de Rudolstadt.*" *Romantisme* 16 (1977): 34–45.

Miller, Nancy K. "Writing (from) the Feminine: George Sand and the Novel of Female Pastoral." In *The Representation of Women in Faction,* edited by Carolyn Heilbrun and M. Higonnet. Baltimore: Johns Hopkins Press, 1981, 124–151.

Moers, Ellen. *Literary Women*. 1963. Reprint: London: The Women's Press, 1980, passim.

Moret, Marc Marcel. *Le Sentiment religieux chez George Sand*. Paris: Marcel Vigné, 1936, 275 pp.

Mozet, Nicole. "Signé 'le voyageur': George Sand et l'invention de l'artiste." *Romantisme* 55 (1987):23–32.

Mozet, Nicole. "Le voyageur sandien en quête d'un lieu d'écriture." *Études Françaises* 24, no. 1, (1988), 41–55

Naginski, Isabelle. "George Sand: Gynographie et androgynie." *Bulletin de la Société des Professeurs Français d'Amérique* (1983–1984): 21–36.

———. "The Serenity of Influence: The Literary Relationship of George Sand and Dostoevsky." In *George Sand: Collected Essays*, edited by Janis Glasgow. Troy, N.Y.: Whitston, 1986, 110–125.

Pailleron, Marie-Louise. *George Sand et les hommes de 48*. Paris: Grasset, 1953.

Pécile, Marie-Jeanne. "George Sand: La Formation et l'éducation d'une femme écrivain." *Nineteenth-Century French Studies* 4 (Summer 1976): 417–437.

Poli, Annarosa. *George Sand et les années terribles*. Paris, Nizet, 1975.

———. *L'Italie dans la vie et dans l'oeuvre de George Sand*. Paris: Colin, 1960, 455 pp.

Pommier, Jean. *George Sand et le rêve monastique. "Spirdion."* Paris: Nizet, 1966, 124 pp.

Powell, David A. "Discord, Dissension, and Dissonance: The Initiation in Sand's *Les Maîtres sonneurs*." *George Sand Newsletter* 6, nos. 3 and 4 (1987): 54–61.

———. *George Sand*. Twayne World Author Series 761. Boston: Twayne Publishers, 1990.

Pritchett, V. S. "George Sand." In his *The Myth Makers: Essays on European, Russian and South American Novelists*. London: Chatto and Windus, 1979, 115–127.

Rambeau, Marie-Paule. *Chopin dans la vie et l'oeuvre de George Sand*. Paris: Les Belles Lettres, 1985, 393 pp.

Rea, Annabelle. "George Sand misogynist?" *George Sand Newsletter* 6, nos. 1 and 2 (1983): 58–65.

Reboul, Pierre. *Errements littéraires et historiques*. Paris: Presses Universitaires de Lille, 1979, 160 pp.

———. "Intrigue et socialisme dans *Le Compagnon du tour de France*." *Romantisme 16 (1977): 56–63.*

Roddier, Henri. "P. Leroux, G. Sand et W. Whitman, ou l'éveil d'un poète." *Revue de littérature comparée* 31 (January–March 1957): 5–33.

Rogers, Nancy. "Slavery as Metaphor in the Writings of George Sand." *French Review* 53 (1979): 29–35.

Schaeffer, Gérard. *Espace et temps chez George Sand*. Neuchâtel: La Baconnière, 1981, 150 pp.

Schor, Naomi. "Female Fetishism: The Case of George Sand." In *The Female Body in Western Culture: Contemporary Perspectives*, edited by Susan Rubin Suleiman. Cambridge, Mass.: Harvard University Press, 1985, 363–372.

———. "Idealism in the Novel: Recanonizing Sand." *Yale French Studies* 75 (1988): 56–73.

———. "Reading Double: Sand's Difference." In *The Politics of Gender*, edited by Nancy K. Miller. New York: Columbia University Press, 1986, 248–269.

Sivert, Eileen Boyd. "Lélia and Feminism." *Yale French Studies* 62 (1981): 45–66.

Sonnenfeld, Albert. "George Sand: Music and Sexualities." *Nineteenth-Century French Studies* 16, nos. 3 and 4 (Spring/Summer 1988): 310–321.

Sourian, Eve. "Amitiés féminines dans *Isidora* et *Constance Verrier*: Polarités et classes sociales." *George Sand Studies* 8, nos. 1 and 2 (1986/1987): 28–37.

———. "L'Influence de Mme de Staël sur les premières oeuvres de George Sand." *George Sand Studies* 7, nos. 1 and 2 (1984/1985): 37–45.

———. "Les Opinions religieuses de George Sand: Pourquoi Consuelo a-t-elle perdu sa voix?" In *George Sand: Collected Essays*, edited by Janis Glasgow. Troy, N.Y.: Whitston, 1986, 127–138.

Szabó, Anna. "La Figure du savant dans les romans de George Sand." *Studia Romanica* 12 (1986): 105–112.

Thomson, Patricia. *Sand and the Victorians. Her Influence and Reputation in Nineteenth-Century England.* New York: Columbia University Press, 1977, 283 pp.

Trapeznikova, Natal'ja. *Romantizm Zhorzh Sand.* Kazan: Isdatel'stvo Kazanskogo Universiteta, 1976.

Vermeylen, Pierre. *Les Idées politiques et sociales de George Sand.* Brussels: Editions de l'Université de Bruxelles, 1984, 372 pp.

Vernois, Paul. *Le Roman rustique de Sand à Ramuz: Ses tendances et son évolution (1860–1925).* Paris: Nizet, 1962, 560 pp.

Vierne, Simone. "George Sand et le mythe initiatique." In *George Sand: Collected Essays*, edited by Janis Glasgow. Troy, N.Y.: Whitston, 1986, 288–305.

Vincent, Marie-Louise. *George Sand et le Berry* 2 vols. 1919. Reprint: Geneva: Slatkine Reprints, 1978.

Wentz, Debra Linowitz. *Les Profils du Théâtre de Nohant de George Sand.* Insel Taschenbuch, no. 565. Paris: Nizet, 1978, 156 pp.

Zellweger, Rudolf. *Les Débuts du roman rustique: Suisse-Allemagne-France, 1836–1856.* Paris: Droz, 1941, 585 pp.

Zimmerman, Dorothy. "George Sand and Willa Cather: Their Pastoral Novels." *George Sand Studies* 7, nos. 1 and 2 (1984/1985): 30–36.

Hofstra Cultural Center

SEVENTH INTERNATIONAL GEORGE SAND CONFERENCE

The World of

GEORGE SAND

George Sand at Nohant
By Françoise Gilot

In celebration of the Tenth Anniversaries of the Establishment of the Hofstra Cultural Center and the Founding of the Friends of George Sand

THURSDAY, FRIDAY, SATURDAY

OCTOBER 16, 17, 18, 1986

Hofstra University gratefully acknowledges the significant support of the National Endowment for the Humanities (NEH) in funding programs of the Hofstra Cultural Center through a Challenge Grant. Since 1983, this generous NEH funding has enabled Hofstra to increase humanities activities on campus for the benefit of the community, students, and faculty.

HOFSTRA
UNIVERSITY
HEMPSTEAD, NEW YORK 11550

THE WORLD OF GEORGE SAND

SEVENTH INTERNATIONAL GEORGE SAND CONFERENCE

In Celebration of the Tenth Anniversaries
of the Establishment of the
Hofstra Cultural Center and the
Founding of the Friends of George Sand

October 16–18, 1986

MARILYN FRENCH
The Joseph G. Astman Distinguished Conference Scholar

NATALIE DATLOF
Conference Director

JO-ANN G. MAHONEY
Conference Coordinator

George Sand Conference Committee

HOWARD CINNAMON
Music, Hofstra University

MARIE M. COLLINS
Modern Languages
Rutgers University/Newark

JEROME H. DELAMATER
Communication Arts
Hofstra University

EDWIN L. DUNBAUGH
History, Hofstra University

JEANNE FUCHS
Comparative Literature & Languages, Hofstra Univeristy

AVRIEL GOLDBERGER
French, Hofstra University

FRANK S. LAMBASA
Comparative Literature & Languages, Hofstra University

ESTELLA LOPEZ
Inter-American University
Puerto Rico

RICHARD MASON
Drama, Hofstra University

WILLIAM A. McBRIEN
English, Hofstra University

DAVID A. POWELL
French, Hofstra University

NANCY ROGERS
National Endowment for the Humanities, Washington, D.C.

GAIL SCHWAB
French, Hofstra University

ALEX SZOGYI
French, Hunter College and
The Graduate Center/CUNY

ALEXEJ UGRINSKY
Comparative Literature & Languages, Hofstra University

George Sand Conference Student Committee

PATRICIA BARTO
Hofstra Cultural Center

MUSA BADAT
Assistant to the Coordinator
Hofstra Cultural Center

CONRAD DAVIES
Hofstra Cultural Center

SI-BUM KIM
Hofstra Cultural Center

WILLIAM KRUEGER
Hofstra Cultural Center

GREG MOSHO
TKE Fraternity

MOHAMED OMAR
Assistant to the Coordinator
Hofstra Cultural Center

DIANE E. PATERSON
Travel Coordinator
Hofstra Cultural Center

JOE PIZZIMENTI
Hofstra Cultural Center

ELISA SCHLOFROCK
President, French Club

TARA STAHMAN
Book Fair Coordinator
Hofstra Cultural Center

BRIAN THEIS
Head, International House

SINAIDA U. WEBER
Hofstra Cultural Center

GEORGE SAND AND THE GENESIS OF A CONFERENCE CENTER

In the beginning there was an idea. It came to the attention of a receptive professor, an understanding dean and a supportive president. It led to a small gathering of scholars marking the 100th anniversary of the death of a writer in 1976: George Sand.

The professor, a man of long standing at the university and highly respected by his peers, called on two of his graduate students. They started working in a small office, on a tempermental typewriter, aided by a half-time secretary.

And history took its course. With the professor's blessing the Heinrich von Kleist bicentennial was celebrated in 1977. In 1978, at the professor's suggestion, we turned again to George Sand and also to William Cullen Bryant. That very year the George Sand Newsletter was born. The rest is indeed history: Trotsky-Stalin, Einstein, Goethe, nineteenth and twentieth century women writers, American presidents, and many more. . . .

And the professor saw his dreams come true — the gathering of scholars from many distant lands, the ambience of discourse, and the broad range of subjects put to study. In 1980 another proud step — the first volume of published proceedings: The George Sand Papers.

And idea begat ideas. Intense planning sessions were held between the professor and the two graduate students: the marking of the anniversary of a significant year or the publication of a milestone book; the study the life and times of American presidents; and finally the celebration of the golden anniversary of this university.

Today, ten years later, we are gathered here at Hofstra University to celebrate the glorious first decade of the Hofstra Cultural Center and to pay homage to George Sand. The Cultural Center is especially proud to welcome back to Hofstra University the distinguished scholars who contributed to the success of the George Sand Conferences here at Hofstra as well as the conferences held in subsequent years at the University of West Virginia, San Diego State University, Bard College and Missouri Western State College.

And the Cultural Center is very grateful for the cooperation and support of the George Sand Conference Committee. More than 80 submitted papers were read and evaluated by Howard Cinnamon, Marie M. Collins, Edwin L. Dunbaugh, Jeanne Fuchs, Avriel Goldberger, Frank S. Lambasa, Estella Lopez, Richard Mason, William A. McBrien, David A. Powell, Nancy Rogers, Gail Schwab and Alex Szogyi.

At the Cultural Center, we can count on an outstanding staff: our conference and seminar coordinator, Jo-Ann G. Mahoney; the conference secretaries, Marilyn Seidman, and Athelene A. Collins, who also doubles as a conference coordinator; the editorial secretary, Jessica Richter; the development coordinator, Donna Testa; the drama coordinator, Al "Tank" Passuello; Marguerite Regan, Curator and Nancy Herb and Anne Rubino of the David Filderman Gallery; the graduate assistants, Musa G. Badat and Mohamed I. Omar; and the irrepressible student aides, Diane E. Paterson, Joseph Pizzimenti and Tara Stahman. To all of these people we extend our deepest gratitude for their spirit, loyalty, good humor and most of all their sincere devotion.

We extend greetings from our "supportive president," James M. Shuart, the pillar of strength of the Cultural Center and from the "understanding dean" of the Hofstra College of Liberal Arts and Sciences, Robert C. Vogt.

Sadly missing is our professor, the late Joseph G. Astman, the man who was our nurturer, our mentor, our friend. He gave us the greatest gift of all — the freedom of creativity. We know he is here with us and to him this conference is dedicated as a living and loving tribute.

He would be honored that Hofstra University's alumna, Marilyn French, is here carrying his banner, the Joseph G. Astman Distinguished Conference Scholar and that our dear colleagues, Georges Lubin and Henri Peyre have returned to Hofstra University to pay homage to George Sand and to share their thoughts with us.

He would elate in thanking the four artists, Françoise Gilot, Maria Cooper Janis, Christiane Sand and Edwina Sandys who so graciously lent their works for our exhibit, "The Friends of George Sand."

He would rejoice in the return to Hofstra of Byron Janis who once again will enchant us with his extraordinary artistry as an interpreter of Chopin's music.

He would delight in the re-creation of George Sand's Salon here at Hofstra and in the première performance of the brilliant play, "Dialectic of the Heart," written especially for this occasion by Alex Szogyi and performed by Byron Janis and Micheline Muselli Lerner. And he would take great joy in the magnificent poster designed by Hofstra's dear friend, the internationally renowned artist, Françoise Gilot, and in the beautiful medal created for the conference by the Soviet emigré artist, Alex Shagin.

He would enjoy, as he always did, the interaction of the disciplines, the blending of the cultures, and the celebration of the arts. In his name we welcome you to the Seventh International George Sand Conference at Hofstra University. Enjoy it in his spirit.

Natalie Datlof

Natalie Datlof
Acting Co-Director
Hofstra Cultural Center
George Sand Conference Director

Alexej Ugrinsky
Acting Co-Director
Hofstra Cultural Center

SEVENTH INTERNATIONAL GEORGE SAND CONFERENCE
THE WORLD OF GEORGE SAND
October 16, 17, 18, 1986

THURSDAY, OCTOBER 16, 1986

9:00 a.m - 5:00 p.m.	**Conference Registration** Hofstra Hall Lobby, South Campus **Book Fair** Hofstra Hall Lobby Coffee

---

CONFERENCE OPENING CEREMONIES

9:45 - 11:00 a.m.	Hofstra Cultural Center Lecture Hall Library — 1st floor **Greetings from the Hofstra University Community**
Presiding:	**Natalie Datlof** Conference Director Acting Co-Director, Hofstra Cultural Center
Greetings:	**J. Richard Block** Assistant to the President **Robert C. Vogt** Dean, Hofstra College of Liberal Arts and Sciences **Greetings from the French Embassy** **Frédéric Berthet** Cultural Attaché French Cultural Services New York, NY
Introduction of Keynote Speaker:	**Avriel Goldberger** Chairperson, French Department Hofstra University
Keynote Address:	**Henri Peyre** Professor Emeritus Yale University and The Graduate Center/CUNY "George Sand Our Contemporary"

THURSDAY, OCTOBER 16, 1986

11:00 a.m. - 12:25 p.m.	Hofstra Cultural Center Lecture Hall Library — 1st floor
Panel Ia	**WORKS: INDIANA**

Moderator: **Isabelle Naginski**
Department of Romance Languages & Literatures
Tufts University

Françoise Van Rossum-Guyon
Universiteit van Amsterdam, The Netherlands
"Le statut textuel de la correspondance de George Sand -- L'Epoque d'Indiana, 1831-1832"

Olivier Urbain
University of Southern California
"Les trois préfaces et Indiana: Constance et sincérité du discours"

Louisette Hamzeh
Bethlehem University, Israel
"Indiana: Passage à écriture"

11:00 a.m. - 12:25 p.m.	Dining Rooms ABC, North Campus
Panel Ib	**GEORGE SAND AND HER CONTEMPORARIES**

Moderator: **David A. Powell**
French Department
Hofstra University

Jeanne Fuchs
Hofstra University
"George Sand and Alfred de Musset: Absolution Through Art in La Confession d'un enfant du siècle"

Eve Sourian
The City College and The Graduate Center/CUNY
"George Sand and Dumas fils"

Janis Glasgow
San Diego State University
"George Sand's Multiple Appearances in Balzac's La Muse du département"

THURSDAY, OCTOBER 16, 1986

12:30 - 2:00 p.m.	Hofstra Cultural Center, Library — 10th floor
	Opening of George Sand Conference Exhibits
	Luncheon in Honor of Georges Lubin
Introduction:	Natalie Datlof
Invitational Address:	Georges Lubin Boulogne-sur-Seine France
	"George Sand: L'Accueil américain de son vivant"
Translation commentary:	Alex Szogyi Hunter College and The Graduate Center/CUNY

2:00 - 3:00 p.m.	Hofstra Cultural Center Lecture Hall Library — 1st floor
Introduction:	J. Richard Block Assistant to the President
Invitational Address:	Marilyn French The Joseph G. Astman Distinguished Conference Scholar
	"The Great Chain"

3:00 - 4:30 p.m.	Hofstra Cultural Center Lecture Hall Library — 1st floor
Panel IIa	PERSPECTIVES OF GEORGE SAND
	Moderator: Gail Schwab French Department Hofstra University
	Naomi Schor Brown University "Recanonizing Sand"
	Jack Kolbert Susquehanna University "George Sand as Depicted by André Maurois"
	Marie J. Diamond Rutgers University/New Brunswick, NJ "The Woman Writer and the Censorship of Female Sexuality: The Example of *Elle et Lui*"

THURSDAY, OCTOBER 16, 1986

3:00 - 4:30 p.m.	Hofstra Cultural Center, Library — Tenth Floor
Panel IIb	**GEORGE SAND AND PROUST**
	Moderator/Commentator: **Elyane Dezon-Jones** Department of French Barnard College/Columbia University
	Frédéric Berthet French Cultural Services New York, NY "Proust avec Sand"
	Antoinette Fouque Founder and Director Les Editions des Femmes Paris, France and La Jolla, Ca "Proust, lecteur de George Sand"
4:30 p.m.	Dining Rooms ABC, Student Center, North Campus
	<u>Cash Bar</u>
Film and Discussion:	**"George Sand, aujourd'hui"**
	Filmmaker: Jose Alvés Office Audio-Visuel Université de Poitiers, France
5:15 p.m.	**Buffet Dinner**
Greetings:	**Christiane Sand** Gargilesse, France Conservateur: Musée de La Châtre Musée de Gargilesse Maison de George Sand
6:30 - 8:00 p.m.	Hofstra Cultural Center Lecture Hall Library — 1st floor
	FORUM: GEORGE SAND AND THE THEATRE
	Moderator: **Richard F. Mason** Dept. of Drama and Dance Hofstra University
	Gay Manifold California State University/Los Angeles Author, <u>A Theatre of One's Own</u>
	Alex Szogyi Hunter College and The Graduate Center/CUNY Author, <u>Dialectic of the Heart</u>
	Uta Wagner Brussels, Belgium Author, <u>George Sand Aujourd'hui</u>

FRIDAY, OCTOBER 17, 1986

8:30 a.m. - 3:00 p.m.	**Conference Registration** and **Book Fair** Dining Rooms ABC, Student Center, North Campus

---

8:30 - 9:00 a.m.	Dining Rooms ABC, Student Center, North Campus **Continental Breakfast**
9:00 - 10:45 a.m.	Dining Rooms ABC, Student Center, North Campus
Panel IIIa	WORKS: THEMATIC ANALYSIS Moderator: **Nancy Rogers** National Endowment for the Humanities Washington, D.C. **Anne Berger** Cornell University "L'Apprentissage selon George Sand" **Oscar A. Haac** SUNY at Stony Brook "A New Religion: Hebronius in <u>Spiridion</u> and Febronius" **Wendell McClendon** Texas Tech University "The Language of Loss in <u>Le Meunier d'Angibault</u>" **Wendy Ann Ryden** Brooklyn College/CUNY "The Divided Self in <u>Lélia</u>: The Effects of Dualism on the Feminine Psyche"
9:00 - 10:45 a.m.	Hofstra Cultural Center Lecture Hall Library — 1st floor
Panel IIIb	RUSSIA, SPAIN AND CUBA Moderator: **Nora de Marval-McNair** Chairperson, Department of Spanish Hofstra University **Nadine Dormoy-Savage** Lehman College/CUNY "The Fabulous Fortune of Sand in Russia" **Kevin J. McKenna** University of Vermont "George Sand's Reception in Russia: The Case of Elena Gan" **Frederick Kluck and Sandra Beyer** University of Texas at El Paso "Sand and Three Hispanic Women Writers" **Tamara Alvarez-Detrell** Allentown College of St. Francis de Sales "George Sand's Influence on Nineteenth-Century Cuban Writers"

FRIDAY, OCTOBER, 17, 1986

10:50 a.m. - 12:10 p.m.	Hofstra Cultural Center Lecture Hall Library — 1st floor
Panel IVa	THE PASTORAL WORKS
	Moderator: **Eve Sourian** Department of French The City College and The Graduate Center/CUNY
	Brigitte Lane Wellesley College "La Petite Fadette: Une dialectique 'féministe' de la tradition"
	Maïr E. Verthuy Université Concordia, Montréal, Québec "La Petite Fadette: Un roman d'apprentissage au masculin et au féminin"
	Jane A. Nicholson University of Tulsa "François Comes of Age: Language, Culture and the Subject"
10:50 a.m. - 12:10 p.m.	Dining Rooms ABC, Student Center, North Campus
Panel IVb	GEORGE SAND AND HER TIMES
	Moderator: **Peter Sourian** Division of Languages and Literature Bard College
	Annabelle M. Rea Occidental College "Healers in Sand's Work"
	George Bernstein Montclair State College "Paris Journalism and the World of Writing: The Opportunities of George Sand"
12:15 - 1:30 p.m.	Hofstra Cultural Center, Library—Tenth Floor
	Luncheon
Introductions:	**James M. Shuart** President, Hofstra University
Speakers:	**Françoise Gilot** New York, NY/La Jolla, CA/Paris, France "George Sand as a Role Model: A Personal Remembrance"
	Gloria Lane Founder and President, Women's International Center San Diego, CA "Leaving a Legacy"

FRIDAY, OCTOBER 17, 1986

1:45 - 3:30 p.m. Dining Rooms ABC, Student Center, North Campus

Panel Va WORKS: CONSUELO AND LEONE LEONI

Moderator: **Avriel Goldberger**
Chairperson, French Department
Hofstra University

Isabelle Naginski
Tufts University
"Consuelo: From Gothic Novel to Novel of Initiation"

David A. Powell
Hofstra University
"Consuelo and Porporino, or the Influence of Change"

Jeanne Goldin
Université de Montréal, Québec
"George Sand et L'Homme Fatal Romantique de Léone Léoni (1834) à l'Uscoque (1838)"

Vera Theisen
Saint John's University/MN
"The Text as Persuasion: Léone Léoni"

1:45 - 3:30 p.m. Hofstra Cultural Center Lecture Hall
Library — 1st floor

Panel Vb INFLUENCE IN GERMANY

Moderator: **Frank S. Lambasa**
Department of Comparative Literature & Languages
Hofstra University

Gisela Spies-Schlientz
Stuttgart, Federal Republic of Germany
"George Sand and the German Vormärz, 1830-1848"

Manfred Kuxdorf
University of Waterloo, Ontario
"The Impact of Sand on German Literature: The Case of Sand and Georg Kaiser"

Hanna B. Lewis
Sam Houston State University
"Fanny Lewald and George Sand"

Aaron Noland
Professor Emeritus
The City College/CUNY
"Nietzsche on Sand: A Note"

FRIDAY, OCTOBER 17, 1986

3:30 - 5:15 p.m.

Hofstra Cultural Center Lecture Hall
Library — 1st floor

Panel VIa

PARALLELS

Moderator: **Edwin L. Dunbaugh**
Department of History
Hofstra University

Margaret E. Ward and **Karen Storz**
Wellesley College
"Fanny Lewald and George Sand"
(Indiana and Eine Lebensfrage)

Lucy M. Schwartz
University of North Dakota
"Intertextuality: Valentine and La Princesse de Clèves"

Murray Sachs
Brandeis University
"Reason of the Heart: George Sand, Flaubert and the Commune"

Mary Rice
Bates College
"George Sand and Flaubert: Inspiration and Divergence"
(Un Coeur Simple and François le Champi)

3:30 - 5:00 p.m.

Student Center Room 145, North Campus

Panel VIb

NARRATIVE

Moderator: **David A. Powell**
Department of French
Hofstra University

Kathryn Crecelius
Massachussetts Institute of Technology
"Narrating Like a (Wo)man"

Pierrette Daly
University of Missouri-St. Louis
"The Metonymy of Women's Relationship to Narratives in Ahura's Tale and in Sand's Les Couperies"

Leyla Ezdinli
Mount Holyoke College
"Surfacing: From 'Collaboration' to Authorship"

FOR THOSE NOT CHOOSING TO ATTEND THE GALA DINNER-THEATRE THERE WILL BE A PERFORMANCE OF: TALKING WITH . . . . by JANE MARTIN

The Little Theatre, South Campus
8:00 p.m. Free Admission

PRESIDENT JAMES M. SHUART

is pleased to welcome

THE PATRONS AND SUPPORTERS

of the

GEORGE SAND CONFERENCE GALA

to

A NINETEENTH CENTURY EVENING
IN THE SALON OF GEORGE SAND

Friday, October 17, 1986

6 p.m. to 11 p.m.

on the occasion of the

SEVENTH INTERNATIONAL CONFERENCE ON
GEORGE SAND

and the

TENTH ANNIVERSARY OF THE FOUNDING OF THE
HOFSTRA CULTURAL CENTER

Under the Patronage of

H. E. The Ambassador of France
and Mme Emmanuel de Margerie

The Consul General of France
Andre Gadaud

The Cultural Counselor of the Cultural
Services of the French Embassy
M. Marc Perrin de Brichambaut

The Cultural Attache of the Cultural
Services of the French Embassy
M. Frederic Berthet

Honorary Co-Chairpersons

Byron Janis and Maria Cooper Janis

Co-Chairpersons

Mr. and Mrs. Maurice A. Deane
Mr. and Mrs. George G. Dempster
Mr. and Mrs. Adolph Eckhardt
Mr. and Mrs. Walter Fillin
Dr. and Mrs. Milton Gardner
Mr. and Mrs. Stefan L. Geiringer
Mme Françoise Gilot
Mr. and Mrs. Robert Kaufman
Mr. and Mrs. George Mallouk
Comm. and Mrs. Raymond Malone
Mme Christiane Sand
Ms. Edwina Sandys
Mr. and Mrs. Clarence M. Schwerin III
Mr. and Mrs. Joseph Sirulnick
Mr. and Mrs. Alexander Smith
Mr. and Mrs. Hamilton Smith
Dr. Alex Szogyi
Mr. and Mrs. Howard L. Weingrow
Mr. and Mrs. Albert Young

The Joseph G. Astman Distinguished Conference Scholar

Marilyn French

George Sand Conference Director

Natalie Datlof

A NINETEENTH-CENTURY EVENING IN THE SALON OF GEORGE SAND

6:00 p.m. **Buffet and Cocktails**

Opening of George Sand Conference Exhibits

FRIENDS OF GEORGE SAND
Honored Artists:
FRANÇOISE GILOT
MARIA COOPER JANIS
CHRISTIANE SAND
EDWINA SANDYS

GEORGE SAND BOOKS, MANUSCRIPTS, AND MEMORABILIA

Hofstra Cultural Center
Hofstra Library, 9th and 10th Floors

7:30 p.m. Gala Dinner-Theatre
Main Dining Room, Student Center

PREMIERE PERFORMANCE
of
"DIALECTIC OF THE HEART"

Written and Directed by
ALEX SZOGYI

Music Direction by
BYRON JANIS

THIS PERFORMANCE IS DEDICATED TO THE MEMORY OF MME. MONIQUE GADAUD

CAST

George Sand . . . . MICHELINE MUSELLI LERNER
Frédéric Chopin . . . . BYRON JANIS
Solange Dudevant Sand Clésinger . . . . MARIA COOPER JANIS
Maurice Dudevant Sand . . . . MICHAEL A. LERNER
Delphine Potocka . . . . ELIZABETH SZCZYGIELSKA CARL
Eugène Delacroix . . . . AL "TANK" PASSUELLO

DINNER MENU CHOSEN FROM AUTHENTIC GEORGE SAND RECIPES

GALA DINNER-THEATRE PLAYBILL

Première Performance

"DIALECTIC OF THE HEART"

Written and Directed *by* ALEX SZOGYI	*Musical Direction* *by* BYRON JANIS

This play attempts to give a fuller assessment of the celebrated relationship of George Sand and Frédéric Chopin than has previously happened in other works devoted to the subject. The need to romanticize this most famous romantic love affair has led writers to falsify the relationship.

There are some elements of the evening's entertainment which have never previously been known to the general public. Chopin never dedicated any of his works to Sand. They collaborated only once when she wrote the lyrics to an already existing song "La Reine des Songes." Byron Janis found the words in the archives of Les Amis de Chopin (of which he is the President). This marks the world première of the song. Elizabeth Carl will sing both this song and a Polish one, "Moja Pieszczotka," op. 74 #12. (I taught her the French and she taught Mr. Janis the Polish.) The play contains quotations from letters previously unknown and unpublished, both by Sand and Chopin. At the end of the play Byron Janis performs Chopin's last work, a Mazurka, op. 68 #4. I wish to thank Gay Manifold and Anne-Marie Mitchell for their fine understanding of George Sand's work. I offer my gratitude to the Research Foundation of City University and the Cultural Center of Hofstra University. All this would not have been possible without the inspiration of Natalie Datlof.

Alex Szogyi

About the Cast

MICHELINE MUSELLI LERNER (George Sand), actress, writer, lawyer, is descended from one of the finest families of Corsica, Muselli Pozzo de Borgo. Her great-great-grandfather was the god-child of Napoleon. She was, at twenty, the youngest lawyer France ever had and is still known there as Maître Muselli. A graduate of the Neighborhood Playhouse in New York, where she worked with Sanford Meisner, she also studied with Lee Strasberg and has acted all over the world. She was the mistress of ceremonies for President Kennedy at the White House in honor of the first visit of the present King of Morocco. Lerner has written two screenplays for NBC and is at present working on her autobiography. She has a Master of Arts as well as a Law degree from the Sorbonne in Paris. Her husband was the late Alan Jay Lerner. She has appeared recently in a play by Alain Malraux, under the direction of Alex Szogyi, at the Ubu Theatre in New York.

BYRON JANIS (Director of Music and Frédéric Chopin), one of the world's great concert pianists, has been a powerful force in the world of music for more than 40 years. A special interest in the music of Frédéric Chopin led Janis to discover two previously unknown manuscripts of Chopin waltzes at Château Thierry, near Paris. Six years later, in a startling coincidence, Janis uncovered two other unknown versions of the same waltzes at Yale University. He also narrated and performed in "Frédéric Chopin: A Voyage with Bryon Janis," a film of his conception, produced by French television and seen around the world. Recent years have seen a deepening and maturing of his art, adding dimension to his legendary virtuosity and leading critics throughout the world to superlatives.

MARIA COOPER JANIS (Solange Dudevant Sand Clésinger) an artist, who is considered to be a major force in American lyrical abstraction, has a unique style which is influenced by Picasso, Fairfield Porter, and David Douglas Duncan, combines elements of Matisse, Porter, and de Kooning. Maria Janis' talent is well adapted to handling subtle surface innuendos with traditional forms superimposed on an outer reality. Not surprisingly, her lyrical abstractions and color-filled paintings are strongly influenced by the musical themes of her life. Her husband is Byron Janis and her father is the late Gary Cooper.

MICHAEL A. LERNER (Maurice Dudevant Sand) is the Foreign Correspondent for *Newsweek* in Paris. He is also a writer in his own right. His parents are Micheline Muselli Lerner and the late Alan Jay Lerner.

HRABINA ELZBIETA SZCZYGIELSKA/ELIZABETH CARL (Delphine Potocka) a Polish countess, opera singer, actress, and Reiki therapist studied at the Warsaw Conservatory, concertized in Poland, Canada and the United States, worked at the Theatre Company of the Banff Center of the Arts. She is in *Who's Who of Outstanding Young Women in America.* She recently gave a recital of Chopin's songs at the Donnell Library in New York. Countess Szczygielska graciously concented to work with Byron Janis in French and Polish for this performance.

AL "TANK" PASSUELLO (Eugène Delacroix) is the founder of two of Hofstra's theatrical companies, The Gray Wig and USA Productions. He has starred in *Fiddler on the Roof, Guys and Dolls, Death of a Salesman, View from the Bridge, Of Mice and Men, Waiting for Godot, Queen and the Rebels, Whisper into My Good Ear,* and the list goes on. Tank is currently working for the Hofstra Cultural Center as the executive director of Hofstra Mid-Season.

ALEX SZOGYI (Playwright and Director) his most recent book, *Molière Abstrait,* became a bestseller in France after his appearance on Bernard Pivot's famous television program, APOSTROPHES. He is one of the few Americans ever to have been invited to speak on France's leading literary talk show. LIRE and PARIS VOGUE have recently written about his life and work. In his 26 years in the professional theatre, he has adapted 45 plays for the stage from many languages. He is the only one in the U.S. to have translated all the plays of Chekhov. He has been Professor of French and Comparative Literature at Hunter College/CUNY for 25 years. He is a founding member of the George Sand Newsletter and has published some 20 articles on George Sand, most recently in three books devoted to Sand. He has been twice decorated by the French Government.

GEORGE SAND GALA COMMITTEE

DR. ALEX SZOGYI, Chair, Gala Buffet and Dinner Committee
MR. AL "TANK" PASSUELLO, Chair, Decorations Committee

Mrs. Madeline Dempster	Mrs. Caroline Smith
Mr. and Mrs. Walter Fillin	Mrs. JoAnne Smith
Ms. Pat Gagliardi	Dr. Donald Swinney
Mrs. Nina Geiringer	Mrs. Graydon Vanderbilt
Ms. Deidre McGuire	Mrs. Muriel Weingrow

TECHNICAL ASSISTANTS

BOB CERRO, Special Events Coordinator
SLOAN MAHONE, Department of Drama and Dance

SATURDAY, OCTOBER 18, 1986

8:15 a.m. - 5:00 p.m.	**Conference Registration** and **Book Fair** Dining Rooms ABC, Student Center, North Campus

---

8:15 - 9:00 a.m.	Dining Rooms ABC, Student Center, North Campus **Continental Breakfast**
9:00 - 10:50 a.m.	Hofstra Cultural Center Lecture Hall Library — 1st floor
Panel VIIa	POETIC IMAGERY

Moderator: **Marie M. Collins**
Dept. of Modern Languages
Rutgers University/Newark

Yi Jai-Hi
Hankuk University of Foreign Studies
Seoul, Korea
"Le Jardin dans l'Histoire de ma vie de George Sand"

Ursula Böhmer
Universität Gesamthochschule Siegen
Federal Republic of Germany
"'Wings of Imagination': George Sand and the Poetics of Flying"

Marie-Jacques Hoog
Rutgers University/New Brunswick
"La Sybille romantique"

Annarosa Poli
University of Bologna
Italy
"George Sand et la mythologie de l'eau douce: Les lacs italiènnes"

9:00 - 10:30 a.m.	Dining Rooms ABC, Student Center, North Campus
Panel VIIb	WORKS: LETTRES D'UN VOYAGEUR

Moderator: **Lucienne Frappier-Mazur**
Department of Romance Languages
University of Pennsylvania

Susan H. Léger
Northern Illinois University
"Lettres d'un voyageur: Travelling with George Sand"

Nicole Mozet
Université Paris VII, France
"Le Voyageur sandien en quête d'un lieu d'écriture"

Mary Anne Garnett
University of South Dakota
"The Imaginary and Symbolic Orders in George Sand's Letter 'Sur Lavater et sur une maison déserte'"

SATURDAY, OCTOBER 18, 1986

11:00 a.m. - 12:20 p.m.	Hofstra Cultural Center Lecture Hall Library — 1st floor
Panel VIIIa	POETICS OF AUTOBIOGRAPHY
	Moderator: **Thelma Jurgrau** Area of Cultural Studies Empire State College/SUNY Hartsdale, NY
	Gita May Columbia University "Histoire de ma vie: George Sand and Autobiography"
	Marilyn Yalom Stanford University "L'Art poétique de l'autobiographie selon Sand"
	Peter G. Christensen SUNY at Binghamton "Positioning the Self in Autobiographical Writing: George Sand as a Model for Marguerite Yourcenar"
11:00 a.m. - 12:20 p.m.	Dining Rooms ABC, Student Center, North Campus
Panel VIIIb	TRANSLATING, PUBLISHING, COLLECTING
	Moderator: **Alexej Ugrinsky** Department of Comparative Literature & Languages Hofstra University
	Joyce Carleton Central Connecticut State University "Maurice Sand's Trip to America, 1861" Readings from Six Mille Lieues à Toute Vapeur Translated by **Mildred Bissinger**, Kentfield, CA and **Joyce Carleton**
	Gaylord Brynolfson Gaylord Brynolfson French Books Boston, MA "On Publishing George Sand"
	Paulette Rose Paulette Rose, Ltd. New York, NY "In Pursuit of George Sand: The Collector's Challenge"

SATURDAY, OCTOBER 18, 1986

12:30 - 2:00 p.m.

Dining Rooms ABC, Student Center, North Campus

Luncheon in Celebration of the Tenth Anniversary of the Friends of George Sand at Hofstra University

Members of the George Sand Newsletter Editorial Board

Marie M. Collins	Natalie Datlof	Thelma Jurgrau
Isabelle Naginski	Nancy Rogers	Alex Szogyi

2:00 - 3:30 p.m.

Dining Rooms ABC, North Campus

FORUM: THE ART OF BIOGRAPHY

Moderator: **William A. McBrien**
Department of English
Hofstra University
Co-author: Stevie: A Biography of Stevie Smith

Oleg Kerensky
New York, NY
Author: Pavlova

Rhoda Nathan
Hofstra University
Author: Katherine Mansfield

Joan Peyser
New York University
Author: Boulez: Composer, Conductor, Enigma
Forthcoming, Spring 1987: Leonard Bernstein: A Life

Renee Winegarten
Middlesex, England
Author: The Double Life of George Sand

SATURDAY, OCTOBER 18, 1986

3:30 - 5:30 p.m.	Hofstra Cultural Center Lecture Hall Library — 1st floor
Panel IXa	ARTISTIC IMPRESSIONS AND INTERPRETATIONS
	Moderator: **Tatiana Greene** Department of French Barnard College/ Columbia University
	Henriette Bessis Paris, France "George Sand critique d'art"
	Lynn Kettler Penrod University of Alberta, Edmonton "Aurore Inscribing Aurore: A Reading of 'La Reine Coax'"
	Doris P. Tishkoff Oregon Institute of Technology "George Sand and the Lyric: The Musical Sketches"
	Gislinde Seybert Universität Hannover, Federal Republic of Germany "Body and Language: 'To the nameless/sexless angel'" (Interpretation of a lyrical fragment)
3:30 - 5:30 p.m.	Dining Rooms ABC, Student Center, North Campus
Panel IXb	REVOLUTIONARY WOMAN
	Moderator: **Jeanne Fuchs** Department of Comparative Literature & Languages Hofstra University
	Wendy Deutelbaum University of Iowa "Political, Familial and Narrative Systems in the Life and Work of Sand"
	Nancy Rogers National Endowment for the Humanities Washington, D.C. "*Nanon*: Novel of Revolution or Revolutionary Novel?"
	Claude Holland Barnard College/Columbia University "*Mademoiselle Merquem*: A Rejection of the Law of the Father. De-mythifying Woman"
5:30 p.m.	**Closing Reception** Hofstra Cultural Center, Library - 10th floor

Hofstra University gratefully acknowledges the generosity of the following friends and corporations:

Conference Donors

Nina and Stefan Geiringer

Françoise Gilot

Christiane Sand

Alex Shagin

* * *

Baccarat, Inc.
New York, NY

Grange Furniture, Inc.
New York, NY

International Wine Gallery
Garden City South, NY

L.F. O'Connell Associates
Garden City, NY

Lufthansa German Airlines
East Meadow, NY

Schaller and Weber
Long Island City, NY

Steinway & Son
New York, NY

Cooperating Institutions

The French Embassy
Washington, D.C.

The French Consulate
New York, NY

French Cultural Services of the French Embassy
New York, NY

Garden City Hotel
Garden City, NY

Island Inn Motel
Westbury, NY

Nassau Library System
Uniondale, NY

New York Public Library System
New York, NY

Suffolk Cooperative Library System
Bellport, NY

THE WORLD OF GEORGE SAND CONFERENCE EXHIBITIONS

Friends of George Sand Art Exhibit
Françoise Gilot, Maria Cooper Janis, Christiane Sand, Edwina Sandys
October 16 - November 3, 1986
Curators: Natalie Datlof and Jo-Ann G. Mahoney

Hofstra Cultural Center, Library — 10th floor
(516) 560-5974
Gallery Hours: Thursday, October 16, 1986 — 9:00 a.m. - 6:00 p.m.
Friday, October 17, 1986 — 9:00 a.m. - 3:00 p.m.
Saturday, October 18, 1986 — 9:00 a.m. - 6:00 p.m.
Sunday, October 19, 1986 — 1:00 p.m. - 5:00 p.m.

October 20 - November 3, 1986:
Mondays, Wednesdays, Thursdays and Fridays — 9:00 a.m. - 5:00 p.m.
Tuesdays — 9:00 a.m. - 9:00 p.m.
Saturdays and Sundays — 1:00 p.m. - 5:00 p.m.

Exhibition of George Sand Books, Manuscripts and Memorabilia
October 15 - November 2, 1986
Curator: Marguerite M. Regan

David Filderman Gallery, Library — 9th floor
(516) 560-5974
Gallery Hours: Wednesday, October 15, 1986 — 9:00 a.m. - 5:00 p.m.
Thursday, October 16, 1986 — 9:00 a.m. - 6:00 p.m.
Friday, October 17, 1986 — 9:00 a.m. - 3:00 p.m.
Saturday, October 18, 1986 — 9:00 a.m. - 6:00 p.m.
Sunday, October 19, 1986 — 1:00 p.m. - 5:00 p.m.

October 20 - November 3, 1986:
Mondays, Wednesdays, Thursdays and Fridays — 9:00 a.m. - 5:00 p.m.
Tuesdays — 9:00 a.m. - 9:00 p.m.
Saturdays and Sundays — 1:00 p.m. - 5:00 p.m.

George Sand Photograph Exhibit
Courtesy of the Cultural Services of the French Embassy in New York
October 16 - October 19, 1986

Hofstra Cultural Center Lecture Hall
(516) 560-5669

Gallery Hours: Thursday, October 16, 1986 — 9:00 a.m. - 8:00 p.m.
Friday, October 17, 1986 — 9:00 a.m. - 5:00 p.m.
Saturday, October 18, 1986 — 9:00 a.m. - 5:00 p.m.
Sunday, October 19, 1986 — 1:00 a.m. - 5:00 p.m.

Images of Women: From Antiquity to Modern Times
From the Hofstra University Museum's Permanent Collection
Curator: Eleanor Rait

On campus
October 15 - December 1, 1986
(516) 560-5672

THE WORLD OF GEORGE SAND BOOK FAIR

Thursday, October 16, 1986 — 9:00 a.m. - 5:00 p.m. Hofstra Hall Lobby, South Campus
Friday, October 17, 1986 — 9:00 a.m. - 3:00 p.m. Dining Rooms ABC, North Campus
Saturday, October 18, 1986 — 9:00 a.m. - 5:00 p.m. Dining Rooms ABC, North Campus

Book Fair Coordinator: Tara Stahman

Academy Press of Chicago
Chicago, IL

AMS Press
New York, NY

Christian Pirot
Saint-Cyr-Sur-Loire, France

Editions de l'Aurore
Meylan, France

Gaylord Brynolfson French Books
Boston, MA

George Sand Books
Los Angeles, CA

George Sand Newsletter
Hofstra University
Hempstead, NY

Greenwood Press
Westport, CT

Harvard University Press
Cambridge, MA

Les Editions des Femmes
Paris, France

Paulette Rose, Ltd.
Fine and Rare Books
New York, NY

Summit Books
New York, NY

University of Amsterdam
Amsterdam, The Netherlands

Whitston Publishing Company
Troy, NY

Name Index

Agoult, Marie d', xxii, 96
Ajasson de Grandsagne, Stéphane, 182
Apuleïus, 16
Arendt, Hannah, 143
von Arnim, Bettina, 156
Arnold, Matthew, xv, xvi, xxi, xxiii
Astman, Joseph G., x, xii
Aucante, Emile, 249
Augustine, Saint, 209
Austen, Jane, xiv

Bach, Johann Sebastian, 120
Bachelard, Gaston, 46, 109
Bakunin, Mikhail, xxii, 227
Balzac, Honoré de, xiv, xxiii, 99, 137, 138, 182, 217–23
Baroli, Marc, 23
Barry, Joseph, xii
Baudelaire, Charles, xvi
Bäumer, Gertrud, 159
Bazouin, Jane (Countess of Fenoyl), 218
Beauvoir, Simone de, xii
Belinsky, Vissarion, 227
Belmont, Nicole, 21
Benjamin, Walter, 237
Berthier, Philippe, 47, 48, 49
Besnard, Micheline, 132
Bettelheim, Bruno, 82
Bloom, Harold, 68, 124
Bodin, Thierry, 218, 219
Bonnet, Henri, 54
Börne, Ludwig, 155
Bossis, Mireille, 182
Bourges, Michel de, xiii
Bouteiller, Marcelle, 186
Bréton, Geneviève, 189
Brombert, Victor, 46
Brontë, Charlotte, xiii, xviii, xxiii
Brontë, Emily, xxiii
Brooks, Peter, 108
Browning, Elizabeth Barrett, xviii, xxiii
Browning, Robert, xviii, xxiii
Bruss, Elizabeth W., 61
Buloz, François, 207
Bunyan, John, 64

Camus, Albert, 86, 89
Cardinal, Marie, 90
Carlyle, Jane, xxiii
Carlyle, Thomas, xxiii
Cassou, Jean, 107, 115
Castex, Pierre-Georges, 220
Chateaubriand, François-Auguste-René de, 164
Chatrian, Alexandre, 182
Chopin, Frédéric, xiv, xxii, 87, 243, 255–61
Cimarosa, Domenico, 120

Clésinger, Jean-Baptiste-Auguste, 260
Cocteau, Jean, 89
Colette, Sidonie Gabrielle, xiv
Comenius, (pseud. Jan Comenski), 63, 64
Constant, Benjamin, 164
Creyancour, Marguerite de (pseud. Yourcenar) *See* Yourcenar, 61

Daly, Pierrette, 49
Datlof, Natalie, xii, 256
Day, William Patrick, 109, 110, 111
Delaborde, Sophie-Victoire, 7, 73, 89, 90–91
Delacroix, Eugène, xxii, 65, 98
De Quincey, Thomas, 209
Deschartres, François, 181
Didier, Béatrice, 47, 87
Dorval, Marie, 65
Dostoevski, Fyodor, xxiii, 99, 227–28
Dudevant, Aurore. *See* Sand, George
Dudevant, Casimir, 87, 265
Dudevant, Maurice, 182, 256
Dudevant, Solange, 182, 186, 256–57, 260–61
Dumas, Alexandre (fils), 243–52
Dumas, Alexandre (père), 244, 245, 247
Dupin, Amantine-Aurore-Lucile. *See* Sand, George
Dupin, Aurore (Lolo), 76, 82–83
Dupin, Gabrielle (Titite), 76
Dupin, Maurice, 6, 7, 62, 64, 73, 89, 90
Dupin de Francueil, Marie-Aurore (née Saxe), 62, 73

Ehrenreich, Barbara, 186, 188
Eliot, George (pseud. Marian Evans), xviii, xxiii
Emerson, Ralph Waldo, xxiii
English, Deirdre, 186, 188
Erckmann, Emile, 182

Farinelli, Carlo, 121, 122
Fauchery, Pierre, 173
Fernandez, Dominique, 119–25
Flaubert, Gustave, xi, xiv, xvii, xxi, xxiii, 75–76, 145–51, 235–40, 245
Foucault, Michel, 115
France, Anatole, xi
Franklin, Benjamin, 86
Frappier-Mazur, Lucienne, 113
Freire, Paulo, 143
Freud, Sigmund, 165–66
Fuller, Margaret, xxiii

Galey, Matthieu, 60, 63, 64
Gan, Elena (pseud. Zeneida R-Va), 228–33
Gaskell, Elizabeth Cleghorn, 264
Gaulmier, Jean, 219
Genlis, Mme de, 88
Gide, André, xi
Gilbert, Sandra, 46, 181
Gilot, Françoise, 256
Grzymala, Albert, 256
Gubar, Susan, 46, 181
Guillemin, Henri, 164
Gutzkow, Karl, xxii, 154–55, 156, 157

Haas, Ferdinand, 159
Hahn-Hahn, Ida Gräfin, 156, 264
Haydn, Joseph, 107, 119, 120
Heine, Heinrich, xiv, xxiii, 153, 154, 155, 156, 264
Herrmann, Claudine, 173
Herwegh, Georg, 156
Herzen, Alexander, xvi, 227
Hoog, Marie-Jacques, 45
Hugo, Victor, xiv–xv, xvii, 23, 137, 138

James, Henry, xix, xxiii, 99–100, 137
Jameson, Fredric, 47
Janis, Byron, 255
Jonsson-Devillers, Edith, 20

Karénine, Wladimir, 218
Kristeva, Julia, 9, 109

Lacan, Jacques, 9, 38, 39, 40, 45, 48
Lafayette, Marie de, 127, 169
Lange, Helene, 159
La Salle, Laisnel de, 186
Laube, Heinrich, 155, 156, 157
Lauth, Frédéric, 82
Le Duc, Violette, 90
Lefebvre, Henri, 212
Lejeune, Philippe, 85
Lemaire, Anika, 40

Lemoine-Montigny, Adolphe, 249
Léonard, Jacques, 182, 184
Leroux, Pierre, xv, xvi, 86
Le Roy, Eugène, 182
Lévi-Strauss, Claude, 39
Lévy, Maurice, 109
Lewald, August, 156, 265
Lewald, Fanny, 156, 158, 263–69
Lewes, George Henry, xxi
Liszt, Franz, 45, 52, 259
Longinus, 97
Lovejoy, Arthur, xxvi
Lubin, Georges, xii, 88–89, 98, 181, 218, 219

Maas, Ank, 85
Malraux, André, xi
Manifold, Gay, 249
Marchal, Charles, 245
Marivaux, Pierre Carlet de Chamblain de, 169
Marix-Spire, Thérèse, xiii
Marx, Karl, xxiii, 157
Maurois, André, xii, xiii, 137, 173
Maurras, Charles, xi
May, Georges, 85
Mazzini, Giuseppe, xxii
Meillant, Françoise, 5
Meininger, Anne-Marie, 217, 218
Menzel, Wolfgang, 154, 155
Meung, Jean de, xxiii
Mill, John Stuart, xxiii, 90
Miller, Nancy K., 127, 132
Moehrmann, Renate, 263, 264, 267
Moers, Ellen, xiii, 111, 112, 181
Montaigne, Michel de, 71
Mozart, Wolfgang Amadeus, 120, 121
Mühlbach, Luise, 156
Mundt, Theodore, 155, 157
Musset, Alfred de, xiv, 51, 52, 163, 207–15, 249
Musset, Paul de, 163, 213
M'Uzan, Michel de, 90

Naginski, Isabelle, xvi
Nelson, Lowry, 110, 116
Nerval, Gérard de, 98, 108

Otto-Peters, Louise, 263

Pagello, Pietro, 51, 52, 163, 208
Papet, Gustave, 182
Pascal, Blaise, 70
Peyre, Henri, x, xi–xx
Pisan, Christine de, xxiii-xxvii
Plath, Sylvia, 90
Plutarch, 103
Pommier, Jean, xvi
Poovey, Mary, 186
Porpora, Nicola, 107, 123
Proudhon, Pierre-Joseph, xi
Proust, Marcel, xviii

Radcliffe, Anne, 108–16
Rea, Annabelle, xii
Renan, Ernest, xvi–xvii, xxiii
Richards, Earl Jeffrey, xxiii
Rimbaud, Arthur, 63
Robert, Marthe, 36, 39
Rollinat, François, xiii, 4, 11
Roubichou, Gérard, 146
Rousseau, Jean-Jacques, 63–64, 65, 67–72, 86, 87, 164, 174, 209
Ruge, Arnold, 157
Ruskin, John, xviii, xxiii

Sachs, Murray, 243
Sade, Donatien Alphonse François (Marquis de), 169
Sainte-Beuve, Charles-Augustin, xxiii, 207, 213
Saint-Pierre, Charles-Irénée Castel, Abbé de, 68
Saint-Surin, Rosa de, 217
Salomon, Pierre, 164
Sand, Aurore, 82
Sand, Christiane, 255
Sand, George. *See* Subject index
Sandeau, Jules, 182, 222
Sartre, Jean-Paul, 89
Saxe, Marie-Aurore de, 62, 73
Saxe, Maurice de, Maréchal de France, 62, 73
Schaeffer, Gerald, xv
Schiller, Friedrich von, 63, 64
Schlientz, Gisela, 255
Schmidt, Julian, 158
Schor, Naomi, 45

Shuart, James M., x, xii, 256
Simon, Heinrich, 263
Staël, Germaine de, 97, 99, 164
Steegmuller, Francis, 145
Steinhauer, Marieluise, 263
Stendhal (pseud. Henri Beyle), xxiii, 99
Stephen, Leslie, xviii
Stern, Daniel (pseud. Marie d'Agoult), xxii, 96
Stirling, Jane, 258
Szogyi, Alex, xix

Taine, Hippolyte, xvii, xxiii, 22
Tanner, Tony, 39, 140, 141
Thackeray, William, xxiii
Thompson, Patricia, 137
Tocqueville, Alexis de, xvi
Tolstoy, Lev Nikolayevich, 63
Trent, W. P., 217
Tricotel, Claude, 146
Turgenev, Ivan, xxiii, 227–28

Valéry, Paul, xi
Van Gennep, Arnold, 22
Varnhagen, Rahel, 156
Vicomte de Launay (pseud. Delphine de Girardin), 99
Vigny, Alfred de, xxii
Voltaire (pseud. François-Marie Arouet), 68

Warens, Mme de, 72, 87
Weinbarg, Ludolf, 155
Wharton, Edith, xxvii
White, Hayden, 54, 56
Whitman, Walt, xviii, xix, xxiii
Wilde, Oscar, xxiii
Winegarten, Renee, xii, xiii, xv
Woolf, Virginia, xxvii, 90

Yalom, Marilyn, 22
Yourcenar, Marguerite, xii, 59–66

Zola, Emile, 89, 137, 182, 235

Subject Index

L'Affaire Clémenceau (Dumas-fils), 249, 250
"Les Ailes du courage" (Sand), 76
Alexis (Yourcenar), 59
L'Ami des femmes (Dumas-fils), 250
Amsterdam, University of, xii
André del Sarto (Musset), 207
Archives du nord (Yourcenar), 59, 60, 61–62
L'Autre (Sand), 183, 189, 249

"Beauty and the Beast," 16
Les Beaux Messieurs de Bois-Doré (Sand), 183, 187–88
Berrichon dialect, 6
Book of Peace, The (Pisan), xxiii
Book of the City of Ladies, The (Pisan), xxiii, xxiv, xxvii
Bouvard et Pécuchet (Flaubert), 149

Les Caprices de Marianne (Musset), 207
"Ce que disent les fleurs" (Sand), 76
Le Château de Pictordu (Sand), 76, 78
Le Château des Désertes (Sand), 100–101
"Le Chêne parlant" (Sand), 76
"Le Chien et la fleur sacrée" (Sand), 76
Les Chouans (Balzac), 137
Claudie (Sand), 249
"Un Coeur simple" (Flaubert), 235, 237–40
Commune, The Paris, xvi, xvii, 145, 146–47, 148, 149–50, 251
La Comtesse de Rudolstadt (Sand), xv, 98, 108
La Confession d'un enfant du siècle (Musset): background of, 207–8; ending of, 213–15; religious vocabulary in, 213; sacred love in, 212; scene of betrayal in, 211, 213; structure of, 210; use of doppelgänger in, 211; use of the word "confession," 208–10
Confessions (Rousseau), 63, 65, 68–69, 70, 71, 86
Confessions of an Opium Eater (De Quincey), 209
Consuelo (Sand), xv, xviii, 104, 185; compared with Fernandez's novel *Porporino*, 119–25; compared with Radcliffe's novel *Mysteries of Udolpho*, 111–16; feminism in, 124, 125; Free-Mason allusions, 122, 123; as a gothic novel, 107, 108, 110, 112–13; as a musical novel, 107, 119–20, 121; as a novel of initiation, 107, 113; road motif in, 114; as a roman-feuilleton, 107

Contes d'Espagne et d'Italie (Musset), 207
Contes d'une grand-mère (Sand), 76
Cosima (Sand), 153

La Dame aux camélias (Dumas-fils), 249
La Daniella (Sand), 185
De l'humanité (Leroux), 86
Le Demi-monde (Dumas-fils), 246
Le Dernier amour (Sand), 183, 185
La Dernière Aldini (Sand), 98, 248
Diary of a Writer (Dostoevski), 228
Die Rauber (Schiller), 63, 64
"Dinah Piédefer" (Balzac), 218
Diogena (Lewald), 264
Le Ditié de Jehanne d'Arc (Pisan), xxiii
Les Don Juan de village (Sand), 249

Education, Sand's views of, 174–75
L'Education sentimentale (Flaubert), xi, xvii, 148, 236
Eine Lebensfrage (Lewald), 267–68, 269
Elle et lui (Sand), 6, 244; background of, 163–64; criticism of, 164; description of, 167–69; marriage in, 170
Emile ou de l'éducation (Rousseau), 174
"En Morée" (Sand), 97, 98–99
L'Entrave (Colette), xiv
L'Epistre du chemin de long estude (Pisan), xxiii

Family history: importance of, 88–89; of Sand, 60, 62–63, 72–73
Faust, Part II (Goethe), xv
"Le Fée aux gros yeux" (Sand), 76
"Le Fée poussière" (Sand), 76
Female sexuality, 163–71
Feminism, xii–xiii, 124, 125, 173–78
La Femme de Claude (Dumas-fils), 250
Le Fils naturel (Dumas-fils), 249
Flaminio (Sand), 244
Flavie (Sand), 245
"La France vue à travers d'Allemagne" (Morin), 158
Francia (Sand), 183
François le champi (Sand), xi, xviii, 3–13, 185; compared with Flaubert's "Un Coeur simple," 235; discussion of art in the avant-propos, 35; foundling/bastard dichotomy, 36–37; incest symbolism in, 39, 40; interweaving of the story of François, 35–36; limited sense of time in, 37; narrative voice in, 37–38, 236–37, 239; Notice in, 36; socializing function of the structure of language in, 38–39; symbolic levels in, 38–40
"A Franz Liszt: Sur Lavater et sur une maison déserte": adoption of male pseudonym in, 46–47; background of, 52–53; compared with Letter One (Musset), 53–56; enclosure/imprisonment images in, 46, 47; ending of, 49–50; images of vegetation in, 47, 48; Lavater's book in, 48–49, 55–56; narrative sequence in, 47; paternal order in, 49
Friends of George Sand, x, 255, 256
"Futile Gift, The" (Gan), 232

"Le Géant Yéous" (Sand), 76
German Reflections (Haas), 159
German Vormärz, 153–160
Germany, influence of Sand in, 153–60
"Le Gnome des huîtres" (Sand), 76
Golden Ass, The (Apuleïus), 16

Histoire de ma vie (Sand), xii, 4, 6–7, 9; adolescence in, 170; family history in, 60, 62, 72–73; images of vegetation in, 47–48; medicine and, 182, 189; purpose of, 86; role of the grandmother in, 49, 73; on Rousseau, 63–64, 67–72; Second Republic in, 65–66
Histoire des treize (Balzac), 220
Un Hiver à Majorque (Sand), 67
Hofstra University, xvi; International George Sand Conferences at, xii, 255
"L'Homme-femme" (Dumas-fils), 250–51

Ideal, The (Gan), 230, 231, 232
Les Idées de Madame Aubray (Dumas-fils), 249–50
Les Idées d'un maître d'école (Sand), 76
Iliad, 96
Les Illuminations (Rimbaud), 63
Les Illusions perdues (Balzac), 99
Illustration, 158
Improvisation: in *Consuelo*, 104; in "En

Morée," 97, 98–99; in *Lélia*, 97, 101–4; in "Le Poème de Myrza," 97, 101; in *Tévérino*, 97, 99–100; use of the term, 99
Indiana (Sand), xi, xiv, xv, 87, 229–30, 263–70
Isidora (Sand), 249

Jacques (Sand), xi, xv, 245
Jeanne (Sand), 4, 5, 98, 187
Jean Ziska (Sand), 157
Journal intime (Sand), 67
Justine (Sade), 169

Le Labyrinthe du monde (Yourcenar), 59, 63
Labyrinth of the World, The (Comenius/Comenski), 63, 64
Laura, ou voyage dans le cristal (Sand), xv
Leaves of Grass (Whitman), xviii
Lélia (Sand): xi, xv, 230; divided self in, 193–97; German translation of, 154; sibyl/mythology in, 97, 101–4
Lettre de Junius (Dumas-fils), 251
Les Lettres à Marcie (Sand), 174–75, 178
Lettres au peuple (Sand), 264
Lettres d'un voyageur (Sand): autobiographical elements, 67; Dumas (fils) and, 244–45; first of the letters (Musset), 51–52, 53–56; "A Franz Liszt: Sur Lavater et sur une maison déserte,"45–50, 52–56
Lorenzaccio (Musset), 208, 209
Lucrezia Floriani (Sand), xiv, 87
Lui et elle (P. de Musset), 163
Le Lys dans la vallée (Balzac), 99

Madame Bovary (Flaubert), xi, 236
Mademoiselle Merquem (Sand): contradiction of heroine's role, 177–78; description of, 174; education of, 175; marriage of, 175, 177; maternal instinct in, 178; quest in, 176; wearing of masculine clothing in, 176–77
Maître Favilla (Sand), 264
Les Maîtres sonneurs (Sand), 189
La Mare au diable (Sand), xi, 10, 245
Le Marquis de Villemer (Sand), 185–86, 245, 248
Marriage, Sand's views of, 40, 157, 170, 175
"Le Marteau rouge" (Sand), 76
Mary Barton (Gaskell), 264
Mauprat (Sand), xv, 9, 10, 247
Le Médecin de campagne (Balzac), 182
Medicine, Sand's interest in, 181–92
Memoirs on the Eighteenth Century and the French Revolution (Genlis), 88
Métella (Sand), 182
Le Meunier d'Angibault (Sand): doctor/care-giver in, 183, 185; education and, 28; importance of, 27–28; literal sense, 28–29; language of loss in Christian terms, 30–31; language of loss in literary terms, 31–32; language of loss in secular terms, 31; Marcelle's relationships with the other characters, 29–30
Mill on the Floss (Eliot), xviii
Mont Revêche (Sand), 183, 185, 248–49
Motherhood, 178
La Muse du département (Balzac), 217; origin of title, 218–19; references to Sand, 219–20, 221–23; source of Dinah's poem, 220–21
Music: Sand's view on, 47, 52–53; used in *Consuelo* (Sand) and *Porporino* (Fernandez), 119–26
Mysteries of Udolpho (Radcliffe): compared with *Consuelo*, 111–17; description of, 108–10

Nanon (Sand): care-giver in, 186; class lines in, 142, 143–44; reconstruction in, 142; states of disorientation and loss in, 139–40; values of work, desire, and love in, 140–41
"Le Nuage rose" (Sand), 76

Oeuvres complètes d'Horace de Saint-Aubin (Balzac), 222
On the Sublime (Longinus), 97
"L'Orgue du titan" (Sand), 76

Le Péché de Monsieur Antoine (Sand), 186, 187, 189
La Petite Fadette (Sand), 6, 10, 15; conceptual level in, 16–18; interpretations of, 199–200; lessons learned from,

203; magic versus science, 18–19; medicine/health in, 188, 189; redemption of Fadette, 201–2; redemption of the twins, 200–201; religion versus magic, 19–20; structural level in, 20–23; thematic level in, 18–20; wise women in, 200, 202–3
Pilgrim's Progress (Bunyan), 64
"Le Poème de Myrza" (Sand), 97, 101
Porporino, ou les mystères de Naples (Fernandez), 119–26
Poverty of Philosophy, The (Marx), 157
La Princess de Clèves (Lafayette), 127–34, 169
La Princesse Georges (Dumas-fils), 250
Pythic Dialogues (Plutarch), 103

Quartre-vingt-treize (Hugo), 137, 138
Quoi, l'éternité? (Yourcenar), 59, 63, 64

"La Reine Coax" (Sand): Bettelheim on, 82; dedication of, 76–77; description of, 77–83
Religion: in *Lélia*, 193–94; Sand's views of, 85–86
"Réponse à un ami" (Sand), 146, 150
Revolution of 1789, *Nanon* and concepts of, 137–44
Revolution of 1848, xvi, xxii, 47–49, 199
Robert, chef de brigands (Schiller), 63, 65
Le Roman de la rose (Meung), xxiii
Rose et Blanche (Sand and Sandeau), 222
Rougon-Macquart (Zola), 235
Russia, influence of Sand in, 227–33

Salammbô (Flaubert), x, xi, xvii, 149
Sand, George: adolescence and, 170; Balzac and, xiv, xxiii, 99, 137, 138, 182, 217–23; Berrichon dialect and, 6; British admirers of, xiii, xviii–xix; childhood of, 6–8; Chopin and, xiv, xxii, 87, 243, 255–61; class lines and, 142, 143–44; Colette and, xiv; Corambé and, 11, 48, 76; doll play of, 165, 166–67; Dumas (fils) and, 243–52; Dumas (père) and, 244, 245, 247; education and, 174–75; family history, importance of, 88–89; family history of, 60, 62–63, 72–73; father of, influence of the, 89–90; female sexuality and, 163–71; feminism and, xii–xiii, 124, 125, 173–78; Flaubert and Paris Commune, 145–52; Flaubert and Revolution of 1848, 147–149; Flaubert's style and, 235–40; German critics and, 153–59; granddaughters and, 75–76; grandmother stories, 76–83; health of, 181; influence of, xxii–xxiii; influence of, on Flaubert, 235–40; influence of, on Gan, 228–33; influence of, on Lewald, 263–69; Leroux and, xv, xvi; Lewald and, 156, 158, 263–69; marriage and, 40, 157, 170, 175; maternal instinct of, 178; medicine and, 181–89; memorialists and, 88; mother and language, 7–10; mother of, 7, 73, 89, 90–91, 164–65; music and, 47, 52–53, 119–26; Musset and, 51, 52, 163, 207–15; mythology/fairy tales and, 95–97; narrative voice and, 37–38, 236–37, 239; Pagello and, 51, 52, 163, 208; peasant language and, 5–6; Pisan and, xxiii-xxv; religion and, 11, 19, 30–31, 85–86; revolution and, 138–44, 147–49, 199; role of reader to, 87; Rousseau and, 63–64, 67–72, 86, 87; Russian admirers of, 227–33; Schiller and, 64–65; styles of autobiography and that used by, 87–89; use of her father's letters, 89, 90; use of men/friends in her works, 87; use of the word solidarity, 86; Voltaire and, 68; Yourcenar and, 59–66
Sand, George (works of): "Les Ailes du courage," 76; *L'Autre*, 183, 189, 249; *Les Beaux Messieurs de Bois-Doré*, 183, 187–88; "Ce que disent les flueurs," 76; *Le Château de Pictordu*, 76, 78; *Le Château des Désertes*, 100–101; "Le Chêne parlant," 76; "Le Chien et la fleur sacrée," 76; *Claudie*, 249; *La Comtesse de Rudolstadt*, xv, 98, 108; *Consuelo*, xv, xviii, 104, 107–8, 110–16, 119–25, 185; *Contes d'une grandmère*, 76; *Cosima*, 153; *La Daniella*, 185; *Le Dernier amour*, 183, 185; *La Dernière Aldini*, 98, 248; *Les Don Juan de village*, 249; *Elle et lui*, 6, 163–64, 167–71, 244; "En Morée,"

97, 98–99; "La Fée aux gros yeux," 76; "La Fée poussière," 76; *Flaminio*, 244; *Flavie*, 245; *Francia*, 183; *François le champi*, xi, 3–13, 35–41, 185, 236–37, 239; "Le Géant Yéous," 76; "Le Gnome des huîtres," 76; *Histoire de la vie*, 4, 6–7, 9, 47–48, 49, 59–66, 67–73, 85–92, 170, 182, 189; *Un Hiver à Majorque*, 67; *Les Idées d'un maître d'école*, 76; *Indiana*, xi, xiv, xv, 87, 229–30, 263–69; *Isidora*, 249; *Jacques*, xi, xv, 245; *Jeanne*, 4, 5, 98, 187; *Jean Ziska*, 157; *Journal intime*, 67; *Laura, ou voyage dans le cristal*, xv; *Lélia*, xi, xv, 97, 101–4, 154, 193–97, 208; *Les Lettres à Marcie*, 174–75, 178; *Lettres au peuple*, 264; *Lettres d'un voyageur*, 45–56, 67, 244–45; *Lucrezia Floriani*, xiv, 87; *Mademoiselle Merquem*, 173–78; *Maître Favilla*, 264; *Les Maîtres sonneurs*, 189; *La Mare au diable*, xi, 10, 245; *Le Marquis de Villemer*, 185–86, 245, 248; "Le Marteau rouge," 76; *Mauprat*, xv, 9, 10, 247; *Métella*, 182; *Le Meunier d'Angibault*, 27–32, 183, 185; *Mont Revêche*, 183, 185, 248–49; *Nanon*, 137–44, 186; "Le Nuage rose," 76; "L'Orgue du titan," 76; *Le Péché de Monsieur Antoine*, 186, 187, 189; *La Petite Fadette*, 6, 10, 15–25, 188, 189, 199–203; "Le Poème de Myrza," 97, 101; "La Reine Coax," 76–83; "Réponse à un ami," 146, 150; *Rose et Blanche*, 222; *Les Sept cordes de la lyre*, xv; *Spiridion*, xv–xvi; *Tamaris*, 183–84, 185; *Tévérino*, 97, 99–100; "Le Toast," 220, 221; *Valentine*, 127–33; *Valvèdre*, 185, 189; *Veillées du chanvreur*, 35

Scenes of Clerical Life (Eliot), xviii

Sibyls/mythology, use of: in *Consuelo*, 104; in "En Morée," 97, 98–99; in *Lélia*, 97, 101–4; in "Le Poème de Myrza," 97, 101; in *Tévérino*, 97, 99–100

Sketches from a Hunter's Notebook (Turgenev), 228

Society's Judgment (Gan), 230, 231, 232

Souvenirs pieux (Yourcenar), 59, 61

Spiridion (Sand), xv–xvi

Le Supplice d'une femme (Dumas-fils), 246

Tamaris (Sand), 183–84, 185

Tévérino (Sand), 97, 99–100

Thousand and One Nights, The, 20

"Le Toast" (Sand), 220, 221

Valentine (Sand), *La Princess de Clèves* compared with, 127–34

Valvèdre (Sand), 185, 189

Veillées du chanvreur (Sand), 35

La Vie de Marianne (Marivaux), 169

La Visite de noces (Dumas-fils), 247

Wally, die Zweiflerin (*Wally, the Doubtress*) (Guzkow), 154

Les Yeux ouverts: Entretiens avec Matthieu Galey (Yourcenar), 59, 60, 63

Young Germany, 154–55, 156, 157, 158

About the Editors and Contributors

ANNE BERGER teaches French literature at Cornell University in Ithaca, New York. She was editor of the French journal *Fruits*. She has a commitment to women's thought and politics and has produced short pieces on Lou Andreas Salome as well as on George Sand. Berger has written extensively on Rimbaud and on poetry in general.

PETER CHRISTENSEN is a Teaching Fellow in the English Department of Marquette University, where he currently teaches American literature. His publications in French studies include articles on Marguerite Yourcenar, André Gide, Jean Cocteau, Paul Nizan, Simone de Beauvoir, and Jean-Luc Godard.

NATALIE DATLOF is Director of Liaison and Creative Development of the Hofstra Cultural Center at Hofstra University. She is the Founder of the Friends of George Sand, established in 1976 at Hofstra University, as well as Co-Editor-in-Chief of the journal *George Sand Studies*, which is published annually. She has edited two volumes of George Sand Conference Proceedings. In 1986 she received a decoration from the French Government: Chevalier dans l'Ordre des Palmes Académiques.

MARIE J. DIAMOND is Associate Professor of French at Rutgers University. Her publications include *Flaubert: The Problem of Aesthetic Discontinuity* (1975) and *Crossings*. She is editor of the forthcoming *Women and Revolution*, a special publication of *Dialectical Anthropology* (vol. 15, nos. 2 and 3).

MARILYN FRENCH has taught English at Hofstra University, Harvard University, and College of the Holy Cross and, in 1976–77, she was a Mellon Fellow at Harvard. Her books include *The Book As World: James Joyce's "Ulysses"* (1976), *The Women's Room* (1977), and *The Bleeding Heart* (1980). Her most recent novel, *Her Mother's Daughter* (1988), was on the Best Seller List. French is currently engaged in writing a history of women from the earliest proto-human emergence to the present.

JEANNE FUCHS is Associate Professor in the Department of Comparative Literature and Languages at Hofstra University. She has also been Associate Dean for Student Academic Affairs for three and a half years. Her main area of research is eighteenth-century French literature, and she is working on a book on Rousseau's *La Nouvelle Héloïse*.

MARY ANNE GARNETT is Associate Professor of French and Chairman of the Department of Modern Languages at the University of South Dakota. Her principal focus of research concerns the development of a female autobiographical tradition in nineteenth-century France. She is currently completing a literary biography of Marie d'Agoult, who wrote under the pseudonym of Daniel Stern.

FRANÇOISE GILOT has worked for over forty years as a painter. She views her task as an artist to transform and extend perceptions and to stimulate viewers toward insights and experiences they might not otherwise obtain. She graciously designed the frontispiece illustration which served as the official conference poster at the George Sand Conference. She is the author of the recent book *Matisse and Picasso: A Friendship in Art*.

JANIS GLASGOW, Professor of French at San Diego State University, has authored *Une Esthétique de comparaison: Balzac et George Sand: "La Femme abandonnée" et "Metella"* (1978) and edited *George Sand: Collected Essays* (1985). She is author of the introduction to *Gabriel* (1988) and of numerous articles on Sand. In 1984 Glasgow was named Chevalier dans l'Ordre des Palmes Académiques by the French Ministry of Education.

CLAUDE HOLLAND has taught at Barnard College and Columbia University and is currently teaching at the Dalton School in New York. She has done extensive research on the feminine novel (from the fifteenth to the twentieth century). Her present field of research focuses on the latest studies on the pedagogy of intelligence conducted both in Paris and in the United States.

MARIE-JACQUES HOOG is Professor Emerita at Rutgers University, where she has served for more than twenty-five years following appointments at Smith and Hunter Colleges. She has written extensively on George Sand's works, is currently finishing a *Suite sandienne*, and is preparing a monograph on the mythology of *La Sibylle romantique et les improvasitrices*.

BRIGITTE LANE is Assistant Professor of French at Wellesley College and has also taught in several universities in the Boston area, including MIT. She has worked extensively on cultures of French expression ranging from France to Africa, to New England, to Quebec. She is currently working on a book, *Essais ethnocritiques*, which analyzes several major nineteenth- and twentieth-century French novels from a perspective based on current ethnological and cultural theories.

SUSAN H. LÉGER is Associate Professor of French at Northern Illinois University. She has published essays on Marguerite Duras and Albert Camus.

GITA MAY is Professor of French and Department Chair at Columbia University. She is author of a number of books, notably *Diderot et Baudelaire, critiques d'art*; *De Jean-Jacques Rousseau à Madame Roland: Essai sur la sensibilité préromantique et révolutionnaire*; *Madame Roland and the Age of Revolution* (winner of the Columbia University's Van Amringe Distinguished Book Award); and *Stendhal and the Age of Napoleon*. She has also published numerous articles, extensive essays, contributions to books and festschriften, as well as reviews and review articles.

WENDELL McCLENDON is Assistant Professor of French at Texas Tech University. He has taught at the University of Oklahoma and at the Glamorgan Polytechnic, Great Britain. His research interests are in the style and themes of nineteenth-century French prose, especially that of Balzac, Zola, and Sand.

KEVIN J. McKENNA is an Associate Professor of Russian in the Department of German and Russian, as well as Director of the International Studies Program at the University of Vermont. His principal research interests include eighteenth-nineteenth century Russian women writers, Soviet political cartooning, and Russian lexicology. He is co-author of *Reading Russian Newspapers* and is currently completing a study entitled *All the Views Fit To Print: Changing Images of the United States in "Pravda" Political Cartoons, 1917–1990*.

ISABELLE NAGINSKI is Associate Professor of French at Tufts University. She has just finished a book entitled *George Sand: Writing for Her Life*, which will be published in Spring 1991.

JANE A. NICHOLSON is Assistant Professor of French and Comparative Literature at the University of Tulsa. Her principal research interests are nineteenth-century French realism and cultural history, literary semiotics, and discourse analysis. She is working on *Rereading Realism: From Language to Discourse*.

LYNN KETTLER PENROD is Professor of French and Associate Dean of Arts at the University of Alberta in Edmonton, Alberta, Canada. Her principal areas of research are French children's literature, French feminism, literary translation, and the interrelationship of literature and law. Her most recent work is *Expériences littéraires*.

HENRI PEYRE was one of the seminal figures of contemporary French scholarship. He was Sterling Professor of French Literature at Yale University until his retirement, then Distinguished Professor of French Literature at the Graduate Center of the City University of New York, as well as the head of the French Doctoral Program. He wrote definitive works on French Classicism, Romanticism, Symbolism, Baudelaire, and many other topics.

DAVID A. POWELL is Assistant Professor of French and Associate Dean of Academic Affairs at Hofstra University. He is the author of *George Sand* in the Twayne World Author Series, as well as several articles and reviews of books on Sand. He is currently researching a book on psychological and semiotic interpretations of Sand's use of music. He is also Co-Editor-in-Chief of the journal *George Sand Studies.*

ANNABELLE M. REA is Professor of French at Occidental College. She has published on George Sand and contemporary Quebec writer Anne Hébert. She served as Visiting Professor at the University of Rennes, II in 1988–89.

MARY RICE is Assistant Professor of French and Acting Chair of the Department of Romance Languages and Literatures at Bates College. She has published on nineteenth- and twentieth-century French literature and is currently at work on a study of the French Revolution of 1848.

NANCY E. ROGERS is the Regional Officer for the Western Region in the Division of State Programs at the National Endowment for the Humanities. She was formerly a member of the faculty at Howard University and at the University of Tübingen in Germany. She is the author of two books on style in American English and has published many articles on nineteenth-century writers, especially George Sand.

WENDY ANN RYDEN is a member of the English and Humanities Departments at Montclair State College and the New Jersey Institute of Technology. Her academic interests include folklore and feminist analysis of literature. A fiction writer, she is co-author and editor of the short story collection *Spirits/Legacies.*

MURRAY SACHS is Professor of French and Comparative Literature at Brandeis University where he has taught since 1960 after having served previously at Williams College, University of California at Berkeley, and Columbia University. His main research interest has been the modern novel and short story, with a specialization on nineteenth-century French writers of fiction such as Balzac, Mérimée, George Sand, Flaubert, Daudet, Zola, Maupassant, and Anatole France, on all of whom he has published studies.

GISELA SCHLIENTZ currently works as an editor and author and was previously the Director of the Foreign Language Department of a major German publishing house. Her publications have focused primarily on French authors of the nineteenth and twentieth centuries, especially Madame de Staël, George Sand, and André Gide. Her most recent book is entitled *'Ich liebe, also bin ich' : Leben und Werk von George Sand.*

LUCY M. SCHWARTZ is Professor of French at the University of North Dakota on leave as Acting Director of Special Programs at Lafayette College. She is the author of numerous articles on George Sand and other nineteenth- and twentieth-century French female novelists. Her edition of Sand's *Le Secrétaire intime* will be published in France in 1991.

EVE SOURIAN is Professor of French at The City College and the Graduate Center of the City University of New York. She has written *Madame de Staël et Henry Heine: Les deux Allemagnes* (1974) and has edited *Nouvelles: La Marquise, Lavinia, Metella, Pauline* by George Sand (1986). She wrote a critical introduction to *Isidora* by George Sand (1990), and has written articles on George Sand and Madame de Staël.

KAREN STORZ is a graduate student in German at the University of Minnesota. Her interests include eighteenth- and nineteenth-century women writers and the construction of gender in literature. She was previously an editor of foreign language textbooks.

ALEX SZOGYI is Professor of French and Comparative Literature at Hunter College/CUNY and was previously President of the American Association of Teachers of French (N.Y.) and Phi Beta Kappa (Hunter) and Chairman of the Romance Languages Department (Hunter). He has translated more than fifty plays from many languages and has written several plays of his own, most recently *Black Snow* adapted from the novel by Bulgakov. His study of Molière, *Molière abstrait*, was published by Nizet. His play *Dialectic of the Heart* was performed at the George Sand Conference, Hofstra University, 1986, where he is one of the founding members of the Friends of George Sand.

MAÏR E. VERTHUY is Associate Professor of French at Concordia University in Montreal, Canada and founding Principal and currently Resident Fellow of the Simone de Beauvoir Institute for Women's Studies at the same university. She is author of *Fenêtre sur cour; voyage dans l'oeuvre humanesque d'Hélène Parmelin* (forthcoming), co-author (with Jennifer Waelti-Walters) of *Jeanne Hyvrard;* editor of *L'espace-temps dans la littérature* (APFUCC, Guelph University, Canada), and *Toute écriture est amour* (texts by Madeleine Gagnon); she has also authored numerous articles on contemporary women writers in Quebec and France.

MARGARET E. WARD is Professor and current Chair of the German Department at Wellesley College in Massachusetts. Her principal research interests include German and French postwar political theater and nineteenth- and twentieth-century German women writers. She has published on Bertolt Brecht and Armand Gatti, is author of *Rolf Hochhuth*, and is completing a biographical study of Fanny Lewald, *Between Rebellion and Renunciation*.

MARILYN YALOM is Senior Scholar at the Institute for Research on Women and Gender at Stanford University. She is the author of *Le Temps des Orages: Aristocrates, bourgeoises, et paysannes racontent* and *Maternity, Mortality, and the Literature of Madness*. She is the editor of *Women Writers of the West Coast* and the Co-Editor of *Coming to Light: American Women Poets in the Twentieth Century* (with Diane Middlebrook) and, most recently, *Revealing Lives: Autobiography, Biography, and Gender* (with Susan Bell).

Recent Titles in
Contributions in Women's Studies

Education for Equality: Women's Rights Periodicals and Women's Higher Education, 1849–1920
Patricia Smith Butcher

Women Changing Work
Patricia W. Lunneborg

From the Hearth to the Open Road: A Feminist Study of Aging in Contemporary Literature
Barbara Frey Waxman

Women, Equality, and the French Revolution
Candice E. Proctor

Serious Daring from Within: Female Narrative Strategies in Eudora Welty's Novels
Franziska Gygax

Verging on the Abyss: The Social Fiction of Kate Chopin and Edith Wharton
Mary E. Papke

The Feminization of Poverty: Only in America?
Gertrude Schaffner Goldberg and Eleanor Kremen, editors

The Dominion of Women: The Personal and the Political in Canadian Women's Literature
Wayne Fraser

Successful Career Women: Their Professional and Personal Characteristics
Cecilia Ann Northcutt

The Life of Margaret Fuller: A Revised, Second Edition
Madeleine Stern

The Sea of Becoming: Approaches to the Fiction of Esther Tusquets
Mary S. Vásquez, editor

Gender Differences: Their Impact on Public Policy
Mary Lou Kendrigan, editor

Hofstra University's
Cultural and Intercultural Studies
Coordinating Editor, Alexej Ugrinsky

Dwight D. Eisenhower: Soldier, President, Statesman
(Editor: Joann P. Kreig)

Goethe in the Twentieth Century
(Editor: Alexej Ugrinsky)

Franklin D. Roosevelt: The Man, the Myth, the Era, 1882–1945
(Editors: Herbert D. Rosenbaum and Elizabeth Bartelme)

The Stendhal Bicentennial Papers
(Editor: Avriel Goldberger)

Faith of a (Woman) Writer
(Editors: Alice Kessler-Harris and William McBrien)

José Ortega y Gasset:
Proceedings of the *Espectador universal* International Interdisciplinary Conference
(Editor: Nora de Marval-McNair)

George Orwell
(Editors: Courtney T. Wemyss and Alexej Ugrinsky)

John F. Kennedy: The Promise Revisited
(Editors: Paul Harper and Joann P. Krieg)

Lyndon Baines Johnson and the Uses of Power
(Editors: Bernard J. Firestone and Robert C. Vogt)

Eighteenth-Century Women and the Arts
(Editors: Frederick M. Keener and Susan E. Lorsch)

Suburbia Re-examined
(Editor: Barbara M. Kelly)

James Joyce and His Contemporaries
(Editors: Diana A. Ben-Merre and Maureen Murphy)